Pittsburgh Series in Composition, Literacy, and Culture

David Bartholomae and Jean Ferguson Carr, Editors

BETWEEN LANGUAGES AND CULTURES

TRANSLATION AND CROSS-CULTURAL TEXTS

Anuradha Dingwaney and
Carol Maier, Editors

University of Pittsburgh Press
Pittsburgh and London

1955

Published by the University of Pittsburgh Press, Pittsburgh, Pa. 15260
Copyright © 1995, University of Pittsburgh Press
All rights reserved
Eurospan, London
Manufactured in the United States of America
Printed on acid-free paper

Library of Congress Cataloging-in-Publication Data

Between languages and cultures : translation and cross-cultural texts
    / Anuradha Dingwaney and Carol Maier, editors.
        p.   cm.
    Includes bibliographical references and index.
    ISBN 0–8229–3858–8. — ISBN 0–8229–5541–5 (pbk.)
        1. Translating and interpreting. 2. Intercultural communication.
    3. Language and culture. I. Dingwaney, Anuradha
    II. Maier, Carol
    P306.2.B48   1994
    418′ .02—dc20   94–39790
                                                                      CIP

For permission to reprint previously published material, we are grateful to the
publishers of three essays: Rosario Ferré's "On Destiny, Language, and
Translation; or, Ophelia Adrift in the C. & O. Canal" is reprinted from *The
Youngest Doll*, by permission of University of Nebraska Press. Copyright ©
1991 by the University of Nebraska Press. Edward W. Said's "Embargoed
Literature" is reprinted from *The Nation* 17 September 1990, by permission
of the author. Copyright © 1990 by Edward W. Said. Anuradha Dingwaney
and Carol Maier's "Translation as a Method for Cross-Cultural Teaching" is
reprinted from *Understanding Others: Cross-Cultural Studies and the Teaching
of Literature*, ed. Joseph Trimmer and Tilly Warnock, by permission of the
authors and the National Council of Teachers of English. Copyright © 1992
by the National Council of Teachers of English.

To my mother and my sons,
Nalin and Jayesh, who have
learned to travel between cultures
at an early age.—A.D.

In memory of Esther Kastner Smith,
Alma Kastner Strack, and
Elsie Emma Kastner, my first
teachers of translation.—C.M.

Contents

III. Examining Translations and Cross-Cultural Encounters

IV. Translation, Pedagogy, and Cross-Cultural Texts

V. Responses

Preface

This collection has its beginnings in a pedagogical imperative. We use "beginnings" to convey the valence Edward Said attaches to the word: a way of delimiting a project, a specification of a particular point of departure, a particular emphasis. Both of us teach (and write about) literatures from and about the so-called "Third World"—Anglophone Africa and the Caribbean, the Indian subcontinent and Latin America—quite literally subjects constituted as the "other" of the West. "Ethnicity," "difference," and the "other" have been so commodified, and are so easily appropriated to the reigning critical fashions of postmodernism, or under the sign of the "familiar," that in order to "respect" the culturally specific contexts from which these literatures arise it is necessary to develop a countermethodology.

The beginning of this collection, then, is located precisely at the point we completed "Translation as a Method for Cross-Cultural Teaching." The essay, which deals with the challenges of teaching and writing about cross-cultural, "Third World" texts, helped us identify translation— or, more precisely, the activities associated with translation—as an enabling method for accomplishing these tasks. It also made us aware of the exciting and sophisticated work being done on translation theory and practice in cultural studies, anthropology/ethnography, postcolonial and "Third World" literatures and texts, and, of course, in the arena of translation studies itself. Wishing to bring some of this work together within the covers of a single volume, we sent out a preliminary proposal to approximately two dozen scholars working in these disciplines to solicit their contributions. Several of these scholars appear in this collection; those who do not wrote back, underscoring the need for such a collection even though previous commitments prevented them from contributing. In putting this collection together, we hoped to contextualize our efforts more fully, to make translation more visible in a variety of situations wider than we could address ourselves.

As the essays for *Between Languages and Cultures* came in, they seemed to fall "naturally" into certain groups, although, as readers will realize, they do not belong exclusively in given sections. On the contrary, there is a great deal of overlap and difference with respect to both style and topic, and we have sought to retain that heterogeneity, believing that translation is not so much a discipline as an interdisciplinary practice that occurs in diverse contexts.

The essays in the first section, "Translators on Translating Across Cultures," foreground decisions made by individual translators who are undoubtedly influenced by various cultural, social, and political imperatives as they seek to render "non"-Western texts into English. The second section, "(Not) Translating Across Cultures," addresses the absence of cross-cultural translation, whether deliberate or inadvertent, where the absence is a function primarily of markedly asymmetrical power relationships. The third section, "Examining Translation and Cross-Cultural Texts," focuses on the problematics—both the impediments and the potential— of translating between the "First" and "Third" worlds. "Translation, Pedagogy, and Cross-Cultural Texts," the fourth section, includes two essays that indicate the classroom as a site where translating subjects are provoked and enabled to move across and between cultures. Finally, the volume concludes with responses that reflect on some of the crucial issues raised by the essays.

As we complete work on this volume, we would like to extend our sincere thanks to the following people. From Oberlin College: Barbara Finnegan for all her help with the preparation of the manuscript; Alfred MacKay, dean of liberal arts, for providing funds to complete the index, and Rachel Schiller for her work on the index. In addition, we are grateful to Lynda Privitera, from Kent State University, for her assistance with Rosario Ferré's essay. We also want to express our gratitude to David Bartholomae and Jean Ferguson Carr for their encouragement when the project was in its early stages. Finally, our thanks to Fred Maier and Larry Needham for reading and commenting on innumerable drafts and for their encouragement.

March 1993

Between Languages and Cultures

Introduction: Translating "Third World" Cultures

Anuradha Dingwaney

"To speak a language," says Frantz Fanon, "is to take on a world, a culture" (38). Of course, Fanon is delineating the dilemma of the colonized—her/his acculturation, through language, to the (French) colonizers' values and ways of being. But Fanon's general point, that language cannot be isolated from the "world" or "culture" within which it is embedded and which it, thus, expresses, can be extended to other situations as well. With respect to translation, for example, Fanon's remark suggests that, in seeking to transport words (and sentences and texts) from one language to another, the translator cannot merely search for equivalent words in the "target" language to render the meaning of the "source." Rather, the translator must attend to the contexts ("a world, a culture") from which these words arise and which they, necessarily, evoke and express. Thus, it seems entirely appropriate that translation theory and practice has, in recent years, turned to both "source" and "target" cultures as something to be studied before the translation of a work can proceed. In translating works in metropolitan languages from what is construed as the "Third World," this imperative acquires even greater significance.[1] In the reflections that follow, I focus primarily on the translation of culture(s), or what can be better defined as a politics of translating ("Third World") cultures.

Before translation can be defined as an enabling means (and methodology) for discussing cross-cultural "Third World" texts, one must examine its potential pitfalls—the "violence," for instance, with which most self-conscious and thoughtful theorists and practitioners of translation associate it.[2]

Translation is one of the primary means by which texts written in one or another indigenous language of the various countries arbitrarily grouped together under the "Third," or non-Western, World are made available in western, metropolitan languages. However, translation is not restricted to such linguistic transfers alone; translation is also the vehicle through which "Third World" cultures (are made to) travel—transported or "borne across" to and recuperated by audiences in the West. Thus, even texts written in English or in one of the metropolitan languages, but originating in or about non-Western cultures, can be considered under the rubric of translation. For this interpretive move, Carol and I, and several of the contributors to this collection, are indebted to certain contemporary critical formulations about ethnography that, as John Sturrock notes, have done much "to fix attention on the question of translation":

In some quarters, ethnography has come to be seen as specifically concerned, no longer with the disingenuous description of other cultures, but with their "translation" into a form comprehensible to ourselves. An explicit "translation" of an alien society's customs, rites, and beliefs is no longer mistakable for the "real" thing, it is a version or account of another culture familiarized for us through the agency of a translator[/ethnographer].[3] (996)

The processes of translation involved in making another culture comprehensible entail varying degrees of violence, especially when the culture being translated is constituted as that of the "other." Talal Asad, whose work has greatly contributed to our understanding of the problems integral to the "translation of [a non-Western] culture," locates this violence in a specific exercise of power—colonial power, for example, and, more generally, the power of the West as it seeks to constitute the "Third World" as an object of its study.[4] In addition, in "Translating Europe's Others," Asad and John Dixon identify the institutional constraints and disciplinary demands of social anthropology and the expectations of the audiences for whom these translations are intended as affecting the translations undertaken. Given these constraints and the asymmetrical relationships of power obtaining between the cultures being studied and those doing the studying, these translations of cultures proceed, not surprisingly, in a predictable, even predetermined, direction: alien cultural forms or concepts or indigenous practices are recuperated (translated) via a process of familiarization (assimilation to culturally familiar forms or concepts or practices) whereby they are denuded of their "foreignness," even, perhaps, of their radical inaccessibility. For Asad and Dixon, therefore, "successful translations are rarer" than, presumably, unsuccessful ones (176). And here Asad and Dixon are insistent that their "argument has nothing to do with pleas for providing *attractive* as against *unattractive* representations, but with the demand that the metaphors being used in translation be *appropriate*." This task entails that the "translator/ethnographer . . . not take it for granted that her language already possesses the necessary concepts" with which to represent another culture (173).

In a recent interview with Nikos Papastergiadis, Ashis Nandy draws attention to a contemporary, spectacular instance of (mis)translation proceeding from what he calls "the bankruptcy of available categories" in the West. Speaking about "the frenzied discussion of [Ayatollah Khomeini's] *fatwa* [directed against Salman Rushdie] in the West," he suggests that this discussion "can be read as an attempt to make it [the *fatwa*] understandable—by turning it into a marker of a known form of insanity." Few people, he says, "were willing to admit that the *fatwa* was an unknown form of communication." For Nandy, the discussion revealed "the process of translation that is brought into play by using these [familiar] categories," for when "an event occurs which is outside the convenient frame of reference, it reveals the limits of the frame" (Papastergiadis, 100). If we accept Nandy's argument, it is possible to surmise that, among those Muslims who did not vociferously denounce the *fatwa*, there were some who did not concur with it at all; instead, they were reacting against and resistant to the West's easy translation of it as a "known form of insanity."

A somewhat different, albeit related, exercise of (Western) power has to do not so much with how non-Western cultures get translated, but rather with what and who gets translated. This has to do with the selection of certain voices, certain views, certain texts—by the publishing industry (presumably in response to what it believes readers will read) and by reviewers and critics—that are then constituted as a putative "canon" of "Third World" texts and/or authors. Tim Brennan, for example, has argued that the privileging of those whom he calls "cosmopolitan" writers as "interpreters and authentic public voices of the Third World" (viii) is a function of these writers' compliance with a "metropolitan audience's tastes" for certain kinds of (postmodern) narratives (37). "Alien, yet familiar," these writers straddle two cultures; attached to specific locales in the "Third World," they address their work primarily to readers in the West, whose tastes they both share and/or appeal to. This dual orientation (and, perhaps, allegiance) of their work makes them the privileged mediators and translators of "Third World" cultures and peoples for Western readers. Indeed, one can also argue that, with a foot in each of two cultures, these writers are themselves, to borrow a phrase from Rushdie, "translated m[e]n" (24).

The power and ability of the West to construct a canon that valorizes certain writers and texts while excluding others is not restricted to what Western readers are encouraged to read, or even what counts in terms of representations of the "Third World" in the West. Rather, this power moves out in ever-widening circles to affect what various "Third World" readers themselves come to see as apt representations of their own and other non-Western cultures. Aijaz Ahmad mentions how certain "canonical" Latin American fictional works arrive in India, mediated not only by translations (in English) commissioned by North American and British publishers, but also by critical commentaries on these works in various academic journals and reviews in the West. Inscribed already with the imprint of Western appropriations and/or interpretations, twice, even three times, removed from the cultures in which they originate or are about, these translations (in more ways than one, surely) are nevertheless often consumed as transparent windows on "Latin American reality" ("The Institution of Comparative Literature"). The stakes for critical (and oppositional) readings of Western translations of non-Western cultures are, therefore, very high, since these translations affect not simply the ways in which non-Western cultures are perceived and discussed in the "First World," but also how they are subsequently recuperated in various parts of the "Third World" as well.[5]

However, to say that translation can be (and often is) a form of violence, and to recognize that translations can be (and often are) tainted by power, time, and the vagaries of different cultural needs, is not to say that translations should, therefore, be scuttled. The fact of the matter is that translations are one of the primary means (not the only means, to be sure) by which cultures travel.[6] And, if we are not to be locked or secured within the bounds of our own culture (if such a thing is at all possible, since many cultures already interpenetrate one another within individuals and communities in virtually all parts of the globe), then translation is both important and necessary.[7] Indeed, all the scholars whose work I have discussed so far—while pointing to the many impediments to successful cultural translation—do not argue for or recommend its hasty demise. Instead, they gesture toward, even indicate, how translation can be made to work, can, in fact, be an enabling means for studying other cultures. Often they quote Rudolf Pannwitz, who is cited by Walter Benjamin in his "The Task of the Translator," to point out the direction translation should take:

Our translations, even the best ones, proceed from the wrong premise. They want to turn Hindi, Greek, English, into German, instead of turning German into Hindi, Greek, English. Our translators have a far greater reverence for their language than for the spirit of the foreign languages. . . . The basic error of the translator is that he preserves the state in which his own language happens to be instead of allowing his language to be powerfully affected by the foreign tongue. . . . He must expand and deepen his language by means of the foreign language. It is not generally realized to what extent this is possible, to what extent any language can be transformed. (72–73)

Thus, for instance, Asad, in a comparable move, claims that the "anthropologist's translation is not merely a matter of matching sentences in the abstract, but of *learning to live another form of life* and to speak another kind of language" ("Concept" 149). Or Lawrence Venuti, acknowledging Schleiermacher, who distinguishes between the translator who chooses a "domesticating method, an ethnocentric reduction of the foreign text to target-language cultural values, bringing the author back home" and the translator who chooses a "foreignizing method, an ethnodeviant pressure on those values to register the linguistic and cultural difference of the foreign text, sending the reader abroad," recommends, as does Schleiermacher, the latter move ("Translation as Cultural Politics" 210). What Pannwitz, Asad, and Venuti, via Schleiermacher, identify are modes of translating the "other" that allow "alien" languages (and ways of life) to interrogate, even radically disrupt the language (and way of life) that the self inhabits by virtue of being embedded within it. This may not (most likely will not) entirely divest the self of its habitual habitation. But it may allow the self to be "powerfully affected" by, instead of merely affecting, the "other," to be transformed and rendered more open to the claims of other languages and cultures. This condition is eminently desirable, indeed necessary, for successful translation between and across cultures to take place.

In response to this need, Carol and I titled this collection *Between Languages and Cultures: Translation and Cross-Cultural Texts.* In our letter to potential contributors we identified our interest

in the complex tension that results when a translator confronts what is alien and struggles to achieve the familiar in the face of otherness, without either sacrificing or appropriating difference. Working with this tension, the translator has a foot in each of two worlds and is able to mediate self-consciously between them. . . . This model of translation can give rise to a potentially disquieting, but highly interactive situation, by insuring that the mediation, including the mediation of reading, will be recognized and scrutinized.

The *between* of our title refers to that space of translation where the self or one culture encounters, and, more importantly, *interacts* with an "other" or another culture. It is a fertile space, and disquieting, because, if explored fully, it proves to be a sphere (or zone) in which one both abandons and assumes associations.

Between also refers to *transculturación,* a term (and activity) that according to Gustavo Pérez-Firmat, who draws on a term coined by Fernando Ortiz, characterizes "the Cuban Condition."[8] "Translational displacements that generate vernacular culture" (13), *transculturación* is Ortiz's rewriting of the term *acculturation,* which he finds "imprecise because it highlights only one aspect of a complicated, multifaceted phenomenon" (21). *Transculturación* can be seen as emerging from the space of translation through which critical criollism "inflect[s] rather than efface[s] European culture" (12). It signifies the "collision of cultures," and insofar as it "designates the fermentation and turmoil that precedes synthesis," it is "a coinage that denotes transition, passage, process" (23)—that "liminal zone or 'impassioned margin' where diverse cultures converge without merging" (25).

Transculturación, insofar as it designates the space within which the dominant language and culture is rewritten, inflected, subverted by the "subaltern," functions as a form of resistance.[9] In this regard, it describes a move similar to the one Homi Bhabha describes (and here I am drawing upon Benita Parry's discussion of Bhabha) when he recuperates those moments where the colonizer's discourse was "interrogated by the natives in their own accents" (Parry 39). According to Bhabha, colonial discourse is already fractured at its moment of enunciation, since, to mention only one such instance of fracture, the Enlightenment belief in the equality of all peoples is at odds with colonial rule. The native subjects exploit this fracture; in the act of rearticulating the colonial script, they (mis)translate it to produce "a qualitatively different thing-in-itself" (Parry 41). In this "hybrid" moment (which is also a moment of translation), "the uncertainties and ambivalences of the colonialist text" are exposed, and its "authorizing presence" is denied (Parry 41).

Between, for the purposes of this collection, is defined in at least two different ways: (1) as that space translators can occupy in response to the "intentions" of the text and/or culture they translate which, then, calls their habitual ways of living and thinking into question and allows them to be "powerfully affected" by another mode of living and thinking; (2) as that space from within which the (colonized) native deliberately (mis)translates the colonial script, alienating and undermining its authority. Regardless of the distinction between the two, each proceeds from an awareness of the "other's" agency and own forms of subjectivity, which "returns" the "other" to a history from which she or he was violently wrenched.

In addition, all the essays in this collection are self-conscious about their own interpretive moves and about the acts of translation they explore or enact. This is in accord with a great deal of current translation theory and practice, which calls for such self-reflexiveness on the part of translators and those who write about translations. As an antidote to translation practiced (or theorized) unaware, Venuti, for example, asserts the need for rendering translations—and the processes leading up to it—*visible* ("Translator's Invisibility" 181). Sturrock makes a comparable case for the value of "translationese," which "could represent, if intelligently used, an honorable refusal on the part of the translator seamlessly to indigenize his source; it could make visible the betweenness in which he is trapped. . . . A voluntary 'translationese,' systematically followed, would be something else, a drawing of our attention to the irrevocably mediate status of the language of translation" (1010).

In the translation of non-Western cultures (and languages), it is imperative that translators/ethnographers make their power and privileged vantage point evident. This task entails not only that they remain aware of their own locations with respect to the cultures they study, but also that they be constantly aware of "the institutional conditions and disciplinary demands" that impinge on their translations, that they understand fully whom they write for, within what contexts, and, more than anything else, the mediated status of their accounts. Fundamentally, this task entails registering those moments when the cultures (and languages) they study and translate are recalcitrant or resistant to the "demands"—or better, "needs"—of their own and those of the culture and language for which these translations are destined.

However, it is important that such self-reflexiveness not "return" the translating subject to the center he or she has implicitly occupied in the past. The cultures, and texts, being translated should, ideally, constrain this move, compelling the translator and her product (translation) to enter into a subtly dialectical interaction with the "source," through which "difference" is both mediated and recorded, not sacrificed or appropriated. The complex tension characterizing between-ness allows the translator to achieve this subtly dialectical interaction.

The significance of this collection is not restricted to a responsible study of other, distant, non-Western cultures. Instead, as Gómez-Peña is so insistent about reminding us, "the colonized cultures are sliding into the space of the colonizer"; multiculturalism "is the very core of the new society we are living in" in North America and other parts of the West (20).[10] Whether dominant culture will interact equitably with these cultures or whether it will compel them to assimilate to its own value systems is significant not merely for the discursive mapping of such a "collision of cultures," but also, and more importantly, for the way it affects the lived realities of those who have been (and continue to be) oppressed by virtue of their "otherness." Obviously, the stakes are high, as the virulent briefs against political correctness and/or cultural diversity/multiculturalism testify.[11] The briefs—which are an index of the power still possessed by dominant culture to define the terms by which the "other" is made to live her life and define her interests—also make clear that power is never just given up, or even shared. But the time has come to re-envision, redefine these terms. This collection, albeit modest in what it sets out to achieve, by focusing on how translation can help remap the task of studying and presenting non-Western cultures, should, nevertheless, contribute to such a redefinition.

Notes

1. Focusing not on cultures but rather on the lack of knowledge of (African and Asian) languages in the West, Aijaz Ahmad remarks on a somewhat different, although related, issue that has some bearing on this point:

Rare would be a literary theorist in Europe or the U.S. who does not command a couple of European languages other than his/her own; and the frequency of translation back and forth, among European languages creates very fulsome circuits for the circulation of texts, so that even a U.S. scholar who does not command much beyond English can be quite well grounded in the various metropolitan traditions. . . . Rare would be . . . a major literary theorist in Europe or the United States who has even bothered with an Asian or African language; and the enormous industry of translation which circulates texts among the advanced capitalist countries comes to the most erratic and slowest grind when it comes to translation from Asian or African languages. ("Jameson's Rhetoric" 4–5)

2. For example, Lawrence Venuti notes that

the violence of translation resides in its very purpose and activity: the reconstitution of the foreign text in accordance with values, beliefs and representations that pre-exist it in the target language, always configured in hierarchies of dominance and marginality, always determining the production, circulation, and reception of texts. Translation is the forcible replacement of the linguistic and cultural difference of the foreign text with a text that will be intelligible to the target-language reader. ("Translation as Cultural Politics" 209).

See also Carol Maier 630.

3. Sturrock identifies Evans-Pritchard as a very influential figure "in establishing this point of view among British ethnographers" (1012n4). More recently, James Clifford, who finds "ethnographic fieldwork" an "unusually sensitive method" for producing responsible "cross-cultural representation," notes how "participant observation obliges its practitioners to experience, at a bodily as well as an intellectual level, the vicissitudes of translation" (23–24). Among these, he mentions "the fact that ethnography is, from beginning to end, enmeshed in writing. This writing includes, minimally, a translation of experience into textual form" (25).

4. See, for instance, Talal Asad's introduction to *Anthropology and the Colonial Encounter*. More recently, Tejaswini Niranjana, who defines "translation as a significant technology of colonial domination," has analyzed the role played by translation in discursively securing and reinforcing British control over India. She points to the translations of Indian texts by "Jones, Wilkins, Halhed, Colebrooke, Ward, and others"—on which James Mill drew to construct his views of "Hindoo nature" in his three-volume *History of British India* (1817)—to argue: "By employing certain modes of representing the Other—which it thereby also [brought] into being—translation reinforce[d] hegemonic versions of the colonised, helping them to acquire the status of what Edward Said calls representation or objects without history" (776, 774). Translating, in this context, entailed "*purifying* the debased native texts," and though the British believed that "Indians should be governed by their own laws," they also believed that

"these laws had first to be taken away from them [Indians] and 'translated' before they could benefit from them" (775). Eric Cheyfitz also argues in similar terms, albeit about the somewhat different colonial conquest of the Americas, when he underscores the integral connections that obtain between translation—as a mode that functions through displacement, dispossession, usurpation—and colonization. His examples point again and again to what he calls "the problems of translation, the complex interactions between cultures and histories" that are evaded or ignored to produce translations of "what were necessarily difficulties, discords, indeed absences of translation, [that were] displaced into fictive accords of communication, composed, except for a scattering of transliterated native tongues, wholly in European terms" (6).

5. Among the far-reaching consequences of the "violence" perpetrated by colonial translations, Tejaswini Niranjana brings our attention to the fact that

European translations of Indian texts prepared for a Western audience provided to the 'educated' Indian a whole range of Orientalist images. Even when the Anglicized Indian spoke a language other than English, 'he' would have preferred, because of the symbolic power attached to English, to gain access to his own past through translations and histories circulating through colonial discourse. English education also familiarized the Indian with ways of seeing, techniques of translation, or modes of representation that came to be accepted as "natural." (778)

Here it is also worth mentioning that Said, in his introduction to *Orientalism*, identifies, among the readers his work is directed to, those from the "Third World" who have internalized "Orientalist" representations of their own peoples and cultures.

6. Edward Said notes: "Human experience is finely textured, dense, as well as accessible enough *not* to need the assistance of extra-historical or extra-worldly agencies to illuminate or explain it. What I am talking about is thus a way of regarding the whole world we live in as amenable to our investigation and interrogation quite without appeals to magic keys, or to special jargons and instruments, or curtained-off practices" ("Figures" 11). Said identifies Hobsbawm and Ranger's *The Invention of Tradition* as providing a method for analysis insofar as it suggests that "all parts of human history are available to understanding and elucidation because they are humanly constructed and designed to accomplish real tasks in the real world" (11). Responsible methods of cultural translation could equally provide exemplary tools for cross-cultural analysis.

7. James Boyd White observes: "The activity of translation offers an education in what is required for this interactive life, for . . . to attempt to 'translate' is to experience a failure at once radical and felicitous: radical, for it throws into question our sense of ourselves, our languages, of others; felicitous, for it releases us momentarily from the prison of our own ways of thinking and being" (257).

8. The term is used by Ortiz in an essay, "Del fenómeno social de la 'trans-

culturación' y de su importancia en Cuba," which, notes Pérez Firmat, "was originally published in the *Revista Bimestre Cubana* (1940) and subsequently included in *Contrapunteo cubano del tobaco y el azúcar* (161n13). Mary Louise Pratt covers some of the same issues; see especially her discussion of transculturation (6–7).

9. See, for example, Samia Mehrez's analysis of "radical bilingualism" as a "subversive poetics"; she notes that it

seeks to create a new literary space for the bilingual, post-colonial writer. It is a space that subverts hierarchies, whether they be linguistic or cultural; where separate systems of signification and different symbolic worlds are brought together in a relation of perpetual interference, interdependence, and intersignification. . . . Such a poetics becomes a statement on the process of decolonization itself, where the latter is to be read as a two-sided rather than a one-sided endeavor; a process in which both colonizer and colonized are implicated, where both parties are constantly written and rewritten. (260)

10. The large-scale scattering and migrations of postcolonial peoples from various parts of the "Third World" to the "First World" have, in turn, produced societies and cultures in the West that are necessarily multicultural.

11. See Needham, "Reimagining Familiar Dichotomies in Reading 'Alternative' Texts."

Works Cited

Ahmad, Aijaz. "The Institution of Comparative Literature and the Post-Colonial World." Lecture, Oberlin College, 5 April 1992.

———. "Jameson's Rhetoric of Otherness and the 'National Allegory.' " *Social Text* 17 (1987): 3–25.

Asad, Talal, ed. *Anthropology and the Colonial Encounter.* Atlantic Highlands, N.J.: Humanities Press, 1988.

———. "The Concept of Cultural Translation in British Social Anthropology." *Writing Culture: The Poetics and Politics of Ethnography.* Ed. James Clifford and George F. Marcus. Berkeley and Los Angeles. U of California P, 1986, 141–64.

———, and John Dixon. "Translating Europe's Others." *Europe and Its Others.* Ed. Francis Barker et al. Colchester: U of Sussex P, 1985. 170–93.

Benjamin, Walter. "The Task of the Translator." *Illuminations.* Ed. with an intro. by Hannah Arendt. Trans. Harry Zohn. New York: Schocken Books, 1969. 69–82.

Brennan, Timothy. *Salman Rushdie and the Third World: Myths of the Nation.* New York: St. Martin's Press, 1989.

Cheyfitz, Eric. *The Poetics of Imperialism: Translation and Colonization from* The Tempest *to* Tarzan. New York: Oxford UP, 1991.

Clifford, James. *The Predicament of Culture: Twentieth-Century Ethnography, Literature and Art.* Cambridge, Mass.: Harvard UP, 1988.

Fanon, Frantz. *Black Skin, White Masks.* Trans. Charles Lam Markmann. New York: Grove Press, Inc., 1967.

Gómez-Peña, Guillermo. "The Multicultural Paradigm: An Open Letter to the National Arts Community." *High Performance* Fall 1989: 18–27.

Hobsbawm, Eric, and Terence Ranger, eds. *The Invention of Tradition.* Cambridge: Cambridge UP, 1983.

Maier, Carol. "Notes After Words: Looking Forward Retrospectively at Translation and (Hispanic and Luso-Brazilian) Feminist Criticism." *Cultural and Historical Grounding for Hispanic and Luso-Brazilian Feminist Literary Criticism.* Ed. Hernan Vidal. Minneapolis: Institute for Study of Ideologies and Literature, 1989. 625–53.

Mehrez, Samia. "The Subversive Poetics of Radical Bilingualism: Postcolonial Francophone North African Literature." *The Bounds of Race: Perspective on Hegemony and Resistance.* Ed. with an intro. by Dominick LaCapra. Ithaca: Cornell UP, 1991, 255–77.

Needham, Anuradha Dingwaney. "Reimagining Familiar Dichotomies in Reading 'Alternative' Texts." *Journal of Midwest Modern Languages Association* 25 (Spring 1992): 47–53.

Niranjana, Tejaswini. "Translation, Colonialism, and the Rise of English." *Economic and Political Weekly* 14 April 1990: 773–79.

Papastergiadis, Nikos. "Ashis Nandy: Dialogue and the Diaspora—A conversation." *Third Text* 11 (Summer 1990): 99–108.

Parry, Benita. "Problems in Current Theories of Colonial Discourse." *Oxford Literary Review* 9 (1987): 27–58.

Pérez-Firmat, Gustavo. *The Cuban Condition: Translation and Identity in Modern Cuban Literature.* Cambridge: Cambridge UP, 1989.

Pratt, Mary Louise. *Imperial Eyes: Travel Writing and Transculturation.* London: Routledge, 1992.

Rushdie, Salman. *Shame.* An Aventura Paperback, 1983.

Said, Edward W. "Figures, Configurations, Refigurations." *Race & Class* 32 (July–September 1990): 1–16.

———. *Orientalism.* New York: Vintage Books, 1979.

Sturrock, John. "Writing Between the Lines: The Language of Translation." *New Literary History* 21 (1990): 993–1013.

Venuti, Lawrence. "Translation as Cultural Politics: Regimes of Domestication in English." *Textual Practice* 7.2 (1993): 208–23.

———. "The Translator's Invisibility." *Criticism* 28 (Spring 1986): 179–212.

White, James Boyd. *Justice as Translation: An Essay in Cultural and Legal Translation.* Chicago: U of Chicago P, 1990.

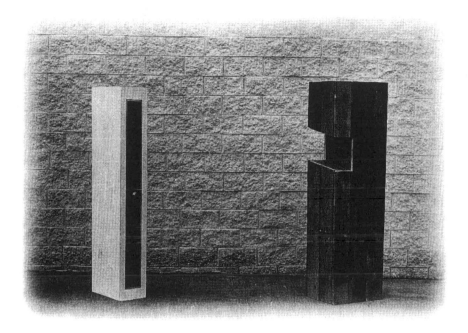

I. Translators on Translating Across Cultures

This section of essays addresses the practice of individual translators, the decisions they make in their work with specific texts, and the cultural, social, and political imperatives that undoubtedly influence those decisions. Although current work in translation theory has begun to draw on various disciplines in order to foreground and explore translation's inevitable mediation, the cross-cultural dimensions of translation practice have yet to be articulated fully. In "Toward a Theoretical Practice for Cross-Cultural Translation," Carol Maier examines the intersections between recent contributions in translation theory and explicit cross-cultural concerns. Stressing a distinction between "difference" and "inequality," she outlines a practice based on altered definitions of intimacy and inquiry, encouraging discussion of translation as an activity that makes cross-cultural power relations more visible and furthers more equitable cross-cultural exchange.

The difficulties inherent in such practice are exemplified in Rosario Ferré's "On Destiny, Language, and Translation; or, Ophelia Adrift in the C. & O. Canal." Ferré defines her "habitat"—as a writer and, frequently, as a translator of her own work—as the "crevice in between" that lets "oneself become the meeting place of [two cultures]." For her, "translation is not only a literary, but also a historical act" which requires a translator who has "experienced the historical fabric, the inventory of felt moral and cultural existence embedded in . . . [the] language [being translated]." In discussing Puerto Rican immigrants to the U.S. who,

19

"fleeing from poverty and hunger," are "forced to be merciless with memory, as they struggle to integrate," Ferré believes it is her duty to translate Puerto Rican texts and culture so that she can "restore" memory to "its true abode."

Sharon Masingale Bell, "In the Shadow of the Father Tongue: On Translating the Masks in J.-S. Alexis," is also concerned with translation as both historical and literary. She examines Haitian literary experiments in French (the official language, language of the colonizers and prestige), in Creole (the vernacular language, assigned less status, and defined as the "language of home and intimacy"), and in French inflected by Creole (instances of code-mixing). For Bell, the choice to use one language or the other, or both, is fraught with political and emotional import, especially in writing, where the choice is assumed to be deliberate. Her essay explores the implications of that choice for writers, translators, and translations. Her own choice to substitute black vernacular for Creole in her translation of Jacques-Stéphen Alexis's *Romancéro aux étoiles*, is implicated in the politics of translating "subaltern" positions/languages constructed through negotiations between "dominant" and "subordinate" languages.

Agha Shahid Ali, like Ferré, reflects on his own work as a translator. In "*The Rebel's Silhouette:* Translating Faiz Ahmed Faiz," he enacts and describes various levels of translation/transformation: from *raga* to *ghazal* and vice versa, from Urdu to English, and, of course, the "translation" inevitable in his own "hybrid" cultural situation as an Indian from the subcontinent writing in English. Possessing an inwardness with the two languages—Urdu and English, whose diverse cultural demands he negotiates with ease—Agha feels virtually no sense of linguistic embattlement or oppressiveness between the two, as Bell registers in her work with French, Creole, and English. Nevertheless, he recognizes and asserts that English has to be "renewed, reworked, 'translated,' even," before it can meet the demands of Faiz's poetry, which is itself engaged in acts of "translation" as it seeks to transform every stock image of Urdu *ghazals* in order to speak urgently about the subcontinent's social and political oppressions and about the need for a (socialist) revolution.

Toward a Theoretical Practice for Cross-Cultural Translation

Carol Maier

"[T]heory's project is to bring to the surface the naturalized, concealed frames of intelligibility that enable cultural enunciation and also to produce new conceptual frames which, by providing new perspectives on the problem, enable (re)thinking in the service of social transformation."
> —Madhava Prasad, "On the Question of a Theory of (Third World) Literature"

1

As a teacher of translation, I have found that one of the topics novice translators first notice and want to discuss in a workshop is the complexity of the translator's role. They usually bring with them the common, unexamined assumption that translation is primarily a question of substitution and unavoidable betrayal. That such assumptions not only misrepresent but actually distort the activity of translation, however, is something beginners pick up on immediately. Translation, they soon point out, implies not so much (failed) exchange as (problematic) interchange that should not automatically be defined as loss.

Not that *loss* is entirely inaccurate, as novice translators argue after only one or two experiences. In the case of translation, however, the strongest associations of *loss* prove not to lie in the impossibility of transferring a given "meaning" from one language to another. Quite the contrary, the loss that beginning translators articulate concerns the practice of translation itself. For what impresses them is not so much the difficulty of finding "equivalents" as the opportunity to explore available possibilities and to discover new ones. With the curiosity and clear-sightedness of those who look for the first time, they are drawn to the crux of the translator's never-static, highly paradoxical activity. They want to discuss it, at times almost obsessively, and they register as loss the fact that the translator's rendering must be offered as absolute, many times without even a nod to the disquieting but potentially enabling flux implicit in all signification.[1]

Despite their recognition of the loss caused by a lack of representations that would portray their work more fully, however, new translators soon begin to move as rapidly as possible through the space "between" languages. Expected by readers and publishers to provide the results of translation rather than a record of their explorations, they assume the translator's nearly habitual stance regarding translation that, however productive in theory, must be abandoned in favor of a solution. This means that the "inner space" defined by translators as consubstantial with the activity of translation tends to be known instead as an "emptiness" (Hirschfield 130), a "no-man's land" (Wuilmart 242; Hewson and Martin 134), or an "abyss."[2]

Consequently, flux becomes identified with defeat rather than with discovery, and translators' notes are often written in apology, as asides, endnotes or footnotes, introductions or afterwards, rather than communications from the "space between." This requires, necessarily, the suppression of the disorientation—at times humorous, at times downright frightening—of a familiar language breaking down under the pressure not only to accommodate but also to transmit the unknown. Hence, there is an almost resolute avoidance of the "between" in which that breakdown occurs and a failure to acknowledge the potential for human interaction that occurs when one language proves inadequate in the presence of another.

2

Recently, in accordance with and informed by current work in literary theory, anthropology, and cultural studies, and particularly with respect to an increased sensitivity to instances of blatant mistranslation between "First" and "Third" worlds, North American[3] translation theorists have begun to call for a scrutiny of practice (see e.g., Venuti, *Rethinking* 1–17). Such scrutiny would focus on translation as activity as well as, or more than, product and thus explore precisely the interaction and ambivalence beginning translators find missing from definitions of translation. Those theorists work from diverse vantage points within a wide range of disciplinary contexts, but they share a certain veering or "turn" in the nature of translation theory. At once expanding the unit of translation from isolated words and sentences to entire texts or even entire cultures (Bassnett and Lefevere 8), and focusing on specific strategies, they have begun to look anew at the "space" in which translation occurs as one of definite "possibilities" (Doyle 25; Hewson and Martin 135–36).

The metaphor of the turn is a promising one that has been developed extensively by Douglas Robinson, who uses it both to indicate a new opportunity for the translator who has too seldom had the chance to speak and to investigate the translator's somatic interaction with a text. Almost simultaneously, however, it has also cropped up elsewhere in situations where its use is less extended but perhaps ultimately more inclusive. Examples would include Dennis Schmidt's "linguistic turn," a "revising gesture that should blast the borders of the Western tradition . . . and recognize the relevance of languages and cultures beyond the walls of the West" (7); Cynthia Roy's study of the interpreter as a participant rather than a "conduit" in turn taking; the "cultural turn" proposed by Mary Snell-Hornby, which "implicitly embraces all kinds of translation" (84; Bassnett and Lefevere 4–5). This last instance, by pointing to translation as an activity that could be termed *interdisciplinary* by definition, also brings to mind examples that can be useful for articulating the "betweenness" so often omitted from discussions of translation: Julia Kristeva's exploration of foreignness and the "uncanny,"[4] Guillermo Gómez-Peña's performances and "border art," and Homi Bhabha's discussion of translation as a hybridity that "represents that ambivalent 'turn' of the discriminated subject into the terrifying, exorbitant object of paranoid classification" ("Signs" 155).

Several other theorists, albeit without employing the same metaphor, also stress the need for a thorough examination of translation's role as a decidedly political practice, even when it is not recognized as such. In this respect, the work, for example, of Eric Cheyfitz, Tejaswini Niranjana, and Lawrence Venuti coincide. Although much of that work studies ways and instances in which translation (as both practice and product) has repeatedly obliterated rather than communicated a "source" culture, it also represents an effort to theorize alternative practices that stress translation's potential for constructing equitable exchange. As envisioned by these theorists, translation acquires a dimension that can be appreciated fully only by returning to the often-lost site of flux, breakdown, and questioning identified by beginning translators. There, translation's potential for prompting an intimacy charged with inquiry can be experienced most immediately.

Such an experience recalls James Boyd White's comment that an examination of translation should not be "about transportable 'content,' but about . . . relations" (255). It also recalls the "border crosser 'subject'" defined by D. Emily Hicks. Pointing to the need for a term that would suggest the altered relation to territory (whether text or terrain) that translation can occasion, Hicks stresses the potential terror or tyrannizing implicit in any allegiance to territory. Thus her "subject," discussed in terms of Deleuze and Guattari's "deterritorialization," "emerges from double strings of signifiers of two sets of referential codes, from both sides of the border" (xxvi). The intent is to trigger what I call "terrortorealization," in which individual allegiance is shed, the allegiances of others are acknowledged, and the potential dangers inherent in all such attachments are experienced.[5] As a term, *terrortorealization* may seem unnecessarily strange, but it responds to the inadequacies of conventional descriptions of the activity of translation. In a large measure because of those inadequacies, as Lori Chamberlain has explained with respect to the binary-directed paradigms of gender, translation practice has been consistently misrepresented, and its potential for accommodating relationships that occur "outside" or "between" languages and cultures has been underestimated. Therefore, Chamberlain and other theorists, in particular feminist theorists like Nicole Brossard, Susanne de Lotbinière-Harwood, Barbara Godard, and Sherry Simon, seek not solely to flaunt translation's mediation (Godard 94) but also to alter the language and the forums in which it is discussed (Homel and Simon, "Feminist Poetics" 43–54).

3

Given the renewed critical attention currently paid to translation, in particular translation as a silencing through violence (Venuti, "Translation as Cultural Politics"), recuperation (Lewis), and imperialism (Cheyfitz) that occurs precisely at the site between languages and cultures, it might seem that a new model for cross-cultural translation has already been proposed. To some extent this is the case, especially with respect to the insistence on a valorization of difference found in the work of both practitioners and theorists. Venuti's work, to cite what is perhaps the most developed example, draws on and applies the writings of Foucault, Derrida, Pound, and Blanchot to call for "resistant strategies" (*Rethinking* 12). Such strategies should enable translation to function as the very "locus of difference" (13) by countering the preference for fluency long prevalent in the West (4, 14*n10*). Further examples would include Niranjana's deliberately "rough" version (185) of a twelfth-century Indian *vacana* or the "simple adjacency" Richard Seiburth proposes as he discusses Walter Benjamin's argument that translation is an activity more metonymic than metaphoric (242–43). Each of these translators works within the definition of respect articulated recently by Noël Valis as "the ability to approach a work knowing you can't explain it away or 'know' it entirely . . . acknowledging that the work does not belong to you, that the work is in some fundamental way alien to you the critic" (415).

"In some fundamental way alien": Even as I copy those words and relate them to the examples of difference noted above, I am reminded of a comment by Madhava Prasad in his remarks on R. Radhakrishnan's identification of the "realities of different and globally unequal histories." "Inequality," Prasad contends, is not synonymous with and may even be considered contrary to "difference"; "inequality is far more resistant to reification, and preserves its rationality." What is more, Prasad suggests, the possibility exists that a focus on difference suppresses discussion of inequality by assuming, perhaps, that the "achievement of difference will automatically erase inequality" (68). In a different context, Radhakrishnan, too, has proffered this caution. Writing about the "plural" (that is, different) "subject" positions in a single South African world, he points out that those positions are "simultaneous but not synchronous." "Whereas the dominant position requires acts of self-deconstruction," he says, "the subordinate position entails collective self-construction" (277). Or, as Ella Shohat notes, "Post-colonial theory's celebration of hybridity" can, and does, serve to "blur" difference rather than define it and the inequalities implicit within it (110). S.P. Mohanty takes this "blurring" even a step further: "Mere difference [which Mohanty contrasts with 'incommensurability'] leads . . . to a sentimental charity, for there is nothing in its logic that necessitates our attention to the other" (23).

The word *inequality* also appears in conjunction with discussions of both fluent translation and the imbalance of power that prevails in discussions about what gets translated and for whom. As Venuti explains, "When the language is contemporary English, transparent discourse sustains grossly unequal cultural exchanges between the hegemonic English-language nations, particularly the United States, and their others in Europe, Africa, Asia, and the Americas" (*Rethinking* 5). His explanation is seconded by Richard Jacquemond, who contends that "inequality is the main feature between Western and Third World languages and cultures" (140) and traces that inequality in translation patterns between what he refers to as languages of the North and those of the South (139). Those "uneven networks of dissemination" are also pointed out by George Yúdice (204) and Ilán Stavans, who has remarked on "a kind of literary I.N.S. that seems to establish quotas on how many south-of-the-border novels can be translated into English annually" (244). Gayatri Spivak, too, speaks of the "sheer authority" enjoyed by certain originals and argues that the "status of a language in the world is what one must consider when teasing out the politics of translation" ("Politics" 189). Andé Lefevere has commented most extensively, perhaps, about the bearing a culture's "relative weight" ("Translation" 19; "Translations and Other Ways") has on the (lack of) translation; his examples rarely include instances from the "Third World," but his discussions of the many ways works are refracted in translation frequently address the factor of inequality.

Lefevere's insistence on discussing as disinterestedly as possible what I refer to as inequality and what he, like Spivak, refers to in terms of authority ("Translation" 15) no doubt responds to his determination to dissociate himself from the prescriptiveness and "pious platitudes" that "invariably surface in discussions of translation" (27). He calls for informed practice but does not advocate particular strategies or propose new models. A similar observation could be made about Robinson, who enumerates various turnings or "versions" available to translators according to the effect and response desired. The "cross-cultural" conversation with which he concludes (258) represents a "paradigm shift" (257) from the conventional goal of one or another form of equivalence to an "open-minded compositional relatedness" (257). Although such a conversation allows for considerations of inequality, those considerations do not figure directly in Robinson's discussion. On the contrary, he suggests that he has deliberately left them implicit (293n19).

Venuti, on the other hand, does advocate particular strategies, propose new models, and acknowledge the importance of power relations in translation. Significantly, however, in discussions of both his own practice as a translator and his presentation of that practice, he stresses not the inequality he mentions in his introduction to *Rethinking Translation* but the crucial link between difference and resistance. Translation's "liberating moment," he suggests, "would occur when the reader of the resistant translation experiences, in the target language, the cultural differences

which separate that language and the foreign text" ("Simpatico" 18).
Venuti here is explaining his work with contemporary Italian poet Milo
De Angelis; he is concerned with the differences between North American
and Italian poetics, which he believes will consign De Angelis to a
"marginal" and "minor" stature in English (8). He is in pursuit of a
"strangeness" (15) that owes to the fact that his translations "resist the
hegemony of transparent discourse in English-language culture" (18).
Neither inequality nor its suggestion arise in his discussion. Nor are the
"cultural differences" he encounters implicated in the "hegemony of
transparent discourse" to an extent that he need speak of either inequality
or the impossibility of finding the "analogous techniques of fragmentation and proliferation of meaning" (10) that will enable him to construct
a version of De Angelis's poetry in English.

Gayatri Spivak's work—in particular her discussion of the "Translator as Reader" in "The Politics of Translation" (178–92)—comes
much closer to offering the translator a model for working cross-
culturally. Not only does she address inequality, she maps out both a
method for translation and what she believes to be the requirements
for considering oneself a reader sufficiently "intimate" with a text, a
language, and a culture to undertake a translation (181, 185). In the
face of what she finds to be a proliferating "with-it translationese" (180),
Spivak's requirements are tough, and her concern is as much to staunch
fluency masquerading as translation as it is to provide a paradigm for
translation itself—indeed, what she stresses in "Translation in General"
("The Politics of Translation" [192–95]) is untranslatability or the
withholding of translation (193). In this way, particularly for the "First
World" translator, her model might better be seen as a caution than
as an attempt to theorize practice; she finds that "the genuinely bilingual
post-colonial [to whom, in the end, she addresses her article] now has
a bit of an advantage" (185). Nirajana's example of the *vacana* might
go further, although that example is brief, and Niranjana, like Spivak,
speaks of (and to?) the "post-colonial translator" (186).

4

Because "First World" translators are only beginning to recognize "the
implicit postulate of an egalitarian relationship between different linguistic and cultural areas," as Richard Jacquemond suggests in his study of

French-Arabic translation (140) and as Marilyn Gaddis Rose indicates in her review of recent works in translation theory ("Hermeneutic" 167), it is no doubt too soon to speak of a theory for cross-cultural translation. At the same time, however, "First World" translators must articulate, as they begin to explore translation's "between" in terms of inequality as well as difference, specific strategies for working with "Third World" texts and the ways in which the practice of translation can prompt a cross-cultural exchange that occurs within an acknowledgment of power relations between "First" and "Third" worlds. With these considerations in mind, I suggest two requisites as primary for the elaboration of such strategies and such a practice: intimacy and inquiry.

Intimacy

"[I]t would be a practical help," Spivak comments, "if one's relationship with the language being translated was such that sometimes one preferred to speak in it about intimate things" ("The Politics of Translation" 181). As I have noted previously, Spivak's suggestion is offered in the face of translations often made quickly and by translators not thoroughly familiar with the language and culture being translated. The result is a homogenization of "Third World" texts, "so the literature by a woman in Palestine begins to resemble, in the feel of its prose, something by a man in Taiwan" (180). (For a further, brief example, think of "Southern Hemisphere" as a section in *Belles lettres* in which appear pieces about works from Africa, the Middle East, Asia, Latin America, and the Caribbean.) As Spivak argues convincingly, a translator needs to "earn the right to become the intimate reader" of a text (181), and this can occur only through the "close acquaintance, association, or familiarity" (*American Heritage Dictionary* 945) that makes intimacy possible.

Spivak's concern with instances of appropriation rather than intimacy leads her to propose a "withholding" of translation in "untranslatable" situations ("The Politics of Translation" 192–95; "Acting Bits" 791–96). Certain experiences or stories, she contends, can only be "passed on" with "the mark of untranslatability" on them ("Acting Bits" 792)—hence the development of resistant strategies that prevent an easy identification devoid of any recognition of inequality. Such strategies will be similar to those proposed by Venuti and others, but they will also be distinct in a significant way: whereas Venuti, for example, seeks to provoke an experience of difference and recognition (of "misrecognition") ("Simpatico" 18), Spivak argues for what is ultimately a severance. Or a silence.

Although I disagree with neither Spivak's examples of homogenization nor her requirements for would-be translators of "Third World" literature, I suggest an altered conception of the relation between intimacy and translation. Because I believe that once translation ceases to be defined in terms of equivalence and one disbands with the determination to "match" phenomena that irremediably cast discussion in terms of translation's product, translation can be considered in terms of a practice in which it is possible to approach both difference and inequality interrogatively. In other words, once translation is made visible and experienced as an activity that occurs within an explicit context or compact (Maier 628) of difference and inequality, one finds oneself involved in a close interaction similar to that of the "linguistics of contact" discussed by Mary Louise Pratt ("Linguistic Utopias" 59–64). Such contact is not best defined in terms of either a tolerance of difference or a silence of separation; rather, as Pratt explains, it emphasizes "copresence, interaction, interlocking understandings and practices, often within radically asymmetrical relations of power" (*Imperial Eyes* 7). Within those relations of power, a certain, redefined intimacy can develop which an informed practice of translation can further. Rather than devise strategies for withholding translation, one must work to redefine expectations for translation by coming up with approaches that will show it as the humbling, disconcerting experience translation can be.

In order to effect such a redefinition of expectations, some of Spivak's strategies will be invaluable, but I would suggest employing and expressing them in terms of translation as a goal rather than as an obstacle or a deception. I would also draw on Venuti's techniques of resistance, although I believe, as noted above, that those techniques have yet to be evaluated in a specifically cross-cultural context. In an essay devoted to strategies similar to Venuti's, which he refers to as "antiabsorptive," Charles Bernstein explains how such resistive techniques can be employed toward "absorptive ends" and a "fuller engagement" (22, 49). The difficulty, of course, is that of creating a context of engagement in which "liberation" (to use Venuti's word) involves not so much Bernstein's "shift" in the "plane of engagement" (56), or Venuti's recognition of "differences" as Pratt's recognition of "contact" with all the potential, heterogeneous interaction it implies.

In this regard, as Niranjana (46) and Sharon Willis (118n7) have indicated, Bhabha's extensive work with "hybridity" has precise and compelling implications for "First World" translators. Not only does it make evident the "hybrid quality of the colonizing culture" (Willis 118*n7*), hybridity is linked, as Bhabha explains to "an aesthetic distance," an "interstial intimacy" that involves estrangement from and subversion of authority ("The World and the Home" 148). A second experience, "Creoleness," and the definition of it as presented by Jean Bernabé, Patrick Chamoiseau, and Raphaël Confiant—"an annihilation of false universality, of monolingualism, and of purity" (892)—can be similarly helpful. Both "hybridity" and "Creoleness," as well as the theoretical essays in which they have been developed, are potentially useful for a translation practice that aims to encourage a move toward a redefined "absorption," "engagement," or "intimacy."

At the same time, however, it must be kept in mind that "hybridity" and "Creoleness," as used in current critical discourse, have arisen in the context of specific political struggles and that to abstract them from that context is to risk compromising the impact of their critique and the nature of the intimacy they propose. The "process of Creolization," as explained by Bernabé and his colleagues, "refers to the brutal interaction . . . of culturally different populations" (893). Bhabha's "hybridity," in turn, is linked not only to "interstial intimacy," but also to "the disjunctive, displaced everyday life of the liberation struggle" of diasporic peoples ("The World" 148) and to a "space of 'translation' . . . where the construction of a political object that is new, *neither the one nor the Other,* properly alienates our political expectations, and changes, as it must, the very forms of our recognition of the 'moment' of politics" ("Commitment" 10–11).

Inquiry

Inquiry is integrally related to "subjectivity" and "identity." It must therefore be addressed with respect to their mutual role in the questioning occasioned by a translation practice that gives rise to the "fractional" intimacy I have just described.

When a translation practice is informed by an acknowledgment of the inequalities that characterize power relations between "First" and "Third" worlds and by a familiarity with the intimacy and heterogeneity that work toward more equitable cross-cultural encounters, subjectivity will be achieved to the extent that identity is problematized. Thus, I believe it is possible to speak of a "translating subject" as one who works deliberately between cultures, enabled by an understanding of identity as a learned or constructed allegiance rather than an innate condition. Aware both that universal terms of identification—*woman,* for example—do not have universal definitions, and that individuals nevertheless employ them as the starting points of their own individual and collective identities, such a translator seeks "new conceptual frames" (Prasad 57–58) that will present one culture to another and does not assume that those frames will be found ready and waiting in either culture.

The word *seeks* is paramount in the previous sentence because it points to the translator's obligation not to fall back on familiar but unexamined frames. This is especially important for cross-cultural translation where the development of "new conceptual frames" might well imply a critique of the "frame" itself as a "promising starting point" (Snell-Hornby 79) for a discussion of translation practice. Even when the frame is presented as "the fabric from which texts are woven" rather than "prefabricated potential texts" (Neubert and Shreve 60), the tendency still persists to speak of "matching cultural frames" (61) as well as mapping the new one that must be created or "organized" (63) in translation. For if translation is defined not as product but as the practice for which I have been arguing, its "end" is the prompting of rather than the resolution of an inquiry. Thus an increase in subjectivity is linked to the problematizing of identity (the "terrortorealization" discussed earlier) and to further investigation of how apparently inexplicable things might be comprehended without making them explicable in familiar terms (and without allowing them to appear simply different).

That even monolingual speakers can be drawn into the activity of translation as I have been discussing it can be illustrated with two brief examples that foreground the use of inequality between languages and cultures as a strategy for provoking translation. The first, found in prose like that of Sandra Cisneros's *"Woman Hollering Creek" and Other Stories* and Tsitsi Dangarembga's *Nervous Conditions,* demonstrates how Spanish or Shona words inscribed in English can communicate not only their "meaning" to a monolingual reader but also their unequal status vis-à-vis an English-speaking "First World."[6] I am thinking, for instance, of the commentary on Spanish and English made by the words of Cisneros's first-person narrator in "Bien Pretty" as she speaks in English and Spanish about making love in Spanish: "To have a lover sigh *mi vida, mi preciosa, mi chiquita,*" she explains, was to make love in a language in which

"Nothing sounded dirty or hurtful or corny" (153). This is not to say that the narrator—or Cisneros's work—implies that nothing nasty ever happens as a consequence of making love "in Spanish"—it can and does in her books. The strategic use of two languages, however, simultaneously excludes a monolingual reader from one (bilingual) reading of the book and triggers another in which that reader begins to translate both individual words and the culture in which they are embedded.

Sadza functions in a similar way in *Nervous Conditions.* Although it is never defined or described, a reader unacquainted with *sadza* cannot but form an idea of what it is, connect *sadza* to the meals prepared and served daily on the farm where Tambu grows up and comprehend its role in her first meal at the mission. *Sadza* is the only food Tambu finds edible there, and she is the only one at the table who eats it. As she struggles to eat with the unfamiliar cutlery, *sadza* clashes as both food and word, inscribing the subordination of an entire culture (82).

Although one could speak of the Spanish endearments in "Bien Pretty" or Dangarembga's use of *sadza* as an example of "withheld" translation, I offer them as examples of translation occasioned and suggest that they be compared with the following instance in which translation was indeed withheld from an audience. That opportunity concerns *Death and the Maiden,* a "dark play involving torture" (Rohter 1) by Chilean playwright Ariel Dorfman. As explained by Benedict Nightingale and Larry Rohter, when the play was staged in London, its specific political context was made explicit; staged in New York, however, the political context was diffused in the hope of pleasing a Broadway audience. Dorfman has summarized as follows the aesthetics of director Mike Nichols, who considered the play "a thriller" (Rohter 32): "Entice them, don't lose them because if you don't cajole them along, they won't bear with it, they'll leave" (Nightingale 34). Dorfman's observation that, as a playwright who collaborated with Nichols, he had "tortured" and "done violence" to the play "for its own good" (Nightingale 34) indicates his evaluation of the "success" of their approach to a difficult translation situation.

Dorfman's observation also suggests the extent to which he and Nichols apparently erred in their assumptions about intimacy and inquiry. Yes, it was necessary to take into account the inequalities between a Chilean context and a North American one, but was it necessary to decide that because a North American audience lacks "a frame" for dictatorship they cannot be prompted to engage in a political drama that addresses the terror of living under a dictatorship? Dorfman called the production a "translation into a language the audience could understand" (Nightingale 34). He might better have said that the production preempted a translation because the audience was denied the opportunity to participate in translation as it might have occurred.

5

The work of anthropologists Ana María Alonso and María Teresa Koreck, who studied the "epidemiology of AIDS among US minorities," led them to realize that their research required the "deconstruction of Anglo-American categories of ethnic identity, such as 'Hispanic,' and of erotic practice, sexual being, and gender" (107). More specifically, Alonso and Koreck learned that, although "equivalents" could be found in Spanish for terms like "homosexuality," "bisexuality," and "heterosexuality," the frames of reference were not interchangeable because "erotic practices and gender identities are differently construed by Mexicans and Anglos" (107). In addition, the implementation of Western "epistemological assumptions and research methodologies" (115) has not been proven to be effective in AIDS research among Latinos because researchers were not asking the appropriate questions, even though they asked their questions in Spanish. Before researchers could conduct their survey, they needed to interrogate their own language and the assumptions operating within it.

My example of the need for a cross-cultural translation of the questions involved in AIDS research should be considered in the context of the "loss" experienced by the novice translators discussed earlier and that the loss they regretted be recovered by the "beginner's mind" or "emptiness" I find in the comments of two very different thinkers, bell hooks and Gayatri Spivak.

In a recent interview, hooks responds to a question about preventing exploitation by describing a "subject-to-subject encounter" of "mutual recognition" reminiscent of those that might occur in Pratt's "contact zones." This recognition both makes inequality apparent and "allows a certain kind of negotiation that seems to disrupt the possibility of domination" (93). hooks also speaks of a genuine "power of knowing" (83) or wanting to know about other people (84) that is linked to a willingness to "empty out the self" (83). She explains that her efforts to encourage such willingness through the basic translation exercises she assigns to her students in order to encourage them to think "globally." "I tell my students," she says, "'In the first two weeks, in order not to think with a First World context—if you eat a steak, you have to take out your pen and paper and write down what goes into producing that steak'" (92).

Although Spivak's comments were made in a theoretical context quite different from that of hooks (and although I in no way want to dismiss or attempt to "bridge" that difference), Spivak too points to such questions as the following as (somewhat paradoxically) an enabling device for "First World" students: "What do you think is the inscription that allows you to think the world without any preparation? What kind of coding has produced this subject?" ("In a Word" 148). Asked with the humility advised by Spivak in her comments ("I will share with you what I have learned about knowing, that these are the limits of what I undertake, looking to others to teach me" [148]), it is a question that can give rise to the separation from oneself that precedes learning.

Such questions can also occasion translation in the context of not only difference but decided inequality.

Notes

1. See Roman Jakobson, for example: "The meaning of any linguistic sign is its translation into some further, alternative sign" (232).

2. I use the word *abyss* because of the response Marilyn Gaddis Rose received from the translators she surveyed about their practice ("Seeking Synapses" 10). Rose found that translators spoke of an "inner space" not clearly identifiable with either language in which they worked (a space she discusses in terms of Jean-François Lyotard's *différand*), but that most translators expressed discomfort in that space and said they tried to pass through it quickly (9, 10).

3. It is important to stress the inclusion of Canadian translators in "North American." See, for example, Simon, "The Language of Cultural Difference," and Homel and Simon.

4. For a discussion of Kristeva's "uncanny" with respect to translation, see Gökberk. I would like to thank Professor Gökberk for allowing me to read and cite her paper.

5. The term *reterritorialization* might come to mind as a restorative move (Hicks xxxi; Venuti, "Simpatico" 18), but it too can be "deadly" (Deleuze and Guattari 61).

6. Interestingly, Cisneros describes herself as a "translator" who writes for both the "Latino" and the "white" communities (Tabor B2).

Works Cited

Alonso, Ana María and María Teresa Koreck. "Silences: 'Hispanics,' AIDS, and Sexual Practices." *Differences* 1.1 (1989): 101–24.

American Heritage Dictionary of the English Language. 3rd ed., 1992.

Bassnett, Susan and André Lefevere, ed. *Translation, History and Culture.* London: Pinter Publishers, 1990.

Bernabé, Jean, Patrick Chamoiseau, and Raphaël Confiant. "In Praise of Creoleness." Trans. Mohamed B. Taleb Khyar. *Callaloo* 13 (1990): 886–909.

Bernstein, Charles. *Artifice of Absorption.* Philadelphia: Singing Horse Press/*Paper Air*, 1987.

Bhabha, Homi. "The Commitment to Theory." *New Formations* 5 (Summer 1988): 5–23.

———. "Signs Taken for Wonders: Questions of Ambivalence and Authority Under a Tree Outside Delhi, May 1817." *Critical Inquiry* 12.1 (1985): 144–65.

———. "The World and the Home." *Social Text* 31/32 (1992): 141–53.

Brossard, Nicole. *Mauve Desert.* Trans. Susanne de Lotbinière-Harwood. Toronto: Coach House P, 1990.

Chamberlain, Lori. "Gender and the Metaphorics of Translation." *Signs* 13.3 (1988): 454–72. Also in Venuti, *Rethinking Translation,* 57–74.

Cheyfitz, Eric. *The Poetics of Imperialism: Translating and Colonization from The Tempest to Tarzan.* New York: Oxford UP, 1989.

Cisneros, Sandra. *"Woman Hollering Creek" and Other Stories.* New York: Random House, 1991.

Dangarembga, Tsitsi. *Nervous Conditions.* Seattle: Seal Press, 1989.

Deleuze, Gilles and Félix Guattari. *Kafka: Toward a Minor Literature.* Trans. Réda Bensmaia. Minneapolis: U of Minnesota P, 1986.

Doyle, Michael Scott. "Translation and the Space Between: Operative Parameters of an Enterprise." Larson 13–26.

Godard, Barbara. "Theorizing Feminist Discourse/Translation." Bassnett and Lefevere 87–96.

Gökberk, Ülker. "Writing 'in Translation': Towards a Hermeneutics of *Ausländerliteratur.*" MLA Convention. San Francisco, 30 Dec. 1991.

Gómez-Peña, Guillermo. "A Bilingual Performance Pilgrimage" and "Border Brujo." *The Drama Review* 35.3 (Fall 1991): 22–45, 49–66.

————. "The Multicultural Paradigm: An Open Letter to the National Arts Community." *High Performance* 12.3 (Fall 1989): 18–27.

Hewson, Lance, and Jacky Martin. *Redefining Translation: The Variational Approach.* London: Routledge, 1991.

Hicks, D. Emily. *Border Writing: The Multidimensional Text.* Minneapolis: U Minnesota P, 1991.

Hirshfield, Jane. "The World Is Large and Full of Noises: Thoughts on Translation." *The Georgia Review* 45.1 (Spring 1991): 125–43.

Homel, David, and Sherry Simon. *Mapping Literature: The Art and Politics of Translation.* Montreal: Véhicle Press, 1988.

hooks, bell. Interview with Andrea Juno. *Angry Women. Re/Search* 13 (1991): 78–97.

Jacquemond, Richard. "Translation and Cultural Hegemony: The Case of French-Arabic Translation." Venuti 139–58.

Jakobson, Roman. "On Linguistic Aspects of Translation." *On Translation.* Ed. Reuben A. Brower. New York: Oxford UP, 1966. 232–39.

Kristeva, Julia. *Strangers to Ourselves.* Trans. Leon S. Roudiez. New York: Columbia UP, 1991.

Larson, Mildred L., ed. *Translation: Theory and Practice, Tension and Interdependence.* American Translators Association Scholarly Monograph Series V. Binghamton: SUNY UP, 1991.

Lefevere, André. "Translation: Its Genealogy in the West." Bassnett and Lefevere 14–28.

————. "Translations and Other Ways in Which One Literature Refracts Another." *Symposium* 38.2 (1984): 127–42.

Lewis, Philip H. "The Measure of Translation Effects." *Difference in Translation.* Ed. Joseph F. Graham. Ithaca: Cornell UP, 1985, 31–62.

de Lotbinière-Harwood, Susanne. *Re-belle et infidèle: La traduction comme practique du réécriture au féminin/The Body Bilingual: Translation as a Rewriting in the Feminine.* Quebec and Toronto: Les Éditions du remue-ménage/Women's P, 1991.

Maier, Carol. "Notes After Words: Looking Forward Retrospectively at Translation and (Hispanic and Luso-Brazilian) Feminist Criticism." *Cultural and Historical Grounding for Hispanic and Luso-Brazilian Feminist Literary Criticism.* Ed. Hernán Vidal. Minneapolis: Institute for the Study of Ideologies and Literature, 1989. 625–53.

Mohanty, S. P. "Us and Them: On the Philosophical Bases of Political Criticism." *Yale Journal of Criticism* 2.2. (1989): 1–31.

Neubert, Albrecht and Gregory M. Shreve. *Translation as Text.* Kent, Oh.: Kent State UP, 1992.

Nightingale, Benedict. "*Death and the Maiden* Becomes a Tale of Two Cities." *The New York Times* 10 May 1992: H1+.

Niranjana, Tejaswini. *Siting Translation: History, Post-structuralism, and the Colonial Context.* Berkeley and Los Angeles: U of California P, 1992.

Prasad, Madhava. "On the Question of Theory of (Third World) Literature." *Social Text* 31/32 (1992): 57–83.

Pratt, Mary Louise. "Linguistic Utopias." *The Linguistics of Writing: Arguments Between Language and Literature.* Ed. Nigel Fabb et al. New York: Methuen, 1987. 48–66.

———. *Imperial Eyes: Travel Writing and Transculturation.* New York: Routledge, 1992.

Radhakrishnan, R. "Negotiating Subject Positions in an Uneven World." *Feminism and Institutions: Dialogues on Feminist Theory.* Ed. Linda Kauffman. Cambridge, Mass.: Basil Blackwell, 1989. 276–90.

Robinson, Douglas. *The Translator's Turn.* Baltimore: Johns Hopkins UP, 1991.

Rohter, Larry. "Dorfman's 'Maiden' Cries Out." *New York Times* 8 March 1992: H1+.

Rose, Marilyn Gaddis. "The Hermeneutic Turn." *Frontiers: Proceedings of the 33rd Annual Conference of the American Translators Association.* Ed. Edith Losa. Medford, N.J.: Learned Information, Inc., 1992. 261–68.

———. "Seeking Synapses: Translators Describe Translating." Larson 5–12.

———. "Translation and Language Games." Schmidt 57–68.

Roy, Cynthia. "Interpreters, Their Role, and Metaphorical Language Use." *Looking Ahead: Proceedings of the 31st Annual Conference of the American Translators Association.* Ed. A. Leslie Willson. Medford, N.J.: Learned Information, Inc., 1990. 77–86.

Schmidt, Dennis J., ed. *Hermeneutics and the Poetic Motion.* Translation Perspectives V. Binghamton: Center for Research in Translation, SUNY Binghamton, 1990.

Seiburth, Richard. "The Guest" Second Thoughts on Translating Hölderlin." *The Art of Translation: Voices from the Field.* Ed. Rosanna Warren. Boston: Northeastern UP, 1989. 244–57.

Shohat, Ella. "Notes on the 'Post-Colonial.'" *Social Text* 31/32 (1992): 99–113.

Simon, Sherry. "The Language of Cultural Difference: Figures of Alterity in Canadian Translation." Venuti 159–76.

Snell-Hornby, Mary. "Linguistic Transcoding or Cultural Transfer? A Critique of Translation Theory in Germany." Bassnett and Lefevere 79–86.

Spivak, Gayatri Chakravorty. "Acting Bits/Identity Talk." *Critical Inquiry* 18.4 (1992): 770–803.

———. "In a Word." Interview with Ellen Roony. *Differences* 1.2 (1989): 124–56.

———. "The Politics of Translation." *Destabilizing Theory: Contemporary Feminist Debates.* Ed. Michèle Barrett and Anne Phillips. Stanford, Calif.: Stanford UP, 1992. 177–200.

Stavans, Ilán. "Roll Over, Vargas Llosa." *The Nation* 22 February 1993:
     244–46.
Tabor, Mary B. W. "A Solo Traveler in Two Worlds." *New York Times* 7
     January 1993: B2.
Valis, Noël. Rev. of *Juan Goytisolo. The Case for Chaos,* by Abigail Lee Six.
     MLN 107.2 (1992): 415–17.
Venuti, Lawrence, ed. *Rethinking Translation: Discourse, Subjectivity, Ideology.*
     New York: Routledge, 1992.
———. "Simpatico." *SubStance* 20.2 (1991): 3–20.
———. "The Translator's Invisibility." *Criticism* 28 (Spring 1986): 179–212.
———. "Translation as Cultural Politics: Regimes of Domestication in
     English." *Textual Practice* 7.2 (1993): 208–23.
White, James Boyd. *Justice as Translation: An Essay in Cultural and Legal
     Translation.* Chicago: U of Chicago P, 1990.
Willis, Sharon. "Mistranslation, Missed Translation: Hélène Cixous' *Vivre
     l'Orange.*" Venuti 106–19.
Wuilmart, Françoise. "Le traducteur littéraire: Un marieur empathique de cul-
     tures." *Meta* 35.1 (1990): 236–42.
Yúdice, George. "We Are *Not* the World." *Social Text* 31/32 (1992): 201–16.

On Destiny, Language, and Translation; or, Ophelia Adrift in the C. & O. Canal

Rosario Ferré

> Language is the most salient model
> of Heraclitean flux . . .
> So far as we experience and realize
> them in linear progression,
> time and language are intimately
> related; they move and
> the arrow is never in the same place.
> —George Steiner, *After Babel*

> What is translation? On a platter
> A poet's pale and glaring head,
> A parrot's screech, a monkey's chatter,
> And profanation of the dead.
> —Vladimir Nabokov, "On Translating Eugene Onegin"

A few weeks ago, when I was in Puerto Rico, I had an unusual dream. I had decided, after agonizing over the decision for several months, to return to the island for good, ending my five-year stay in Washington, D.C. My return was not only to be proof that Thomas Wolfe had been wrong all along and that one *could* go home again; it was also an anguishedly mulled over decision, which had taken me at least a year to arrive at. I wanted to come in contact with my roots once again; to nurture those hidden springs of consciousness from which literary inspiration flows, and which undoubtedly are related to the world we see and dream of as infants, before we can formulate it into words.

In my dream I was still in Washington, but was about to leave it for good. I was traveling on the C. & O. Canal, where horse-towed barges full of tourists still journey picturesquely today, led by farmers dressed up in costumes of Colonial times. I had crossed the canal many times before, entering the placid green water which came up to my waist

39

without any trouble, and coming out on the other side, where the bright green, African daisy–covered turf suspiciously resembled the Puerto Rican countryside. This time, however, the canal crossing was to be definitive. I didn't want my five professionally productive years in Washington to become a false paradise, a panacea where life was a pleasant limbo, far removed from the social and political problems of the island. I felt that this situation could not continue, and that in order to write competently about my world's conflicts, as war correspondents have experienced, one has to be able to live in the trenches and not on the pleasant hillocks that overlook the battlefield.

As I began to cross the canal, however, and waded into the middle of the trough, I heard a voice say loudly that all the precautions of language had to be taken, as the locks were soon to be opened and the water level was going to rise. Immediately after this someone opened the heavy wooden gates of the trough at my back and a swell of water began to travel down the canal, lifting me off my feet and sweeping me down the current, so that it became impossible to reach either of the two shores. At first I struggled this way and that, as panic welled up in me and I tried unsuccessfully to grab onto the vegetation which grew on the banks, but I soon realized the current was much too powerful and I had no alternative but to let it take hold of me. After a while, as I floated face up like Ophelia over the green surface of the water, I began to feel strangely at ease and tranquil. I looked at the world as it slid by, carried by the slowly moving swell of cool water, and wondered at the double exposure on both shores, the shore of Washington on my right and the shore of San Juan on my left, perfectly fitted to each other and reflected on the canal's surface like a traveling mirror on which I was magically being sustained.

The water of the canal reminded me then of the mirror on the door of my wardrobe when I was a child, whose beveled surface entranced me when I crawled up to it because, when one looked closely into its edge, left and right fell apart and at the same time melted into one. The canal had the same effect on me; in it blue sky and green water, north and south, earth and vegetation ceased to be objects or places and became passing states, images in motion. The water of words, the water in the C. & O. Canal where "all the precautions of language had to be taken," was my true habitat as a writer; neither Washington nor San Juan, neither past nor present, but the crevice in between. Being a writer, the dream was telling me, one has to learn to live by letting go, by renouncing the reaching of this or that shore, but to let oneself become the meeting place of both.

In a way all writing is translation, a struggle to interpret the meaning of life, and in this sense the translator can be said to be a shaman, a person dedicated to deciphering conflicting human texts, searching for the final unity of meaning in speech. Translators of literary texts act like a writer's telescopic lens; they are dedicated to the pursuit of communication, of that universal understanding of original meaning which may one day perhaps make possible the harmony of the world. They struggle to bring together different cultures, striding over the barriers of those prejudices and misunderstandings which are the result of diverse ways of thinking and of cultural mores. They wrestle between two swinging axes, which have, since the beginning of mankind, caused wars to break out and civilizations to fail to understand each other: the utterance and the interpretation of meaning; the verbal sign (or form) and the essence (or spirit) of the word.

I believe that being both a Puerto Rican and a woman writer has given me the opportunity to experience translation (as well as writing itself) in a special way. Only a writer who has experienced the historical fabric, the inventory of felt moral and cultural existence embedded in a given language, can be said to be a bilingual writer, and being a Puerto Rican has enabled me to acquire a knowledge of both Spanish and English, of the Latin American and of the North American way of life. Translation is not only a literary but also a historical task; it includes an interpretation of internal history, of the changing proceedings of consciousness in a civilization. A poem by Góngora, written in the seventeenth century, can be translated literally, but it cannot be read without taking into account the complex cultural connotations that the Renaissance had in Spain. Language, in the words of George Steiner, is like a living membrane; it provides a constantly changing model of reality. Every civilization is imprisoned in a linguistic contour, which it must match and regenerate according to the changing landscape of facts and of time.

When I write in English I feel that the landscape of experience, fields of idiomatic, symbolic, communal reference are not lost to me, but are relatively well within my reach, in spite of the fact that Spanish is still the language of my dreams. Writing in English, however, remains for me a cultural translation, as I believe it must be for such writers as Vladimir Nabokov and Vassily Aksyonov, who come from a country whose cultural matrix is also very different from that of the United States. Translating a literary work (even one's own) from one language to another curiously implies the same type of historical interpretation that is necessary in translating a poem of the seventeenth century, for example, as contemporary cultures often enclaved in different epochs of time coexist with each other. This is precisely what happens today with North American and Latin American literatures, where the description of technological, pragmatic, democratic modern states coexists with that of feudal, agrarian, and still basically totalitarian states. Translating literature from Spanish into English (and vice versa) in the twentieth century cannot but take into account very different views of the world, which are evident when one compares, for example, the type of novel produced today by Latin American writers such as Carlos Fuentes, Gabriel García Márquez, and Isabel Allende, who are all preoccupied by the processes of transformation and strife within totalitarian agrarian societies, and the novels of such North American writers as Saul Bellow, Philip Roth, and E. L. Doctorow, who are engrossed in the complicated unraveling of the human psyche within the dehumanized modern city-state.

Translating has taught me that it is ultimately impossible to transcribe one cultural identity into another. As I write in English I am inevitably translating a Latin American identity, still rooted in preindustrial traditions and mores, with very definite philosophical convictions and beliefs, into a North American context. As Richard Morse has so accurately pointed out in his book *Prospero's Mirror, a Study in the Dialectics of the New World,* Latin American society is still rooted in Thomistic, Aristotelian beliefs, which attempt to reconcile Christian thought with the truths of the natural universe and of faith. Spain (and Latin America) have never really undergone a scientific or an industrial revolution, and they have never produced the equivalent of a Hobbes or a Locke, so that theories such as that of pragmatism, individual liberty, and the social contract have been very difficult to implement.

Carlos Fuentes's novel *Terra Nostra,* for example, tries to point out this situation, as it analyzes the failure of the Latin American totalitarian state (the PRI in Mexico), founded both on the Spanish tradition of absolute power established by Philip II during the seventeenth century and on the blood-soaked Aztec Empire. Fuentes' case, however, as well as that of Alejo Carpentier, can be said to be exceptions to the rule in the Latin American literary landscape, as both writers make an effort in their novels to escape arbitrary descriptions of their worlds, and often integrate into their novels rationalistic analyses which delve into Latin American traditions from diverging points of view.

Translating my own work, I came directly in contact with this type of problem. In the first place, I discovered that the Spanish (and Latin American) literary tradition permits a much greater leeway for what may be called "play on words," which generally sounds frivolous and innocuous in English. In Puerto Rico, as in Latin America, we are brought up as children on a constant juggling of words, which often has as its purpose the humorous defiance of apparent social meanings and established structures of power. In undermining the meaning of words, the Latin American child (as the Latin American writer) calls into question the social order which he or she is obliged to accept without sharing in its processes. This defiance through humor has to do with a heroic stance (*el relajo, la bachata, la joda*) often of anarchic origin which is a part of the Latin personality, but it also has to do with faith, with a Thomistic belief in supernatural values. It is faith in the possibility of Utopia, of the values asserted by a society ruled by Christian, absolute values rather than pragmatic ends, which leads the Puerto Rican child to revel in puns such as "Tenemos mucho oro, del que cagó el loro" ("We have a lot of gold, of the kind the parrot pukes"), or "Tenemos mucha plata, de la que cagó la gata" ("We have a lot of silver, of the kind the cat shits"), which permit him to face, and at the same time defy, his island's poverty; or in popular Puerto Rican sayings of the blackest humor and unforgiving social judgment such as, "El día que la mierda valga algo, los pobres nacerán sin culo" ("The day shit is worth any money, the poor will be born without assholes").

But faith in the magical power of the image, in the power to transform the world into a better place through what Lezama Lima calls the "súbito," is only one of the traditions that enable Latin American writers to revel in puns and wordplay; there is also a historical, geographic tradition which I believe helps to explain the elaboration of extremely intricate forms of expression. It is not casually or by expediency that the literary structures in Alejo Carpentier's *Los pasos perdidos* (*The Lost Steps*), João Guimarães Rosa's *Grande Sertão: Veredas* (*The Devil to Pay in the Backlands*), or Nélida Piñón's *Tebas no meu coração* (*My Beloved Thebes*) often remind us of the baroque altarpieces of the churches of Brazil, Mexico, and Peru, where baroque art reached its maximum expression. When the Spanish conquerors reached the New World in the fifteenth and sixteenth centuries they brought the Spanish language and tradition with them, but that language and tradition, confronted by and superimposed on the complex realities of Indian cultures, as well as the convoluted forms of an equally diverse and till then unknown flora and fauna, began to change radically. In this sense Spanish literature in itself had received, by the seventeenth century had come around, considerable cultural influence from the Latin American continent. Don Luis de Góngora y Argote, for example, who never visited the Spanish colonies, would probably never have written *Soledades* (Solitudes), a poem considered the apex of baroque literary expression, in which a shipwrecked traveler reaches the shores of a Utopian New World, if Spanish had not been the language in which Mexico and Peru were discovered and colonized. None has put it more clearly than José Lezama Lima, the Cuban poet, in an essay entitled "La curiosidad barroca" (Baroque Curiosity). Lezama points out there how the baroque literary art of Góngora, as well as that of his nephew, the Mexican Don Carlos de Sigüenza y Góngora and of the Mexican nun Sor Juana Inés de la Cruz, evolves parallel to the carved altarpieces of Kondori, an Indian stonecarver from Peru, which represent "in an obscure and hieratic fashion the synthesis of Spanish and Indian, of Spanish theocracy with the solemn petrified order of the Inca Empire." Lezama's own novel, *Paradiso,* whose linguistic structure is as convoluted as the labyrinths of the Amazon jungle, remains today the most impressive testimony to the importance of baroque aesthetics in the contemporary Latin American novel.

A third characteristic that helps define Latin American tradition vis-à-vis North American tradition in literature today has often to do with magical occurrences and the world of the marvelously real (*lo real maravilloso*), which imply a given faith in the supernatural world which is very difficult to acquire when one is born in a country where technological knowledge and the pragmatics of reason reign supreme. We are here once again in the realm of how diverging cultural matrices determine to a certain extent the themes that preoccupy literature. In technologically developed countries such as the United States and England, for example, the marvelous often finds its most adequate expression in the novels of writers like Ray Bradbury and Lord Dunsany, who prefer to place their fiction in extraterrestrial worlds where faith in magic can still operate and the skepticism inherent in inductive reasoning has not yet become dominant.

As I began to translate my novel, *Maldito Amor (Sweet Diamond Dust),* the issues I have just mentioned came to my attention. The first serious obstacle I encountered was the title. "Maldito amor" in Spanish is an idiomatic expression which is impossible to render accurately in English. It is a love that is halfway between doomed and damned, and thus participates in both without being either. The fact that the adjective *maldito,* furthermore, is placed before the noun *amor,* gives it an exclamative nature which is very present to Spanish speakers, in spite of the fact that the exclamation point is missing. *Maldito amor* is something very different from *amor maldito,* which would clearly have the connotation of "devilish love." The title of the novel in Spanish is, in this sense, almost a benign form of swearing, or of complaining about the treacherous nature of love. In addition to all this, the title is also the title of a very famous *danza* written by Juan Morell Campos, Puerto Rico's most gifted composer in the nineteenth century, which describes in its verses the paradisiacal existence of the island's bourgeoisie at the time. As this complicated wordplay would have been totally lost in English, as well as the cultural reference to a musical composition which is only well known on the island, I decided to change the title altogether in my translation of the novel, substituting the much more specific "Sweet Diamond Dust." The new title refers to the sugar produced by the De Lavalle family, but it also touches on the dangers of a sugar which, like diamond dust, poisons those who sweeten their lives with it.

The inability to reproduce Spanish wordplay as anything but an inane juggling of words not only made me change the title; it also soon made me begin to prune my own sentences mercilessly like overgrown vines, because, I found, the sap was not running through them as it should. How did I know this? What made me arrive at this conclusion? As I faced sentence after sentence of what I had written in Spanish hardly two years before (when I was writing the novel), I realized that, in translating it into English, I had acquired a different instinct in my approach to a theme. I felt almost like a hunting dog which is forced to smell out the same prey, but one which has drastically changed its spoor. My faith in the power of the image, for example, was now untenable, and facts had become much more important. The dance of language had now to have a direction, a specific line of action. The possibility of Utopia, and the description of a world in which the marvelously real sustained the very fabric of existence, was still my goal, but it had to be reached by a different road. The language of technology and capitalism, I said to myself, must above all assure a dividend, and this dividend cannot be limited to philosophic contemplations, or to a feast of the senses and of the ear.

Thus, I delved into a series of books on the history and sociology of the sugarcane industry in Puerto Rico, which gave me the opportunity to widen the scope of the novel, adding information and situating its events in a much more precise environment.

Is translation of a literary text possible, given the enormous differences in cultural tradition in which language is embedded? I asked myself this, seeing that as I translated I was forced to substitute, cancel, and rewrite constantly, now pruning, now widening the original text. In the philosophy of language and in reference to translation in general (not necessarily of a literary text), two radically opposed points of view can be and have been asserted. One declares that the underlying structure of language is universal and common to everyone. "To translate," in the words of George Steiner, "is to descend beneath the exterior disparities of two languages in order to bring into vital play their analogous and . . . common principles of being." The other one holds that "universal deep structures are either fathomless to logical and psychological investigation or of an order so abstract, so generalized as to be well-nigh trivial." This extreme, monadistic position asserts that real translation is impossible, as Steiner says, and that what passes for translation is a convention of approximate analogies, "a rough-cast similitude, just tolerable when the two relevant languages or cultures are cognate."

I lean rather more naturally to the second than to the first of these premises. Translating literature is a very different matter from translating everyday language, and I believe it could be evaluated on a changing spectrum. Poetry, where meaning can never be wholly separated from expressive form, is a mystery which can never be translated. It can only be transcribed, reproduced in a shape that will always be a sorry shadow of itself. That is why Robert Frost pronounced his famous dictum that "poetry is what gets lost in translation" and Ortega y Gasset evolved his theory on the melancholy of translation, in "Miseria y esplendor de la traducción" (The Misery and the Splendor of Translation). To one side of poetry one could place prose and poetic fiction, where symbolic expression may alternate with the language of analysis and communication. Here one could situate novels and prose poems which employ varying degrees of symbolic language and which are directed toward both an intuitive *and* an explanatory exposition of meaning. On the far side of the spectrum one could place literary texts of a historical, sociological, and political nature, such as the essays of Euclides Da Cunha in Brazil, for example, and the work of Fernando Ortíz in Cuba or of Tomás Blanco in Puerto Rico. These texts, as well as those of literary critics who have been able to found their analytic theories on a powerfully poetic expression (such as Roland Barthes), are perhaps less difficult to translate, but even so the lacunae which arise from the missing cultural connotations in these essays are usually of the greatest magnitude.

Translating one's own literary work is, in short, a complex, disturbing occupation. It can be diabolic and obsessive: it is one of the few instances when one can be dishonest and feel good about it, rather like having a second chance at redressing one's fatal mistakes in life and living a different way. The writer becomes her own critical conscience; her superego leads her (perhaps treacherously) to believe that she can not only better but surpass herself, or at least surpass the writer she has been in the past. Popular lore has long equated translation with betrayal: "Traduttore-traditore" goes the popular Italian saying. "La traduction est comme la femme, plus qu'elle est belle, elle n'est pas fidèle; plus qu'elle est fidèle, elle n'est pas belle" goes the chauvinst French saying. But in translating one's own work it is only by betraying that one can better the original. There is, thus, a feeling of elation, of submerging oneself in sin, without having to pay the consequences. Instinct becomes the sole beacon. "The loyal translator will write what is correct," the devil whispers exultantly in one's ear, "but not necessarily what is right."

And yet translation, in spite of its considerable difficulties, is a necessary reality for me as a writer. As a Puerto Rican I have undergone exile as a way of life, and also as a style of life. Coming and going from south to north, from Spanish to English, without losing a sense of self can constitute an anguishing experience. It implies a constant recreation of divergent worlds, which often tend to appear greener on the other side. Many Puerto Ricans undergo this ordeal, although with different intensity, according to their economic situation in life. Those who come from a privileged class, who form a part of the more recent "brain drain" of engineers, architects, and doctors who emigrate today to the States in search of a higher standard of living, can afford to keep memory clean and well tended, visiting the site of the "Lares" with relative assiduity. Those who come fleeing from poverty and hunger, such as the taxi drivers, elevator operators, or seasonal grape and lettuce pickers who began to emigrate to these shores by the thousands in the forties, are often forced to be merciless with memory, as they struggle to integrate with and become indistinguishable from the mainstream. It is for these people that translation becomes of fundamental importance. Obliged to adapt in order to survive, the children of these Puerto Rican parents often refuse to learn to speak Spanish, and they grow up having lost the ability to read the literature and the history of their island. This cultural suicide constitutes an immense loss, as they become unable to learn about their roots, having lost the language which is the main road to their culture. I believe it is the duty of the Puerto Rican writer, who has been privileged enough to learn both languages, to try to alleviate this situation, making an effort either to translate some of her own work or to contribute to the translation of the work of other Puerto Rican writers. The melancholy of the Puerto Rican soul may perhaps this way one day be assuaged, and its perpetual hunger for a lost paradise be appeased. Memory, which so often erases the ache of the penury and destitution suffered on the island, after years of battling for survival in the drug-seared ghettos of Harlem and the Bronx, can, through translation, perhaps be reinstated to its true abode.

I would like now to talk a bit about the experience of being a woman writer from Latin America, and how I suspect being one has helped me to translate literary works. As a Latin American woman writer I feel a great responsibility in forming a part of, and perpetuating, a literary tradition which has only recently begun to flourish among us. I feel we must become aware that we belong to a community of countries that cannot afford to live at odds with each other; a community whose future, in fact, depends today on its ability to support and nurture itself, helping to solve each other's problems. A sense of belonging to a continental community, based on an identity which was first envisioned by Simón Bolívar, must rise above nationalistic passions and prejudices. In this respect, Brazilian women writers have always been at the forefront, for they were the first to write not solely for the women of Brazil, but for all those Latin American women who, like the feminine protagonists of Clarice Lispector and Nélida Piñón in stories like "Uma gallina" (A Chicken) and "Torta de chocolate" (Chocolate Cake), have suffered a stifling social repression.

As a woman writer who has lived both in Anglo America and Latin America I have had, like Ophelia drifting down the canal or the child that looks into the beveled mirror of her wardrobe, to be able to see left become right and right become left without feeling panic or losing my sense of direction. In other words, I have had to be able to let go of all shores, be both left-handed and right-handed, masculine and feminine, because my destiny was to live by the word. In fact, a woman writer (like a man writer), must live traveling constantly between two very different cultures (much more so than English and Spanish), two very different worlds which are often at each other's throats: the world of women and the world of men. In this respect, I have often asked myself whether translation of feminine into masculine is possible, or vice versa (here the perennial question of whether there is a feminine or a masculine writing crops up again). Is it possible to enter the mind of a man, to think, feel, dream like a man, being a woman writer? The idea seems preposterous at first, because deep down we feel that we cannot know anything but what we are, what we have experienced in our own flesh and bones. And yet the mind, and its exterior, audible expression, language or human speech, is mimetic by nature. Language, in Leibnitz's opinion, for example, was not only the vehicle of thought but its determining medium. Being matterless, language (thought) can enter and leave its object at will, can actually become that object, creating it and destroying it as it deems necessary. In this sense the cabalistic tradition speaks of a logos, or a word which makes speech meaningful and is like a hidden spring which underlies all human communication and makes it possible. This concept of the word as having a divine origin confers upon it a creative power which may perhaps justify the writer's attempt to enter into modes of being (masculine, Chinese, extraterrestrial?) in which she has not participated in the course of her own human existence.

I like to believe that in my work I have confronted language not as a revelation of a divine meaning or of an unalterable scheme of things, but as a form of creation, or recreation of my world. If writing made it possible for me to authorize (become the author of) my own life, why may it not also permit me to enter into and thus "create" (translate?) the lives of other characters, men, women, and children? These are questions I ask myself often, which I may never be able to answer, but I believe it is important to try to do so.

In the Shadow of the Father Tongue:
On Translating the Masks in J.-S. Alexis

Sharon Masingale Bell

I

The reflections presented here grew out of my translating Haitian writer Jacques-Stéphen Alexis's collection of nine short stories, *Romancéro aux étoiles*. The language of these short stories based both on traditional Haitian folklore and on the Western literary tradition includes instances of Creole embedded in an otherwise standard, literary French, embedded so subtly that readers unfamiliar with Haitian language and culture might not be aware that they are reading representations of another language. I came to believe that these instances of Creolization in Alexis's literary language represent episodes of deliberate code-mixing, a phenomenon which commonly occurs in communities where two or more languages find themselves in contact. As such, they needed to be translated into English in such a way that the code-mixing was preserved. I chose Black English as a target language for the translation of what, following Henry Louis Gates, I shall call Alexis's linguistic masks. As I struggled to discover and to understand as many of Alexis's masks as I could, I began to reflect upon what it means to multilingual speakers to possess a vernacular tongue and to function in it in a situation where that vernacular exists in the shadow, as it were, of an official language, or, as in the case of African Americans, of a standard dialect beside which the vernacular language has the status of "basilect," the language of lowest social prestige.

In this analysis of my choice of Black English for translating the Creole embedded in the narratives of Alexis's *Romancéro aux étoiles*, I will demonstrate that the two languages have similar functions within their respective dominant languages and communities. My purpose, however, is not merely to provide an inventory of such similarities, but rather to reflect on the political, cultural, and social import of code-mixing and code-switching within both communities. For example, what emotional coloring is carried by the use of these respective tongues for native speakers? How does the choice of a vernacular word or locution in otherwise standard speech alter communication? What is the political significance of a writer's choice to write in the standard dialect, and how is it altered by the occasional embedding of vernacular language? I wish to demonstrate here that the encoding of vernacular language forms within standard or "official" language allows writers the possibility of informing the official languages in which they write with a subtext that takes on the characteristics of vernacular language use within their respective cultures.

Code-mixing is defined as the insertion of words on phrases from one of the given languages in contact into an utterance primarily enunciated in the other. When speakers alternate between languages in longer utterances—for example, when they change languages on switching topics or interlocutors—the process is called code-switching (Olshtain and Blum-Kulka 59, 60). Both are such frequent phenomena in bilingual communities that finding them reflected in the speech of characters in literatures that emerge from, and variously inscribe, contact with colonialism (and which, at least in the countries of the African diaspora, nearly always arise out of a situation where two or more languages are in contact) strikes one as the normal experience of a common speech habit. One of the preconditions of code-mixing is that the speaker actually speak both languages. Thus, my discussion here will concern fairly small groups of speakers in Haiti and in African-American speech communities, which fact, in turn, has implications about who is actually producing discourse in Alexis's fiction.

In Haiti, the group that is capable of true code-switching between French and Creole is identified by Valdman as the "bilingual urban élite," who number at most between 5 and 10 per cent of the entire population.[1] In the United States, no one is sure exactly how many African Americans are proficient speakers of standard English, and of these how many also are willing or able to function to some degree in Black English vernacular. My guess is that the former group is less than a majority of African-American speakers, and the latter, smaller still. Furthermore, while Haitian Creole is a fully formed language separate from French—neither a "patois" nor "broken French"—Black English is not a separate language, but a dialect of English (of which standard English is a dialect as well). This fact means that some linguists would consider it inappropriate to call alternation between Black English and standard English "code-mixing" or "code-switching"; John Baugh, for one, prefers to call this phenomenon "style-shifting" (58–59). However, the fact that Black English is a dialect and not an autonomous language in the sense that French or Creole is does not diminish the complexity or significance of its functions for African Americans. To those of us who speak it, it *feels* like a language. It has affective levels for us that standard English does not have; it reflects our history and connects us to our past in America, linking us to speakers of other New World creoles and even to Africa in ways that standard English cannot; it is, for some members of our community, the last uncoöpted place in the psyche. To speak Black English is to enter a space where values and modalities are different from those expressed by standard English: sometimes we must reframe the very way in which we think in order to frame a Black English utterance. It is in this affective, symbolic sense that Black English functions for many bidialectal African Americans. Black English also serves the symbolic function of expressing our intergroup unity and our separateness from other groups in American society.

In order to understand why I chose to translate Creole by Black English in code-mixed utterances, I will first examine the status each seems to occupy for monolingual speakers. Creole is the sole language of some 85 to 90 per cent of Haitians (only members of the elite and educated Haitians speak French, which, outside of the elite class, is learned primarily through formal education). Moreover, linguists, a growing number of whom are Haitians addressing an educated Haitian audience, unanimously consider Creole to be a language fully formed and adequate for any purpose for which language is used. Yet members of the Haitian elite class insist that Creole is not a "real" language, that it is nothing more than broken French, that it has no grammar and is inadequate for the expression of abstract ideas and technical concepts (Fleischman 112; Lofficial 27; cf. Bennett 334 et passim). Even though a number of Haitians feel that Creole is "appropriate for many of [their] interactions with the world outside," and that it serves their "intellectual, psychological, and social needs," they realize that speaking and/or writing in French represents social mobility and access to economic and political power (Valdman, "Linguistic Situation" 79, 81–82). Some of the negative attitudes about Creole are also attached to Black English and its speakers in America. Black English, for example, is blamed for the poor progress of many inner-city children in school, and the widely held belief that Black English is a "deficient" language has led to the corollary belief that the thinking processes of its speakers are deficient as well. But in the case of both Creole and Black English, their basilect status ultimately derives from the relative lack of power of the people who speak them rather than from imputed deficiency or ugliness in the languages themselves; they are languages of low social prestige because their speakers have low social prestige in their respective countries (Baugh 6–9; Lofficial 44–45).

Leaving aside their status as basilects, there are rather striking similarities in the way each language is used within its culture. Each is a language of national identity and cultural unity, an evident fact with Creole in Haiti, perhaps less so with Black English. The very members of the elite who proclaim that Creole is not a real language demonstrate a deep attachment to their mother tongue at the same time. Thus, there is the "widely shared view that there is a particularly Haitian level of understanding and communication bound to the Creole language . . . which is 'national' . . . [and] excludes the foreigner" (Fleischmann 112). The situation in the United States is slightly more complicated by the fact that not all African Americans speak Black English (though Smitherman (2) asserts that some 80 to 90 per cent use it at least some of the time). But all African Americans exist in a family relationship with Black English—they know it for what it is when they hear it and are moved by it on several emotional levels; they participate in a shared culture of music, formal oratory, and informal speech acts, all informed by Black English structure and style. Sociolinguistic literature has amply pointed out an evident fact of language usage in the black community, that even people who cannot use Black English grammatical structures will occasionally use words from the Black English lexicon to emphasize their belonging to the culture. But most use much more than isolated words and phrases. Black English and Creole, then, are, first of all, badges of belonging to the communities that speak them.

In bilingual societies, the use of vernacular languages in code-mixing by people capable of using the official or standard language can have political significance as well, for the contact languages in colonial and postcolonial situations are rarely equal in status. In such situations, some degree of competition for the privileges and power available in the society usually occurs; often, one of the languages in contact is the language of access to power, prestige, and opportunity for social mobility; in the Caribbean, this has almost always been the language of the former colonizer. Evidently, access to these attributes is not equally shared among speakers of the languages concerned. Under these circumstances, a speaker's choice to use the vernacular would appear to be to choose some degree of identification with monolingual speakers of that language. That choice can exact a heavy price, both psychologically and socially. For vernacular languages in the United States and in the Caribbean, as I argue below, are used as what Olshtain and Blum-Kulka call "'we' codes as opposed to the 'they' code of the major language group which is perceived as more formal, stiff and distant" (60). Yet use of the vernacular can be socially and economically limiting simply because, realistically speaking, it is the language of those with less education. But refusal to use it when one is linguistically capable of doing so signals a distancing away from the group which speaks it. Thus, a speaker's choice of a language is seen to be an index of her or his chosen allegiances and self-image, and choosing to mix or switch codes can constitute "a sensitive stylistic device, for [it signals] subtle changes of roles and attitudes among interlocutors" (Valdman, "Language" 314). Sometimes speakers of a nation's two languages varieties find themselves pulled between self-interest and love of home in its most intimate sense.

Creole and Black English are both languages of intimate communication, of the "restricted context" *(le réseau fermé)* (Fattier-Thomas 112). Among bilingual Haitians, Creole is the predominant language of relations in the family, between close friends, among colleagues, with neighbors, and with "home people"—anyone, in short, with whom one can assume a certain level of familiarity. French would be used with people one knows less well, especially on first meeting; in a business or official setting; in education; and in any situation where it is expedient for the speaker to make a positive impression by his or her social status and education. French, then, is the predominant language of the "larger context" *(le réseau ouvert)*, where one is "in the presence of speakers of diverse origins who need to establish a consensus in their interaction, who do not share a common history and a relatively unified system of values" (Fattier-Thomas 112, 113 et passim; translation mine here and throughout). Put another way, French is used in the domain of "public (impersonal or representative)" and "formal (formally prescribed) behavior," while Creole serves for "private (personal or nonrepresentative)" and "informal (not formally prescribed) behavior" (Valdman, "Language" 313).

Among African Americans who are prone to use both dialects, one can safely say that Black English is also the language of intimacy and closeness, more likely to be used in informal settings, within the family, and with friends. Standard English, or varieties of Black English closer to it, would be used in the larger context, and especially with speakers not black or not from the culture. I might add, however, that any informal gathering of black people constitutes a restricted context, particularly if characterized by impassioned involvement (an athletic event, for example, or a church service or concert) or by the relaxation that permits joking or badinage (say, in a club or bar, or at a party). In such situations, people may rather quickly switch to the structure, lexicon, and stylistic forms of Black English, even where they do not know each other well. In fact, the ability, or willingness, to function in these forms can constitute a kind of shibboleth by which a person's demonstrated willingness to be considered part of the community is measured.

Creole and Black English are the languages in which subjects proper to the particular cultures are discussed, either because the requisite vocabulary doesn't exist in the official or standard language, or because those languages cannot express the proper nuances. This use of vernacular language becomes especially significant when we remember that folklore, believed to encode a culture's most cherished beliefs in symbolic form, comments on subjects pertinent to the community and reinforces its values, norms of behavior, and ways of thought. Thus, Creole and Black English are preeminently the languages of folklore in their respective cultures. In the United States, there exist well-documented collections of jokes, of word games such as "sounding" and "the dozens," of the elaborate rhymed stories known as toasts, of folk songs, gospel music, folk sermons, adages and proverbs, even superstitions and recipes for magic, collected from African–American urban and rural informants and transmitted primarily in Black English. As for Haitian folklore, Price-Mars remarks succinctly: "It is through Creole that our oral traditions exist, are perpetuated, and are transformed" (66).

Fattier-Thomas names Creole as the language used to transmit strong emotion: great surprise, intense pain, or profound sadness would be much more likely to be expressed in Creole than in French. As for Black English, strong emotion is probably one of the uses mass media representations of African-American culture have made it best known for. One of the characteristics of black discourse in general is deep personal involvement in the argument one is enunciating. Moreover, other marks of strong feeling, such as the use of cursing, profanity, and intensifiers, are common in informal discourse, especially that of men. And when a speaker's express purpose is to insult or tell someone off, put a person in his place, or express other strong feelings, Black English possesses ammunition admirably suited to the purpose. Participants in vernacular culture are masters of the innuendo, the sarcastic putdown, the ritual insult, and hyperbole.[2]

Yet another similarity in the use of vernacular language in the two speech communities has to do with the fact that the use of one's mother tongue can sometimes indicate a singular earnestness about what one is saying; what is uttered in the vernacular in an act of code-switching is meant to be taken very seriously indeed. Thus, the Haitian proverb "Sé kréyòl m-ap palé avè-ou, oui?" ("I'm speaking Creole to you now") indicates that whatever statement is attached to it is meant to be taken as serious (Hall 132). And most bidialectal African Americans can relate at least one experience where switching to Black English convinced listeners that they were deadly serious about what they were saying.

In black intracommunity speech, there has historically been a use of language for secret communication and survival. Slaves found ways to communicate highly sensitive information to each other so that overseers and slavemasters were not privy to the information. In the American South, the spirituals are believed to have been used at times to pass on information in code. Moreover, the very language the slaves spoke came to include discrete instances of change away from the standard speech of the planter class in order to encode resistance in such a way that the masters would be unaware of what was being said. David Dalby identifies several ways in which this might have occurred. New words might be added to the English the slaves spoke by a direct borrowing from their African languages; or words or terms in wide usage in the indigenous language of some segment of the slave community might be calqued, translated directly into their English—hence, "to bad-mouth," meaning to slander, which has direct parallels in both Hausa and Mandingo. Or else, convergence might occur between words from an African language and English words having similar sounds, so that for the African-American speaker these words would grow to acquire a different meaning from their standard English definitions. (One example is "to dig," meaning "to understand," corresponding to Wolof deg, dega, "to understand.") And whereas the overt use by slaves of African words to obfuscate meaning would have called attention to itself and perhaps brought down retribution, the use of English words whose meanings had been changed, either by a deliberate inversion of English words so that in black speech they had the opposite meaning, or by the above-mentioned process of convergence, could pass unnoticed (Dalby 174; on inversion, see Holt 154–55). The nonstandard language of the slaves, then, came to include instances of resistance that would have been foolhardy to make in an overt manner.

Even today, some African Americans claim to be able to speak in the presence of outsiders so that what they are saying is perfectly clear to the blacks who are present but perfectly incomprehensible to the outsiders. There is an analogue to this speech behavior in Haiti called *palé andaki*, which might be used against interlocutors, whether Haitians or outsiders, who are not part of the speakers' own group (Fleischmann 117*n9*).

Both languages in a contact situation are heavy with significance for the entire community, for both monolingual speakers and bilinguals. For bilingual Haitian speakers, Creole, as we have seen, symbolizes the soul of the nation and encodes that which is most truly Haitian. Since the American occupation (1915–34), it has also become a powerful symbol of an authentic African past, and as such, a site of resistance. Yet the French language also acquired an important symbolic value during that time: French was "the expression of a cultural link inherited from the colonial past which is still highly valued and which is perceived as protecting Haiti from American cultural imperialism" (Valdman, "Decreolization" 85). Add to this its symbolic value in Haitian culture as the language of power and prestige, and it is clear that for monolinguals, who for the most part have no access to French, it can sometimes take on an almost magical aura, symbolizing the material and social progress that supposedly accrue to the speaker who masters it. At the same time, Albert Valdman found among his peasant informants not only a healthy respect for the Creole language, but a resentment of French as a social barrier and mark of social stratification and a feeling that it is an imposed language, the "relic of an externally imposed social order" (Valdman, "Linguistic Situation" 83, 85). One might say that, for Creole, comfort and familiarity are mingled with a subliminal contempt in Haitian culture, a contempt that colors attitudes toward monolingual speakers. Black English among African-American speakers likewise is the language of home, of community solidarity, of heritage, and of a difference that has come more and more to be celebrated rather than concealed—but sometimes the ties of home are felt to bind too closely. In the two situations, neither of the languages in contact entirely escapes negative dimensions either for those who speak them both or for those who speak only one.

II

In the fact of code-mixing, Jacques-Stéphen Alexis found a phenomenon which served him as an apt symbol of Haiti's historical situation in several ways. We have seen that, according to Valdman, for a Francophone Haitian, the act of speaking Creole is sometimes a political act, a claim of solidarity with the monolingual masses. But the possibilities of political and cultural symbolism go even further. The Négritude movement, which saw New World blacks as having been robbed of their culture, heritage, language, and status as a free people, emphasized the violence perpetrated against blacks during slavery and colonial partition. Cataloging the wrongs of the colonial powers, the movement sought to transform the black man from the status of victim to that of accuser. It insisted on purity of racial heritage—made possible through a recovery of a "pure" African past—as the sign of cultural authenticity. Alexis, however, evolved a different vision of Haitian identity, a vision based on the acceptance of multiple origins without shame, on a celebration of the mixture of bloods and of cultures which together constituted the Haitian ethos. While that blended self might not always be experienced by given individuals without fragmentation, the possibility of the existence of a new image of the Haitian personality existed and was symbolized by the very nature of Haitian linguistic diversity. Thus, to accept Creole as a language equal to other languages in its aptness to fill any social need, to accept the fact that Haitian French was changed by its contact with Creole so as to be different in subtle ways from metropolitan French,—in brief, to reject the notion of "pure" language—was metaphorically to embrace that idea of a fused Haitianity, of a new self born of multiple forebears. As Alexis writes in a Creolized French in *Romancéro aux étoiles,* he celebrates in his very writing, he venerates, as it were, the two ancestors, the French and the African, who have contributed to the modern Haitian amalgam—indeed, three ancestors, for in some of the stories, Taino Indian words are also prominent; and the principal narrator of the collection is not called "Le Vieux Vent Caraïbe" (the Old Carib Wind) by accident. And so in his very language Alexis claims the multistrand braid that links his people to a past where many sources came together to produce the new product that is modern Haitian culture.

I believe that Alexis's use of Creolized forms embedded in standard French served as a form of interpellation, hailing his audience of choice and establishing that a text belongs to a shared community in a way in which it is simply not open to an outsider. Thus, whereas Alexis was undoubtedly sure that the largest number of his readers would be non-Haitian, his use of Creolized French ensures as well that there are levels of affective interaction in his texts to which that non-Haitian readership is not privy. Thus, this kind of language use marks his text as ultimately belonging to a limited community. This dimension has not been lost even on a new generation of younger Haitians living in exile, some of whom feel that terms hermetic to the non-Haitian in modern Haitian literature should not be explained in notes, for in a sense such translation (virtually always initiated by the author, not the publisher) betrays the relationship between the Haitian writer and his or her ideal audience (Jonassaint 316). Alexis's coded masks constitute a kind of secret discourse, a *palé andaki*, in instances where he discusses issues particularly pertinent to Haitians' situation as a nation under siege, or comments on peculiarly Haitian characteristics and foibles. Finally, Clandia Mitchell-Kernan suggests that the introduction of black language or stylistic features in an act of code-mixing marks the fact "that what is being engaged in is a black speech act. This serves a function other than simply emphasizing group solidarity; it signals to the hearer that this is an instance of black verbal art and should be interpreted in terms of the subcultural rules for interpreting speech acts" (328).

Henry Louis Gates's conception of the mask may help us understand some of the ways in which the embedded vernacular speech in *Romancéro* functions for Alexis's larger narrative purposes. Gates describes the mask in African-American literature as the use of dialect: words, locutions, and cultural referents that very succinctly, very powerfully reflect African-American tradition and evoke the realities of African-American experience, thus creating an especially intimate level of communication with the writer's own people, his audience of choice (92–94 et passim). The situation in postcolonialist writing such as Alexis's is often parallel. Even though a writer's works might be published in a language not in his own vernacular (in the case of the Caribbean writer, most often the language of his former colonizer, with whose political and cultural hegemony his own country still finds itself linked) and read in the main by readers not from his culture, the presence of masks—words and locutions borrowed outright or adapted from another language— recreates the official language in such a way that it can be said to belong to the linguistic community of the poet. Gates asserts that the poet "has in this mutation . . . an accessible linguistic system that turns the literate language upon itself, that exploits the metaphor against its master" (94). The use of vernacular language in *Romancéro aux étoiles* constitutes a mask that makes Alexis's French prose carry an entire complex of meaning for a Haitian audience.

III

I have already established that the use of the vernacular can serve to signal that we are participants in an act of speech (or writing) that must be interpreted in terms of vernacular performance norms. But what, in writing, is Black English or Creolized French? In other words, what signals to a reader that writing is meant to be read as vernacular? Aside from the American tradition of dialect writing—a tradition that exists as well in Haiti (I refer here to Creole written long before that language had anything approaching a standardized orthography, and where it was often transcribed as deformed French, a move that must have diminished its status and dignity as an autonomous language)— there are other clues. One fairly obvious one would be the use of calques (loan translations), which often strike one as odd in the standard language; another is the more-or-less direct transcription of words, terms, or locutions known to belong to the vernacular tongue. The grammar of Black English is fairly easy to spot. But even suggestions of the pronunciation typical of the vernacular are enough to trigger a reading as being Black English, or Creole, instead of standard English or French. Thus, Gates asserts that the word *gwine* in a spiritual evokes a complex tapestry of meaning for an African-American audience (113–14), just as Alexis's having village children call an American marine "bôzô"[3] ("Le sous-lieutenant enchanté" 196) may well have produced in his Haitian readers smiles of recognition.

It is perhaps fitting to begin a discussion of my use of Black English in *Romancéro aux étoiles* with "La romance du Petit-Viseur" ("The Ballad of Little Sharp-Shot"), the tale in which I discovered the first instance of language that I knew could not be French and which thus required a different translation strategy: "Le ventre du Petit-Viseur avait crevé et, avec un grand éclat de rire, l'Oiseau de Dieu en jaillit, s'envola *dret* vers le forêt, filant sur le même filao où il était perché le matin même" (224). That one word, *dret*, so small as to be almost unobtrusive, clamored its difference from the rest of the sentence. I came up with what I thought was an ingenious solution at the time and translated that sentence: "The belly of Little Sharp-Shot popped open, and with a great shout of laughter, the Bird of God sprang out, flew *dreckly* into the forest, and slipped onto the same filao tree where he'd been perched that very morning." Though it's debatable whether "dreckly" would be found in any Black English lexicon, it has some of the characteristics by which some English words are thought to be taken into Black English: suppression of the unaccented vowel of the first syllable, and the gliding of the final *t* of the second syllable into a *k*. Like Alexis's aptly coined spelling of *bôzô*, my coinage fits a pattern of pronunciation known to exist in Black English.

But this word in nonstandard English, slipped into a translation written totally in standard English, stuck out like a sore thumb, and that observation touched off the series of reflections recorded in this essay. Later versions of that first translation have included Black English in other places as well, partly because I began to perceive Creolized French where I had not seen it when I began the project. Another reason, however, was simply that I realized that Black English seldom occurs as just one word in a long, standard English utterance. Moreover, the narrator of that story possessed an idiolect in French in which code-mixing was quite believable. We know from other stories in the collection that the Old Carib Wind has several strings to his linguistic bow; his various texts reveal him to be a code-mixer par excellence, not only of French and Creole, but of Taino as well. My task as translator was to demonstrate that virtuosity in English, creating an idiolect for the the Old Carib Wind in keeping with his bilingual character.

In his introduction to "La romance du petit-viseur," the Old Carib Wind declares his intention of singing the ballad of Little Sharp-Shot to prove that all living things are linked together in a brotherhood and that life cannot be annihilated. The line in which he states his intention reads, "Pour l'illustrer, si cela est encore nécessaire, je te chanterai cette chantefable: 'La Romance du Petit-Viseur'" (215). Now, the *chantefable* is a well-known genre in medieval French literature, and a venerable genre in Haitian folklore as well, called the *kont chanté*. Thus,

Creolophone culture slips into the introduction in that last word; yet, it is a code word, in a sense, because the reader unfamiliar with Haitian mass culture will not know that its referent is a well-known Haitian tale form. In my translation, I could not express the double-sidedness of this referent, for although the *chantefable* is very much alive in African-American folklore (and in folklore all over the world, for that matter), it has no particular name among its African-American practitioners; it is simply a story that features a repeated refrain, whether sung or not. In translation, then, the Old Carib Wind says: "To illustrate—if that's even necessary—I'm gon' sing this fable-song: 'The Ballad of Little Sharp-Shot.'" Even as I write it here, the word *sing* is pronounced in my mind as *sang*—keyed by the first instance of Black English grammar, the rest of the utterance becomes Black English as well. The bilingualism is retained, though in a different form.

Other parts of the narrative bear many marks of Black English discursive style in translation. Sometimes these are not direct translations of Creolized French, but serve to create the idiolect of a narrator capable of saying "dret" in the penultimate line of the story. Others, however, translate features of Alexis's French text. The following are some examples.

Little Sharp-Shot's adventure begins when he wakes up one day feeling particularly contrary. The Old Carib Wind muses, "Tel jour, on se lève du pied gauche et, bougon, on ne dit pas bonjour au soleil. Tel jour, on se lève du pied droit et, gaillard, on claironne tout le monde" (220). In my English translation, he says:

"One day you get up on the wrong side of the bed, all *evil,* and don't even tell the sun good morning. Another day, you get up on the right side, gay as anything, and hail everybody." *Evil* is a good Black English word which simply means in a bad mood, ill-humored.

Further on, we are told that as he first sees the Bird of God in a filao tree: "l'oeil du Petit-Viseur se mit à méringuer, son nez à remuer et son doigt à frétiller" (220). I translated this as, "Little Sharp-Shot's eye started doing a *meringue,* his nose started twitching, and his finger (pronounced *fang-*a) started itching." Here, I was able to translate two parts of the three-part rhyme of the original. I am certain that the rhyme in French either translates a stylistic device of Creole, or else compensates for qualities in the oral narration which most transcribers of folk narration in Creole admit are almost impossible to render by words alone. In English, the line partakes of a classic and widespread Black English rhetorical technique. There was one other instance of rhyme: "Qui donc a entendu chanter un oiseau? Qui ose l'affirmer?" (219). ("But who has ever *heard* a bird *sing?* Who'd dare to declare it?")

Alliteration is another classic rhetorical device of Black English. The first example here was actually the accidental translation of alliteration where there was very little in the French. But the second was a deliberate recreation of alliteration in the original:

Tudieu! quel oiseau que celui-là! Minuscule arc-en-ciel de couleurs radiants qui *tintinnabulaient* l'une contre l'autre. (220)

[God, what a bird this was! Miniature *r*ainbow of *r*adiant colors that *j*ust about *j*angled against each other.]

Je *m*'empressai d'emporter toutes ces *m*agnifiques plumes qu'on *m*'abondonnait, car neveu, me faisant *V*ieux *V*ent Caraïbe de *p*lus en *p*lus, je suis frileux en hiver et j'en voulais faire un *bon beau bonnet bien* chaud pour ma tête. (223)

[I rushed to carry off all those magnificent feathers he was throwing my way. You see, son, I get chilly in winter, as I'm becoming the *Old* Carib Wind *m*ore and *m*ore, and I wanted to *m*ake *m*e a *cozy, comfortable, cushy cap* for my head.]

Alliteration, too, inserts the Old Carib Wind's text in English into a Black rhetorical tradition, continuing to confirm a nonstandard subtext.

In one instance, the Old Carib Wind abundantly uses alliteration that I could not duplicate in English. I translated it by using a different Black English rhetorical strategy:

Caramba, quel maestro [speaking of the Bird of God], neveu! Les grands filaos-musiciens de la forêt eux-mêmes en étaient jaloux. Ce *porte-plume coquet, croque-notes et coquecigrue* venait pour les narguer. (221)

[Caramba! What a maestro, son! Even the great filao-musicians of the forest were jealous of him. This *no-singing, jive-talking, dandified turkey* was always coming around to mess with them.]

A term like *no-singing,* creating a negative adjective from a gerund, is a common construction in Black English, as is *dandified,* which creates an adjective from a past participle—in this case, the past participle of a nonstandard verb. These two terms, then, use Black English grammar, though the terms themselves are certainly not coined; both already exist in Black English. *Jive-talking*, too, has been well-known for more than fifty years. This same passage goes on to include another Black English feature, the use of language that can sometimes be emotionally loaded for black speakers:

Depuis le matin les filaos se taisaient, balançant leurs longues crinières de filaments vert mordoré. Chut! on ne sait jamais avec ces grands nègres qui fréquentent et sont à tu et à toi avec les puissants du ciel ou de la terre! (221)

[Since morning the filaos had been keeping quiet, nervously swaying those long, stringy, greenish-brown manes of theirs. 'Cause hush!—you never know with these high and mighty folk who are close to and close with the powers of heaven and earth!]

Here the English evokes a thread that often runs through the fabric of African-American folk literature, the necessity to be discreet around people who have more power than oneself and can possibly provoke real harm. There is certainly the suggestion of a preoccupation on the part of relatively powerless people with questions of inclusion and access to power. I read in it even the healthy respect, still found in parts of the black community, and spoken of in Haiti as well by Hurston, Métraux, and other observers, for the powers of the conjurer. The whole affair of conjure is fraught with secrecy and fear, and people who live in communities where conjure is still believed in learn not to offend those in a position to cause them harm.

The most striking instance of the use of Creolized French in this tale is the voice of the Bird of God. Here is his first utterance; all his subsequent ones repeat the same warning, simply adding a new step each time to the process of killing and cooking him:

Han! Hé! P'tit-Viseur, eh!
Han! Hé! P'tit-Viseur, eh!
P'tit-Viseur, "pin'ga" me viser!
Han! Hé! P'tit-Viseur, eh!
P'tit-Viseur, "pin'ga" me viser! (221)

[Ho! Hey! Li'l Sharp-Shot, hey!
Ho! Hey! Li'l Sharp-Shot, hey!
Li'l Sharp-Shot, you *bet'* not aim at me!
Ho! Hey! Li'l Sharp-Shot, hey!
Li'l Sharp-Shot, you *bet'* not aim at me!]

This passage is almost a direct transliteration from the Creole; only *me viser* is French. In the sense that the rhythm and the Black English equivalents for the Bird of God's Creolized words were readily available in Black English tradition, it was an easy passage to translate into an idiomatic and powerful Black English. What is most striking about it as it appears in the narrative is that the most powerful character in the tale is a speaker of Creole: the Bird of God *demands,* in no uncertain terms, not to be oppressed in the first place, and then demands an end to his oppression; neither does he stop his demands in the face of repeated defeat. His is the preeminent voice of resistance, the resistance of a spirit which literally never says "die." Symbolically, the Bird of God's death and triumphant resurrection suggest that the spirit of the Haitian people is indomitable and indestructible—a message fittingly transmitted in that people's community language.

We might say that in the previously cited passages, wherein the Bird of God demands his rights, Alexis has given the Haitian masses a voice, a voice which resonates courage, awareness of the prevailing political situation, and the confidence of human beings who have fully assumed their personhood. In another passage, from "Le dit d'Anne aux longs cils" ("The Tale of Anne-with-the-long-lashes"), we see another strong representation of the voice of the common people. But whereas in "The Ballad of Little Sharp-Shot" the message proclaimed by that voice seems to be directed to the world outside, in "The Tale of Anne-with-the-long-lashes" it is almost as if we hear the voice of a people at play in the context of their intimacy as members of one community—a community speaking to each other about their own concerns, unconscious of an audience outside their borders.

The passage of "The Tale of Anne-with-the-long-lashes" where this community dialectic occurs claims our attention for a number of reasons. "The Tale of Anne-with-the-long-lashes," told by the young, human narrator, is recounted primarily in standard French, and a sophisticated, literary French at that. As he pronounces his own discourse, this narrator mixes codes, but rather sparingly. One of the more striking instances occurs at the very beginning of the tale, where he enunciates, first, a list of the putative fathers and mothers of Anne-with-the-long-lashes:

Caillou rose, cri de cricri, poil de comète, scarabée, rayon d'argent, sucrin, clin d'oeil d'enfant malicieux, poisson-docteur, rire de clochette, pétale de lune, écaille d'arc-en-ciel, lézard enchanté furent les pères d'Anne aux longs cils et sa mère, une pépite d'or, une écrevisse, une escarbille de charbon, une *poule-à-jolie,* une chanson d'avril, une goutte de lait, une "*maîtresse-de-l'eau*" morte d'amour. (54; emphasis added)

[Pink pebble, cricket's cry, a comet hair, a scarab, a ray of silver, a sugary melon, the wink of a mischievous child, a surgeon-fish, a bell's laughter, a moon petal, a scale from a rainbow, an enchanted lizard, were the fathers of Anne-with-the-long-lashes; and her mothers, a gold nugget, a crayfish, a cinder of flint, an ancient joy, charcoal dust, a poule-à-jolie, an April song, a drop of milk, a water mistress dead from love.]

Two of these terms, *poule-à-jolie* and *maîtresse-de-l'eau,* are Haitian names designating, respectively, a kind of bird and an important figure of Haitian mythology, the siren. In another passage, the narrator creates a second list, this time of the individuals who together make up the "folk," the common people of Haiti. This list, again recounted in standard French, nevertheless uses many local terms for occupations and types found within the community. This kind of code-mixing often occurs among Francophone Haitians either because these local terms are felt to be natural, whereas French equivalents would be seen as pretentious, or because there are no French terms (Pompilus, *Langue* 137–38). Through his style of code-mixing, then, the narrator typifies middle-class Haitian speakers who range freely between French and Creole as their expressive needs dictate.

But the passage that concerns us here is a section of the story where the peasants and the land—which is personified as Creole, like the people of the countryside—interact with the narrator and with each other. The narrator, having returned home from traveling all over the world in search of knowledge, is eager to see and speak with the land and the people whom he loves. As he interacts with the physical features of his island, the land and the people speak to him in a language which, at first glance, appears to be standard French informed by dialect—that is, a nonstandard dialect of France. But a deeper examination reveals instances of language which belong to the linguistic geography of rural Haiti:

A mon approche, les chapeaux coniques des montagnes du Nord se soulevèrent amicalement:

«Bonjour, frère! dirent-ils . . . Et la santé? . . .
—Bonjour, frères! leur répondis-je . . . On se débat . . . Et vous?
—Comme ça! . . . Quessi quemi! Car les pluies sont amères» (59)

The phrase "et la santé?," asking about the interlocutor's health with no previously intervening question having been asked, is a type heard frequently in Haiti. "On se débat," which would be unusual usage in French, is a calque from the Creole. But "Comme ça" and "Quessi quemi" are French, as is the rest of the utterance where they appear.

But for me, the fact that this dialogue takes place in rural Haiti, as well as certain cues further along in the same passage that show that a speech encounter in Creole is taking place, indicated that the use of Black English was sociolinguistically appropriate for the translation of the passage, and my translation of the section cited above reads:

At my approach, the northern mountains raised their conical hats in a friendly gesture:
    "Good morning, brother!" they cried. "Hi'a you?"
    "Good morning, brothers!" I answered. "I think I'a make it. How 'bout you?"
    "Tol'ably . . . fair-to-middlin'. The rains are bitter, you see."

The next few passages I translated as Black English discourse may appear problematic. In these portions of the French text, the peasants of rural Haiti participate in discourse with each other and with nature itself. The appearance of each month causes animated discussion in the peasant community because the weather is anomalous. Yet, except for the signal that we are witnesses to country people talking to each other, there is very little Creolized French in the entire passage, which extends over some eight pages. Now, the French that is used in the narration of the peasants' conversation has some distinctive characteristics. Its register is very familiar, even popular. It is fast-paced, highly rhythmical, and replete with slang. Yet the familiar register and the slang are French. My translations of these passages make significant use of Black English, but it is in precisely these passages that I find that I have deviated most from the letter of the original. Let me discuss several representative examples.[4]

Surprise nouvelle, Février arriva [mais visiblement changé]. . . .
    «On dit bonjour madame, et c'est le monsieur qui est là! dirent les prud'hommes sentencieux . . . Ouvrez l'oeil! Guettez bien, car il y a des menteries dans l'air. Février est un gamin mal élévé, s'il rit c'est qu'il va mordre et s'il pleure, c'est pour rire!» (65)

[Another surprise—February arrived [visibly changed] . . .

"You say 'Good morning, ma'am,' and *a man be standing there*," pronounced the elders sententiously. "*Y'all open y'all's eyes*. Look out, *'cause it's lies flying about!* February is a half-raised urchin; if he laughs, it's because he's about to bite, and if he cries, it's from laughter."]

Here, while my translation remains lexically quite close to the words of the original French, I have introduced instances of what is easily recognized as Black English grammar:

Mars chassa Février à coups de pieds au derrière. [. . .] Cette fois-ci, les *papaloas* s'inquiétèrent tout de bon: «*Mirez* donc, *petit monde!* . . . Voilà Mars qui s'amène comme un malotru. [. . .] On dit que les grands sorciers blancs ont encore fait péter dix grosses bombes afin de voir s'ils sont capables de faire crever un «décallion» de chrétiens vivants d'un seul coup. Ils ont détraqué pour tout de bon cet incorrigible Mars qui n'avait déjà pas la tête très solide!» (66)

[March chased February out with kicks in the behind. [. . .]

This time, the *papaloas* were seriously upset:

"*Chi'ren, look-a here! Here come March falling in here* like some chump. . . . They say the great white sorcerers have exploded ten more big bombs *to see can they kill* a decallion of living Christians with a single blow. They've gotten that incorrigible March off track for good and all! And he never was rowing with both oars in the water!"]

In this excerpt, we find five lexical items borrowed from Creole. *Papaloas,* which is one of the Creole words for a *vaudou* priest, is an instance of a Creole word inserted directly into the French text. Since it is foreign to French, I left it untranslated, and that foreignness is preserved in the English version. *Chrétien,* which transliterates the Creole *krétyin,* meaning a person, a soul, was likewise foreign to French in this sense, and I kept "Christian" in the English translation for the same reason. *Mirez* is a loan translation of the Creole verb *miré,* look, and *petit monde,* that of the Creole word for children, *ti-moune.* Black English had available equivalents by which I was able to render their difference from the rest of the citation in translation. As for "Here come March falling in here like some chump" and "to see can they kill a decallion of living Christians," both characterized by recognizable Black English grammar, the wording I chose serves to establish, again, that we are in the presence of black speakers.

La gracile et jeune mai s'achemina, métamorphosée en petite vieille percluse de fièvre:
. . . «Tip! Tap! . . . Tip! Tap! . . . *Le corps se débat!*» (68)

[Graceful, young May came along, transformed into a little old woman crippled with fever.
. . . "Tip-tap! Tip-tap! *I'm doing pretty po'ly today, thank ye just the same!*"]

Again, "Le corps se débat" is the transformation of a Creole expression, as was "on se débat" above. I translated it into a sentence one might hear on the lips of just such an old woman in rural East Texas. Except for "po'ly," the words May utters might not be recognizable as African-American speech in another context—the words themselves might belong to other American dialects. But the context of the encounter—rural Haiti, and an elderly female speaker responding politely to an implied interlocution—marks them as fitting within the context of a black speech act.

Juin le Valiant Piroguier vint à la tête de toutes les pluies qui puissent s'imaginer. [. . .]
«Juin le Piroguier nous a sauvés,» dirent les anciens, «mais l'horloge des saisons est bel et bien dérangée. Les blancs ont encore fait péter quelque méchanceté dans les airs! . . . Juin est bon, mais jadis il était plus modéré et combien plus judicieux.» (69)

[June the Valiant Canoeman came in leading all the rains imaginable. [. . .]
"June the Canoeman has saved us," the ancient ones said, "but the clockwork of the seasons *sho' is* off track. *Them white people have gone and exploded some more of they mess* in the air! Nothing wrong with June, now, don't get me wrong, but *seem like* in the old days it was better behaved and had so much more good sense."]

Here, there is no perceivable Creolization of the French of the original; yet, this was one of the passages where my inner ear heard Black English most strongly. My use of Black English grammar in the translation of the passage is obvious. But there is another element from rural black culture here, a subtle insistence on order and seemliness. Thus, the fact that the white people have exploded "mess" in the air, the subject of how June "behaved" and had "good sense," were all topics—and terms— only too familiar in the context of rural child rearing during my girlhood in the 1950s.

Why did I feel so free to use a free-form strategy in these passages, where generally my aim as translator is to remain very close to the wording of the original text?[5] Part of the reason, I believe, was that several cues signaled that the peasants' conversation in these eight pages was a vernacular speech act. Cued by the fact that the speakers are, in fact, peasants, and that their discourse in some of the latter citations is characterized by a great deal of verbal play and emotional unrestraint, I felt that Black English was the target language of choice, that it translated the *soul* of these speakers' discourse, that rural African Americans would not speak otherwise in English.

But a corollary question arises. Having identified his characters as country people—by implication speakers of the dialect of Creole that is least like French and most highly stigmatized—why did Alexis have them speak in a French virtually unmixed with Creolized forms or content? Could it be that his use of argotic, rhythmic, emotional French in a popular register was intended to represent a *pure* Creole—that is, a Creole unmitigated by code-mixing, which the peasants of the remote countryside are in little position to do? If that is the case, then we are dealing in these citations with what amounts to an act of covert translation: Alexis has translated for us the discourse of his peasant characters from Creole into French. Moreover, vernacular speakers speak their own language perfectly, fluently; that fluency is suggested by the fast pacing of these passages of French vernacular, and the flawlessness of their command of their language is suggested by the seamlessness of the French, the feeling that not one word could be changed without doing harm to the entire structure. If we are looking at Creole translated into French in these passages, we can regard the code-mixing that exists in them in a different sense: perhaps one of its purposes is to inform us that we are readers of a kind of linguistic doubling. Like the tips of icebergs in an ocean, they advise us that beneath the surface lies something of moment.

The use of the official language to represent the vernacular, actually fairly common in Haitian literary tradition, is not unknown in other black literatures. The rural speakers of several of the stories of Jean Toomer's *Cane,* for example, as well as his urban, working-class characters, are also made to speak and to think (in interior monologues) in a highly poetic, standard English which, in the world outside their novelistic universe, would probably not be available to them. And the Igbo villagers of Achebe's *Things Fall Apart* speak an elegant English virtually unmixed with any Igbo forms, except for the occasional use of concepts for which no words exist in English. To say, then, that Alexis's use of French in this instance is actually a symbolic use of Creole, is to arrive at a reading that is by no means without precedent in the fiction of peoples at the confluence of several postcolonial languages. Thus, as translator, when I used Black English in the translation of these passages, my intention was to go beyond the French words printed on the page in order to render the multilingual subtext of Alexis's peasant speakers' discourse, revealing the interplay of language and of heritage which characterizes modern-day Haitian Creole culture.

Notes

1. The traditional definition of *bilingualism* has been that a speaker be perfectly competent in two languages. Valdman asserts that "balanced bilinguals" in Haiti constitute no more than 5 per cent of the population ("Linguistic Situation"), and Pompilus suggests that many Haitians who have in fact been educated in French are competent in it only in certain domains (*Contribution* vi). But Fattier-Thomas argues for a broader definition, one which takes into consideration the capacity of an individual to alternate between two or more languages (100); she argues that such a conception of bilingualism would change the way in which Haitian bilinguals have traditionally been numbered.

2. At the same time, it is my impression, unconfirmed by research, that to proffer a reproach in Black English softens the reproach, whereas to do so in standard English makes it harsher. Claudia Mitchell-Kernan has observed that using an ordinarily harsh word like *nigger* in the context of black English has the effect of " 'smiling when you say that' " (328); perhaps this principle applies to my observation about reproaches as well.

3. *Bôzô* (elegant and vain) is the kind of word unlikely to have had a wide currency in writing—hence the unexpected delight of seeing the oral in print. Alexis had to coin a representation of its sound, as Creole orthography was not yet standardized in Haiti at the time he wrote.

4. Instances of Creole or Creolized French in the original, and black English in the translation, are italicized for purposes of illustration.

5. As I discuss my strategy here, I have to admit in all honesty that not all of it was conscious; when I proofread these passages, comparing them with the French, I was quite surprised to find that they contained so little Creolized French in the original.

Works Cited

Achebe, Chinua. *Things Fall Apart.* London: Heinemann, 1958.

Alexis, Jacques-Stéphen. *Romancéro aux étoiles: Contes.* Paris: Librairie Gallimard, 1960.

———. *Carried on the Wind: Tales from the Haitian Tradition.* Trans. Sharon Masingale Bell. In press.

Baugh, John. *Black Street Speech: Its History, Structure, and Survival.* Austin: U of Texas P, 1983.

Bennett, Ernest. *Du rire aux larmes.* Port-au-Prince: Les Editions Fardin, 1981.

Dalby, David. "The African Element in American English." Kochman 170–86.

Fattier-Thomas, Dominique. "Portraits de bilingues francophones haïtiens: Hommage au linguiste Pradel Pompilus." *Conjonction: Revue Franco-Haïtienne* 176 (Supplement 1987): 97–125.

Fleischmann, Ulrich. "Language, Literacy, and Underdevelopment." Foster and Valdman 101–17.

Foster, Charles R., and Albert Valdman, eds. *Haiti—Today and Tomorrow: An Interdisciplinary Study.* Lanham, Md.: UP of America, 1984.

Gates, Henry Louis. "Dis and Dat: Dialect and the Descent." *Afro-American Literature: The Reconstruction of Instruction.* Ed. Dexter Fisher and Robert Steptoe. New York: MLA, 1978. 88–119.

Hall, Robert A. *Pidgin and Creole Languages.* Ithaca, N.Y.: Cornell UP, 1966.

Holt, Grace Sims. "'Inversion' in Black Communication." Kochman 152–59.

Jonassaint, Jean. "Les productions littéraires haitiennes en Amérique du nord (1969–1979)." *Etudes littéraires* 13, 2 (août 1980): 313–32.

Kochman, Thomas, ed. *Rappin' and Stylin' Out: Communication in Urban Black America.* Urbana, Ill.: U of Illinois P, 1972.

Lofficial, Frantz. *Créole-français: une fausse querelle: Bilinguisme et reforme de l'enseignement en Haïti.* LaSalle, Québec: Collectif Paroles, 1979.

Métraux, Alfred. *Voodoo in Haiti.* Trans. Hugo Charteris, 1959. Rpt. New York: Schocken Books, 1972.

Mitchell Kernan, Claudia. "Signifying, Loud-talking and Marking." Kochman 315–35.

Olshtain, Elite and Shoshanna Blum-Kulka. "Happy Hebrish: Mixing and Switching in American-Israeli Family Interactions." *Variation in Second Language Acquisition. Volume I: Discourse and Pragmatics.* Ed. S. Gass, C. Madden, D. Preston, and L. Selinker. Philadelphia: Multilingual Matters, Ltd., 1989. 59–83.

Pompilus, Pradel. *Contribution à l'étude comparée du créole et du français à partir du créole haïtien: Phonologie et lexicologie.* Port-au-Prince: Editions Caraïbes, 1973.

———. *La Langue française en Haïti.* 1961. Rpt. Port-au-Prince: Editions
        Fardin, 1981.
Price-Mars, Jean. *Ainsi parla l'oncle.* 1928. Rpt. Montreal: Leméac, 1974.
Smitherman, Geneva. *Talkin' and Testifyin': The Language of Black America.*
        Detroit: Wayne State University Press, 1977.
Toomer, Jean. *Cane.* 1923. Rpt. New York: Liverwright, 1951.
Valdman, Albert. "Decreolization or Dialect Contact in Haiti?" *Development
        and Structures of Creole Languages: Essays in Honor of Derek Bickerton.*
        Ed. Francis Byrne and Thom Heubner. Philadelphia: John Ben-
        jamins Publishing Co., 1991. 75–88.
———. "Language Standardization in a Diglossia Situation: Haiti." *Language
        Problems of Developing Nations.* Ed. J. A. Fishman, C. A. Ferguson,
        and J. Das Gupta. New York: John Wiley and Sons, Inc., 1968.
        313–26.
———. "The Linguistic Situation of Haiti." Foster and Valdman 77–99.

The Rebel's Silhouette: Translating Faiz Ahmed Faiz

Agha Shahid Ali

My first sensuously vivid encounter with Faiz Ahmed Faiz: the voice of Begum Akhtar singing his *ghazals*. She sang Urdu poets, particularly him, as no one has since her death in 1974, ten years before he died. What other singer can give, the way she did, a *raga* to a *ghazal* and then make the *raga*, that melodic archetype, feel grateful for being a gift?

Passion, attachment, something that has "the effect of coloring the hearts of men"—that is what the Sanskrit term *raga* literally means. (One interpretation of *ghazal* is "whispering words of love.") An incipient melodic idea that uses at least five tones of the octave, each *raga* has "strict rules of ascent and descent, prescribed resting places, characteristic phrases and a distinct ethos of its own" (Dhar 84–86). What Begum Akhtar did was to place the *ghazal* gently on the *raga* until the *raga* opened itself to that whispered love, gave itself willingly, guiding the syllables to the prescribed resting places, until note by syllable, syllable by note, the two merged compellingly into yet another aesthetic ethos for the Urdu lovers of the Indian subcontinent. She, in effect, allowed the *ghazal* to be caressed into music, translated as it were: "You've finally polished catastrophe, / the note you seasoned with decades / of Ghalib, Mir, Faiz," I said in my elegy for her (Ali, "In Memory of Begum Akhtar," 15–17, *Half-Inch*). For unlike other *ghazal* singers, who clothe words until they can't be seen, she stripped them to a resplendent nudity. If she clothed them at all, it was in transparent muslins, like the Dacca gauzes: "woven air, running / water, evening dew" (Ali, "The Dacca Gauzes," 1–3, *Half-Inch*).

The *ghazal,* a form that in its present shape is eight hundred years old, traces its origins to pre-Islamic Arabia. (García Lorca wrote several *ghazals,* acknowledging in his catholic manner the Arabic influence on Spain.) Composed of thematically autonomous couplets that are linked together strictly through rhyme and meter, the *ghazal* in its opening couplet establishes a scheme that occurs in both lines. As John Hollander says, "For couplets the ghazal is prime; at the end / Of each one's a refrain like a chime: 'at the end' " (1–2). Having seen this couplet, the reader would know that the second line of every succeeding couplet would end with "at the end" (called *radif*), the refrain preceded by a word or syllable rhyming with "prime" and "chime" (called *qafia*). Thus, Hollander continues: "But in subsequent couplets throughout the whole poem, / It's the second line only will rhyme at the end" (3–4). Hollander has done something remarkable here, for he has captured the peculiar fragrance of the form of the *ghazal,* its constant sense of longing. Further, in subsequent couplets, not only has Hollander maintained the form but he has resisted the Western insistence on unity. (His one departure is that he has not maintained syllabic consistency in his line lengths.) The form of the *ghazal* is tantalizing because it gives the poet the freedom to engage in different themes, issues, and attitudes while keeping himself gratefully shackled. Let me offer one more of Hollander's couplets: "You gathered all manner of flowers all day, / But your hands were most fragrant of thyme, at the end" (13–14).

Before the partition of the subcontinent, Faiz had stayed in our house in Srinagar, the summer capital of Kashmir. Some decades later, Begum Akhtar too was to stay in our home the summer before her death. When I was six or seven, Faiz sent my father a copy from Lahore of his then latest volume—*Zindan-Nama.* My father often quoted Faiz, especially his elegy for the Rosenbergs:

> It's true—that not to reach you was fate—
> but who'll deny that to love you
> was entirely in my hands?
> So why complain if these matters of desire
> brought me inevitably to the execution grounds?
> ("We Who Were Executed," 18–22, *Rebel's Silhouette*)

I must have then begun to internalize Faiz, repeating to myself the original of this, as well as other passages of his. Without any clear understanding of the lines, I somehow *felt* the words, through their sounds, through my father's rhythmic, dramatic voice. So perhaps my first sensuous encounter with Faiz was not through Begum Akhtar but at home, during childhood.

Poetry was part of the air we breathed. In Srinagar during the summer of 1989 (when my mother helped me to translate Faiz), my grandmother, then eighty-eight, quite by chance quoted Milton during a conversation. In English. Ever since I can remember, she quoted Shakespeare, Keats, and Hardy in English; Hafiz and Rumi in Persian; Ghalib and Faiz in Urdu; Habba Khatun, Mahjoor, and Zinda Kaul in Kashmiri. But I'd never heard her quote Milton. I was ecstatic: once again I didn't need proof of my rights to the English canon (which, in any case, was created by the British in India). Significantly, not only was my training in school in English (I mean I grew up with English as my first language), but, paradoxically, my first language was/is not my mother tongue, which is Urdu. When I wrote my first poems, at the age of ten, they were in English. I did not "choose" to write them in English, it just happened that way. Naturally.

Someone of nearly two equal loyalties must lend them, almost give them—a gift—to each other and hope that sooner or later the loan will be forgiven and they will become each other's. My double loyalty has, after all, rescued rather than hampered me—by giving me *The Rebel's Silhouette*. In a prefatory-note to the book, I wrote:

Though the poems here are taken from various Faiz volumes, for my selection (which is arranged chronologically) I have chosen to adapt the title of his first volume, *Naqsh-e-faryadi* (*Sketch of the Plaintiff* or *Outline of the Plaintiff* or *Features of the Plaintiff*)—a phrasing that captures the spirit of his entire output. However, because Faiz does not recognize the moral authority of man-made courts, he is a plaintiff only in the courts of the universe. Clearly, a rebel. (*Rebel's Silhouette* xi)

This explanation reveals my simultaneous love of Urdu and of English. Neither love is acquired; I was brought up a bilingual, bicultural (but never rootless) being. These loyalties, which have political, cultural, and aesthetic implications, remain so entangled in me, so thoroughly mine, that they have led not to confusion, but to a strange, arresting clarity. I thus now qualify an assertion I made, at twenty, in a poem:

> call me a poet
>   dear editor
> they call this my alien language
>
> i am a dealer in words
>   that mix cultures
>   and leave me rootless
>   ("Dear Editor," 1–6, *Belovéd Witness*)

Rootless? Certainly not. I was merely subscribing to an inherent, dominative mode that insisted one should not write in English because it was not an Indian language. But in those lines I had implicitly begun to protest this notion of English as alien, questioning the "they" who "call this my alien language." Perhaps I was subconsciously aware that subcontinental English needed renewal and reworking, "translation" even, before I and other poets could use it to meet the demands of a "hybrid" cultural situation. But it was mine, ours.

Why did I choose to translate Faiz? Oh, for a mess of reasons, some of them quite certainly concerned with the poetic ego. Could I make English behave outside its aesthetic habits? But more immediately: When I came to the United States in 1976, no one seemed to have heard of Faiz (at that time, some people had begun to hear of Nazim Hikmet—a friend of Faiz's and like him a winner of the Lenin Peace Prize for Literature; Faiz had translated some of Hikmet's poems into Urdu). To have to introduce Faiz's name, to explain who he was, seemed an insult to a very significant element of my culture. As Edward Said says,

The crucial thing to understand about Faiz . . . is that like Garcia Marquez he was read and listened to both by the literary elite and by the masses. His major—indeed it is unique in any language—achievement was to have created a contrapuntal rhetoric and rhythm whereby he would use classical forms (*qasida, ghazal, masnavi, qita*) and transform them before his readers rather than break from the old forms. You could hear old and new together. His purity and precision were astonishing, and you must imagine therefore a poet whose poetry combined the sensuousness of Yeats with the power of Neruda. He was, I think, one of the greatest poets of this century, and was honored as such throughout the major part of Asia and Africa. (Blurb to *The Rebel's Silhouette*)

So here was this poet whose work I had grown up reciting and hearing recited by heart, a poet who has continued to be sung by the leading singers of the subcontinent, a poet who was such a master of the *ghazal* that he transformed its every stock image and, as if by magic, brought absolutely new associations into being, and yet he was not known in this part of the world. So I made attempts, imbibing some methods Adrienne Rich and W. S. Merwin (see Ahmad) had adopted in translating Ghalib, whom Faiz often echoed, but my attempts were feeble, my results uneven.

And then, quite by chance, I came across five of Naomi Lazard's excellent translations of Faiz's poems in *Kayak*. Because the world—at least of poetry—is delightfully small, a series of coincidences led me several months later to a phone conversation with her and, shortly after that, a meeting in Manhattan. I learned that she had met Faiz at an international literary conference in Honolulu in 1979—one of the two times he was allowed into the country. Otherwise, the McCarran-Walter Act had kept him from these shores. As Carlo Coppola says,

A spokesperson for the world's voiceless and suffering peoples—whether Indians oppressed by the British in the '40s, freedom fighters in Africa, the Rosenbergs in cold-war America in the '50s, Vietnamese peasants fleeing American napalm in the '60s, or Palestinian children living in refugee camps in the 1970s—Faiz wrote painfully, stunningly and compassionately of the human aspiration for freedom: a hallmark of his verse and, more than once, an excuse to refuse him entry into the United States (97).

On meeting Faiz, Lazard says, she immediately knew she was in the presence of a poet of world stature, one who must be brought to the attention of her compatriots. And so the translation process began, right there at the conference. Lazard writes:

We established a procedure immediately. Faiz gave me the literal translation of a poem. I wrote it down just as he dictated it. Then the real work began. I asked him questions regarding the text. Why did he choose just that phrase, that word, that image, that metaphor? What did it mean to him? There were cultural differences. What was crystal clear to an Urdu-speaking reader meant nothing at all to an American. I had to know the meaning of every nuance in order to recreate the poem. (28)

What were these cultural differences? I presume Lazard had to learn the nuances of images that would seem too lush to an American poet— images that recur shamelessly in Urdu poetry, among them the moon, the rose, the moth, the flame. She needed to learn their modern implications as well as their uses over the centuries, a formidable task. For example, the Belovéd—an archetype in Urdu poetry—can mean friend, woman, God. Faiz not only tapped into these meanings but extended them so that the Belovéd could figure as the revolution. The reader begins to infer, through a highly sensuous language, that waiting for the revolution can be as agonizing and intoxicating as waiting for one's lover. How is the translator to get all this across? Victor Kiernan, the first to translate Faiz into English, says: "Of all elements in foreign poetry, imagery is the easiest to appreciate, except when, as often in the Persian-Urdu tradition, it has symbolic and shifting meanings" (14). Lazard's translation process continued across continents, through the mail; on a few occasions she was able to meet Faiz during his visits to London. When he died she already had enough poems for *The True Subject,* her volume of Faiz translations. By way of an epigraph to her book, Lazard offers a ring of quotations regarding the true subject of poetry:

> Faiz Ahmed Faiz to Alun Lewis, Burma, circa 1943:
> "The true subject of poetry is the loss of the beloved."

> Alun Lewis, in a letter to Robert Graves
> before Lewis was killed, Burma, 1944:
> "The single poetic theme of Life and Death—the question
> of what survives of the beloved."

> Robert Graves, in *The White Goddess,*
> quoting Alun Lewis, 1947:
> "The single poetic theme of Life and Death—the question
> of what survives of the beloved."

> Naomi Lazard to Faiz Ahmed Faiz, Honolulu, 1979
> (having read *The White Goddess* many years before
> and misquoting
> the line attributed to Alun Lewis:
> "The true subject of poetry is the loss of the beloved."

Someone in a mood to mystify may offer this ring of quotations as yet another kind of translation, one engaged in by destiny. But let me not tempt myself.

Born in Sialkot, in undivided Punjab in 1911, Faiz earned a master's degree in English literature and another in Arabic literature. In a sense, he had embarked on his own inner translations and, later, did translate into Urdu the Turkish poet Nazim Hikmet and the Kazakhstani poet

Omar Uljaz Ali Suleiman. After independence, which accompanied the partition of the subcontinent in 1947, he chose to live in Pakistan and became editor of the *Pakistan Times*. In 1951, along with several left-wing army officers, he was arrested on the charge of planning a Soviet-sponsored coup; he spent four years in prison, mostly in solitary confinement under sentence of death, but was released in 1955. He returned to work on the *Pakistan Times*.

In 1958, he was removed from that post and jailed when Ayub Khan's military government took over. Interestingly, when UNESCO was approaching governments to nominate the representative writers of their countries—so they could be translated into various "major" languages—Faiz's was the first name Ayub Khan mentioned. After translations of his work appeared in Russian, he was awarded the Lenin Peace Prize (1962). Appointed chair of the National Council on the Arts during Zulfikar Ali Bhutto's prime ministership, he lost the position after Bhutto's overthrow by Zia ul-Haq. He then lived in Beirut until the Israeli invasion of 1982 and edited *Lotus*, the journal of the Afro-Asian Writers' Association. His death in Lahore in November 1984 was reported, sometimes in banner headlines, on the front pages of newspapers in India, Pakistan, the Soviet Union, and throughout the Middle East.

Given Faiz's political commitments, particularly his Marxist understanding of history, audiences may hastily assume that he was a poet of slogans. His genius, however, lay in his ability to balance his politics with his (in some ways stringently traditional, often classical) aesthetics without compromising either. He once advised a poet to avoid didactic and rhetorical gestures. He also said that

the future of the *ghazal*, like the future of all poetry, depends above all on the talent of its future practitioners. Pedantically speaking, there is nothing good or bad in any poetic form, but that the poet makes it so. . . . [For] some insight into the future of this much maligned and much admired form of expression, it were best to look at its past. Not the distant past when its excellence was unquestioned but the recent past when its *raison d'etre* was first brought into question. This was in the mid-nineteenth century when in Ghalib's phraseology, "the last candle of freedom anguished by the ending of the convivial night flickered and died"; when the last battle for liberation was fought and lost. In the breast-beating that followed, poetry, which was then synonymous with the *ghazal* was denounced as one of the factors responsible for this debacle. ("Future of *Ghazal* Poetry" 53–55)

But, Faiz emphasizes, the *ghazal* survived and continues to.

Perhaps this is so because the *ghazal*'s "rigidity of form," in Faiz's words, "is coupled with an equal if not greater freedom in the use of not only Empson's seven but innumerable forms of 'ambiguity'" ("Future of *Ghazal* Poetry" 55). It manipulates the "meaning of meaning, i.e., endowing a word or sign with a number of concomitant referents explicable only in a particular textual or social context" (Kiernan 14). The form embodies, in Kiernan's words, "a kind of stream-of-consciousness, and might prove helpful to Western writers caged in their framework of logic, which they have tried to break out from by discarding metre, and sometimes sense as well" (14). One couplet of a *ghazal* may be political, another tragic, one religious, another romantic, and so on. Comprising at least four couplets, it has no maximum limit. In the hands of a master, this seemingly "light" form has more grandeur than a sestina and more emotional compression than a sonnet. Ghalib's *ghazals,* for example, reveal a great tragic poet and Faiz's a great political one (in the most generous, inclusive sense).

Because translating a *ghazal* formally is just about impossible (beyond my powers, in any case), I have adopted loose, free-verse stanzas (along the lines of Merwin's versions of Ghalib; see Ahmad) to suggest the elliptical power of Faiz's couplets. But the magic of the form is missing, often heartbreakingly so. Desperation, however, can lead one to freer ways of approximating magic, and mine led me back to Aijaz Ahmad's edition of the *Ghazals of Ghalib,* a collaboration with Thomas Fitzsimmons, William Hunt, W. S. Merwin, David Ray, Adrienne Rich, William Stafford, and Mark Strand. Ahmad simplified Ghalib into literal versions and added necessary scholarly explanations. He sent this material to the poets and asked them for versions of the ones they liked. What emerged was sometimes spectacular, sometimes magical, sometimes passable—but always interesting. Merwin's and Rich's efforts struck me as particularly compelling, some of which have inspired me in my attempts. They have shown me how one may at times use free verse in translation to capture the essence of a poem, even if the original is in a stringent form. One of my favorite couplets by Ghalib was transliterated by Ahmad, who maintains the passive arrangement of the original:

> To him comes sleep, belongs the mind (peace of mind),
> belong the nights
> On whose arm you spread your hair.   ("*Ghazal* XV" 5–6)

This is how Merwin tackled it:

> Sleep comes to him
>> peace belongs to him
>> the night is his
>
> over whose arm you spread your hair   (11–14)

Adrienne Rich:

> Sleep is his, and peace of mind, and the nights belong to him
> across whose arms you spread the veils of your hair.   (5–6)

William Stafford:

> Sleep comes, peace, quiet of rest,
> for one who holds an arm under your hair.   (5–6)

None of these quite suggests the emotional desperation, however quiet, of the original. How to convey that this person, because of whom your world is in absolute turmoil (the word for "spreading your hair" evokes that in Urdu), is undisturbed, absolutely in control, asleep peacefully while you are lying restlessly on his arm? Merwin made another attempt:

> He is the lord of sleep
> lord of peace
> lord of night
>
> on whose arm your hair is lying   (10–13)

Though "hair is lying" doesn't quite do it, I cannot think of any way his use of "lord" can be improved upon. It conveys everything, for the passive voice in Urdu is not passive; rather, it can be quite imperious. "Lord" captures that imperial moment, the control this lover has, his habit of taking for granted the one whose hair is lying on his arm. How I wish Merwin knew Urdu so he could realize his aesthetic victory here; he could then hear Begum Akhtar's rendering of these lines in *Raga Bhairavi* and be put under a spell. This is quite an irony: someone who doesn't know the language he is translating from can never truly know the extent of his failure or triumph.

Faiz's regular poems (that is, not the *ghazals*) are somewhat easier for me to translate. But how to point out to exclusively English speakers the

moment when what they see merely as exotic is actually challenging the
"exotic"? In "Don't Ask Me for That Love Again," Faiz breaks radically
from Urdu's usual manner of looking at the Belovéd, asking that his
social commitment be accepted as more important than their love:

> That which then was ours, my love,
> don't ask me for that love again.
> The world then was gold, burnished with light—
> and only because of you. That's what I had believed.
> How could one weep for sorrows other than yours?
> How could one have any sorrow but the one you gave?
> So what were these protests, these rumors of injustice?
> A glimpse of your face was evidence of springtime.
> The sky, wherever I looked, was nothing but your eyes.
> If you'd fall into my arms, Fate would be helpless.
>
> All this I'd thought, all this I'd believed.
> But there were other sorrows, comforts other than love.
> The rich had cast their spell on history:
> dark centuries had been embroidered on brocades and silks.
> Bitter threads began to unravel before me
> as I went into alleys and in open markets
> saw bodies plastered with ash, bathed in blood.
> I saw them sold and bought, again and again.
> This too deserves attention. I can't help but look back
> when I return from those alleys—what should one do?
> And you still are so ravishing—what should I do?
> There are other sorrows in this world,
> comforts other than love.
> Don't ask me, my love, for that love again.
>   (*Rebel's Silhouette* 5; my translation)

This was a revolutionary poem, envied by many Urdu poets who
wished they had first brought the socialist revolution into the realm of
the Belovéd, setting the archetype against itself, as it were. In this poem,
Faiz announces that poetry, without dismissing tradition, must take on
political themes consciously. Notice that Faiz did not discard the tradition: the poem clearly establishes the importance of the Belovéd and her
beauty. But its speaker does some plain speaking (almost like Cordelia
to Lear), granting love its due, but no more. That Faiz had emphasized
political commitment here did not, of course, mean that he would not,

in other poems, address the Belovéd in the manner of love-poetry, showing how the speaker's life depended entirely on her or him. But often when he addresses the Belovéd, he is also addressing a figure that may very well be the revolution—revolution as a lost lover, or a cruel lover refusing to return.

In "Don't Ask Me for That Love Again," I took two recognizable liberties. One of the lines, literally translated, could read: "When there's your sorrow, what is this struggle of the world?" "Your sorrow" in Urdu can mean both "the sorrow you've caused me" and "the sorrow you feel." Further, "struggle of the world" does not quite suggest the nuances Faiz was striving for. I enlarged that one line into three:

> How could one weep for sorrows other than yours?
> How could one have any sorrow but the one you gave?
> So what were these protests, these rumors of injustice?   (5–7)

I also bypassed two lines of the original, which Victor Kiernan has translated as:

> Flesh issuing from the cauldrons of disease
> With festered sores dripping corruption—   (14–15)

Later, I was delighted to discover that in subsequent editions Faiz himself had deleted those very two lines. Did he also, like me, find them excessive, as I had, if not outrightly gratuitous? There is this kinship among poets, I will insist, this ability at times to see through craft, ironically because of the craft, to the essence.

My translation process, as is clear, was quite different from Lazard's. I knew, both because of her Faiz and because of Merwin's and Rich's Ghalib, that not knowing the original is not necessarily a handicap. Not knowing the original may even be an advantage of sorts as long as one is working with very good literal versions. Merwin, after all, had set a standard for me with one line, against which I had to measure myself. My distinct advantage was that I could "hear" and say the originals to myself, as I translated, something Rich and Merwin just couldn't do. My particular problem was how to "pretend" that I was not burdened with a dual loyalty, to ignore that I was negotiating the demands of two cultures, both of which I felt in my bones, that I was responding to the sounds of two languages simultaneously. Even though the final product does not show it, I was constantly aware of my dual loyalties. But I decided: Wasn't this absence of a pure agenda an advantage? I had an inwardness with two languages: my loyalty to Urdu made me want to bring across its exquisite power to sway millions of people with its poetry, and my loyalty to English made me (as a poet in the language) want to create poetry in English. To what extent would I compromise Faiz's voice? I finally attacked the task with no theoretical inhibition, letting each poem dictate itself, which often resulted in my fashioning for Faiz an English that is by turns dry and lyrical. But I always heard the music of the original, and that was fruitful, for some people have mentioned that there is a metrical "feel" to my translation, of which I was quite unaware.

I wrote to Faiz in 1980 in Beirut, where he was living in exile, into which he had been forced by the military regime of Zia ul-Haq. He had "found a welcome of sorts in the ruins of Beirut. His closest friends were Palestinian" (Said 50). Besides asking for permission to translate him, I told him that I would be taking liberties with the originals. But what I really did was to bribe him with a sort of homecoming. I reminded him that he had, years before my birth, stayed in our home in Kashmir. I created nostalgia: Begum Akhtar, too, had stayed in our house. I tempted him: I had rare tapes of Begum Akhtar singing his *ghazals* in private concerts. In exactly a month he wrote back: "I certainly knew your father and I am glad to have news from you. You are welcome to make your adaptations of my poems which I shall be happy to receive. Also some of your own poems and the tape or cassette of Begum Akhtar which you have kindly offered to send."

My "Homage to Faiz Ahmed Faiz" underscores my experience as a translator and also reveals some of my strategies for rendering Urdu into English. In one stanza, I incorporated a couplet of Ghalib's in the following manner:

> You knew Ghalib was right:
> blood must not merely follow routine, must not
> just flow as the veins' uninterrupted
> river. Sometimes it must flood the eyes,
> surprise them by being clear as water.   (21–25, *Half-Inch*)

Ghalib's two lines may be transliterated: "I do not approve of a mere running and loitering in the veins. / If it isn't spilled from the eye, then how can it be called blood?" My weaving it into a poem meant explaining it—"You knew Ghalib was right"—paraphrasing it, even.

Sometimes explanation may be the best way to translate. Here is my literal version of one of Faiz's couplets: "Got an occasion to sin, that too for only four days. / I've seen the courage of God Almighty." I had to fill in the elliptical moments and adopted a free-verse stanza, a strategy I have used quite often with the *ghazals:*

> You made it so brief our time on earth
> its exquisite sins this sensation Oh Almighty
> of forgetting you
> > We know how vulnerable you are
> > We know you are a coward God   ("Ghazal" 11–15)

Will something be borne across to exclusively English readers through my translations? I also hope that those who know both languages will find some pleasure in my moments of literal fidelity to Faiz as well as in those moments (of fidelity, I insist) when I am unfaithful. As for purists, I hope they will be generous and welcome the times when I had no choice but to adjust, especially in the *ghazals,* the letter of Faiz's work—a letter to which I have a visceral attachment. But only in the original Urdu. As Salman Rushdie says in *Shame,* "Omar Khayyam's position as a poet is curious. He was never very popular in his native Persia; and he exists in the West in a translation that is really a complete reworking of his verses, in many cases very different from the spirit (to say nothing of the content) of the original. . . . It is generally believed that something is always lost in translation; I cling to the notion—and use, in evidence, the success of Fitzgerald-Khayyam—that something can also be gained" (24).

In "In Memory of Begum Akhtar," I wrote: "Ghazal, that death-sustaining widow, / sobs in dingy archives, hooked to you. / She wears her grief, a moon-soaked white, / corners the sky into disbelief" (11–14, *Half-Inch*). I could use the same words for Faiz. Begum Akhtar comes back to me in strange moments, at times unexpectedly. So does Faiz; often, they come back together.

In a recent poem, "Snow on the Desert," I narrate driving my sister to Tucson International Airport in a terribly thick January morning fog. Suddenly, the sliding doors of the fog opened and the sun-dazzled snow, which had fallen all night, blinded us. All the cactus plants were draped in a cocaine-like whiteness. I told my sister to imagine that we were driving by the shores of the sea, for the Sonora Desert was an ocean two hundred million years ago. At the airport I stared after her plane until the window was again a mirror. And then,

As I drove back to the foothills, the fog

shut its doors behind me on Alvernon,
and I breathed the dried seas

                    the earth had lost,
their forsaken shores.

                                        (*A Nostalgist's Map of America* 52–56)

   I thought for weeks that I had nothing to compare that moment
with, nothing to contrast it with. How could I *translate* that moment?
Months later, as I struggled with the poem, I remembered

            another moment that refers only
            to itself:

                    in New Delhi one night
            as Begum Akhtar sang, the lights went out.

            It was perhaps during the Bangladesh War,
            perhaps there were sirens,

                            air-raid warnings.
            But the audience, hushed, did not stir.

            The microphone was dead, but she went on
            singing, and her voice

                            was coming from far
            away, as if she had already died.

            And just before the lights did flood her
            again, melting the frost

                    of her diamond
            into rays, it was, like this turning dark

            of fog, a moment when only a lost sea
            can be heard, a time

                    to recollect
            every shadow, everything the earth was losing,

            a time to think of everything the earth
            and I had lost, of all

that I would lose,
of all that I was losing.

(*A Nostalgist's Map of America* 57–80)

The only way to translate that moment was to find one that could not be compared with or to another. But in that untranslatable fraction of time, I did manage a translation by pointing out its impossibility.

Was Begum Akhtar singing Faiz when the lights went out? He is always with me, often in her voice. I have brought them to America with absolute ease, taken them back to the subcontinent, then again brought them back to America. I have not surrendered any part of me; rather, my claims to both Urdu and English have become greater. The way the *raga* and the poem became the other's for Begum Akhtar, so have Urdu and English become for me. My two loyalties, on loan to each other, are now so one that the loan has been forgiven. No, forgotten.

Begum Akhtar stripped words until they were revealed in the glory of their syllables, each syllable made an integral note of her chosen *raga*—so often a tantalizingly unclichéd *Bhairavi*. She knew the *ghazal* at its heart has a circularity of meaning, created seductively by its *qafia* and *radif* in couplet after couplet. She knew how to time this circularity so it seemed we were at the stillpoint of the revolving circle, especially when she was interpreting a great poet. No translation can hope to do that. But "nothing's lost. Or else: all is translation / And every bit of us is lost in it / Or found" (Merrill, "Lost in Translation," 208–10). For me, translating Faiz has led to its own moments in which I am sometimes at the stillpoint of the turning circle, sometimes part of its revolution. Sometimes the circle comes to a dazzling halt, and I manage to find my meaning as a translator.

Works Cited

Ahmad, Aijaz, ed. *Ghazals of Ghalib*. New York: Columbia UP, 1971.

Ali, Agha Shahid. *The Belovéd Witness*. New Delhi: Viking Penguin, 1992.

———. *The Half-Inch Himalayas*. Middletown, Conn.: Wesleyan UP, 1987.

———. *A Nostalgist's Map of America*. New York: W. W. Norton, 1991.

Coppola, Carlo. "Faiz Ahmed Faiz." *Poetry East* (Spring 1989): 96–97.

Dhar, Sheila. "Hindustani Music: An Inward Journey." *Temenos* 7 (1986): 83–93.

Faiz, Faiz Ahmed. "Future of *Ghazal* Poetry." *Sonora Review* (Spring 1985): 53–55.

———. *Poems.* Trans. Victor Kiernan. London: George Allen & Unwin, 1971.

———. *The Rebel's Silhouette.* Trans. Agha Shahid Ali. Layton Utah: Peregrine Smith Books, 1991.

———. *The True Subject.* Trans. Naomi Lazard. Princeton: Princeton UP, 1987.

Hollander, John. *Rhyme's Reason.* New Haven: Yale UP, 1989.

Kiernan, Victor. "Iqbal: A Translator's Confessions." Iqbal Centenary Meeting. Urdu Society. Birmingham, England, 1980.

Lazard, Naomi. "Translating Faiz." *Columbia: The Magazine of Columbia University* (June 1985): 26–30.

Merrill, James. *Selected Poems.* New York: Alfred A. Knopf, 1992.

Rushdie, Salman. *Shame.* New York: Alfred A. Knopf, 1983.

Said, Edward W. "The Mind of Winter: Reflections on Life in Exile." *Harper's* (September 1984): 49–55.

II. (Not) Translating Across Cultures

This section foregrounds those moments of absence or lack, of deliberate or inadvertent mis(sed)translation, when texts, languages, cultures construed as subordinate (and subjugated) do not get "borne across" on their own terms or on terms congenial to those cultures perceived as dominant. As such, the essays in this section disclose, in part at least, the markedly asymmetrical power relationships that obtain between what are seen as "strong" (or colonizing) and "weak" (or colonized) languages and cultures. Thus, for instance, Edward W. Said's "Embargoed Literature," while providing a survey of several important contemporary works in Arabic, reflects on the sustained and deliberate refusal by U.S. publishers to undertake translations of Arabic literary texts because "'the problem,' I was told 'is that Arabic is a controversial language.'" In the event these translations are undertaken, they go largely "unnoticed and unreviewed," and this lack, says Said, is a function of attempts "to interdict any serious attention to texts that do not reiterate the usual clichés about 'Islam,' violence, sensuality, and so forth."

Lawrence Needham's "'Goody Two-shoes' / 'Goosee Shoo-shoo': Translated Tales of Resistance in Matthew Lewis's *Journal of a West India Proprietor*" focuses on the seemingly unmotivated erasures and elisions as Lewis sets out, in his transcriptions of "Nancy" stories, to constitute the "primitive in life and art." Insisting on these transcriptions as forms of translation that depend on the "signifying systems of colonial power" enables Needham to return the stories to the "contradictory site of their production." For when Lewis "situates his writing at a utopian point purportedly removed from social determinations, not pressure points between systems of meaning," he, argues Needham, deliberately "dissipates the tensions and contradictions inherent in translations." In addition, a recuperation of context and performative markers, such as the one Needham undertakes, allows readers to witness what might well be the "native" storyteller's "sophisticated, double-voiced performance . . . in a hybrid" tongue that, through inflection, "both meets the needs of dominant discourse and refuses to be bound by its (in)appropriate power."

Jacinto R. Fombona I.'s "Writing Europe's 'Orient': Spanish-American Travelers to the 'Orient'" is also concerned with the power of European colonial representations and the erasures and displacements they necessarily generate. He analyzes turn-of-the century Spanish-American travel narratives, especially Enrique Gómez Carrillo's *De Marsella a Tokio* to disclose a "very special moment for the discursive construction of traveled space." His essay focuses on how Spanish-American texts about travel to the "Orient" are always already mediated by, indeed "translations" of, prior European texts about travel to the "Orient." Signifying the desire to "assign and acquire social and cultural distinction" that being (or becoming) European implies in this context, Spanish-American travelers achieve this distinction by inscribing "their privileged access to the [textualized] space of Europe's Other." However, even though "the European text of the 'Orient' becomes the guideline while facing the Other," it is purged of the "political dangers that facing the colonial might imply." Hence, the focus on a purely aesthetic space in Spanish-American travel narratives.

Tim Brennan's "The Price of Happiness: C.L.R. James in New York, 1950" begins by presenting James as a "translated man," although not so much because of the "ontological state of mixing and matching identities" referred to in Salman Rushdie's well-known phrase as because of a "critical selectivity after the fact." Focusing on James's "The Struggle for Happiness" (which has only recently been published as *American Civilization*), Brennan examines him as an appropriate(d) "model-for-use" employed by cultural theorists in the United States who have tended "creatively to misrepresent earlier Left structures of feeling . . . in much more doctrinally consistent forms than we are often led to believe." At the same time, in his skeptical reading of James's American project, Brennan describes James himself as a translator whose "struggle" reveals an "unexpected identification with the United States as an adopted home," a "desire to live where the future was unfolding," and a determination to become a successful writer in his new world. James's translation of the United States conveys his belief that the American workers were "poised for victory on the crest of a vast media wave." This belief, Brennan suggests, is premised on the inevitable suppression and evasion of a host of "realities," among them both the "colonial question" and "the crazyhouse of U.S. intellectual consumerism."

Mahasweta Sengupta's "Translation as Manipulation: The Power of Images and Images of Power" focuses explicitly on that aspect of translation which Niranjana has called a "technology of colonial domination." Sengupta examines "the tyranny and power of 'images'" of "India" evident in the nineteenth century, where natural, "simple" or "primitive," and "essentially spiritual" representations of India were circulated to justify the "civilizing mission" of the British colonizers. In the second part of her essay, she turns to the auto-translations (in English) of Tagore, who deliberately recycled colonial stereotypes about Indians, thereby denuding his poems of their richness, ambiguity, and heterogeneity to cater to the tastes of his English readers. This motivated assimilation to the colonizers' tastes underscores, for Sengupta, the power of colonial hegemony.

Embargoed Literature

Edward W. Said

Eight years before Naguib Mahfouz won the Nobel Prize in Literature, a major New York commercial publisher known for his liberal and unprovincial views asked me to suggest some Third World novels for translation and inclusion in a series he was planning. The list I gave him was headed by two or three of Mahfouz's works, none of which was then in circulation in the United States. True, there were a few novels by the Egyptian master available in England, but these had never gained entry into the United States, and even in Europe were principally known only by a few students of Arabic. Several weeks after I submitted my list I inquired which novels had been chosen, only to be informed that the Mahfouz translations would not be undertaken. When I asked why, I was given an answer that has haunted me ever since. "The problem," I was told, "is that Arabic is a controversial language."

What, exactly, the publisher meant is still a little vague to me—but that Arabs and their language were somehow not respectable, and consequently dangerous, *louche,* unapproachable, was perfectly evident to me then and, alas, now. For of all the major world literatures, Arabic remains relatively unknown and unread in the West, for reasons that are unique, even remarkable, at a time when tastes here for the non-European are more developed than ever before and, even more compelling, contemporary Arabic literature is at a particularly interesting juncture.

An amusing sign of the disparity between the interest taken in Arabic literature and that in other literatures outside the Atlantic world can be seen in the treatment afforded Mahfouz and his work in English after he won the Nobel in 1988. Doubleday acquired the rights to much of his work and in 1990 began to introduce a handful of his stories and novels, including the first volume of his major work, the *Cairo Trilogy*, in what appeared to be new editions. In fact, with one exception, the translations were exactly the ones that had been available all along in England, some quite good but most either indifferent or poor. Clearly the idea was to capitalize on and market his new fame, but not at the cost of a retranslation.

Second, and more comically symptomatic, half a dozen profiles of Mahfouz appeared in American magazines, including *Vanity Fair. The New Yorker*, and *The New York Times Magazine*. In effect, they were the same article rewritten over and over. Each talked about his favorite café, his modesty, his position on Israel (in the second sentence of its story on his Nobel Prize, *The New York Times* thoughtfully expressed the opinion of the Israeli consul in New York), his orderly and extremely uninteresting life. All of the authors, some of them reasonably accomplished essayists, were innocent of both Arabic and Arabic literature. (In *The New Yorker*, Milton Viorst delivered himself of the thought that "Arabic, an imprecise language, requires most writers to choose between poetry and clarity.") All regarded Mahfouz as a hybrid of cultural oddity and political symbol. Little was said about his formal achievements, for instance, or about his place in modern literature as a whole.

Third, now that the act has worn thin, Mahfouz has more or less been dropped from discussion—without having provoked even the more venturesome literati into finding out which other writers in Arabic might be worth looking into. Where, after all, did Mahfouz come from? It is impossible not to believe that one reason for this odd state of affairs is the longstanding prejudice against Arabs and Islam that remains entrenched in Western, and especially American, culture. Here the "experts" on Islam and the Arabs bear considerable blame. Their so-called *doyen*, Bernard Lewis, still blathers on in places like *The Wall Street Journal, The Atlantic*, and *The American Scholar* about the darkness and strangeness of Muslims, Arabs, their culture, religion, etc. Israeli or Jewish scholars are commonly asked to comment on things Islamic while the reverse—an Arab commenting on Hebrew literature or Israeli policy—is seldom risked. Princeton University, one of the leading American centers of Arab and Islamic studies, does not have on its faculty a single native speaker teaching Arabic language or literature. Critics, book reviewers, and journal editors studiously avoid discussion of Arabic books even as they attempt prodigies of reading and interpretation where, for instance, Czech and Argentine literatures are concerned.

The bald fact is, the unavailability of Arabic literature in translation is no longer an excuse. Small but conscientious publishing houses like Al-Saqi and Quartet in England, Sindbad in France, and Three Continents Press in the United States have assembled a diverse cross section of contemporary work from the Arab world that is still overlooked or deliberately ignored by editors and book reviewers. In addition, some larger publishers (Penguin, Random House, and a handful of American university presses) have recently put out some truly first-rate literary work that has gone unnoticed and unreviewed, as if indifference and prejudice were a blockade designed to interdict any attention to texts that do not reiterate the usual clichés about "Islam," violence, sensuality, and so forth. There almost seems to be a deliberate policy of maintaining a kind of monolithic reductionism where the Arabs and Islam are concerned; in this, the Orientalism that distances and dehumanizes another culture is upheld, and the xenophobic fantasy of a pure "Western" identity elevated and strengthened. (Some of these reflections have been partially instigated by the truly disgraceful level of reporting on the Iraqi military aggression in Kuwait. Most of what has passed for journalistic and expert commentary in the United States media has been simply a repetition of appalling clichés, most of them ignorant, unhistorical, moralistic, self-righteous, and hypocritical. All of them derive unquestioningly in one way or another from U.S. government policy, which has long considered the Arabs to be either terrorists or mindless stooges to be milked for their money or abundant and inexpensive oil.) What is disappointing is how little compensating pressure there is from the culture at large, one that seems automatically to prefer the Mahfouz rewrites and the Islamic stereotypes to almost anything else.

The irony is that there is a good deal in recent literary material to complicate and make more interesting the current Arab scene. In less than a year three books of unique literary distinction have appeared in fine translations yet gone virtually unnoticed. Each, in its own way, is both a dissenting or oppositional work and also a work by an author well-known and admired within the Arab and Islamic tradition. In other words, while each of these works treats Arab culture as something to be fought over and contested, thereby opposing orthodoxy, unjust authority, and uncritical dogma, none of them expresses the kind of alienation and estrangement from the culture that is at work in attacks by Western Orientalists.

The most intellectually stimulating of the three is Adonis's *An*

Introduction to Arab Poetics, from Al-Saqi, translated with uncommon intelligence by Catherine Cobham. Adonis is today's most daring and provocative Arab poet, a symbolist and surrealist who is like a combination of Montale, Breton, Yeats, and the early T. S. Eliot. In this compilation of four essays originally given as lectures at the Collège de France, he reinterprets the whole massive Arab tradition, from pre-Islamic poetry through the Koran, the classical period, and on into the present. Arguing that there has always been a literalist, authoritarian strain in the literature, Adonis presents the thesis that this has usually been opposed by poets and thinkers for whom modernity is renewal rather than conformism, transgression rather than nationalism, creativity rather than fundamentalism.

Far from being simply an academic statement, *Arab Poetics* is an uncompromising challenge to the status quo that is held in place by official Arab culture. In no uncertain terms Adonis identifies the latter equally with religious and with secular authority, clerics and bureaucrats whose retreat into either a reliquary past or the arms of a foreign patron has brought us to the cultural crisis that we as Arabs face today. Adonis's command of the texts is astonishingly true, as is the simple brilliance of his argument. One would have thought it as important a cultural manifesto as any written today, which is what makes the silence that has greeted the work so stupefying.

The two other recent works are Edwar al-Kharrat's *City of Saffron* and the Lebanese feminist novelist Hanan al-Shaykh's *Women of Sand and Myrrh,* both published by Quartet, the first translated admirably by Frances Liardet, the latter with her customary fluency by Cobham. Kharrat is a Coptic Egyptian writer whose early years in Alexandria form the subject of this semi-autobiographical text, which bears a formal resemblance to Joyce's *A Portrait of the Artist as a Young Man.* Readers who have swallowed the journalistic myth that Copts and Muslims hate each other will be informed otherwise by these meditative yet subversively intimate ruminations about childhood. One feels not only the *non serviam* of the budding artist but also a warmly confident exploration of life in a working-class Coptic family beset with physical dislocation, unhappy sex, political upheaval. Here too it is possible to read Kharrat's revelations as very much a part of contemporary Egyptian culture without ever forgetting that he disputes the official establishment's facile versions of what "realism" and social responsibility are all about. Hanan al-Shaykh's novel is a complex and demanding story of women in the Persian Gulf—

oppressed, manipulated, sexually tormented, and confused. Far from simple romance, *Women of Sand and Myrrh* is both breathtakingly frank and technically difficult, taking on such experiences as homosexuality and patriarchy with unexpected power. Would that more Western feminists attended to writers like Shaykh and not just to the overexposed (and overcited) Nawal el-Saadawi.

It is less the explicit subject matter than the formal and technical achievement of these three works that is so striking, and so accurate an index of how excitingly far Arabic literature has come since Mahfouz was at his peak about twenty-five years ago. The best of today's writers are oppositional figures who frequently use literary virtuosity to form an oblique critique of life in the various Arab states, where tyranny and atavism are common features of daily existence but where a large number of writers are still committed to live. But, one should add, these writers are neither alone nor unaware of what surrounds and has preceded them. Other excellent translations (again, ignored by the Anglo-American literary world) have appeared of: Abdel Rahman Munif's monumental *Cities of Salt,* by Peter Theroux for Random House's Vintage Books, the only serious work of fiction that tries to show the effect on a gulf country of oil, Americans, and local oligarchy; Gamal al-Ghitani's *Zayni Barakat* in the best of all translations, by Farouk Abdel Wahab, for Viking Penguin, a superbly elegant Jamesian novel about sixteenth-century Cairo, in effect an allegory of Nasser's rule with its combination of honest reformist zeal and political paranoia and repression; Elias Khoury's *The Little Mountain*, in Maia Tabet's spare translation for the University of Minnesota Press, a postmodernist fable of the Lebanese civil war; and Emile Habiby's great *Secret Life of Saeed the Ill-Fated Pessoptimist*, the surreal Palestinian masterpiece, in only a passable version by Trevor Le Gassick and Salma Jayyusi published by Readers International, which is nevertheless astonishing in its wit and dark inventiveness.

Other recent Arabic works include Hussein Haddawy's distinguished new translation for Norton of the *Arabian Nights;* the Sudanese Tayib Salih's *Season of Migration to the North,* in an edition by the leading Arabic-English translator of our time, Denys Johnson-Davis, done for Heinemann in England and republished in the United States by Michael Kesend; Ghassan Kanafani's *Men in the Sun,* in Hilary Kilpatrick's rendition for Three Continents, a prescient parable of three Palestinian refugees trying to smuggle themselves from Iraq to Kuwait in a tanker truck, dying of asphyxiation and heat at the border post; the collection of poems by Mahmoud Darwish, Samih al-Qassim (today's leading Palestinian poets), and Adonis, *Victims of a Map,* in a bilingual Penguin edition rendered capably by Abdullah al-Udhari. Salih's novel can bear extremely favorable comparison with V. S. Naipul's *A Bend in the River;* despite their common source in Conrad's *Heart of Darkness,* Salih's work is far less schematic and ideologically embittered, a novel of genuine post-colonial strength and passion.

There are also the enormous compilations by Salma Jayyusi being published over several years by Columbia University Press, of which *Modern Arabic Poetry: An Anthology* was the first to appear. It is fortunate that this relatively high number of recently translated Arabic works coincides with their importance and literary reputation in the Arab world. Nevertheless, it is also sadly the case that Arab writers themselves (as well as their publishing houses, ministries of culture, embassies in Western capitals) have done hardly anything to promote their works, and the discourse of Arab culture, in the West; the absence of an Arab cultural intervention in the world debate is thus depressing and tragic. I write these lines as the horrific waste and potential violence of today's gulf crisis focus all efforts on war and confrontation. Is it too much to connect the stark political and military polarization with the cultural abyss that exists between Arabs and the West? What impresses one is the will to ignore and reduce the Arabs that still exists in many departments of Western culture, and the unacceptable defeatism among some Arabs that a resurgent religion and indiscriminate hostility are the only answer. It may seem pathetically utopian to offer the reading and interpretation of contemporary literature as meliorative activities, but what is so attractive about the war now going on between Baghdad, the former Abbasid capital, and the entire West?

"Goody Two-shoes" / "Goosee Shoo-shoo": Translated Tales of Resistance in Matthew Lewis's *Journal of a West India Proprietor*

Lawrence Needham

Playwright, translator, poet, and collector of tales, Matthew Gregory Lewis also was a novelist whose notorious, erotically charged gothic romance, *The Monk* (1794), earned him the sobriquet "Monk Lewis," by which he is remembered even today. He was author, as well, of *Journal of a West India Proprietor,* a relatively obscure work that to this day has disappointed Samuel Taylor Coleridge's expectation that it would "live and be popular" as a book of "travel and touring" (297). Increasingly, however, Lewis's *Journal* has been given a second life by social historians who, mining it for information on Jamaican plantocratic culture and slave life, have uncovered invaluable evidences of slave resistance, particularly among women.

Their acts of resistance, sometimes sensational—as in the commission of dread poisonings—sometimes unobtrusive—as in private acts of reproductive control—included discursive practices that challenged metropolitan and colonial representations of "Negro" culture in the course of articulating African-Caribbean culture under plantocracy. Among these practices were the oral performances Lewis transcribed and published as texts in his *Journal* as evidence of "primitive" culture, but which can be read as instances enacting textual resistance to dominant modes of representation or as rehearsing alternative possibilities to life under domination.

Reading Lewis in this way entails remarking on his textualization of "Negro" culture and inscribing features of performance which he systematically omits from his account. It requires noting as well that the tales Lewis recounts as pure products of authentic "primitive" culture, are, in fact, the end products of multiple translations involving numerous mediations: Caribbean variants of African folktales, articulated in a Creolized tongue to satisfy a master's pleasure, the stories Lewis collects are borne across, or translated, for British consumption. As transcultural or cross-cultural texts, they retain traces of diverse sites of genesis and reception, foregrounding as a problem the social determinants of their production and raising as an issue the precise identity and relationship of "source" and "target" languages and cultures in a colonial context.

Begun shipboard, 8 November 1815, during passage to Jamaica, Lewis's *Journal* is an account of two years spent actively overseeing the Cornwall and Hordley estates he inherited in 1812. His 16 March 1816 letter to an unnamed correspondent indicates that early on he intended to publish it; he mentions "a sort of journal I have in petto . . . meaning it for publication on my return to England."[1] We may surmise that his desire to go public was intended, in part, to extenuate his position as proprietor of a West Indian sugar plantation—in the *Journal* he stresses that his enlightened, humane practices distinguish him from other slave owners.[2] Yet, despite the differences he urges on his readers, Lewis is, as his title acknowledges, a West Indian proprietor, and he recognizes owners as a legitimate ruling class whose existence guarantees a social order beneficial to slaves and proprietors alike. Though "in no sense a political manifesto," but "concerned with Lewis's personal experience" (Wilson 7), the *Journal* mobilizes that experience to demonstrate that slaves wanted and required the benevolent stewardship of masters. It makes the case of owners against those who wanted the emancipation of slaves to follow upon the abolition of the slave trade.[3]

On its face, however, the *Journal* most likely was meant to capitalize on contemporary taste for, and fascination with, the "primitive" in life and art, fueled by antiquarian researches and Romantic primitivism. Lewis himself had combined antiquarian interests and literary ambitions in collecting and publishing European ballads and legends; presenting "Negro" customs and culture was consistent with his practice of promoting "folk" materials, but with the advantage of circulating novelties in a market already surfeited on Old World materials.[4]

Of particular interest to Lewis—and, he hoped, to readers—were the "Nancy" stories he envisioned as the main attraction of his journal. Involving magic, shapeshifting, and the supernatural, the various narratives Lewis collected as "Nancy" stories were related, at least by name, to *Anansesem,* or Anancy tales, folktales of the spider Anancy, a guileful and cunning trickster figure. Broadened by Lewis to be the categorical equivalent of European tales of wonder, the "Nancy" stories were "choice morceaux" for public consumption, the gustatory metaphor suggesting public appetite for such "primitive" tales, and we may speculate that he included them to garnish his account with the accents of "Negro" culture. The Nancy stories were, in fact, separable from his journal, the first "published" specimen appearing in the 16 March letter attempting to create a taste for more of the same in the journal he promised to publish. The stories eventually printed in the *Journal* are themselves presented as discontinuous with the narrative of his first year's stay in Jamaica; recollected and recorded in transit to English, filling up journal entries for the period between his first and second visit to Jamaica, the Nancy stories are suspended, as if within parentheses, between periods of his active engagement with "native" informants.

Adrift between cultures as he recorded these tales (though projected toward England), Lewis literally and figuratively was in translation, occupying a paradoxical "no-place" removed from, yet engaged with, different cultural systems. Ultimately, however, Lewis situates his writing at a utopian point ostensibly removed from social determinations, not at the pressure point between systems of meaning. By decontextualizing the Nancy tales and presenting them as pure textual products of a timeless "Negro" culture, by positioning himself as a transcendent subject outside the stories he relates, he dissipates the tensions/contradictions inherent in translation. In order to read those stories with their full resonance and meaning, it is necessary to return them to the contradictory site of their production, the tensions of which can then be reinscribed into new re-markings/re-writings/translations. Fortunately, we are able to do so because of the details of performance Lewis records in the one Nancy story he describes outside his journal—the story of the "Neger Vithout 'ed," narrated by "Goody Two-shoes," otherwise affectionately known by Lewis and her fellows as "Goosee Shoo-shoo."

In brief, Shoo-shoo's "true and marvelous history of a 'lilly niggerman born vithout hed'" (213) recounts the story of a "nigger woman's" (214) efforts to secure for her son a head so that he might court a mate.

She turns to a tutelary owl ("massa") for help, yet lies about the circumstances surrounding her son's unfortunate condition, with a disastrous result: run off from a courting ritual amid the laughter and ridicule of the crowd, her son loses the head he received upon following the owl's instruction. Forced at last to disclose the sad truth about her son, the woman is sent to the king, whose power and influence assure her son's acceptance by a courtly retinue who exclaim, in the king's presence, "Nebber was sush ed—sush fine ed!" (220). Acceding to this judgment, "his Majesty's" daughter agrees to marry the "nigger vithout a 'ed," fulfilling the king's imperative that, despite her initial resistance, "you *sall* marry de man!" (219).

The moral of the story—"that telling lies will prove the worst cement for preserving heads of any description" (220), which Lewis appends to the account—is neither gratuitous nor inappropriate once we locate the genesis of the tale in plantocratic culture. Restated in the more specific terms of the story, the moral cautions "nigger" men and women to be truthful and obedient to "massa" in order to find surety under his protection and authority. The sentiment "massa provides" is reinforced when the story concludes with the assurance that the married couple "lib berry appy, and ab plenty rum and backy, de rest of dere day!" (220). Reduplicating the story's conclusion, it is enacted when Lewis provides Shoo-shoo, who obediently has given "massa" what he wanted, with rum and "backy." And, like the "nigger vithout a 'ed," the tale, "Neger Vithout 'ed" is completed when Lewis attaches sense, or a moral, to its sensible parts.

Yet it is precisely the plantocratic context Lewis displaces when he aestheticizes Shoo-shoo's story as a "pretty" narrative or a "picturesque" tale. To do otherwise would imply it lacked "authenticity," that it was fabricated to meet the demands of the moment or to serve his interests as a collector and proprietor. Rather, the case for stewardship of "nigger[s] vithout a 'ed" is insinuated by presenting Shoo-shoo's account as the natural expression of a childlike culture; that is, by framing it as a nursery tale for full-grown "piccaninnies," the " 'piccaninny' nearest to her, and grinning with extension from ear to ear, being a fellow above six feet, proportionately stout, and apparently between thirty and forty years of age" (213).

Read as a literary remain or survival—like "Jack the Giant-Killer," "Cinderella," and "Little Red Riding Hood" to which it is compared—the "Neger Vithout 'ed" opens a window on "primitive culture," which is the baseline from which to calculate loss or, in this case, gain in the progress of civilization. However, its value as an artifact of "Negro" culture or mind is directly tied to its perceived authenticity; hence, Lewis is at pains to insist that he conveys her story with the "true gusto of Shoo-shoo's precise words" (213).

Shoo-shoo's voice and "precise words" are given in what seems to be an exact transcript of her recitation, excepting those parts "taken up by Mat, in the best manner he is able" (213), when memory falters. Lewis's authorial (and sometimes editorial) intrusions, rather than raising questions, actually secure the "truthfulness" of his transcription; the alteration of her voice and his words, her pidgin English and his graceful writing establishes, by contrast, the "authenticity" of the original and the fidelity of his transcription. Consider, for example, the beginning of "Neger Vithout 'ed":

"Vonce on time, my piccaninnies" (the "piccaninny" nearest to her, and grinning with extension from ear to ear, being a fellow above six feet, proportionately stout, and apparently between thirty and forty years of age), "vonce on time there live voman under cotton-tree, ab lilly son, born vithout ed. So ven she see her son ab got no ed, the woman say, Vat I do now? my son ab no ed; and I 'fraid him look particular, and ebbery body take notice: beside, him no talk—him no hear—him no see—him no yammee (eat)—so what I do now?" (213)

Lewis's mediations as commentator on, and translator of, Shoo-shoo's story are contained within parentheses, the use of which throws her language into prominent relief as originary and prior to his secondary, derivative discourse. The authenticity of Shoo-shoo's words is assured by quotation marks demarcating the precise places where her words end and his begins. Yet the marks fostering the illusion of the immediate presence of her words also betray the mediated nature of Lewis's transcript. As typographical devices, they substitute for and approximate, not reduplicate, the texture of voice in its absence. Lewis's transcript—like all transcriptions—is, in fact, a translation, the substitution of one set of signifiers for another. It is the record of choices made under pressure of diverse social determinations, chief among them the need to re-present an alien language and culture to meet the demands, expectations, and tastes of a target culture.

For example, Lewis's decision to re-produce the asyndetic quality of Shoo-shoo's pidgin English cannot be divorced from the contemporary expectation that "primitive" speech was a crude, undeveloped instrument.[5] By contrast—one Lewis insists on by offsetting Shoo-shoo's fractured tale with the flourishes of his in-text commentary—"modern" English was thought to be lexically richer, syntactically more advanced, and logically more coherent, distinctions Lewis maintains by omitting or suppressing features of an original performance which make it fully intelligible. Textualizing Shoo-shoo's performance and separating out the contexts informing it, Lewis reduces speech to writing, anticipating anthropological reductions of "primitive language" to print in interlinear translations, which, as John Sturrock notes in a different context, through "the decontextualization of the native utterances" on the page made native speakers "sound not only strange but, relative to our own linguistic expectations, naive" (1003).

Considered underdeveloped and impoverished in important areas, "primitive" language nonetheless was described as more colorful, figurative, and expressive—in short, more childlike—than "modern" language, a characterization arising from a widespread, then-contemporary belief in cultural evolutionism and the progress of languages and societies.[6] While said to naturally produce figurative language, "primitive speakers" were thought to be unaware of the metaphoric nature of their utterances, mistaking the literal for the figurative, just as they confused matter and spirit in practicing idolatry and fetishism. Incapable of understanding the symbolic, "primitive" peoples produced rich allegories, the significances of which fell to collectors like Lewis who did not hesitate to provide the moral. (For example, Shoo-shoo's story seemingly borders on the ridiculous and nonsensical until Lewis draws out the appropriate moral.)

Colorful, demotic, presented as a literary survival, "Neger Vithout 'ed," in addition to being likened to a nursery tale, is offered as a specimen of the "picturesque," a word Lewis frequently uses to convey his impressions of Jamaican topography, plantation life, and "Negro" culture. An aesthetic category celebrating irregularity, discontinuity, variety *and* unity in composition, the picturesque was a liberal art form that encouraged license within limits, freedom within constraints. From one perspective— one that presupposes Romantic expressivist and organicist assumptions about language production—Shoo-shoo's tale is picturesque simply because it embodies the qualities of its picturesque speaker. From another, it is picturesque because the language of its articulation—pidgin English—intermixes languages and linguistic registers and, by comparison to Lewis's "standard" English, is discontinuous, irregular. Of course, the historical and social exigencies necessitating pidgin English are occluded; though itself a product of translation—hence, of active mediation—between cultures violently brought together, pidgin English, in Lewis's account and others, is presented as directly encoding "primitive" language, or, at the very least, of expressing the deep structure of the "primitive" mind.

The attempt to visualize/spatialize "primitive" consciousness through typographical display is related, in this particular case, to the tendency of the picturesque to empty out the sociopolitical/moral content of a composition, substituting for it a "highly specialized experience of *form*" (Liu 65). Displacing *istoria* and narrative underpinnings, and foregrounding the arrangement and patterning of surface details, the picturesque object invited *apatheia* and repose at the same time that its intricacy, variety, contrasts, and partial concealments excited curiosity and active recreation. In his suggestive analysis of the formalism of picturesque painting, Alan Liu argues that "the picturesque . . . forgot half the Classic picture—the narrative—to focus exclusively on the landscape mapping interpretation," yet, "without narrative reference . . . the very fact of interpretation became unapparent. Thus, I suggest, arose picturesque form: unapparent interpretation is form" (75–76). Keeping this in mind, the features of Shoo-shoo's picturesque speech—its halting syntax, lexical shortcomings, and colorful idioms—constitute Lewis's motivated interpretation of the "primitive mind," though, as in landscape painting, his interpretation, or point-of-view, is unobtrusively naturalized in what is offered as organic expression; motives become natural motifs devoid of historical reference.

Yet traces of narrative reference, intimated in static scenes of frozen violence and arrested desire, charged the picturesque experience with erotic and/or sadistic energies, activating the "detached" observer's prurient curiosity.[7] Shoo-shoo's "Neger Vithout 'ed," for example, interjects momentary *frisson* into its colorful, humorous picture of "Negro" culture and mind when "massa king" commands, "'bring de vip for floggee,' and directly two ear came all so quick, my piccaninnies, two bootiful big broad ear, so black, so shinee, lay upon him shoulder, all ready for stick gold ring" (220). His violent act, suggestive of the violence at the heart of plantocratic culture (emblematized by the whip) is fearful/repulsive, yet is only one detail of an aestheticized scene that fascinates in depicting the pleasurable exercise of arbitrary, absolute power without consequence. The suppressed sadism of the scene has a counterpart in the veiled sexuality of the story as a whole, which, at one level, concerns

the attempts of a black male to secure his mate. Castrated, impotent,
sticking his makeshift head into places "where it has no business" (220),
the "nigger vithout a 'ed" finally secures his marriage bed with the
blessings of "his Majesty" who legitimizes and makes a man of him.
Ultimately at issue in the story—importantly so, for the maintenance of
a plantocratic culture facing crisis—is reproductive control and possession
of the potentially wayward black female body.

Prurient interest in the control of the black female body is, in fact,
excited by Lewis's explanation of how he came to possess Shoo-shoo's
"quaint" tale (211). Full of double entendres and smarmy suggestiveness,
Lewis's characterization of his knowledge of Shoo-shoo and her "acquire-
ments" includes his tongue-in-cheek confession that she is "a most irresistible little woman," "wonderfully adroit in her profession" (212).
Her "profession" involves the commodification of her "pretty" tale for
"a glass of rum, or a roll of 'backy'" either of which is "sure to unpack
Goosee Shoo-shoo's budget" (212), and Lewis flaunts the power of his
privileged position in noting his easy access to her purse.

Of course, the economic basis of their intercourse betrays the interested nature of the exchange and calls into question the authenticity of
Shoo-shoo's "choice bit of originality" (213). We already have seen how
Lewis interprets "Neger Vithout 'ed" to thematize universal ideas, which
also happen to favor the class interests of West Indian proprietors, though
Lewis is at pains to "naturalize" their expression in the guise of presenting
a Nancy story in "Shoo-shoo's precise words." The tendency of her story
to mimic sentiments of dominant discourse and mirror the images of
Lewis's desires raises the possibility that Shoo-shoo is "putting on massa"
in a way rife with irony: the tale that cautions "nigger" men and women
that "telling lies will prove the worst cement for preserving heads" is an
artful fabrication designed to turn "massa's" head, while providing an
example of how to get ahead.

The idea that Shoo-shoo's recitation is, in fact, a command performance negotiating the exigencies of the moment, or that Shoo-shoo is a
self-conscious narrator using her tale to advantage, unsettles the notion
that "Neger Vithout 'ed" is the organic expression of a simple culture. It
suggests, rather, that her story is a sophisticated, double-voiced performance addressing multiple audiences in a potentially subversive hybrid
tongue.[8] This suggestion, reinforced whenever Lewis recognizes Shoo-
shoo as "shrewd" (212) or "cunning" (220), is precisely what Lewis suc-
cessfully blurs in translating her story as the picturesque equivalent of a

nursery tale or as the natural expression of the "Negro" mind. It is also a suggestion that Lewis studiously avoids when, in the *Journal,* he presents his collection of Nancy stories divorced from context and stripped of performative markers. For that reason, "Neger Vithout 'ed" is a valuable document; pointing to the social determinants of its genesis, it intimates alternate readings/interpretations to the one implicit in Lewis's translation, and it opens a window on how to read and remark on Lewis' other translations of Nancy tales, recorded in his *Journal* at some remove from the site of production of those tales.

The "traditional" beginning of "Neger Vithout 'ed"—"Vonce on time, my piccaninnies"—at once frames Shoo-shoo's story as something other than commonplace discourse and establishes its social orientation: It is directed at auditors, Shoo-shoo's "sable audience," and Lewis himself, though, in recounting it, Lewis assumes the dual role of detached participant-observer and commentator outside the charmed circle "squatted round her" (212). It is clear, nonetheless, that Lewis belongs to the context of performance; he solicits and pays for a performance requiring his attendance among the "piccaninnies" surrounding her. The experience is leveling and disquieting; Lewis remarks that it "seems strange" to be among servants who "grin at [his] jokes, pass remarks, & c., yet still consider themselves as slaves" (212), and it is evident that he finds their informal comportment and familiarity a bit unsettling. Though not quite the "world upside down," the free and easy contact of master and slave is reminiscent of the subversive, antihierarchical impulse of carnival; indeed, the relaxation of normal proprieties and prohibitions is occasioned, in this instance, by an "entertainment" which suspends the normal work regime and is recreational, if not festive.

A holiday mood pervades the context of performance and Shoo-shoo's actual recitation, confusing the boundaries between the two; colorful remarks, passing humor, and casual gossip—part of Lewis's picturesque scene of happy, carefree natives—provide dynamic conditions for Shoo-shoo's ribald and, it must not be forgotten, interactive tale. In this atmosphere, Shoo-shoo's "nursery tale" (211) assumes the contours of quite adult entertainment; it's hardly surprising that, in the end, Lewis identifies her story, not as a fairy tale, but as a "specimen of negro *facetiae*" (221). The question is, of course, who is the focus or butt of such facetious humor?

The question arises because, read as a specimen of "carnivalized" literature, Shoo-shoo's story becomes multivalent and polyphonic, its articulation and meaning deeply ambivalent. Consider, for example, some details of its formulaic opening: " 'Vonce on time, my piccaninnies' (the piccaninny nearest to her, and grinning with extension from ear to ear, being a fellow above six feet, proportionately stout, and apparently between thirty and forty years of age)" (213). What is one to make of the "piccaninny" responding to Shoo-shoo's call to performance? Is he the childlike creature Lewis pictures him to be, grinning "with extension" out of natural-born stupidity and foolishness? Or is he an actor, grinning "from ear to ear" in self-conscious awareness that he plays a part, enacting, in present tense, the "vonce on time" of "primitive" simplicity. In a context of general merriment and indecorous behavior, the very real possibility exists that Shoo-shoo's forty-year-old piccaninny is "puttin' on massa," providing an entertainment that is literally and figuratively at Lewis's expense—he not only commissions a performance, but is the object of its humor.

As part of the audience called to performance, Lewis, structurally at least, performs the same function as the "piccaninnies" "squatted round her"; he assumes as well their childlike posture in attending to a nursery tale. For her part, "Goosee Shoo-shoo"—formerly "Goody Two-shoes," the name given by Lewis but transmuted by the slave community—assumes her new identity as a teller of tales who unburdens herself in delivering nursery tales for full-grown children. In this context, Goosee Shoo-shoo is both mother and Mother Goose to "Mother Goos'es Son," a sarcastic reference to Lewis from private correspondence, intended to characterize his "flighty" nature, but suggesting, as well, his credulity and proclivity for chasing after fantastic stories.[9] Lewis's reversion from patriarch to child, reinforced to the extent that his slaves are "kidding him" with their performance, is part of a process temporarily undermining his authority—in the context of a story upholding the authority of "massa" and "his Majesty." It's no small irony that the supercilious attitude of his retrospective account of Shoo-shoo's "primitive" tale has its counterpart in the grins and knowing winks of the "piccaninnies" participating in the performance.

Yet, despite its opening formula, the balance of Shoo-shoo's story, showing how the "nigger vithout a 'ed" finds surety and satisfaction at "massa's hand," hardly seems ambivalent or subversive at all; it appears, in fact, to support the counsel, favorable to proprietors, that slaves be truthful and obedient to masters. Nonetheless, in articulating the sentiments of dominant discourse, Shoo-shoo's distinct patois and location gives them a different inflection, producing a discourse not quite identical with an original, and, through distortion, raising the possibility of diverse interpretations.[10] Consider, for example the slippage between "Goody Two-shoes" and "Goosee Shoo-shoo," which is also the distance between her two significations: Goody, the obedient charge and Goosee, the subversive storyteller. Her mimic discourse, given by virtue of her subject position, reflects as well her tenuous position as a black woman empowered to speak within the constraining limits of plantocratic culture. Her recitation before a mixed audience is by necessity a double-voiced discourse embodying contradictory impulses to disguise and disclose, to hide and to reveal. Her mimicry is one resource of "voice under domination" which insinuates resistance into what James C. Scott has called the "public transcript," or the record of interaction between subordinates and those who dominate.[11] Such resistance, rarely openly declared, is offered in a tone or gesture that leaves no record, or is given in a cryptic, or ambiguous, form open to a subversive or innocuous interpretation, and is always subject to disavowal. Consider, for example, the ambivalence of "massa's" power and authority in "Neger Vithout 'ed." Though his word is law, the basis of "massa's" power and authority ultimately resides, not in wisdom and intelligence, but in force, emblematized by the lash he wields. That singular image is at once a vivid reminder of the price of dissent and an occasion of resistance in that it cuts against the grain of a story portraying "his Majesty" as the source of all surety and contentment. It is, as well, a backhanded slap at Lewis who proposed banishing the whip on his estates but turned to it as an instrument of last resort.

"Voice under domination" might be said to thematize the content of the other Nancy story I will consider, as well as to characterize the situation of the narrative itself. "The Story of Sarah Winyan" relates how Sarah, a young black child, is betrayed into captivity but ultimately freed from bondage by her brothers. Cheated of her inheritance, she is turned over, "by contract," to Tiger, the "enormous black dog" (247) who spirits her away. Forbidden to speak or sing, Sarah manages, nonetheless, to whisper her complaint; as a result, she is rescued from captivity by her half-brothers, who decapitate the "monster" (249) after recognizing Sarah in her plaint:

> Ho-day, poor me O!
> Poor me, Sarah Winyan, O!

> They call me neger, neger!
> They call me Sarah Winyan, O!   (247)

In the context of a plantocratic culture that still retained slavery after the abolition of the slave trade and that desperately required able bodies in the face of declining slave population, "The Story of Sarah Winyan" begs to be read as an exemplum of successful verbal and physical resistance to degrading/dehumanizing bondage "by contract." Thematizing call and response in the context of what, based on the details of Shoo-shoo's recitation, was an interactive performance, the story invites recognition on the part of its enslaved auditors of their common oppressed condition and an appropriate response, potentially of the kind intimated by its violent ending.

As with "Neger Vithout 'ed," however, it's an interpretation that Lewis, like Tiger, either can't hear or won't allow. His translation of the story removes it from any sociopolitical context, framing it, instead, as a representative example of "Negro notions" of the preternatural and childlike credulity in ghosts and shape-shifting supernatural attendants like Tiger, who is interpreted, in this instance, as the familiar of an aunt (suspected of Obeahism), who appropriates Sarah's property. In addition, Lewis classifies "The Story of Sarah Winyan" as a "Just-So" story, a near cousin of the nursery tale (and a favorite of Kipling's), which, through the narrative unfolding of mythic events, displays the simple logic of "primitive" thinking about the origins of things—in this case, an explanation of how dogs came to be domesticated in Jamaica. That Tiger might be identified with the masters or overseers who dogged their charges, or be associated with the dread beasts used to hunt runaways and intimidate the slave population, that his violent end might signify a symbolic inversion—the bloody, riotous carnival of the world turned upside down—is never countenanced in a presentation that prefers (for good reason) mythic to historical reference and explanation. Of course, both readings are valid if one envisions a context of performance in which a narrator directs a double-voiced discourse to a mixed audience of slaves and masters to achieve different ends. Such a context—provided in "Neger Vithout 'ed," omitted elsewhere—should be invoked to remark upon Lewis's journal translations of Jamaican Nancy stories.

In remarking upon the Nancy stories Lewis records, I have tried to keep in mind that they are cross-cultural texts in at least two senses. First, they are translations—textual (hence mediated) actualizations of oral performances which were scripted and borne away for domestic consumption. As translations, they mediate powerful systems of meaning, yet as Talal Asad reminds us, in a colonial context, languages and systems of meaning are never equal, and practices of cultural mediation like translation tend to reproduce the asymmetrical relations informing them. Through his additions and omissions, Lewis effectively "colonizes" his sources, making them conform to the contours of a dominant discourse on the "primitive." Yet to leave the argument at that would be to restate the tautology that "domination dominates" (Porter 49) and to reproduce the colonizing gesture whereby "alien" voices are introduced to confirm a rehearsal of cultures where "marginal" voices are "always already subordinated, dominated, othered" (Porter 57). I have suggested ways that Lewis's translations of Nancy stories not only reproduce colonialist ideology, but also unwittingly preserve features of performance that subvert and/or displace the dominant discourse of the target language. Evoking the features of previous linguistic performances enables us to reread his texts as productive sites of conflict and new signification rather than re-productive sites of hegemonic control.

Yet, the Nancy stories Lewis records are cross-cultural in another, more fundamental sense. They emerge out of what Mary Louise Pratt has labeled the *contact zone,* the "space of colonial encounters, the space in which peoples geographically and historically separated come into contact with each other and establish ongoing relations, usually involving conditions of coercion, radical inequality and intractable conflict" (6). These stories are not simply borne across cultures for domestic consumption, but are born in the crucible of cultural confrontation and interpenetration. They are marked by, and remark on (if subtly and surreptitiously), dominant discourse and culture and exist not as "survivals" of "primitive culture" or "Negro culture"—or, for that matter, of "African culture," if only "purified" of their Eurocentric excrescences—but as sketchy textual realizations of a Creole culture itself in translation, constantly negotiating complex intercultural demands for particular occasions or situations.

Consequently, in crossing over and returning the Nancy stories to the sites of their production, I have insisted on the fundamental dialogism and rhetoricity of Shoo-shoo's performance. Directed at a mixed audience of slaves and masters, her double-voiced discourse in a hybrid tongue both meets the needs of dominant discourse and refuses to be bound by its (in)appropriate power, particularly the power of its representations.

Seen not simply as convenient receptacles for preexisting discursive fields and representations—a view tending to silence and arrest historical subjects as already spoken for or already contained by the language that enfolds them—the Nancy stories perhaps are best understood as modes of action. As such, it is possible—and productive—to read the texts of their performances not so much for what they represent or signify (while offering alternative readings to counter Lewis' own, I do not claim to offer up *the* meaning of each story), but for what they suggest about the effectual force of prior discursive events; events which, in the act of their unfolding, mediated inequitable social relations, ensured survival, provided solidarity, and enacted resistance in a context of domination.

Notes

1. Reprinted in the 1929 edition of Lewis's *Journal*, the 16 March letter is taken from *The Life and Correspondence of Monk Lewis* (1839), published anonymously by Henry Colburn. In *The Life*, this letter is recorded as being written at Cornwall on 16 March 1815, though it's clear that Lewis never had visited Jamaica before 1816. All references to the *Journal*, first published in 1834, are from the 1929 edition.

2. Lewis's reforms and "humanitarian" practices were not as unusual as he would lead readers to believe, but were part of a policy of amelioration on the part of some owners following the abolition of the slave trade. Fearing a labor shortage in the wake of abolition, these owners sought to maintain the supply of slaves through improved conditions and incentives to reproduce.

3. With some exceptions, there was no immediate ground swell to free the slaves following abolition. State efforts were directed at enforcing and extending prohibitions on slave trade. Abolitionists like William Wilberforce believed that the instruction and conversion of slaves were prerequisites for emancipation. Nonetheless, many supported freeing the slaves and anticipated its future reality. In the context of debates about the ultimate status of slaves, the *Journal* makes the case that slaves desired and needed the paternal supervision of owners and that religious instruction was wasted on backward "Negroes."

4. Lewis published *Tales of Wonder* (1801) and *Romantic Tales* (1808). His borrowings and appropriations of European ballads and ballad collections led some critics uncharitably to dub his first book "Tales of Plunder."

5. Hugh Blair, whose *Lectures on Rhetoric and Belles Lettres* was widely reproduced during the nineteenth century, wrote that among the "rude and uncultivated" first men, the use of "language, in its infancy, must have been

extremely barren" (63). In his essay, "On Language," Thomas De Quincey argues that the language of "semi-barbarous" tribes were "uncultivated and rude in a degree corresponding to the narrow social development of the races who speak them." Those races were in a "state of imperfect expansion, both civilly and intellectually" (248–49).

6. Blair, for example, considers language "in its primitive state" to be "more barren," but "more picturesque" than language in its modern condition (62–63). In his lecture, "Origin and Nature of Figurative Language," he argues that primitive language abounded in tropes as compensation for its inadequacies. It also expressed the sentiments of races given to wonder and astonishment; in sum, it was "bold, picturesque, and metaphorical" (152).

7. See Liu (61–65) on the arrest of motive in the picturesque. My discussion of the picturesque is indebted to his chapter, "The Politics of the Picturesque: An Evening Walk."

8. Henry Louis Gates discusses double-voiced discourse arising in a context of white domination in *The Signifying Monkey*. His notion of signification in which texts by a black writers repeat with difference texts by white writers is suggestive in the context of Shoo-shoo's mimicking of dominant discourse.

9. Postmarked 23 February 1815, the letter alluding to Lewis as "Mother Goos'es Son" (260) is reprinted in Louis Peck's *A Life of Matthew G. Lewis*.

10. Given her subject position, Shoo-shoo's repetition of dominant discourse inevitably distorts it. For a discussion of such mimicry, see Homi Bhabha's "Signs Taken for Wonders."

11. The terms are taken from James C. Scott's stimulating *Domination and the Arts of Resistance*. For his discussion of the insinuation of resistant voices into the publically sanctioned discourse of dominant groups, see his chapter, "Voice Under Domination: The Arts of Political Disguise."

Works Cited

Asad, Talal. "The Concept of Cultural Translation in British Social Anthropology." *Writing Culture: The Poetics and Politics of Ethnography*. Ed. James Clifford and George Marcus. Berkeley: U of California P, 1986. 141–64.

Bhabha, Homi K. "Signs Taken for Wonders: Questions of Ambivalence and Authority Under a Tree Outside Delhi, May 1817." *Europe and Its Others*. Ed. Francis Barker et al. Colchester: U of Essex, 1985. 89–106. 2 vols.

Blair, Hugh. *Lectures on Rhetoric and Belles Lettres*. Philadelphia: James Kay, Jun. and Brother, 1833.

Coleridge, Samuel Taylor. *The Table Talk and Omniana.* With a note on
        Coleridge by Coventry Patmore. London: Oxford UP, 1917.
De Quincey, Thomas. *Selected Essays on Rhetoric.* Ed. Frederick Burwick.
        Foreword by David Potter. Carbondale, Ill.: Southern Illinois P, 1967.
Gates, Henry Louis, Jr. *The Signifying Monkey: A Theory of Afro-American
        Literary Criticism.* New York: Oxford UP, 1988.
Lewis, Matthew G. *Journal of a West India Proprietor.* Ed. Mona Wilson.
        Boston: Houghton Mifflin Company, 1929.
———. *Romantic Tales.* London, 1808.
———. *Tales of Wonder.* London: J. Bell, 1801.
Liu, Alan. *Wordsworth: The Sense of History.* Stanford, Calif.: Stanford UP, 1989.
Peck, Louis F. *A Life of Matthew G. Lewis.* Cambridge, Mass.: Harvard UP, 1961.
Porter, Carolyn. "Are We Being Historical Yet?" *The States of "Theory": His-
        tory, Art, and Critical Discourse.* Ed. David Carroll. New York:
        Columbia UP, 1990. 27–62.
Pratt, Mary Louise. *Imperial Eyes: Travel Writing and Transculturation.* Lon-
        don and New York: Routledge, 1992.
Scott, James C. *Domination and the Arts of Resistance: Hidden Transcripts.*
        New Haven: Yale UP, 1990.
Sturrock, John. "Writing Between the Lines: The Language of Translation."
        New Literary History 21 (1990): 993–1013.
Wilson, Mona, ed. Introduction. Lewis.

Writing Europe's "Orient": Spanish-American Travelers to the "Orient"

Jacinto R. Fombona I.

The following is a passage from Enrique Gómez Carrillo's *De Marsella á Tokio:*

Helo aquí mi Japón. ¡Amaterasu, diosa del sol y patrona del Yamato, bendita seas! ¡Y tú también, milagrosa Kamiya San-no-inari, tú que curas todos los males y proteges á los que aman; tú también sé bendita! Al apearme del tren, mientras un atleta amarillo acomoda mi equipaje en un kuruma, mi ensueño se realiza. De pie en la puerta de la estación, una musmé me sonríe, ó mejor dicho, se sonríe á sí misma. Es delgada, pálida, de un color de ámbar claro y transparente, con las venas finísimas marcadas en el cuello desnudo. El óvalo de su rostro es perfecto. Sus ojos, no grandes pero largos, muy estrechos y muy largos, tienen una dulzura voluptuosa que explica el entusiasmo de aquellos antiguos poetas nipones que compusieron las *tankas* en las que las pupilas femeninas son comparadas con filtros de encantamiento. . . . Yo la contemplo absorto. Y gracias á ella, á su belleza extraña, á su gracia lejana, á su esplendor de leyenda, la vulgaridad de esta plaza de estación desaparece y un Japón admirable surge ante mis ojos extasiados.

["Tis here my Japan. Amaterasu, goddess of the sun and patron of Yamato, bless'd you! And also you, miraculous Kamiya San-No-Inari, you, who heals all sorrows and protects those who love; also you, be bless'd! As I step down from the train, while a yellow athlete sets my luggage in a kuruma, my reverie comes true. Standing at the gate of the station, a musmé smiles to me, or better smiles to herself. She is slender, pale, of the color of clear and translucent amber, with the finest veins marking her naked neck. The oval of her face is perfect. Her eyes, not large, but long, very narrow and very long, have a voluptuous sweetness that explains the enthusiasm of those ancient Nipon poets who composed the

119

tankas in which feminine pupils are compared with charming potions. . . . I contemplate her entranced. And thanks to her, to her strange beauty, to her distant grace, to her legendary splendor, the vulgarity of this railroad station disappears and an admirable Japan rises before my ecstatic eyes."] (149–50)[1]

Gómez Carrillo's arrival in Tokyo provides us with a moment for the discursive construction of the traveled space. A narrative technique, an ekphrasis, the coming to life through language of an art object, is applied to the photographic instant provided by the smile of a woman dressed in a kimono—a special smile because it immediately summons the image of the Japanese print to the mind of the reader. In terms of the performative in language, Gómez Carrillo's encounter produces an object that fits into his (and the audience's) expectation of the Japanese. I want to stress the idea of the production and reproduction of an object from the discourse on Asia as the "Orient" provided by this text, because it relates to the Spanish-American traveler's overall strategy when writing Europe's Orient.

The image that haunted me from Gómez Carrillo's encounter with "his" Japan, the smile of a *musmé*, is an aesthetic encounter, an attempt to narrate the aesthetic experience that had eluded him since his arrival in Yokohama. Such an encounter is also an encounter with the Japan of the Japanese print of which Utamaro is probably the best known exponent.[2] The fashion for Japan arrived in the Spanish America of the nineteenth-century bourgeoisie from a direction opposite that from which the *Nao Philipina* used to arrive in Acapulco every year. It came from Spanish America's very own "Orient," namely Europe, and it was associated with the social prestige, or "distinction" as Pierre Bourdieu puts it, that its European origin gave it. By the time the Oriental fashion became part of the Spanish-American discourse it was a semiotic system of a second order: a text on a text, a "mythology" in the Barthean sense—a cultural production that is appropriated and recontextualized into a new semiological system with an existence that appeals to a particular group of readers, in this case interestingly foreign and yet close to Europe (Barthes). Moreover, in the case of Spanish America, it is also a translation, interestingly enough, of a "discourse on the Other" whereby the Spanish-American author adopts those characteristics that would allow him or her to belong to the European (particularly French) discourse.

According to Angel Rama and Tulio Halperín Donghi, a great part of the cultural production of turn-of-the-century Spanish America can be understood as a coming to terms with its newly found place in the colonial order of nineteenth-century capitalism (see, e.g., Rama; Halperín Donghi). The bourgeois nineteenth century that established the rhetoric of European dominance in terms of positive progress and liberal mercantilism brought for the Spanish American the idea of modernity, and of "present," as a place beyond: Europe for the criollo becomes the space where the future is already at work. In modernity's conflicting relationship with its own past, its present, and its future, it is not surprising that Spanish-American culture was the first Western culture to use the term *modernism (modernismo)* to denote the cultural (mostly aesthetic) outcome that was brought forth as a result of facing Europe in terms of "our" history.[3]

There is also a Deleuzian *rhizome* that shows one of its shoots here; thus, when one considers the text of the Orient as a mythology mediated or predigested by Europe, one is forced to consider the cultural mechanics involved. "We are Europeans, yet we are not Europeans," says Octavio Paz in his 1990 Nobel Prize lecture (6). Referring to the Americans, Paz brings forth, once again, an issue that was born five hundred years ago. This Europeanness outside of Europe which drives the intellectual debate—the "Europeans of America," as Bolívar's call to action put it in 1816—is seen by Paz as a "consciousness of being separate," a "wound" that at times causes us "to go forth into the outside world and encounter others" (10). As a form of understanding his or her place in the world, the drive of the criollo bourgeois to appropriate from, and "create," Europe is particularly evident in turn-of-the-century Spanish America.

An aspect of such a drive is Paz's call to "encounter others," which finds its outlet within Spanish-American culture through travel texts. As cultural artifacts they allow for a play, an articulation of the elements that informs the imaginary world of the traveler and his or her culture; they are a "minor" literary genre that could easily fit into what Paz calls "transatlantic reflections of European literatures" (5), and thus be easily dismissed. However, it is precisely this "translation," a misreading of Europe and its texts, that permits an analysis of Spanish-American travel texts as cultural artifacts: they repeat the displaced Europeanness of their authors to the extent that they can be made to speak of those misreadings or, rather frequently, those "better readings," as Sylvia Molloy suggests, referring to Domingo Sarmiento's readings of Europe's texts (22–35).

In the prologue of *De Marsella á Tokio,* Rubén Darío writes that its author, upon returning from Japan, showed up one day in Darío's house in Paris and said, "Aquí le traigo á usted un álbum de amores torturados, una oración thibetana, una estampa de Utamaro" ("I bring you here an album of tortured loves, a Tibetan prayer, an Utamaro print.") To which Darío comments, "Para mí un hombre que vuelve del Japón es siempre interesante; y si, como en este caso, ese hombre es un poeta, el hecho me resulta encantador" ("For me, a man who returns from Japan is always interesting; and if, as is the case this time, that man is a poet, the event is indeed charming") (vii). Darío's prologue to Gómez Carrillo continues with a recurrent display of what the call to "encounter with others," or rather, the "prescribed" encounter set by the readings of Europe's texts means for the Spanish-American writer. What is interesting in Darío's textual reveries about Japan is his reaction to the objects, the souvenirs: He already has a mediated knowledge of what they are, of what they metonymically represent, but they become specially valued (*valor precioso,* "preciously valued," says Darío) because of a further, yet closer, mediation. That mediation imbues them with the proximity of the eye, since they have been brought by

El compañero que ha tenido la suerte de ver con sus ojos de artista el Yoshivara, los puentes de bambú y las lindas muñecas todas sedas y genuflexiones y sonrisas, que apenas he podido yo amar en los biombos, abanicos y lacas de los ichibanes de occidente, y en las secciones exóticas de las exposiciones universales.

["the companion who has had the luck of seeing, with his own eyes of an artist, the Yoshivara [sic], the bamboo bridges, and the pretty dolls, all silk, genuflections and smiles, that I have barely been able to love in the screens, fans, and lacquers of Western ichi-bans, and in the exotic sections of Universal Expositions."] (vii–viii)

Aside from the extremely bourgeois ideology of this text, Darío's mediated knowledge of the exotic "Orient," attained as he says through representations and displaced imitations alone, displays the Spanish-American writer's textual strategy for assigning and acquiring social and cultural distinction. This knowledge is presented as the result of a privileged access to the space of Europe's Other, through the distinction these mediations have of being French (and European). It should come as no surprise that attitudes toward the "Orient"—and here I am drawing from Edward Said's concept of Orientalism—attitudes that conceive of the Orient as a space of fantasy and of an incomplete textuality, the Freudian *Enstellung*, reappear in the Spanish-American re-writing of the text of Europe's Orient. However, the cultural consumption or appropriation of these texts was filtered out, by the turn of the century, toward what has been considered the purely aesthetic space of art and literature, drawing from one of many aspects of European Orientalism. Thus the Orient becomes the space portrayed by the novels of the Goncourt brothers and Pierre Loti, along with Kipling, Lafcadio Hearn, and Parcival Lowell, novels that are avidly read by the criollo bourgeois from the space Paz would call the historical in-betweenness of Spanish America, while the travel text becomes the space in which to face not only the Orient, but Europe itself, through a dialogue with these texts.

Modernismo as an aesthetic stance on modernity finds a rich vein in the "Orient," especially rich for the Spanish-American traveler in terms of the metaphor of the "penetrated space," or, as Homi Bhabha puts it, the "hybridity" of the colonial space (98); the Orient is both the space of the colonial presence and the written space of and for literature. Like Darío's longing for a more direct experience of Japan, the travel text of Spanish-American writers opens a double space signed by a double displacement, a text in which a performance takes place. The writer as traveler is a witness to a space that has been made textual prior to his visit, but this text is a European text, a text translated and consumed by Spanish-American culture in such a way that travel writing for the Spanish American will always imply a displaying and a re-writing of those European texts, always the same texts, marked by their original European gesture.

At this point, I am tempted to take a structuralist approach and apply the mathematics of Ron H. Atkin's Q-analysis. This method of analysis, used in geography and the social sciences, is based on the notion of a hierarchy in which terms at the top of the hierarchy cover or include those below, thus defining the nature of the events that can take place in a given set. The hierarchy in question in this case is the one that establishes the precedence of the European traveler and his texts over the Spanish-American experience of the traveled space. In such a way, a structure of Spanish-American textual (re)productions of the "Orient" is posited as a direct function of current, or given, "canonical" European texts: the "Goncourts" and "Lotis" of a particular moment. What results as a consequence is the Borgesian declaration that there is but one text and its re-writings of Spanish-American travel to the Orient. Writing the

Orient for the Spanish American thus becomes a textual repetition of a textual gesture in which any given author repeats the commonplaces given by European literature. Such repetition is part of the author's cultural "backcloth," an "allowing and forbidding, but not requiring, geometry"—as Q-analysts put it—that sets the parameters of one's cultural production. Thus, the Spanish-American traveler who writes, having seen the Japan of Loti or Kipling, produces his or her version of that which the cultural hierarchy established for and within the traveler's culture, since, as Q-analysis implies, there is no other India or Japan to be seen that would fit the terms of the traveler's colonial dependence.

This is, however, quite a simplified and incomplete picture of the cultural production of which these travel texts are a part, a picture that is only helpful in illustrating a first approach to these texts. To return to the in-betweenness of the region, these travel texts are written from the so-called "margins" of Western culture, as is so often said of Spanish America. But, more importantly, they are part of the cultural production of certain social classes mostly associated with the mercantile bourgeoisie, who functioned, in turn-of-the-century Spanish America, as both colonized and colonizing classes. During most of the nineteenth century, their ideological stance sought the leveling-off of differences through the rhetoric of a national program under their patronage, while they became, at the same time, agents of the mercantile and neocolonial interests of industrial powers (see Sommer). In terms of the cultural production of these classes, however, the sought-after social distinction could only be attained through a constant "deterritorialization," to use Deleuze and Guattari's notion, in which one's own culture becomes displaced or detached from its territory. A "translation" proper takes place in which Europe is construed as both the familiar and the desired, and the local as the place to inform and give shape in terms of the European.

The stance of the *modernista* author toward these social classes is also a deterritorialized situation; these classes are the consumers and the patrons of a literature that by the turn of the century was produced by "professionals," and the reaction to European rhetoric of dominance became an occasion for the author to "enter" and "leave" the European discursive space through appeals to the aesthetic. Thus, while the European text of the "Orient" becomes the guideline for the response when facing the Other, this text and its discourses are purged of the political dangers implied by facing the colonial. Such is the aesthetic choice Gómez Carrillo makes between Loti and the "serious" French journalist and advocate of colonial imperialism, Paul Leroy-Beaulieu. Gómez Carrillo's selective sight performs a putting aside of what he does not to wish to see but must nonetheless mention: anything or everything that stands in contrast to the aesthetic realm established by the European text. Thus Gómez Carrillo writes in a letter to Darío about Japan: "los Loti tienen siempre razón. Es un país de muñecas y de sonrisas, el Yamato. Fuera de Yokohama que es internacional, fuera de los métodos industriales y de los sistemas guerreros que son europeos, todo sigue lo mismo que antes." ("The Lotis are always right. The Yamato is a country of dolls and smiles. Aside from Yokohama, which is international, aside from the methods of industrial production and war systems, which are European, everything is the same as before") (viii). Gómez Carrillo's "before" is the textual "before" of Loti's novel, *Madame Chrysanthème*, which is also a textual, and a safer, frivolous space. The colonial imagination of the bourgeois (or cosmopolitan) writer requires the exotic space to fit what are often called "illusions" that haunt the traveler who, "instead of feeding from logical realities, lives off phantasmagoric hopes and suffers the unavoidable disappointment" (147–48). Gómez Carrillo performs this task brilliantly in accordance with the bookish construction of Spanish-American discourse on the Orient, seeking the existence of the exotic Japan as something fixed and pervasive, yet hidden: "Desde mi ventana veo pasar á Madame Crisantema envuelta en un kimono claro. Detrás de ella va un samuray á quien no le falta para ser un personaje de Kiuiso, sino el sable tradicional" ("From my window I see Mme. Chrysanthème pass by wrapped in her light colored kimono. Behind her goes a samurai who only lacks the traditional sword to be a character from Kiuiso") (viii). If, according to Roland Barthes, the utmost bourgeois travel guide is "an agent of blindness" that overpowers and masks the real spectacle of human life and history (76), then Spanish-American consumption of the European text functions as a built-in travel guide, an internal device of selective sighting that provides the sought-after illusion of stability and continuity of the conservative ideology.

But what happens when the Spanish-American traveler faces the colonial in terms of the political? The visit to Japan is, after all, a visit to the nation that defeated Russia in 1903, a defeat that was "welcome" among many Spanish-American intellectuals, and a visit to a country that, after the Meiji restoration, had embraced a policy of modernization that was part of the "project" of the Spanish-American liberal bourgeois.

Gómez Carrillo puts it very clearly when he arrives in Yokohama and his travel companions perplexedly ask him:

—Francamente, ¿qué le parece á usted? . . . Todos mis compañeros de viaje me hacen, al cabo de dos horas de paseo por las calles de Yokohama, la misma pregunta. Y por el tono y por el rostro, se comprende desde luego que están desilusionados. Esto que vemos, no es lo que ellos querían ver. Los libros les habían hablado de progreso, de europeización, de modernidad. No importa. Un misterioso instinto decíales que, a pesar de todo el progreso, los antiguos trajes, las antiguas costumbres y las antiguas calles debían subsistir. . . . No era aquello, no. Pero las ilusiones son tenaces en las almas de los turistas. Un paseo de playa puede esconder una ciudad rara.

["Frankly, what do you think? . . . All my travel companions ask me the same question, after two hours walking in the streets of Yokohama. And through their tone of voice and their faces, one easily understands they are disenchanted, deeply and incurably disenchanted. What we see is not what they wanted to see. Books have told them of progress, of Europeanization, of modernity. It does not matter. A mysterious instinct told them that, in spite of all the progress, the old customs, the old costumes, and the old streets, had to survive. . . . That was not it, no. But illusions are tenacious in the tourists' souls. A beachwalk can hide a rare city."] (139).

Gómez Carrillo's dismissal of his travel companions as "tourists" is followed by his own dismissal of the landscape of Yokohama as a non-Japanese city, an impression that he, as a better reader, already had "figured" ("ya me lo había figurado") before his arrival. The others, the English tourists, "han pasado cuarenta días en un buque . . . han gastado cinco mil francos en el billete de ida y vuelta [y] se han resignado á no oir la plática evangélica por cinco semanas" ("have been forty days aboard a ship, . . . spent five thousand French francs round trip, [and] have given up listening to evangelical preaching for five weeks") (142), expecting to see Rudyard Kipling's impression of the Japanese policeman dressed European style, drinking tea with a fan in his hand.

But, as Gómez Carrillo puts it, "Esto no debía extrañareme, puesto que ya lo sabía" ("This should not surprise me since I already knew that) (152), and adds "Acaso no había leído antes de venir mil descripciones detalladas y escrupulosas? . . . Sí. Lo que veo ahora en la realidad, ya me era por los libros y las estampas familiar" ("Hadn't I read before arriving a thousand detailed and fastidious descriptions? . . . Yes. What I see now in actuality, was for me already familiar through books and prints") (153).

This statement, which leads Gómez Carrillo into a discussion that describes the "reality" of what he sees as "más completa, más intensa que la visión [familiar]" ("more intense, more complete, than the [familiar] vision") (153), textually places him as the reader of European texts—even in the presence of other Europeans. This is precisely the Deleuzian *rizoma* of Spanish-American intellectuals: "con el libro en la mano" ("book in hand"), the writer—according to Sylvia Molloy—is continuously narrating scenes of reading, or of encounters with reading. The Spanish-American traveler is no exception, and his or her chronicles from abroad for Spanish-American audiences constantly set the travelers in their texts as readers of the European book, or the "European archive" (Molloy 22).

If one excepts Japan, using a gesture that recalls Gómez Carrillo himself, since Japan belongs to a level of the hierarchies that has been purely textualized and depoliticized by the choice of Loti over Leroy-Beaulieu, the occasions on which the Spanish-American writer faces the hybridized native in the colonized space provide an insight into what it means to face the political in terms of the aesthetic. Gómez Carrillo again provides the blueprint of behavior: behave like a Frenchman; like Marx in 1853, praise the English civilizing power in India; admire the "Invisibility" of the English and their ability "to make themselves forgotten" ("se hacen olvidar") in the landscape of the colony (69). Thus the presence of the native is emphasized as "standing alone, filling the space with his fine coppery silhouette" (69), and the questions of domination and colonialism dismissed by the author who answers his own search for visual clues, "¿Qué es aquí inglés? ¿Qué indica una dominación? ¿Qué hace ver el yugo?" ("What is English here? Where are the signs of domination? What shows the yoke?") with a quirkish "Nada, nada" (69). This space is, however, a space derided and devoid of the mobility that belongs to the space of trade, since "everything that denotes movement of gold, material effort, practical intelligence . . . is English" (69). There is a yielding to the status quo of colonialism that reflects both the discourse of European Orientalism and the ideology of the Spanish-American bourgeois: the space of the native is fixed and nonthreatening, since, for the Spanish-American traveler, the disappearance of the civilizing control of colonialism will only result in a feared and well-known anarchy.

Thus the avoidance of anarchy, through the preservation of the civilized order, becomes for Gómez Carrillo a manner of being civilized and a manner of performing the role of the European to the extent that what is real, what defines reality for the author, is his European experience. Gómez Carrillo's text of his arrival in Saigon illustrates the vision of the Orient as the space where the traveler enters a state of reverie as an open, unfinished, and dreamlike space which disappears when the reality of Europe enters its landscape. Thus Gómez Carrillo's arrival in Saigon is an "awakening" into the reality of Paris:

Media hora más tarde, cuado el cochero anamita os abre la portezuela de su «malabar», os figuráis despertar de un ensueño de exotismo. Vuestro viaje de más de un mes, vuestros paseos por las callejuelas de Aden, pobladas de árabes que agonizan de sed bajo el sol implacable; vuestros entusiasmos entre las palmeras de Colombo; vuestra estupefacción infantil en las calles chinas de Singapur, olorosas á ajo, á miel, á vainilla y á grasa: todo lo visto y todo lo entrevisto, los cielos blancos del trópico, los celajes de Oriente las mañanas celestes y las noches claras, sin luna, claras de estrellas; todo, todo fué un ensueño.

["Half an hour later, when the Annamese coachman opens the door of his 'malabar', you feel you are awakening from an exotic reverie. Your trip of over a month, your promenades through the narrow streets of Aden, populated by Arabs in agony from thirst under the implacable sun; your excitement under the palm trees of Colombo; your childish astonishment in the Chinese streets of Singapore, smelling of garlic, honey, vanilla, and fat: everything seen or glimpsed, the white skies of the tropics, the sunset clouds of the Orient, the celestial mornings, and the clear moonless nights, clear from the light of the stars; everything, everything was a reverie."] (108)

Gómez Carrillo's reason: "La realidad, hela ahí: estáis en París, no habéis salido de París" ("The reality is this: you are in Paris, you have never left Paris") (108). The traveler in the tropical space, the threatening space of the tropics which is also the space of the colonies, and which, interestingly, disappears from Darío's prologue and is only hinted at as the space to be filled by the book's title, faces the presence of civilization as an honest-to-God modern man should, as the space of movement which yields when night falls. The extreme fragility of civilization quivers then and in Saigon's dusk, "Hay, en el silencio, en el calor, algo de asiático. Estamos, en verdad, lejos de París. La civilización es como la educación: cambia el aspecto de los pueblos y de los seres que se mueven; pero desparece en cuanto unos y otros se adormecen. Estamos en Extremo Oriente" ("there is, in the silence, in the heat, something Asian. We are, truly, far from Paris. Civilization is like education: it changes the appearance of the peoples, and of the moving beings; but it disappears as soon as one and the other lull. We are in the Far East" (111). But Saigon, because of its successful Parisian effect, does not allow this sensation to remain. The artificiality of the make-up worn by women passing by will break the Asianness with a substitution that parallels the effect of "education" as a fragile layer that covers the true nature of the tropical night. So the thoughts of exoticism disappear: "Apenas lo hemos pensado, un cuchicheo ligero nos hace volver la vista. Es el cortejo galante que principia. Chicas elegantes, con ojos azules y labios pintados, pasan sonriendo, como en París. El perfume de sus cabelleras hace desaparecer los aromas vagos de la Naturaleza. El señor Lubin se sobrepone á Budha" ("No sooner have we thought of this than a light whispering makes us turn around. It is the gallant procession that starts. Elegant girls, with blue eyes and made-up lips, go by, smiling, like in Paris. The fragrance of their hair makes the vague scents of Nature disappear. Mr. Lubin takes over Buddha" (111).

Gómez Carrillo further insists that "Es París, os digo" ("it is Paris, I tell you") (111). But the traveled space has never been otherwise, the blue eyes and perfumed hair of the women passersby are presented in the Gómez Carrillo text as signs of Europeanness that suggest the idea of a European, in this case Parisian, space that the author privileges over the traveled colonial space. The question of whether the women are indeed European is irrelevant for the Spanish-American traveler who seeks not the reverie (ensueño) of the Oriental space, but rather the possibility of civilization as conceived by the Spanish-American bourgeois surviving outside Europe. So, as is the case of Gómez Carrillo in De Marsella á Tokio, the travel to the Orient of the Spanish-American writer is performed on a construction of the discourse on the Orient that has always been a translation of the Parisian: it has indeed "never left Paris."

Notes

1. De Marsella á Tokio is a collection of chronicles that Gómez Carrillo wrote as travel correspondent for La Nación of Buenos Aires and El Liberal of Madrid. I will quote from this edition. The term musmé derives from the Japanese musume: girl or daughter. In this translation I retain the original's use of italics which only sporadically signals the presence of another language.

2. The history of the Japanese print, or ukiyoé, is rather appropriate in this case, since there is a mediation that brings us to the subject of this essay. The

art of the print, the *ukioe,* or the floating world, was in Japan a menial, albeit popular, element of everyday life, condemned to disappear after it had circulated, in the form of a wrapper for fish or vegetables from the market. It was, after all, a floating and frail world. Europe comes into the story as the mediating agent that assigns an artistic value to this "foreign" and "exotic" element of another culture's everyday life. Interestingly, to date, the largest collections of Japanese woodprints are in Europe. See Illing, *The Art of Japanese Print.*

   3. For a discussion of the term's history, see Calinescu. For the "modernity" of Spanish-American cultures, see Anderson. See also Alonso's discussion of Spanish-American modernity.

Works Cited

Alonso, Carlos. *The Spanish American Regional Novel.* Cambridge: Cambridge UP, 1990.

Anderson, Benedict. *Imagined Communities.* London: Verso, 1983.

Atkin, Ron H. *Mathematical Structure in Human Affairs.* New York: Crane Russak, 1974.

Barthes, Roland. *Mythologies.* Trans. A. Lavers. 1957. New York: Hill & Wang, 1986.

Bhabha, Homi. "Signs Taken for Wonders: Questions of Ambivalence and Authority Under a Tree Outside Delhi, May 1817." *Europe and Its Others: Proceedings of the Essex Conference on the Sociology of Literature.* Ed. Francis Baker et al. Colchester: University of Essex, 1985.

Bourdieu, Piere. *Distinction: A Social Critique of the Judgment of Taste.* Trans. R. Nice. Cambridge: Harvard UP, 1984.

Calinescu, Matei. *Five Faces of Modernity.* Durham: Duke UP, 1897.

Deleuze, Gilles, and Felix Guattari. *A Thousand Plateaus.* Trans. Brian Massumi. 1980. Minneapolis: U of Minnesota P, 1987.

Gómez Carrillo, Enrique. *De Marsella á Tokio.* Paris: Garnier Hermanos, 1905.

Halperín Donghi, Tulio. *Historia contemporánea de América Latina.* 1969. Madrid: Alianza Editorial, 1990.

Illing, Richard. *The Art of Japanese Print.* London: John Calamann and Cooper, 1980.

Molloy, Sylvia. *At Face Value: Autobiographical Writing in Spanish America.* Cambridge: Cambridge UP, 1991.

Paz, Octavio. *In Search of the Present.* Trans. A. Stanton. New York: Harcourt Brace, 1991.

Rama, Angel. *Rubén Darío y el modernismo.* Caracas and Barcelona: Alfadil Ediciones, 1985.

Said, Edward. *Orientalism*. New York: Vintage Books, 1978.

Sommer, Doris. "Irresistible Romance: The Foundational Fictions of Latin America." *Nation and Narration*. Ed. Homi Bhabha. London: Routledge, 1990.

The Price of Happiness:
C.L.R. James in New York, 1950

Tim Brennan

In 1950, soon after a divorce, James set out to write a study of U.S. popular culture. Already aware of government plans to deport him as a political undesirable, and eager to leave the cramped theorizing of the previous decade, James assumed in the work a tone of urgency. But in spite of some initial interest from friends (he circulated the work in typescript), the study was never published, and within a few years he was forced to flee the country.[1]

Not as autobiographical as *Beyond a Boundary* whose composition was still more than a decade away, "The Struggle for Happiness" is an important missing piece of James's life and thought.[2] Composed in a concentrated burst of activity over several weeks, the brilliant and bulky draft was a philosophical meditation on a specifically national desire—what James saw as the characteristically American expectation to be happy. It capped the brittle theorizing of the American years (1938–1953) and colored them beyond recognition even as it continued many of their obsessions. Although his concerns in those years had been wide-ranging, his focus had been on the assimilationist role of the "Negro" in the American mainstream and on the "state capitalist" character of the Soviet state. "The Struggle for Happiness," however, reveals two aspects of James's thought about which even the recent prolific scholarship on his work has remained silent: his unexpected identification with the United States as an adopted home and his bid to become a "popular" author in the market sense of that term.[3] Although the American project is largely unknown even by James specialists, threads of its argument available elsewhere (particularly in the work of the less desperate period of *Beyond a Boundary*) have given some critics the warrant to misstate his political intentions—misstatements that are aided by his own theoretical wanderings in the early fifties as he struggled to adapt traditional Leninist positions to the era of McCarthyism (a task, it must be said, in which he was in great measure successful).[4] Taken whole, the study reasserts the "classical" side of James at the same time that it adds new reasons to question his coherence as a whole—problems related to the pressures of living in the United States as an adopted "American."

James's study is therefore paradigmatic of much more than a strangely understudied moment in his personal career. Instead, it captures a tendency within current U.S. cultural theory to creatively misrepresent earlier Left structures of feeling that, far from suppressing our present cultural turn, fully enabled it, although in much more doctrinally consistent forms than we are often led to believe. We have read so much lately about the migrant sensibility of the third-world intellectual abroad that we tend to blanket that sort of experience with Salman Rushdie's famous phrase about being a "translated man." But the most pertinent kind of "translation" is not perhaps so much an ontological state of mixing and matching identities as a critical selectivity after the fact. Such practice tends to excise uncomfortable continuities with the past found in the writing of key cultural innovators, who are then presented as example of a radical break. This has occurred most strikingly with Antonio Gramsci—another communist militant—but in a New World context, James is perhaps the clearest case. The matter, however, is more complicated than mere misreading. That is, James's own experience in the early fifties looks forward to a pattern of self-censorship and terminological maneuvering faced by the U.S.-based critics once they attempt to enter an anticommunist public sphere.

James's motives, however, in "The Struggle for Happiness" are deeply conflicted. One of the most salient features of the project lies in his desire to use the book to establish himself as a commercially viable author of "philosophical" volumes on popular themes accessible to a mainstream reading public. At least one of James's intentions was to have the book demonstrate to the immigration authorities that, loving America so, he could not be an alien and therefore could not be undesirable. The other, inevitably personal, reasons for fighting deportation were in this case inseparable from the genesis of the project itself. James's whole style of living had become bound up with the crazy media saturations of American postwar life. After a day of solitary reading, his greatest pleasure was to slip away at midnight to see a film in Times Square; he was a man who, covered by newspapers and opened books, would write in bed at midday with the TV on. The United States could not be left behind so easily. For it was also the home of the model and activist Constance Webb, James's lover and confidante, with whom he discussed the proposed book's contents in a long and intimate correspondence. In these letters, the project's new turn and new emphases were starkly apparent:

Some pseudo-Marxist has been getting at you, telling you that what you should do is join a party and work in a factory? Just tell them to go to hell, that's all. I worked at literature for years and made my own way to where I am. Nobody taught me; and, thank Heaven, I find that I am still making my own way while so many others are floundering around.[5]

"The Struggle for Happiness" is crucial to a contemporary accounting of the cultural left in other respects as well. It challenges the view of the Left's tardy arrival at a systematic study of cultural politics. In it, James launches the first of his many pioneering comments on scholarly practices that have arisen since: sport as the popular art of a national character; the distance of intellectuals from the correctives of "everyday life"; the cultural interdependence of Europe and its colonies. He does precisely what Marxist intellectuals are repeatedly described as not doing: showing concern not only with issues of property, wages, or parties in conflict, but with the deep social and psychological needs of modern life. "The Struggle for Happiness" is explicitly set up to do this *as against* the vulgar materialism of the liberal critics of his day. What is more, the manuscript forces one to remember that American debates on popular culture in the thirties and forties were already rich, varied, and (by the fifties) quite general. James already can be seen talking in detail about what is called today (with unintentional irony) the "new social movements." Large sections of the manuscript are dedicated to the special demands, histories, and organizational requisites of women, youth, and blacks—a fascinating passage that culminates in an analysis of the political importance of "homosexuality" in American life, in which James lays out a proto-program of gay rights.

Most important of all, however, is precisely what is *not* new in James's typescript. European and Latin American intellectuals had for centuries seen the United States as a place of utopian refuge from imaginative staleness and class fixities. The rhetorical family James joins in the manuscript is a familiar one, and one that was enjoying a huge popularity in precisely the years he was writing. James's fight to stay in New York reminds one of the attachments to California of postwar German film directors and recent French poststructuralist professors, as though they were surrounding themselves with a future that the world's others would inevitably be forced to live. There was the matter of personal taste, in other words, but also an imperceptible conflation of taste with the stimulations of historical necessity: to live where the future was unfolding.

The early fifties, then, marked a transitional moment in James's career. He was finding a new voice after a long (and perhaps necessary) preparation of pamphleteering and exhausting theoretical debates within tiny, isolated far-left groups. At a personal level, it seems likely that he sought a return to the prolific *anni mirabili* of the 1932–39 period in Britain where his best work had been written.[6] The startling conceptual leaps, the elegance and assurance of phrasing, the immense theoretical originality of *The Black Jacobins,* for example—belong to personal as well as intellectual inspirations that coalesced at the point of his American debut as a professional writer. In the earlier years, James thought of himself as a novelist, and he wrote with a novelist's care. The arrival in England on its own would have been enriching enough for a Trinidadian devoted to cricket and English literature. But in addition to the excitements of arrival were the unforeseen intellectual discoveries. He read Marx there for the first time, and that reading seemed especially vital given his involvements in the Independent Labour Party, which seemed to bear those bookish prophecies out. He hung out with Karl Korsch and Daniel Guerin, and met George Padmore and Jomo Kenyatta. The new ideas seemed to gather force in his extensive pub talk with the workers of Nelson, Lancashire, where he was then living with the cricketer Learie Constantine. Indeed, his setting off to do research in the Parisian libraries—as the text of *The Black Jacobins* shows through numerous contemporaneous allusions—had been motivated by a desire to bring Marxism and African independence together, to make them part of the same constellation of thought. The linkage itself was enabled by another event of these years which more than any other had been a catalyst for the intellectual turn to Africa: the Italian invasion of Ethiopia in 1935. In 1950, these communities and conjunctures were simply missing.

"The Struggle for Happiness" was, of course, equally a creature of its age, but raw enthusiasm and high-talking hopes now substituted for actual movement. There is, I think, a certain sadness in James's uncircumstanced optimism. And there is certainly much of dubious warrant. James saw the American workers poised for victory on the crest of a vast media wave; popular culture was not the "mind-forged manacles" of an ascendant corporatism but final proof that the common people had in a sense already won: that *their* image and *their* values were now regnant. In this James presaged a libertarian politics of style that today marks the outlooks (and liabilities) of American left criticism—a criticism whose authority has been enhanced by the prominent work of foreign intellectuals resident here, who share many of the study's drawbacks. The non–U.S. commentator on "America"—an intellectual type from before Tocqueville—is very much with us, as is the tendency to exaggerate, if not idealize, American popular culture's vaunted futurisms and potentials.[7]

But here as elsewhere James has become a model-for-use. To what extent did he deserve to be? Adopting a style of reference appropriate to James's own sources, one might recall nothing so much as the passage in the *Communist Manifesto* in which the authors speak of cultural "translation." Here they refer to the importation of "communist literature" from France into a Germany that was widely felt to lag behind the more novel theoretical work of its Western neighbors:

The work of the German *literati* consisted solely in bringing the new French ideas into harmony with their ancient philosophical conscience, or rather, in annexing the French ideas without deserting their own philosophic point of view. This annexation took place in the same way in which a foreign language is appropriated, namely by *translation* (62, my emphasis).

If the actors today have reversed, the effects are just as Marx and Engels described them. That is, contemporary critics often translate James so that, like the German critics of 1848, they transform social materialities into the philosophical notions that most matter to them. In Marx and Engels's terms, they transform the "criticism of the economic functions of money" into the "Alienation of Humanity," and the "criticism of the bourgeois state" into "Dethronement of the Category of the General." And this is how James has become today a "deconstructionist," an "artist," and an "independent" radical.[8]

The principle deviations in James from a standard interwar Marxist historiography were the result of his attempts to demonstrate the compatibility of Leninism to a libertarian populism; they were not the result, as Cedric Robinson argues, of James's interest in forging a distinct "black radical tradition." The point here is not to credit nostalgia or preserve the sacred, but simply to remark how his very prescience and originality were bound up with a stubbornly classical position.

Indeed, the traditionalism of James's study reveals itself in his literary models. Seeing his book as a contribution to an established genre on the American social character, he explicitly cites Tocqueville's *Democracy in America* and the Viscount James Bryce's *American Commonwealth* while bringing them into a postwar recognition of the new stakes of "in-dividuality" in a media society. Less about than *in* that social character, the typescript is almost quaint in its motives. It was to be the first of a series of books designed for the public to read "on a Sunday or on two evenings," a profound and embattled philosophical reflection in the form of a fireside novel.

I. *The Struggle for Happiness*—What People Want

The project is in many ways a more thorough and sustained example of James's applied cultural theory than *Beyond a Boundary* (1963), which is usually seen as the place to learn about this side of his thinking. Both works talk about the artistic tastes of ordinary people in a language of rhetorical enthusiasm, giving them a status usually reserved for the museum and the concert hall. James had a name for this process of linkage, which he defined elsewhere as "the coalescence of the cultural tradition with the popular audience," or simply "integration," a concept he derived ultimately from his understanding of ancient Greece. The Athenian festivals placed judgment in the hands of "sausage vendors" rather than professional critics.

Unlike his first book on the Trinidadian labor leader Arthur Cipriani, or his future book on cricket, "The Struggle for Happiness" speaks to a global English-speaking audience. The grand narratives to which James was typically drawn, and which he had enlivened with the oddly obscure case studies of a Trinidadian unionist and a sport unknown outside the commonwealth, were now linked to a popular cultural language of American images and characters that was beginning to be known, as it is now known, virtually everywhere. His aspirations to be more like the great popular artists of history—Shakespeare, Aeschylus, Chaplin—had shifted from the idiosyncratic to the symptomatic. He finally had a topic that could reach millions: the "cultural tradition" as an unbroken line running from Greek tragedy through Dick Tracy was a precise record of the very outlooks and designs of history's great revolutions. The spirit exalted there was the spirit of Dessalines, John Brown, and Lumumba.

And yet if the contemporary site of productive upheaval was the United States, James was unavoidably—like Tocqueville and Bryce—a foreigner. The energy behind the project—and the particular charge infusing the word "American" throughout—lay in James's decisive contrasting of the term with Europe. The primary ideological conflict for him was New World versus Old, not first world versus third, and the United States was the only fully realized New World society. His preferences are very easy to misinterpret, however. Refusing to be sentimental, and faithful to what he saw as the "science" of politics, James saw the United States—in spite of its imperial involvements—as a standard: the place where any fight worth the name would occur. That calculation empowered his optimism in spite of such insistently contrary details as the Platt Amendment, the occupations of Haiti, the railroading of Garvey, and the creation of the Panama Canal.

Far from oblivious to these precedents, he nevertheless chose to direct his anger at that brand of American cultural groveling before Europe that was then evident in one strain of the mass culture debate. Not unaware of the contradictions of doing so, he wanted to disrupt the pattern of American radicalism as an immigrant affair. He wanted to develop a way of thinking about political change that relied entirely on indigenous American traditions. These had not been theorized adequately, he argued, because America's intellectuals (both right and left), cowed by Europe, had not given them sufficient attention. The point was not simply to battle over what was aesthetically pleasing in popular culture by exposing the prejudices of the opponents of "kitsch." The argument mattered only as a means of demonstrating that popular culture provided documentary evidence for an American "happiness"—an uncompromised hunger for what (in his view) socialism alone could provide. The revisionary impertinence of the thesis is appreciable when one grasps the return here to the classical notion of the revolutionary leadership of the most "advanced" countries—a highly strange thesis, in fact, for a man who had been involved in African decolonization in the thirties. Predicting in so many other ways the obsessions of the sixties—the rise of "youth," of non-Party forms of organizing—the study directly contests the writing of Fanon, the ideology of peasant war and third-world encirclement—a rarely noticed corollary of his message.

The intended sting of that message cannot be felt without recovering the prominence at this time of the thesis of "American exceptionalism"— a very widely and publicly debated issue that James takes up in order to stand it on its head. The question for us to ask, however, goes to the heart of the migrant intellectual abroad: how well did James understand the United States? Proposing to enter mainstream publishing on the eve of his incarceration at Ellis Island (which immediately preceded his departure from the country), James seemed almost self-flagellating. The typescript comes off with a numbing desperation. The selflessness and moral vigor of the move alone seemed to justify it; to become "popular"— not merely to comment upon the popular—was to realize practically the critical emphasis he had placed on "audience" in his earlier readings of the European literary classics. The polemical point was in this sense embodied in the project rather than explicitly argued in its pages. The key political questions are always posed "from below"; they are the ones so obvious that the cultivated flee from them, thinking them banal. Thus the intentionally naive framing of the study itself: "What do the people want? What makes them happy?" (*AC* 166).

His answer to these questions in the opening movements of the outline, however, suggest some of the difficulties of adopting "America" for his purposes, and these too are problems of cultural translation: of the foreign intellectual faced by U.S. centrality of power and resources seeking to kill two birds with one stone—to acknowledge that power, but then, in an act of subversive interpretation, to convert it. What people want, he writes, is "to manage and arrange the work they are doing without any interference or supervision by anybody . . . to work and love handling the intricate scientific masses of machinery" (*AC* 167). What a synthesis! The vision might be called "industrial-pastoral." It attempts to splice a typically American frontier scorn for government interference with a very different tradition of workers' control from the socialist movement.

Leaving aside the historical issue of whether the movements James revered (among them, the early Bolsheviks, Cipriani's Labor movement) ever believed in a workplace without "supervision by anybody," the statement elides progressive and reactionary desire. In the United States, "government interference" had already in Reconstruction a resonance James unexplainably forgets in his eagerness to locate a univocally progressive American populism. Nor would this resonance change in coming years in the school desegregation battles of Little Rock or in today's stand-offs at the abortion clinics. By tapping into an instinctively anarchist response to an overbearing state, James was making the same gestures familiar in today's culturalism—a gesture in which the "state" is doubly damned as an object of desire. It is for one thing the code word for what failed in the Soviet experiment; it is for another the nemesis of the methodology at work here: a viewing "from below." And yet what James is doing here is punning on the notion of workers control to draw on the vocabulary of Marxism by applying it to a specifically national conception of freedom that was, in many ways he chose not to discuss, hostile to his sort of Marxism.[9] A similar slippage occurs in his focus on individual happiness, the book's central concept.

The typescript begins with the thesis that individual happiness had found in the United States a fuller expression than anywhere else in the world and that, as a social expectation, individualism had the force (unlike in Europe) of rallying mass movements: "Freedom of the individual . . . cannot be abstracted from the nation. It is the peculiar, the special contribution of the United States to international civilization" (AC 106). This beguiling observation is put so energetically that one almost forgets to add the obvious provisos. It is not only a looking backward from the 1980s that allows one to complain about this unguarded way of putting the matter; to say that individualism in its American form has also meant cars rather than cheap mass transportion, picket fences rather than public housing, the lottery rather than guaranteed health care is to say only what Lewis Mumford and Thorstein Veblen had been saying before the war.

It is not that James does not remark on the potential contradictions of his thesis. He just neglects to explore them fully. For example, the book sets out to distinguish between two eras. One of them is characterized by the enviable individualism of the pre–Civil War days of Jacksonian democracy, Tocqueville's yeoman farmer, and the abolitionists, all of whom he sees collectively embodied in Melville in much the same way that medieval Europe had been embodied in Dante. To this he opposes the cant of the rising northern magnates after the Civil War who, in a sense, colonized the idea of freedom. Their unwitting mouthpiece for James was Whitman, who becomes in the book Melville's alter-ego and whose poetry is compared to "Voice of America" broadcasts.[10] The last one hundred pages of the four-hundred-page manuscript are dedicated to an ambivalent reading of John L. Lewis and the CIO, in which he criticizes the union for being limited to narrow material demands, rather than the larger, and more insubstantial, social issues—the quality of life issues.

In the early sections of the manuscript, James explores the paradox of American society that Tocqueville had already recognized in the 1830s: its authoritarianism alongside its outbursts of mass democratic protest and its cultural expressions of an undying hunger for individual happiness that had been reduced to general prognoses on the "boredom of freedom" and prosperity by existentialist intellectuals and *Partisan Review* contributors (whom he loathed). Tocqueville thought that America was unique because of the individual—that "puny" thing of the self—as against the social stratification of Europe; the American individual has a "capacity for free association," "individuality and universality achieve a fusion unknown elsewhere" (*AC* 48). And yet, by contrast, the rule of the majority was dominant, leading to an apparently untroubled conformity: "I know of no country in which there is so little independence of mind and freedom of discussion as in America" (*AC* 48). Taking these observations of Tocqueville and reapplying them to the present, James predictably blames this conformity on the routines of life brought about by the social regimentations of the captains of industry, but also, and less predictably, on the communist and trade-union bureaucracies whose unimaginative choices emphasizing social "security" rather than "freedom" failed to challenge the vicious system of industrial peonage and its attendant welfare "statism."

At this point, James steps into novel territory, for he concludes that this factor of "individual freedom," although apparently evanescent, had been precisely what powered Jacksonian democracy, as well as the uprising of Denmark Vesey, the first National Negro Convention of 1830, and finally (and following their inspirations), abolitionism itself in the form of William Lloyd Garrison's *Liberator* (1831) and the great speeches of the New England radical, Wendell Phillips—the clear hero of James's early chapters.[11] James had always angrily denied that the moral imperative of freeing slaves had only been a cover story for the investment designs of northern federalists in the Civil War. Linking the high drama of abolitionism with the jeremiads of Melville, James subsumes both in a striking association under the subheading of "Nineteenth Century Intellectuals." He establishes an indigenous American radicalism that had proven itself the equal of revolutions everywhere, thereby venturing into a dimension of the doctrine of "American exceptionalism" that was not a customary part of it:

Out of America, with no assistance from any alien tradition but from the very genius of the country emerged this clearly recognizable replica of the early Christians, the Puritans, and later the early Bolsheviks, types which have appeared only when fundamental changes are shaking a society to its depths (AC 91).

A homegrown idealism grounded in a stubborn resistance to threats against the sanctity of the person had given abolitionism a resilience and a clarity that Europe no longer had.

The novelty of James's thesis arises when he actually theorizes the need to recover the now-distant and diluted passion of this era by excavating mid–twentieth-century popular culture. Capitalist social "rationality" (and for James this would have included, of course, life in the "capitalist" Soviet Union as well) was not simply "the daily grind of the assembly-line workers. It is that the whole of productive life is tuned to this pattern" (AC 115). If opposition to this broad web of disciplinary culture, marching to the rhythms of the factory, had become increasingly narrow and defensive in the hands of economistic union leaders, there were abundant signs that the workers themselves had not lost their memory of "freedom." Workers were continually striking, not for wages, but for the dignity of free association.

What James develops, then, is the proposition that American popular culture, particularly the pre–1928 cinema, the detective novel, and the "serious" comic strip of Al Capp and Chester Gould, did not reflect an impoverishment of the human spirit; it was, by contrast, the direct descendant of the pre–Civil War classics of American literature. Popular culture expressed a desire for individuality that could be found in present American society in a twisted rhetoric of enterprise hiding a new authoritarianism:

Melville has left no serious descendents . . . [one must turn to] radio and the comic strip, to Charles Chaplin, Rita Hayworth, Sam Spade, Louis Armstrong, Dick Tracy and Gasoline Alley . . . after the writers of the middle of the 19th cent., [these] are the first genuine contributions of the U.S. to the art of the future and an international art of the modern world. (AC 35)

What is unique about James's take on the matter is (1) his linking of the classics of nineteenth-century American literature with mass art, where the latter is actually portrayed as the fulfillment of the former; (2) his finding the motor of development of mass art not in "technology" or the demands of advertising or wartime lessons about the uses of propaganda (the then familiar lines), but in the fundamental character of American society—"individualism"; and (3) his clear formulation, at this very early date, that culture, like politics, was "concentrated economics" and could give direction to political activity:

Where formerly we had to look at the economic relations of society, the political and social movements and the great artistic expressions to get a whole, complete and dynamic view of the society, while as far as the great mass was concerned, we had to guess; today it is not so. The modern popular film, the modern newspaper (the *Daily News*, not the *Times*), the comic strip, the evolution of jazz, a popular periodical like *Life*, these mirror from year to year the deep social responses and evolution of the American people in relation to the fate which has overtaken the original concepts of freedom, free individuality, free association. (*AC* 118–19)

Popular culture was not something for the Left simply to exploit; nor was the issue to give popular culture its due as entertainment. For James, popular culture was an unsullied archive of popular desire. It provided a space for intellectuals to readjust their sights, wake up from their reveries. With an enormous confidence in the wisdom of the people and their trudging power, James felt that the future glimmered back at one from the dancing images of the commercial cinema. What interested him, and what he found historically new, was the "day-to-day correspondence between the ordinary experiences of many millions of human beings and their transmutation into aesthetic form" (*AC* 139). In watching popular culture, the people watched themselves, and liked what they saw.

II. James's Art

The conflicting combinations that James embodied—Victorian theorist of cultural studies, third-world European, anarcho-Leninist—rose up fully in his plans for "The Struggle for Happiness." It would be not only fireside reading for the petit-bourgeois listeners of Walter Winchell, but a sort of handbook for a new politics. While the going debate in mass art criticism was, predictably, over "taste" and the decline of art (which the current "political correctness" debates show has force still), James was busy redefining what a discussion of aesthetics ought to be about.

Apart from an open hostility to the literary modernists—he called them "magists, textualists, and metaphoricals" (*The C.L.R. James Reader* 258)—and a primary emphasis on audience, there are two aesthetic categories that recur in James's work with impassioned emphasis: "rhythm" and "simplicity." The latter has an obvious bearing on audience. As for "simplicity," James applies that concept to the genres standing midway between highbrow reflection and public contact— another way of stating, perhaps, his earlier category of "integration."

In a letter to Constance Webb in 1946, James laid out what he believed to be rhythm's "positive universal." Prompted by the viewing of a film starring Jennifer Jones whose lines, James believed in an epiphanic moment, were "our modern poetry," his observations detail the great directive of art to repeat the accomplishments of Shakespeare using "the prosaic sharp disjointed urban speech of our time" (*C.L.R. James Reader* 151). It is a fascinating passage, not only for its technical detail (which James's criticism often lacks), but for its privileging of "America" over the Caribbean, an odd focus when the subject is "rhythm." The Caribbean—the home of the *son, rumba, bomba, guaracha*—is the site of rhythmic superabundance.

With puzzling evasion, he speaks instead of "the great rhythms of history," which he took to be "the Greek hexameter, the Elizabethan blank verse, the heroic couplet." But the point here is not James's quirky Eurocentrism; these rhythms were "expressions of the human soul" and, as such, social, and they came each in their own way through a process of distilling the "'normal' speech at the time."[12] What excites him about the United States is that "the people's speech . . . distilled into poetic rhythm . . . becomes not only echoes but positive expressions towards the freedoms, powers, sentiments, etc., of previous generations enjoyed by only a few" (*C.L.R. James Reader* 152). In other words, the authenticity given popular speech by the ritualized fame of the cinema confers power on the ones who are represented.

This audience, though, is different from those of the past, argues James, in that its knowledge of the past and present can only be learned "in art, and above all, literature." By stressing the saturated nature of representation in a period of media control, James significantly departs from his emphasis on art as cultural infrastructure. A major postwar statement of his more typical position is in "Lenin and the Problem," where James admiringly remarks how Lenin, when speaking about culture, ignored Pushkin and Chekhov—those men who "even outside of

Russia were acknowledged as the greatest artists of the nineteenth century" (*C.L.R. James Reader* 332), and instead speaks of education. Following Lenin's lead, James finds the major tasks of cultural study to be universal literacy and the curbing of the power of governmental bureaucracy. The latter refers not only to the classical problem of the Soviet state but, step for step, to the postcolonial African elite, an aspect of his thought that, again, is pushed aside both in recent cultural nationalist and postmarxist appraisals of his work.[13]

III. American Exceptionalism

How did James's study of popular culture differ from those of the time? James had already collaborated with Dwight MacDonald—the founder of *Partisan Review*—on Irving Howe's journal *Labor Action* in the early forties. James had also mingled with the New York intellectuals, but never felt a part of them, given their identifications with the avant-garde and their fascination with psychoanalysis, both of which he detested. Although too alien in temperament and outlook to call him a friend, James had coffee more than once with Theodor Adorno in the lunchroom of the New School for Social Research.

James's study was, in this sense, deliberately contemptuous of academic production. The tenor of the typescript evolved from a deep and precious resentment. In 1950, he was writing defensively and out of worry he would not be heard, but from a position, nevertheless, that he believed to be a privileged one. Although he had early won Trinidad's prestigious scholarships, and his impressive archival performances in *The Black Jacobins* and *The Life of Captain Cipriani* had suggested something of the acclaim he might have won in the university, he had thrown all of that away because it would isolate him from "ordinary people." His pain and his anger are apparent in his correspondence with Melville scholar Jay Leyda or, later, Lionel Trilling and Frank Kermode who do not see what he sees, but who he fears will take him for a crank. "The whole thesis of this book," he writes, is to show that

the American intellectuals have nothing to say that is new. They will make no special contribution to the future of American society. . . . Not only are they powerless before the process [of bureaucratization]. The intellectuals contribute to it, and then either drown themselves and their doubts and hesitations in it or desperately seek a retreat in their own individual psyches. (*AC* 225)

His outline was written in the middle of (or a little before) an enormous outpouring of work by U.S. intellectuals on popular culture. The European predecessors had been, for example, José Ortega y Gasset, the Frankfurt School, and (through the *Partisan Review*) George Orwell. In the United States, the chief predecessor had been particularly Veblen (1899). Some characteristic American work of the period included MacDonald's "A Theory of Popular Culture" (1944), Clement Greenberg's "Avant Garde and Kitsch" (1946) and Edmund Wilson's "Who Cares Who Killed Roger Ackroyd" from *Classics and Commercials,* a book that is exactly contemporaneous with James's manuscript in 1950.[14]

In as much as the mass culture debate was about aesthetics, the familiar complaint was with popular culture's insincere imitations of high artistic raw material. More relevant to James, predictably, were the arguments about social effects—arguments not at all unique to him in kind. The mass culture debate was littered with them. James's innovation was to pinpoint the reversal at work within the troubled notion of a U.S.-centered "popularity." Without denying its apologetic covering for the principle of freedom as market "choice," he saw no reason to recoil from the principle of individuality itself. It was too precious for that. "American exceptionalism" had long been the theoretical slogan summoned to explain the weaknesses of a progressive politics. But in the face of the charge (willingly repeated by the mainstream press) that the United States was "exceptional" in the sense that it was immune to revolution because of its racially divided working class and its high standard of living—James countered by turning the thesis around. His historical rereading of the abolition movement was conducted with precisely that goal in mind.

The country was the best, not the worst, site for socialism because of its racial divisions. In America, the African diaspora had reached its fullest sense of self; African Americans would either lead the revolution or the revolution would not be. James echoed Garvey before him: "The American Negro is the peer of all Negroes, the most progressive and the foremost unit in the expansive chain of scattered Ethiopia" (Henrik Clarke 89). What poorer countries were struggling for, what decolonization was (and would be) mainly about, was achieving what already existed in the United States (*C. L. R. James Reader* 352, 367–69).

Intellectually, though, the all-important tone of his arguments came from his personal life, and are perhaps responsible for an overstatement of potential within popular culture that diminishes the validity of the claims. James's letters to Constance Webb between 1939 and 1948 were both a courtship and a literary preparation. It is true that through this correspondence James worked his way out of his sectarian milieu, but the study's almost millenarian optimism offers to all but the most careful reader the temptation to mistake James for an advocate of a purely culturalist politics. Hinted at and even loosely outlined in the letters from about 1944 onward, "The Struggle for Happiness" became in a sense the culmination of his relationship with Webb, a relationship that was not by any means only intellectual (they had a son) but which depended a great deal on the free association of intellectual desire James felt uniquely able to employ in her imagined presence.[15]

The Webb letters do not suggest that there were not other, hardly personal, motives; but they do put an appropriate emphasis on personality (a key historical category for James), which in a touchingly vulnerable letter betrays the extent to which James dramatized his own:

Curious the affinity I find myself always making now with you and the proletariat. . . . If I write to you I will in time write better for the proletariat. And if the proletariat does act and a voice is needed to give its actions their fullest implications, I not only know that I will do it, but that I'll write to you as never before. No one will ever write as I shall write then. No one. The revolution is a release of power—and release for me too, in every direction. (Webb Letters, 1 March 1946, 1)

In this sense, "The Struggle for Happiness" is a record of this type of sublimation: Constance becomes the working class just as the libertarian dream of the United States is translated into being the true goal of socialism. Constance, militant and model, brought together for James the symmetrical ends of the manuscript as a photo of the "real mind" of the working class in the thoroughly American, thoroughly marketable form of the "good read."

In still other ways, the originality of the study points to its potential influence. First of all, "The Struggle for Happiness" combines two familiar genres of the time and so is unique in combination. It fits in not only with the popular culture media work being done, but with other types of study as well: general, prognostic explorations of the American "character" which virtually flooded the market at this time.[16]

One of these was *The New Image of the Common Man* (1950) by Carl J. Friedrich. A battling liberal, Friedrich declares himself against the condescension with which the image of the "common man" is widely treated. His point: the common man is not someone else—it is you and I—a not un-Jamesian point. According to Friedrich, only the critics of democracy itself, like Ortega y Gasset or, before him, Nietzsche, speak of the "incompetence of the masses," and these today are food for the witch hunts "now sweeping the country" (Friedrich 8). In one section entitled "Independence of Thought and Propaganda," Friedrich attacks elitism and pleads, much like James, for a Veblenian "sense of workmanship" (Friedrich 9).

The similarity of his approach does not end here, either. Friedrich looks back to the nineteenth century to discover, much like James discovered in Melville's use of Anacharsis Clootz, a general movement among the intellectuals from "nationalism to cosmopolitanism," an idea that is central both to the priority James gave "America" over Europe (its classlessness in *culture*) and to his understanding of the distinctive mixing of the West Indian character (its unity despite a linguistic and racial heterogeneity).

In 1950, the only really new twist possible to give to the genre of Bryce and Tocqueville would have been the discovery of the "masses." However much one toys with the liberalizing intent of these two books, a cold reminder of their contents (as well as their uses since) places James in a hard position. We could say he was merely taking the genre over, but his precursors mark the genre with inherent hostility toward social "leveling" and with paeans to entrepreneurship. They were basically the work of admiring snobs. Thus, in invoking them, how can James say in the age of Henry Luce and Douglas MacArthur that "America is the greatest country in the world," as he does repeatedly in the typescript? "The Struggle for Happiness" is much more of a continuity than a departure. Such a book had to be written, he seems to say, not by a European, who dissects the country from the vantage point of imperial experience and a settled culture, but by an "American" who is to the United States what the United States was to Europe then: raw, mixed, energetic, new.

As I suggest above, the contribution of James's America project is not found so much in its insights (which were already in the air in the late forties and fifties), but in its *location*. The typescript's resilience derives in part from its tone. The ecstatic drive of the narrative, its rigorous but plain-speaking enthusiasms are based on a conception of an American social and artistic conscience in evolution. Both derive from James's assumption of place *within* the ranks of everyday people, whom he conceived, unlike Friedrich's pan-humanist "you and I," as a class that stood in opposition to the "industrialists." This aspect of being in a class, and in solidarity with it, is completely absent in the other books. His location ensured "integration" in the simultaneously aesthetic and political sense of the term: "I have sat for hours in America, listening to people, all sorts of poor working people, telling me all about themselves. It is indispensable for any understanding of anything. It must go side by side with the books" (*AC* 225). If the separate sections of the larger study had echoes in the work of others, they are altogether different in James because he fits America into an apocalyptic narrative of global liberation from an explicitly Marxist point of view.

The unmistakable feel of mass culture criticism in the 1950s, like the postmodernism debate today which repeats it in a barely modified language, is that of helpless witness: recording by inches the approach of something too powerful to resist. In these accounts, the evils conjured—the leveling of value and standardization—are horrible *precisely because* they are popular; that is, a vestigial memory of Marx's focus on the "working class" produces in the researcher a terrifying loneliness since "they" (ordinary workers) have willingly joined the anonymous culture of the machine, making the latter's victory certain.[17] How different all this looks in James, where he talks instead of a colonization of American ideology by businessmen. And here really is the key to James's reconciliation of this era of detour in his work with the rest of his career. "Individualism" itself begins to appear very much like a collectivism; individualism equals a collectivism *without centralized leadership*. Mass art portrayed what people were, and what they wanted with complete faithfulness. But mass art also revealed to the people the commonality of their class desires:

It is the writer's belief that in modern popular art, film, radio, television, comic strip, we are headed for some such artistic comprehensive integration of modern life, that the spiritual, intellectual, ideological life of modern peoples will express itself in the closest and most rapid, most complex, absolutely free relation to the actual life of the citizens of tomorrow. (*AC* 150)

In a good deal of the mass culture debate, the ugliness of "standardization" was the real complaint. The civic component of the argument—

that standardization led to totalitarianism—was merely strategic. For James the case is just the opposite—not good taste but new society. For him, the thrill of mass culture lay in its documentary testimony of a people grasping at fleeting individuality. Media art was integrating "all aspects of the life of modern man" by projecting into a new public forum both "ordinary" life and "the great social and political events of the day," allowing the one to belong to the other.

Weakly, perhaps even fatally, James complains about the excessive focus on declining values while neglecting to address the problem of libidinal enslavement. Despite the currently fashionable attacks on the Frankfurt school, Leo Lowenthal, writing at exactly the same time, points out what surely must be accounted for, but was not in James's study: that mass culture has always been inextricably bound up with advertising; while it gives expression to vivid desires, the desires have the effect of pacifying the audience: "Wherever revolutionary tendencies show a timid head, they are mitigated and cut short by a false fulfillment of wish dreams, like wealth, adventure, passionate love, power, and sensationalism" (Lowenthal 55).

More debilitating was James's rhapsodies over an imaginary American "worker." The appeal of the industrial-pastoral took over his mass culture analysis. He was somehow of the opinion that American workers generally believed in a nonsectoral, unified world community; that religion had no serious hold on them, and that the prevailing opinion was that everyone had "the right to the best possible education." With his analysis of the Soviet Union, it was impossible to maintain a position without these appealing fictions. The usually careful historian, so original in his reading of the nineteenth century, overlooks the country's origins as refuge for religious zealots, its opening of doors to conservative exiles, and its consistent ideology of "go-it-alone" individualism and governmental noninterference. For a time, James had even brought himself to believe it reasonable to rally the United States to aid anticolonial liberation movements following the war (Worcester, "American Century" 29).

The price of optimism—that plausible, but finally preposterous weight he gave to "happiness"—was to suspend the colonial question. By the time he wrote *Mariners, Renegades, and Castaways*, this neglect had become extreme. There he quotes Melville who, tongue in cheek, praises the great "naked Nantucketers" who would "overrun and conquer the watery world like so many Alexanders; parcelling out among them the Atlantic, Pacific, and Indian oceans, as the three pirate powers did

Poland." In the face of this remarkable passage, James offers the following preface without a hint of irony: "Melville understands what America has given to the world—none better. He has chosen whaling for his unit of demonstration. And in a brilliant page he sums up the grandeur of the American past!" (36).

These lines have a very different emphasis from those he would write only a few years later in Britain about the "seeds of the new society" planted by the imperial diaspora—the fertile invasions, as it were, of the metropolis from without. Without wanting to, "The Struggle for Happiness" suggests that the greatest problem of the twentieth century is, apart from the color line, the beguiling image of American liberty itself.

It would be wrong to suggest that his theses on "American exceptionalism" were confined to this moment of transition. He retained them throughout his life. In a letter to Maxwell Geismar in 1961, for example, he is again planning an essay on "American character." The difference, he says, between Americans and Europeans (always his major point of contrast), can be "crudely" pinpointed in the fact that "Americans expect to be happy."[18] James punned on that image of happiness (and of "America") as an urge that is intensified by a milieu of evident and growing unhappiness.

His reading was brilliant, but too subtle, and the largely unconscious repetition of many of his findings in current cultural theory misses the joke. Its transformation today—or better, unwitting echoes—in various theories about the politics of style, of subversive consumption, and of the opportunities for resistance opened up by the new technologies, leave all of his ironies behind. In part, of course, the reasons for this are not hard to find: they are generational; they have to do with lacking James's cross-generational experiences, with poststructuralist fallout, and with the ever-looming power of the United States itself in the wake of combined colonial and second-world defeats. But I am suggesting something else as well: the existential disorientation of writing, without an outside base, in the crazyhouse of U.S. intellectual consumerism. For a variety of reasons that I have sought to cover here, that disorientation affected even the likes of C.L.R. James.

Notes

1. The outline, however, has recently appeared as *American Civilization,* edited by Anna Grimshaw and Keith Hart. Since this essay was written before *American Civilization* was published, I refer to it as "The Struggle for Happiness," which was Grimshaw and Hart's title (taken from James's original title of his chap. 6) for an earlier version of his work. But for the sake of convenience, I cite from *American Civilization,* since differences between it and James's original typescript are insignificant.

2. Apart from some descriptive notes by the keepers of the James archives, and one projected essay, no critical study of the book exists, and in the lengthier biographical treaments, "The Struggle for Happiness" gets barely a mention. See Grimshaw and Hart, "C.L.R. James and the *Struggle for Happiness,*" and Worcester, "American Century." The latter, at any rate, does not deal with James's cultural profile, only his political one.

3. Included in the recent revival are Wynter, "Beyond the Categories of the Master Conception," *C.L.R. James's Caribbean,* Henry and Buhle, eds., 63–91; Robinson, *Black Marxism,* 447; Grimshaw, *"C.L.R. James: A Revolutionary Vision";* Buhle, *C.L.R. James: The Artist as Revolutionary;* Worcester, *C.L.R. James: A Political Biography;* McLemee, "Afterword," in McLemee and Le Blanc, *C.L.R. James and Revolutionary Marxism.*

4. This is not to say that *Beyond a Boundary* does not have a special claim to place in the James canon. Apart from being the autobiography he never wrote, its boastful mastery of cricket lore, its rude catholicity of outlook in which the entire Commonwealth becomes a family in sport gives the proper feel of a man who was, despite his reach and range, a West Indian. This West Indian sensibility, this fleeting concession to that which is "indigenous" in him, is intentionally suppressed in James's American years.

5. The James-Webb letters, 1 Sept. 1943, 1. For an opposing emphasis, see McLemee, "In the American Tradition": "Every significant line of thought in the 1950 document had been anticipated in the pages of James's literary productions for the Trotskyist press over the decade previously" (2). For another dimension of the personal, see Weir, "Revolutionary Artist," who writes of James's "need to be in a major industrial society which contained a significant Black population" (180).

6. James's productivity in these years is recorded best in Hill (69–80). The best short account of James's career can be found in Cudjoe, "Forever Mellow" (17–35) and Cudjoe, "C.L.R. James Misbound" (124–36).

7. The semipoetic, apocalyptic snapshots of Jean Baudrillard's *America,* and the chatty arcana of U.S. "underground" technocultures in Andrew Ross's *Strange Weather* are very different sorts of examples of current nonnative hypostatizations of U.S. popular culture—the United States as a European myth.

Because the authority of both writers derives in part from their European backgrounds, they are (in this sense) quite unlike James.

8. For the argument that James shares the views of deconstruction, see Wynter; for the view of his "independence" from traditional Marxism, see Robinson.

9. According to Look Lai, when James found himself with actual governmental authority for the first time in Trinidad under Eric Williams, his positions on workers' control were much more guarded and conservative (196).

10. The following passage is typical: "Today in the 'cold war' the picture of America which is being presented to the world by the rulers of America is Whitman's picture. Free individuals, free enterprise, science, industry, democracy—that is the Voice of America and this at a time when every thinking mind in America is pondering over the outcome of precisely what these terms signify for American and human civilization. . . . His 'body beautiful' and 'body electric' and 'seminal wetness' are the reservoir from which advertisers of foods, toothpaste, vitamins, deodorants draw an unending source of inspirations by which to cheat and corrupt the American people" (AC 46).

11. His view of American political potential is contained more or less whole in his comments on Phillips: "Phillips developed a political policy for Abolitionism which to this day remains ignored . . . yet seen in its context, it is perhaps the highest peak reached by the U.S. intellectuals in the foreshadowing of the future of the world of today and in indicating how deeply all great world currents are integral to the U.S. as a nation" (AC 91).

12. But James's preferences for European art cannot be explained away by pointing to his admiration for the postwar West Indian novel, or by saying that the postcolonial mixture of cultures renders all claims to a purely "European" or "indigenous" art spurious. In fact, only in his semiofficial capacity as nationalist commentator for the Nation in Trinidad did he, rather colorlessly, express his admiration for carnival, and even here one feels that he wants to like it much more than he actually does.

13. For the charge that Marxism aided and abetted imperialism—not in the actions of this or that individual, but at the level of its very foundational ideas—see Young (4, 9) and Miller (38). James's comments on George Padmore (James 1992, 288–95) and Kwame Nkrumah (James 1992, 331–46) seem to be an appropriate first response to these now familiar canards.

14. The sort of view James opposed is familiar enough. Quoting Greenberg, though, gives a faithful reminder not only of the tenor, but of the typical linkage at the time between good taste and socialism: "It is one of the tragedies of our time that solicitude for any of the arts forces one to be a snob. The mass public of industrial countries, wittingly or unwittingly, asks for such concessions to the limitations of its tastes as cannot but debase the arts. The real trouble lies deeper, of course—in the causes of these limitations. The fact is that most people in our

society lack the security, leisure, and comfort indispensable to the cultivation of taste; and only a socialist society can provide security, leisure, and comfort" (Greenberg 64).

15. See James letters, March 1, 1946: "I feel that by bringing my full powers to bear on you, I can illuminate you and develop you. Because a genuine exploration and adventure develops both the explorer and the territory."

16. These included Friedrich's *The New Image of the Common Man* (1950); Gorer's *The American People* (1948), which James mentions in his manuscript; and Commager's slightly more academic *The American Mind* (1950).

17. It is interesting to compare James's project with the almost contemporaneous one of Raymond Williams in England, who was also fundamentally literary in his Marxist effort to account theoretically for mass culture. In a little known public lecture, James in *Marxism and the Intellectuals* reviewed *Culture and Society* (1958) and *The Long Revolution* (1960). In "The Creative Power of the Working Class," he says, "Mr. Williams is the most remarkable writer that the socialist movement in England has produced for ten years or perhaps twenty . . . of working class origin but with a university education. . . . He has developed the idea of culture from an exclusive possession of the educated and intellectuals and shown that the only meaning the word has for today is a *total way of life of the whole people*" (5). However, he goes on to add, "Marxists have to show large and grave gaps in Mr. Williams' work, and in his thinking" (5). What makes a worker a worker, says James, is work itself, the labor process. Socialism, then, is primarily about the reorganization of work: "It plays a very small part in Mr. Williams' two books" (11).

18. Letter to Maxwell Geismar, 11 Apr. 1961 (unpublished). New York: The C.L.R. James Institute and Cultural Correspondence.

Works Cited

Baudrillard, Jean. *America.* London: Verso, 1988.

Bryce, James. *The American Commonwealth.* Vol. 2. London: Macmillan & Co., 1889.

Buhle, Paul. *C.L.R. James: The Artist as Revolutionary.* London: Verso, 1988.

———, ed. *C.L.R. James: His Life and Work.* London: Allison & Busby, 1986.

Commager, Henry Steele. *The American Mind.* New Haven, Conn.: Yale UP, 1950.

Cudjoe, Selwyn. "For Ever, Mellow: Selected Treasurers of C.L.R. James's Intellectual Legacy." *The C.L.R. James Journal* Winter 1992: 17–35.

———. "C.L.R. James Misbound." *Transition* 58, 124–36.

Fiedler, Leslie. "The Middle Against Both Ends." *Encounter* 5, (1955): 16–23.

Friedrich, Carl J. *The New Image of the Common Man*. Boston: Beacon Press, 1950.

Gorer, Geoffrey. *The American People: A Study in National Character*. New York: Norton, 1948.

Greenberg, Clement. *The Collected Essays and Criticism*. Vol. 2. Chicago: U of Chicago P, 1986.

Grimshaw, Anna. "C.L.R. James: A Revolutionary Vision for the Twentieth Century." New York: The C.L.R. James Institute, 1991.

———, ed. *The C.L.R. James Reader*. Oxford: Blackwell, 1992.

Grimshaw, Anna, and Keith Hart. "C.L.R. James and *The Struggle for Happiness*." New York: Desktop publishing by Jim Murray of *Cultural Correspondence*, 1991.

Henrik Clarke, John, ed. with the assistance of Amy Jacques Garvey. *Marcus Garvey and the Vision of Africa*. New York: Vintage, 1974.

Henry, Paget, and Paul Buhle, eds. *C.L.R. James's Caribbean*. Durham: Duke UP, 1992.

Hill, Robert A. "In England, 1932–1938." Buhle, *Life and Work:* 61–80.

James, C.L.R. *American Civilization*. Eds. Anna Grimshaw and Keith Hart. Cambridge, Mass.: Blackwell, 1993.

———. *Beyond a Boundary*. London: Hutchinson, 1963.

———. *The Black Jacobins: Toussaint L'Ouverture and the San Domingo Revolution*. 1938. New York: Vintage, 1963.

———. Anna Grimshaw, ed. *The C.L.R. James Reader*. Oxford: Blackwell, 1992.

———. Letters to Constance Webb. New York: The Schomburg Center for the Study of Black Culture.

———. *Mariners, Renegades, and Castaways: The Story of Herman Melville and the World We Live In*. New York: privately published, 1953.

———. *Marxism and the Intellectuals*. J. R. Johnson [James's pseudonym]. Detroit: Facing Reality Publishing Committee, 1962.

———. "Notes on American Civilization: The Struggle for Happiness." Unpublished typescript, 1950. All page citations are from the typescript available at the C.L.R. James Institute and Cultural Correspondence, New York.

———. *Notes on Dialectics: Hegel, Marx, Lenin*. 1948. London: Allison & Busby, 1980.

Jameson, Fredric. *Marxism and Form*. Princeton: Princeton UP, 1971.

Look Lai, Walter. "C.L.R. James and Trinidadian Nationalism." *C.L.R. James's Caribbean*. Ed. Paget Henry and Paul Buhle. Durham: Duke UP, 1992: 174–209.

Lowenthal, Leo. "Historical Perspectives of Popular Culture." *Mass Culture:*

The Popular Arts in America. Ed. Bernard Rosenberg and David
Manning White. Glencoe, Ill.: The Free Press, 1957. 46–58.

McLemee, Scott. "In the American Tradition: A Provocation Regarding the
Ecole Grimshaw and Related Matters." Unpublished essay, 1992.

———. "Afterward." Scott McLemee and Paul Le Blanc, eds. *C.L.R. James
and Revolutionary Marxism: Selected Writings 1939–1949.* New
York: Humanities Press, 1993.

Marx, Karl, and Frederick Engels. *Manifesto of the Communist Party.* 1848.
New York: International Publishers, 1983.

Miller, Christopher. *Theories of Africans: Francophone Literature and
Anthropology in Africa.* Chicago: U of Chicago P, 1990.

Robinson, Cedric. *Black Marxism: The Making of the Black Radical Tradition.*
London: Zed Books Ltd., 1983.

Ross, Andrew. *Strange Weather.* London: Verso, 1992.

Souvarine, Boris. *Stalin: A Critical Survey of Bolshevism.* Trans. C.L.R. James.
London: Secker & Warburg, ca. 1939. In French, 1936.

Tocqueville, Alexis de. *Democracy in America.* 1835. New York: Signet, 1956.

Weir, Stanley. "Revolutionary Artist." Paul Buhle, ed. *C.L.R. James: His Life
and Work,* 180–84.

Wilson, Edmund. "Who Cares who Killed Roger Ackroyd?" *Mass Culture:
The Popular Arts in America.* Ed. Bernard Rosenberg and David
Manning White. Glencoe, Ill.: The Free Press, 1957. 149–53.

Worcester, Kent. "C.L.R. James and the American Century: 1938–1953." Selwyn Cudjoe, ed. *C.L.R. James and His Intellectual Legacies.* Amherst:
University of Massachusetts, 1994.

———. *C.L.R. James: A Political Biography.* Unpublished manuscript.

Wynter, Sylvia. "Beyond the Categories of the Master Conception: The
Counterdoctrine of the Jamesian Poeisis." Henry and Buhle 63–91.

Young, Robert. *White Mythologies: Writing History and the West.* London:
Routledge, 1990.

Translation as Manipulation: The Power of Images and Images of Power

Mahasweta Sengupta

Translations of texts from cultures that are not civilizationally linked, and among which exists an unequal power relationship, manifest extremely complex processes. Some recent studies on translation emphasize the role of culture and history over a purely formal and linguistic approach; they bring into focus the position of a translated text within the intersecting networks of a culture and the manipulations behind a given positioning—of the translator, her or his culture, and the text/culture being translated. It is important to recognize that translations often operate under varied constraints and that these constraints include manipulations of power relations that aim at constructing an "image" of the source culture that preserves or extends the hegemony of the dominant group (Lefevere 15–27). In fact, these "images" construct notions of the Other and formulate an identity of the source culture that is recognizable by the target culture as representative of the former—as "authentic" specimens of a world that is remote as well as inaccessible in terms of the target culture's self. The nature and quality of these representations or rewritings, therefore, are of immense importance for cultural studies in general and translation studies in particular.

In the colonial situation, this process assumes added significance; while choosing texts for rewriting, the dominant power appropriates only those texts that conform to the preexisting discursive parameters of its linguistic networks. These texts are then rewritten largely according to a certain pattern that denudes them of their complexity and variety; they

159

are presented as specimens of a culture that is "simple," "natural," and in the case of India, for example, "other-worldly" or "spiritual" as well. Such a rendition clearly justifies the colonizer's "civilizing mission," through which the inherent superiority of the colonizer's culture is established.

The tyranny and power of these "images" constructed by the colonizer can only be grasped fully if one examines translations of "native" works done by the colonized and sees how pervasive colonial hegemony is. By formulating an identity that is acceptable to the dominant culture, the translator selects and rewrites only those texts that conform to the target culture's "image" of the source culture; the rewriting often involves intense manipulation and simplification for the sake of gaining recognition in and by the metropole. For, of course, the discursive parameters of the dominant power are such that they restrict the entry of texts that do not fit into their idea of the Other. The result of such a process of exclusion is that the source or the dominated culture is homogenized and domesticated, the polyphony of its existence obliterated, and a unified, monolithic view of that culture is created as truly legitimate.

I will first examine how the British constructed a certain "image" of India through a selective rendition of texts since the early days of contact between the two cultures. The dominant power consistently and methodically created boundaries in its discourse regarding this part of the so-called Orient; as a result, only certain signifying processes appealed to it while a large body of signs was excluded because it could not be rewritten into "images" that were acceptable to the English. I will then examine the autotranslations of Rabindranath Tagore to explore how he manipulated his own works to conform to the "image" of the East as it was known to the English-speaking world of the West.

The English Orientalist scholars first familiarized the West with what they regarded as the treasures of the "East"; their conscious effort was to retrieve a "golden age" of the Indian past that existed before the medieval period and the coming of the Islamic rulers to the subcontinent. Apart from the legal documents and specifically religious scriptures, these translators limited themselves to some very specific kinds of literary texts. The foremost scholar who located and translated the literature of the "Orient" for the West was Sir William Jones, president of the Asiatic Society of Bengal and a pioneer in Orientalist scholarship. Working from the premise of cultural superiority and faith in the advanced nature of European civilization, Jones divided the world into two spheres, where "reason and taste [were] the grand prerogatives of the European minds," whereas the "Asiatics soared to loftier heights in the sphere of imagination" (3: 12).

Jones believed in the Enlightenment notion of the two faculties of the human brain and was happy to concede the "Asiatic" the domain of the imaginative and exotic because it did not fit into the Cartesian world of rational discourse. The two specific literary translations Jones undertook were Jayadeva's *Gitagovinda* (1792) and Kalidasa's *Sakuntala* (1789). Both were enormously popular in England and in Europe and were largely responsible for creating an "image" of India that came to be regarded as an authentic representation of her culture. *Gitagovinda* was a Sanskrit *kavya* (long poem) consisting of lyrics about the divine love of Radha and Krishna written around the tenth or eleventh century. It is highly significant and typical that Jones designated the text as *mystical* and grouped it with the mystical poetry of the Sufi poets of Islam.

In the Hindu tradition, however, the *Gitagovinda* was more human than mystical, combining the devotional, erotic, and intensely poetic at the same time. Jones did not mention anything about the human appeal of the text that is vital in the subcontinent's culture even now and prefaced his translation with an essay "On the Mystical Poetry of the Persians and the Hindus." His description of the method he adopted clearly stated his ideological inclinations:

After having translated the *Gitagovinda* word for word, I reduced my translation to the form, in which it is now exhibited; omitting only those passages which are too luxuriant and too bold of an [sic] European taste, and the preparatory ode on the ten incarnations of Vishnu, with which you have been presented on another occasion: the phrases in Italicks are the *burdens* of the several songs; and you may be assured, that not a single image or idea has been added by the translator. (7: 115)

While Jones as a translator declared that he had not added "a single image or idea," he certainly had denuded the original of its richness and variety in order to make this poem conform to an "image" acceptable to "European taste." In his translation, the highly erotic, intensely poetic lyrics of Jayadeva became devotional prayers steeped with mysticism, and that was how his English constituency situated "India" within the domains of their discourses.

The other literary translation that played a major role in shaping the "image" of India was Kalidasa's *Sakuntala,* written around the first century BC. Jones and the European Romantics were fascinated by one particular aspect of the play: the "simplicity of Sakuntala the Protagonist, the peacefulness of Kanva's ashram" (Mukherjee 115). One specific theme of the play—the intimate bond between the human and the natural world, the dependence and interpenetration of the two—was foregrounded, displacing all other issues inherent in the text. This pioneering translation of *Sakuntala* was one of the earliest attempts to propagate an image of the "natural" yet "civilized" existence of India in ancient times. More significant was the attempt to privilege and emphasize the simple and the natural in the translation at the expense of the immensely complicated images of court life as well as the problems of relationship that Kalidasa had built into the original.

The notion of a primitive innocence, of simplicity and naturalness, and above all of mysticism or spirituality became the basic notes of all future rewritings about the cultures of India. These were domains in which the colonized could be safely contained and the colonial mission justified. Ashis Nandy maintains that colonialism legitimized itself by drawing parallels "between primitivism and childhood." Certain societies were supposed to be infantile, and their discourse was considered relevant to demonstrate the need to help them grow up (15). Once the cultural stereotype of the colonized race as childlike, innocent, and primitive was constructed through translations, the constituent subject could be safely contained within a discursive domain that did not clash with the more advanced and "civilized" or sophisticated cultures of the West.

H. T. Colebrook, a later Orientalist, summed up the characteristic domain of Orientalist discourse when he commented that the most important feature of "the arts" in Asia was their "simplicity"; however, he found that the study of those texts would be beneficial to his countrymen who might learn something about a value they seemed to lack (1: 389). Later translations that followed the work of Jones did not cross the legitimate boundaries of discourse regarding the culture of the colonized; the texts that were translated were either religious or spiritual, saturated with mysticism, or portrayed a simple and natural state of existence that was radically different from the metropolitan self of the target culture. More than the difference, these translations constituted the "image" of the source culture as safely tame, singularly other-worldly, and quite domesticated in relation to the self of the dominant power.

Later translators continued the trend established by the Orientalists. Edwin Arnold enjoyed considerable popularity during the last few years of the nineteenth century. Arnold's program was to render into English the "Pearls of Faith" of the "Orient." In the "Advertisement" to the first American edition of an anthology of that name, published in *Indian Idylls,* he wrote:

I have thus at length finished the Oriental Trilogy which I designed. In my "Indian Song of Songs" I sought to transfer to English poetry a subtle and lovely Sanskrit idyl of the Hindu theology. In my "Light of Asia" I related the story and displayed the gentle and far reaching doctrines of that great Hindoo Prince who founded Buddhism. I have tried to present here ["Pearls of the Faith"], in the simple, familiar, and credulous but earnest spirit and manner of Islam, and from its own point of view, some of the thoughts and beliefs of the followers of the notable Prophet of Arabia.

Texts that appealed to the English were basically those that spoke of the "faiths" of the "Orient," and Edwin Arnold was committed to a program that served his culture with palatable dishes of the food that were agreeable to their taste and were perceived as coming from "that unchanging and teeming population which Her Majesty Queen Victoria rules as Empress of Hindustan" ("Preface" 5). Arnold also translated parts of Jayadeva's *Gitagovinda* again, and episodes from the two epics of *Ramayana* and *Mahabharat.* The only text which could be considered as "secular" and did not belong to the religious tradition in particular was *Hitopodesha,* a collection of fables dealing with moral choices.

Translations from the vernaculars, particularly Bengali, repeated the same pattern of representation. The Asiatic Society of Bengal sponsored projects for translating Mukundaram Chakravarti's narrative poem *Chandimangal Kavya,* a tale of the prowess of goddess Chandi.[1] Translators were interested in religious literature in general, and in the 1920s several collections of Bengali religious lyrics were published. Edward J. Thomson and Arthur Marshman Spencer translated an anthology entitled *Bengali Religious Lyrics/Sakta* in 1923. J. A. Chapman brought out *Religious Lyrics of Bengal* in 1926, and Atul Chandra Ghosh translated *Deathless Ditties from Candidas and Other Bengali Poets* (1921).

The "image" of India that came through these translations was quite consistent with the image that Macaulay portrayed earlier in his (in)famous "Minute on Indian Education" (1835). In fact, Macaulay had no doubt about the correctness of his understanding about the indigenous forms of knowledges; and he had, he clearly stated, formed that knowledge from translations:

I have no knowledge of either Sanscrit or Arabic. But I have done what I could to form a correct estimate of their value. I have read translations of the most celebrated Arabic and Sanscrit works. I have conversed both here and at home with men distinguished by their proficiency in the Eastern tongues. I am quite ready to take the Oriental learning at the valuation of the Orientalists themselves. I have never found one among them who could deny that a single shelf of a good European library was worth the whole native culture of India and Arabia.

It will hardly be disputed I suppose, that the department of literature in which the Eastern writers stand highest is poetry. And I certainly never met with any Orientalist who ventured to maintain that the Arabic and Sanscrit poetry could be compared to that of the great European nations. But, when we pass from works of imagination to works in which facts are recorded and general principles investigated, the superiority of the Europeans becomes absolutely immeasurable. It is, I believe, no exaggeration to say that all the historical information which has been collected from all the books written in the Sanscrit language is less valuable than what may be found in most paltry abridgements used at preparatory schools in England. (241)

Macaulay's assessment of the literatures of Arabic and Sanskrit was derived from his reading of "translations" and one wonders what he had read to construct such an estimate of two of the richest languages of the world. In fact, like William Jones, even while granting the "Eastern" writers some credit in the domain of imaginative literature, Macaulay categorically ruled out the possibility of any comparison between the Europeans and the Indians. Ignorant yet arrogant, this reading clearly constructed an "image" of India from a position of power, and the power of this "image" held sway over many minds for a long time to come. The passage of time could not alter the power of this "image" of the culture the English represented through translations.

The hegemonic power of these images becomes obvious when one examines the translated works of someone from the colony writing in English, someone who seeks to enter the "symbolic order" of the English language, where meaning and signification are already fixed according to the differential network of relations.[2] The "symbolic order" is the "antecedent linguistic structure" (Taylor 88–89) in which a subject finds himself; it cannot be altered or constituted by an individual, it is a system that patterns and regulates all thought and action within a given discursive field. Therefore, when a writer from the colony seeks to enter the domain of the colonizer, he seems to have no option but to deploy the symbolic order of the English language which already has an existent repertory of discourse defining the alterity of the East.

The autotranslations of Rabindranath Tagore's (1861–1941) poetry in English clearly reveals the hegemonic power of the "images" that existed in the discourse of the English language regarding the imaginative literature of India. Rabindranath Tagore was the first Asian to receive the Nobel Prize for Literature, which he won in 1913 for an anthology of translated poems. The poet had written and translated these poems around the first decade of the twentieth century. He became tremendously popular in England in the second decade of the century, but his popularity waned as meteorically as it had risen. An innovator and pioneer who shaped the modern period of Bengali and other literatures, he presents a very different facet of himself in his translations. Rabindranath himself appeared to be conscious of this split in his identity when he started translating his immensely rich Bengali originals into English around 1910.[3] His scattered remarks concerning the process of translation and the metaphors he used to make sense are clearly indicative of a poetics that was adjusted to the demands of the colonizing power. Rabindranath was conscious that the process of rewriting from Bengali to English involved not just literal translation but a new creation; a creation that could be judged according to the parameters existing in the English language about literature from India. His comments to the *Christian Science Monitor* of October 16, 1916, reiterate this notion of a rupture that is involved in formulating an identity recognizable to the English-speaking world. The *Monitor* quotes the poet from Seattle: "I wish you might read it in the original Bengali. My English translations are not the same. Each country has its symbol of expression. So when I translate my work, I find new images" (Rabindra Bhavana archive). That the poet was aware of the vicissitudes of translating from one culture to another is revealed in the comments strewn among his letters, and it is clear that he responded to the two cultures in distinctly different ways. In a letter to Alice Rothenstein he admits that he was tempted to join his friends at Carutza, Caux sur Montreux, but he was afraid to cancel his other engagements:

I have to prove, so long as I am in the West, that Indians are also punctual in their habits and know the value of time and in the language of their conducts they observe the same accents and idioms as you do. In fact, we have to translate ourselves—otherwise you do not understand us, or what is far worse, misunderstand. If I were the original Rabindranath of the east I could come to you this moment and my people would laugh and say the fellow has forgotten the date. But the translation has to observe a different grammar and be very correct. (Lago 330)

These "accents and idioms" that Rabindranath was compelled to observe in the West were undoubtedly foreign to his "original" self, and he was aware of the fact that the "grammar" of one language did not work for the other. What is striking is his consciousness of the process involved in representing a self that was constituted by foreigners to cater to the grammar of a foreign audience.

This sense of a split is a characteristic mark of a colonized psyche, and Rabindranath was simply foregrounding that aspect of his self that was recognizable to the English through earlier literature that had been translated from the Indian languages. In a letter to William Pearson, who was translating a novel, Rabindranath comments on his understanding of the demands of an English audience:

I believe that in the English version some portions of it may profitably be left out, for I find that English readers have very little patience for scenes and sentiments which are foreign to them; they feel a sort of grievance for what they do not understand—and they care not to understand whatever is different from their familiar world. This is the reason why you find translations from oriental works in Germany and France and very few in England.[4]

It is clear that Rabindranath's reading of the demands of English culture proceeded from his understanding of the discursive boundaries of the English language, and when he manipulated the translations of his poems to suit the prevailing notions about the "poet-prophet" from the "East," he was simply submitting to the hegemonic power of "images" that had been constructed through translations of a particular kind.

The most important and characteristic feature of the changes that Rabindranath undertook while translating *Gitanjali* and five other anthologies of poems published between 1912 and 1921 is the predominance of the spiritual or devotional at the expense of all other moods of the original Bengali poems.[5] This was the domain that was familiar to the English as truly "Oriental" or "Eastern"; poets from Asia were, to the English, more like prophets who dealt with transcendental rather than with material issues which were part of their everyday struggle in the colony. The enormous variety of matter, mood, and mode of the

Bengali originals was reduced to one simplified tone of devotion to a personal god in the English translations, and Rabindranath naturally fell into the stereotypical image of the saint from the "East" who spoke of peace, calm, and spiritual bliss in a troubled world entering the cauldron of the First World War.

Examples of this process of reduction will make the point clear. Let us consider a poem from the first English anthology of Rabindranath, which became paradigmatic of his later attempts at translation because of its enormous success and the popularity brought by the Nobel Prize. Poem no. 3 in Rabindranath's translation in "simple" language reads:

> I know not how thou singest, my master!
> I ever listen in silent amazement.
> The light of thy music illuminates the world. The
> life breath of thy music runs from sky to sky. The
> holy stream of thy music breaks through all stony
> obstacles and rushes on.
> My heart longs to join in thy song, but vainly
> struggles for a voice. I would speak, but speech
> breaks not into song, and I cry out baffled. Ah,
> thou hast made my heart captive in the endless
> meshes of thy music, my master!

Note the repeated use of the word "master," and the emphasis on the mood of surrender to a higher authority that rules the world. A literal translation of this poem would read:

> How do you sing genius [guni]
> I listen with amazement.
> The light of your music envelops the world,
> The breeze of melody fills the sky
> Streams of music break out of solid rocks
> and flow torrentially
>
> I wish to sing like you,
> I do not find melody in my voice.
> I wish to say something, but do not find the words;
> My heart cries because of the defeat;
> What is this trap you have caught me in?
> I weave the net of music all around me.　　　(My translation)

Certain changes are glaring and obvious: the original has the Bengali word *guni* in the first line, which comes back as a refrain when the poem is sung, and which designates someone who is a genius. The meaning can be extended to include the sense of the divine Creator, but the original leaves it ambiguous. In the English translation, Rabindranath chose to use the word *master,* which certainly alters the tone of the entire poem and establishes a power relationship between the devotee and the Almighty. The ending of the English version also does not conform to the original; in the Bengali version, the poet is trapped by his intense desire to sing like the Creator, and in spite of his inability to achieve this he tries his best. In the English rendering, Rabindranath changes the sense of anguish and tension to a simple desire to surrender to the "master" because his heart is a "captive . . . in the meshes of [the master's] music."

The original Bengali poems, chosen from various anthologies of verses, are characterized by their immense variety and complex texture; they range from simple love poems to devotional poems that embody a spiritual calm rare in the entire career of the poet. In the English translations, however, a single basic principle seems to have dictated the choice of matter and manner: the demands of an English readership. Rabindranath repeatedly reiterates his conviction regarding the need to represent himself in a manner that would be familiar to the culture of the colonizer; he alters not only the style by translating the poems in "simple" language, but also radically changes the imagery, the tone, and the register of his language to cater to the discursive parameters of English. This process of reduction and simplification occurs in almost all the English versions, and poem no. 31 of *Gardener* will make the issue clear; it is the translation of a song from the Bengali *Kori o Komol,* an anthology of poems that is intensely sensual and rich in images and metaphors. In Rabindranath's "simple" rendering, the poem titled "Heart-sky" reads:

> My heart, the bird of the wilderness,
> Has found its sky in your eyes.
> They are the cradle of the morning,
> They are the kingdom of the stars,
> My songs are lost in their depths.
> Let me but soar in that sky, in its
> Lonely immensity.
> Let me but cleave its clouds and spread wings in its sunshine.

In a literal English translation the poem would read:

I have surrendered, bird of the sky
I have found a new sky in your eyes.
What are you hiding under your lashes?
The traces of dawn appear when you smile.
Heart desires to fly there alone
To dwell in the land of the eye-star.
That sky has made me sing
This climax of music wants to lose itself here.

The sky of your heart is endless and lonely—
It is calm and beautiful.
If I cross that expanse
And reach there with my golden wings,
My heart will be a *chatak* and beg for tears,
My soul will crave for the light of smiles.[6]

The English version is considerably reduced in line length, it is truncated and simplified. It does not try to reach anywhere near the complexity of the images of the original and does not render even a trace of the sense of intense longing or the sense of anxiety at the prospect of a refusal. The metaphor of the bird *chatak* is dropped in the English translation; the significance of the image of a bird who cries out for water but is unable to drink it when it rains is compelling and haunting in the original. The English translation gets nowhere near the intricate ambiguity of the original poem.

It is not difficult to multiply examples of such manipulation from the translations of Rabindranath; he took enormous liberties while rendering his own works into English. He explains this method of rewriting himself and expressed his confidence in the entire procedure:

I have realized that it does not help unless one translates his own writings. Since the melody and rhythms of the Bengali language cannot be transferred into English, the inner beauty of the poem only comes out if one translates the essential substance in simple English. This task is easy for me, because I cannot but write simple English, and at least I myself comprehend the essential nature of my poems. There is no chance of making a mistake in that. There is an advantage in having incomplete knowledge of the English language. . . . I discard what is beyond my powers of expression, I circumvent areas that offer resistance. I can only do this because these are my own creations. . . . It does not matter if the translations are good enough; there is no option but to be one's own translator. (Rabindra Bhavan archive, letter to Dineshchandra Sen)

Though this might have been a confession made out of a sense of modesty, there is no doubt that the poet felt sanguine that only the writer himself was empowered to translate his own works because the "essential substance" of his work was more accessible to him than to anyone else. However, this "substance," Rabindranath categorically stated, required a complete overhaul if it were to be made to enter the discursive world of another language, another world.

Elsewhere, Rabindranath compared this process of simplification in a more elaborate manner, and here denuding the poems of their richness and complexity was raised almost to a virtue. It is worth quoting the entire argument, from his letter of March 13, 1913, to Ajit Chakrabarti, in order to grasp the conviction that guided this poet from the colony:

Nobody in this country would accept that these are translations—everyone says that they would not believe that these were originally written in Bengali and that they are much better in their original form. I cannot disapprove of their opinion as entirely false. In fact, one cannot just translate one's own works. Because my right regarding my own works is not of an adventitious kind. If that was the case, I would have to answer for every deviation from a word. I do not do that. I try to represent in English the essential meaning of the poem. That creates a gulf of difference. You would not even be able to identify a poem unless I tell you which it is. Many of the poems have naturally become much shorter in the process. When a poem is expressed in Bengali, it appears with all the majesty of the language; she cannot but display her patrimonial wealth in public. But all these ornaments become a burden when carried in a trip to a distant land. Whatever it is, jewellery and beautiful dresses are not meant for pilgrimages. That is why I am engaged in the act of divesting my poems of their adornments—she has not given up the signs of her marriage like the vermilion mark or the iron bangle, she has not turned into an [sic] European lady, but shorn of her ornaments, she is wearing a completely new attire. (Rabindranath Bhavan archive)

This description elaborates the process of translation in which the majestic wealth of the original has to be pruned in order to be "borne across" to a "distant land"; in the English translations, the original Bengali poems are sometimes unrecognizable because they are mutilated beyond recognition. They had to be "simple" and mystically inclined to be the authentic voice of the poet from India.

Rabindranath continued to translate his own works in this manner until quite late in his life, and even when he became conscious of the duplicity involved in the process, he could not but submit to the hegemonic power of the "images" that constituted the identity of the "native" from the colonized world. Later in his life, he regretted his venture badly and more or less abandoned the idea of translating from one culture to another in the way he did during 1912 to 1921. But, whenever he did want to translate, he would resort to the "symbolic order" of the English language and culture. The tyranny of representation was so strong that even a genius like Rabindranath Tagore had to succumb to the power of the "image" of the "Orient" as it had been produced by the English. Toward the end of his life, in 1935, when there was an attempt to publish a collected edition of his works, Rabindranath wrote a letter, dated June 11, 1935, to Sturge-Moore that quite candidly described his earlier efforts to translate for the English:

I am no longer young and I have had ample time to realise the futility of going out of one's own natural sphere for winning recognition. Languages are jealous sovereigns, and passports are rarely allowed for travellers to cross their strictly guarded boundaries. What is the use of my awkwardly knocking my head against their prohibitions specially when I have the cause to feel sure of having contributed something acceptable to the world literature through my own mother tongue. I ought to remain loyally content with her limitations that are inevitable and yet which afford the only hospitality to the larger world.

In India, circumstances almost compel us to learn English, and this lucky accident has given us the opportunity of an access into the richest of all poetical literatures of the world. . . .

Translations, however clever, can only transfigure dancing into acrobatic tricks, in most cases playing treason against the majesty of the original. I often imagine apes to be an attempt by the devil of a translator to render human form in the mould of his own outlandish idiom. The case may be different in European languages which, in spite of their respective individual characteristics, have closely similar temperaments and atmosphere, the Western culture being a truly common culture. . . .

As for myself, I ought never to have intruded into your realm of glory with my offering hastily giving them a foreign shrine and certain assumed gestures familiar to you. I have done thereby injustice to myself and to the shrine of the muse which proudly claims flowers from its own climate and culture. There is something humiliating in such an indecent hurry of impatience clamouring for one's immediate dues in wrong time and out of the way places. (Rabindra Bhavana Archive. Unpublished correspondence with Thomas Sturge-Moore)

This is perhaps the best self-reflexive analysis of what the poet sought to accomplish through translations, but even then it does not recognize the compulsory nature of his efforts. It was difficult for him to be aware of the larger networks of power that were at work in the shaping of his attitudes toward English culture, and even when he realized the futility of translating in terms of categories imposed by the colonizer, he could not but act otherwise when actually translating a poem.

Translation in such a situation became a process of manipulation, a submission to the hegemonic power of "images" created and nurtured by the target culture as the authentic representation of the Other. This trend exists even today; a cursory review of what sells in the West as representative of India and its culture provides ample proof of the binding power of representation; we remain trapped in the cultural stereotypes created and nurtured through translated texts.

Notes

Thanks are due to the Rabindra Bhavan authorities for granting me access to the correspondence of Rabindranath Tagore. This essay is part of a larger project on cultural perceptions and the way they work through translations. Research for the project was carried out partly through a grant from the American Institute of Indian Studies during 1988–1989.

1. See, for example, E. B. Cowell, *Three Episodes from the Old Bengali Poem "Candi."*

2. Jacques Lacan explains how meaning is always constructed through reference to another meaning; in that sense, translations that enter a linguistic system necessarily abide by the rules of that system to make sense. Meanings, therefore, are constructed over a period of time through reference to known signifiers within the culture.

3. I am using the Bengali convention of referring to a person by his first name and not by his surname.

4. Rabindra-Bhavan Archive, Santiniketan. There is no date written on the letter except the printed date of 1922, and a note on the top reads: "I wrote this letter two days ago and was under the impression that it had been posted. I found it today in a most unlikely place."

5. *Gitanjali: Song Offerings* (1912) brought Tagore the Nobel Prize for Literature in 1913. Then appeared *The Gardener* (1913); *Crescent Moon: Child*

Poems (1913); *Fruit Gathering* (1916); *Lover's Gift and Crossing* (1918); and *The Fugitive* (1921).

6. It is extremely difficult to translate the connotations of the images that are culturally specific, though I have tried to be as faithful as possible.

Works Cited

Arnold, Edwin. *Indian Idylls: From the Sanskrit of the Mahabharat.* Boston: Robert Brothers, 1884.

Chapman, J. A. Selected, edited, and translated. *Religious Lyrics of Bengal.* Calcutta: The Book Company, 1926.

Colebrook, H. T. *Miscellaneous Essays.* 3 vols. London: Trubner, 1873.

Cowell, E. B. *Three Episodes for the Old Bengali Poem "Candi."* Calcutta: Asiatic Society of Bengal, 1902.

Ghosh, Atul Chandra, trans. *Deathless Ditties from Candidas and Other Bengali Poets.* Calcutta: M. C. Sarkar, 1921.

Jones, William. *The Works of William Jones.* 13 vols. London: John Stockdale and John Walker, 1807.

Lacan, Jacques. "The Insistence of the Letter in the Unconscious." *Modern Criticism and Theory: A Reader.* Ed. David Lodge. London: Longman, 1988.

Lago, Mary. *Imperfect Encounter: Letters of William Rothenstein and Rabindranath Tagore.* Cambridge, Mass.: Harvard UP, 1972.

Lefevere, André. "Translation: Its Genealogy in the West." *Translation, History, and Culture.* London: Pinter Publishers, 1990. 15–27.

Macaulay, Thomas Babbington. *Selected Writings.* Ed. with an intro. by John Clive and Thomas Pinney. Chicago: U of Chicago P, 1972.

Mukherjee, S. N. *Oriental Jones.* Cambridge: Cambridge UP, 1968.

Nandy, Ashis. *The Intimate Enemy: Loss and Recovery of Self Under Colonialism.* Oxford, Delhi: Oxford UP, 1983.

Tagore, Rabindranath. In English translation: *The Crescent Moon: Child Poems.* New York: Macmillan, 1913; *Gardener.* New York: Macmillan, 1913; *Gitanjali: Song Offerings.* London: India Society, 1912; New York: Macmillan, 1913; *Fruit Gathering.* New York: Macmillan, 1916; *The Fugitive.* New York: Macmillan, 1921; *Lover's Gift and Crossing.* New York: Macmillan, 1918. In the original Bengali: *Rabindra Rachanabali.* The centenary edition in 15 vols. Calcutta: Government of West Bengal, 1961.

———. Letter to William Winstanley Pearson. n.d. William Winstanley Pearson file. Rabindra-Bhavana Archive. Santiniketan, India.

————. Letter to Thomas Sturge-Moore. 11 June 1935. Rabindra-Bhavana
    Archive. Santiniketan, India.
Taylor, Mark. *Altarity*. Chicago: Chicago UP, 1987.
Thomson, Edward J. and Arthur Marshman Spencer. Selected and translated.
    Bengali Religious Lyrics/Sakta. London: Oxford UP, 1923.

III. Examining Translations and Cross-Cultural Encounters

This section focuses on texts in translation—on the impediments and the potential of translating between the "First" and the "Third" worlds. In "Aimé Césaire's Subjective Geographies: Translating Place and the Difference It Makes," Indira Karamcheti directs her attention to Césaire's "linguistic re-occupation of the land" and his attempt to inscribe a "Black Martinician subject matter into the dominant codes of French." Césaire's, says Karamcheti, is a "double-pronged project" that seeks to "de-exoticize" a Martinican landscape and subject rendered exotic in (French) colonial representations *and* to "re-mythologize" them by "self-consciously creating myths of origins, a genesis and a genealogy" that pits his textualization against that of the European colonizers. Such a project, she argues, runs the risk of re-inscribing the code of the exotic. Karamcheti is also concerned with translating Césaire into English, more especially with defining the "nature of translative fidelity to [his] colonizing intention." She wonders whether such linguistic transfer won't in fact end up subverting Césaire's subversive texts. By way of a "solution," she offers strategies of "opaque" translation—excessive or no translation—that "by refusing fluency can guide the reader to question the easy codes of the exotic," compelling a "reading with cognitive holes."

Like Karamcheti, Harsha Ram writes as a translator whose practice is inseparable from an effort to historicize or "spatialize" his work. The particular project that gave rise to his essay is an anthology of "Poems Beyond Russia" with poems by Mikhail Lomonosov, M. Yu. Lermontov,

177

Velimir Khlebnikov, and Gennadii Aigi. Ram's primary concern in "Translating Space: Russia's Poets in the Wake of Empire," however, is to explore the space crossed as his examples are "brought into English." He locates his translations at the conjunction of three histories: that of poetic translation in English and the overriding—and now, he believes, exhausted—preoccupation with temporality that he discerns, albeit in different ways, in Ezra Pound and Walter Benjamin; that of Russian poetry, with its "deep national-linguistic valency" and "sustained engagement in the fact of power"; that of the Caucasus and Central Asia, which, like other regions of the Russian empire, have recently become autonomous but have been characterized by "their canonical assimilations within the body of Russian literature." Through a discussion of the sublime and its manifestations in European and Russian literature, Ram outlines a spatially oriented translation by probing the gap "between language as a natural patrimony and the project of empire" he finds within the original Russian texts.

The next two essays are also concerned with exploring the "space" crossed in translation, although they are focused more concretely on the "mechanics" of specific choices and the preparation of individual translations. Amel Amin-Zaki's essay studies the changes traditionally undergone by Shakespeare's texts as his translators adapted his work to the cultural heritage and the sensibilities of Arabic readers. Based on Amin-Zaki's wide readings of translations, "Religious and Cultural Considerations in Translating Shakespeare Into Arabic" examines the ways in which Arabic translators have both compensated for their readers' unfamiliarity with Elizabethan literature and culture and adapted Shakespeare's frequently bawdy and blasphemous language so as not to offend a Muslim audience. Drawn from many plays, Amin-Zaki's examples focus primarily on the Islamization of Shakespeare's oaths and his ribald witticisms, wordplays, and puns. She also addresses changes she finds in the tolerance of current Arabic/Islamic audiences and in the work of recent Arabic translators who may have a more thorough preparation in Western literature than their predecessors, but who are less familiar with their own heritage.

Cultural sensibilities and their role in all aspects of translation are also foregrounded in "A Gift of Tamil: On Compiling an Anthology of Translations from Tamil Literature," by Paula Richman and Norman Cutler. Their discussion of the intricacies of preparing a crosscultural gift reflects on "a number of seemingly intractable problems." Transliteration practices, the issue of representation, and the question of categorization all had to be dealt with as Richman and Cutler edited an anthology of Tamil literature to honor an ailing teacher, friend, and critic "whose own life had involved moving back and forth between Indian academic culture and American academic culture." Some of the problems had to do as well with the fact that two American scholars were compiling an anthology for diversely located readers; still others arose from the need to negotiate the sometimes competing "demands" of their granting agency and the anthology's publisher—all within severe time constraints.

In "Translation, Cultural Transgression and Tribute, and Leaden Feet," Mary N. Layoun deals with specific texts in translation. Her interest, however, lies principally in the ways in which the translation that occurs within those works might offer new strategies for moving between cultures, what she calls "other notions of language." Focusing on two novels of "translation"—Etel Adnan's *Sitt Marie Rose* and Elias Khoury's *Al-jabal al-saghir/The Little Mountain*—Layoun finds that the multiple forms of translation contained in those novels encourage "other ways of thinking (and practicing) translation/carrying across." Analyzing these novels allows her to reflect on questions of gender, nationality, dominance and counter-dominance, and history and to suggest, as a teacher, that translation can prompt the learning of new languages.

Aimé Césaire's Subjective Geographies: Translating Place and the Difference It Makes

Indira Karamcheti

While France was under siege during World War II, Aimé Césaire and René Ménil produced a literary journal called *Tropiques: Revue culturelle,* from Fort-de-France, Martinique, a French colony. Under their editorship, the journal worked toward cultural and artistic decolonization, and proposed itself as an agent for the construction of a specifically Martinican, Caribbean subjectivity. Suzanne Césaire, Césaire's wife and a fiery speaker for Martinican cultural independence, contributed to its conceptualization and its production. In its pages in 1942, she lambasted the imitative, exoticized poetry of Martinique. In an article titled "Misère d'une poésie," she castigated it as deeply trivializing, deeply implicated in colonialism and commodification, calling it "literature of the hammock. Literature of sugar and vanilla. Tourism literature. . . . Not poetry." Ironically enough for an article situated in a journal titled *Tropics,* she rejected easy, familiar, stereotypical tropicalism, saying, "the hell with hibiscus, frangipani, bougainvillea. Martinican poetry will be cannibal or will not be" (my translation, 50).

The situational ironies do not end with the journal's title. I imagine the following scene supplementing Suzanne Césaire's manifesto: Immediately after denouncing by name the hibiscus, frangipani, and bougainvillea that function as metonyms for exoticism, she turns to the window to see—affronting her vision like Isabella Archer affronting her destiny—hibiscus, frangipani, and bougainvillea.

For me, this imagined scene, in its demonstrated difference between

181

speech and sight, representation and presentation, the revolutionary intention and the recalcitrance of "reality," emblematically represents the
problematic of translating place in Aimé Césaire's work. His struggle to
name and inhabit the local place—Martinique rather than a French
colony, the Caribbean rather than *outre-mer*—and to make them Black,
is conducted against the power structures inherent in language, as in all
representational systems. To move his texts from one language to another,
as translation does, entails a confrontation with yet another, perhaps
similar or related, system of representational power. Any cross-cultural
text is by definition translative; an untranslated text that announces itself
to be decolonizing in intent is doubly translative, evoking and transforming referential codes. The linguistic translation of such self-announced
decolonizing texts is enormously challenging, enormously complicated.
I hope to explore here the nature of such translation and the nature of
translative fidelity to that decolonizing intention. Focusing throughout
on Césaire's treatment of Martinican landscape, flora, and fauna, I will
first discuss the subversive nature of Césaire's cultural translation (carrying over) of Black Martinican subject matter into the dominant codes of
French. Second, I will examine the potential of translation into English,
another dominant language, to subvert Césaire's subversion.[1] Third, I
will suggest ways that an "opaque" translation can respect Césaire's subversive intentions.

Aimé Césaire's place in the genealogy of decolonization and the
genesis of negritude needs little rehearsal. His is a performative life; in
fact, his biography and canon have been constructed as one grand narrative of decolonization, resistance, and liberation. From *Discourse on
Colonialism* to *Letter to Maurice Thorez,* he has deconstructed colonial
ideologies and entered into the battle for the rights of political and
discursive self-representation. From his early epic poem, *Notebook of a
Return to the Native Land,* to the four plays which create a local, transnational history for the Black diaspora, to the collections of surrealistic
poetry that have fueled his literary production, he has been consistently
engaged in the creation of a Martinican, a Caribbean, a Black subjectivity.

Césaire's is both a deconstructive and a constructive project. Like
Suzanne Césaire, he deconstructs the cult of the exotic which transforms
the Caribbean—the place and its inhabitants—into commodities
fetishized by the European.[2] Césaire's work is simultaneously an originary
discourse, self-consciously constructing a Caribbean subject by creating
myths of origins, a genesis, and a genealogy. For Césaire, one way to

construct subjectivity is to discursively appropriate geographic place. In this, he shares an aim and a technique with other writers confronting colonialism. As Edward Said points out in "Yeats and Decolonization,"

if there is anything that radically distinguishes the imagination of anti-imperialism it is the primacy of the geographical in it. Imperialism after all is an act of geographical violence through which virtually every space in the world is explored, charted, and finally brought under control. For the native, the history of his or her colonial servitude is inaugurated by the loss to an outsider of the local place, whose concrete geographical identity must thereafter be searched for and somehow restored. (77)

Within the Caribbean, the geographic appropriation must be articulated differently. Since there was no felt historical "original" ownership of local place which was then lost to an outsider, Césaire legitimates his claim to a land whose original owners are themselves lost. He is in fact asserting his right to represent that land, to name and occupy it. As Gayatri Chakravorty Spivak puts it, he is "worlding . . . a world on a supposedly uninscribed territory" (1); that is, he is putting himself and *his* textualization in direct competition with European colonizers. In Spivak's words, "When I say this, I am thinking basically about the imperialist project which had to assume that the earth that it territorialised was in fact previously uninscribed. So then a world, on a simple level of cartography, inscribed what was presumed to be uninscribed. Now this worlding actually is also a texting, textualising, a making into art, a making into an object to be understood" (1). In claiming the right to "world," "textualize" his world, Césaire is combating the colonizers' geographic violence, their right to explore, chart, and finally bring the world under control. Said calls this desire on the part of the native to (re)claim the local place, both imaginatively and discursively, the "cartographic impulse."

From the title on, *Notebook of a Return to the Native Land* is a textbook example of the cartographic impulse, filled with subversions of exoticism, replacing tropical tropes of irresponsibility, liberty, libertinism, and expansiveness with insistent images of smallness, disease, causality. It enacts a linguistic reoccupation of the land, as critics like Michael Dash have pointed out, building an incremental mass sedimented out of the repetition of the specifics of place, from a cartographic tracing of the little road that wanders through the "inert town" to the naming of Mont Pelée, the *mornes, cecropias, bananiers, balisiers,* mangoes, and so on.[3]

Within the work, Césaire himself represents his generative project as the Adamic rite/right of naming this tropical place:

I would rediscover the secret of great communications and great combustions. I would say storm. I would say river. I would say tornado. I would say leaf. I would say tree. I would be drenched by all rains, moistened by all dews. I would roll like frenetic blood on the slow current of the eye of words turned into mad horses into fresh children into clots into curfew into vestiges of temples into precious stones remote enough to discourage miners. Whoever would not understand me would not understand any better the roaring of a tiger. (*Notebook* 43, 45)

Here, he conflates the act of naming, the spoken words, the named place, and the subject created by enunciation. His discursive claims on names and local habitation not only decolonize, but also attempt to remythologize: speaking creates place creates speaker. Césaire's narrator is a *vates* and more than *vates:* the poet is both the divine force transforming matter into subjective being and the unformed matter being infused with subjective breath. Place, speech, and being are inextricably fused. To fuse the speaker/poet/Black-Martinican subject with Martinique is, in effect, to replace Adam in Eden.

However, in his proposed construction of a specific Martinican subjectivity based on the specifics of Martinican space, Césaire runs risks particular to cross-cultural, subversive texts, risks inherent in translating, carrying across cultural matter of which the audience is ignorant. His proclaimed decolonizing intention means that he wishes to reclaim the Martinican landscape, both de-exoticizing it, and remythologizing it. On the face of it, this double-pronged action seems self-defeating. First, the desire to subvert the cult of the exotic means to make the Martinican geography ordinary, to discursively deflate it. But to remythologize means to remake it as extraordinary, legendary, discursively inflated. This is not really a contradiction, however. Rather, Césaire removes the false glamor of the exotic, which is in effect the insertion of Martinique and "Blackness" as a commodity into the exchange circuit of literary tourism. He simultaneously reglamorizes the landscape with symbolic, spiritual content. In the movement between the two, Césaire runs the specific risk of re-inscribing the code of the exotic.

Subversive representation is closely connected to translation. While it can be argued that all acts of representation are perforce acts of translation from being to saying, experience to memory, presence to absence, subversive representation is more precisely translative. Like translation, subversion is always a twice-written discourse, transforming an original text by supplementation. Like translation, subversion is always referential to another text, conceding priority, even if only chronological, to that other text, and negotiating some kind of dominant/submissive relationship with it. But unlike linguistic translation, subversion seeks to displace, replace, or deface the original text rather than seeking primarily to supplement it. Césaire desires to subvert the exotic, translating a colonial into a decolonizing discourse, rewriting one text into another, an othered, an Other's, text. His urge toward cultural and literary translation, appropriation and supplantation, is far more totalizing than linguistic translation, which retains some deference, of whatever degree, toward the priority of the original text.[4]

Linguistic translation complicates cultural translation further, threatening to subvert Césaire's subversive text, recolonizing that transformed work through the imperialistic nature of language. Jorge Klor de Alva reminds us that "language encodes power relations" and that, in the colonial context, language use is highly politicized because of the dominance of one language group over another (143). Césaire's text can subvert the dominance of metropolitan French speakers over black Francophone speakers. But translation can undo that subversion through the structures of dominance embedded in English. Because domination arms language with its own power, the desire to decolonize contends not only with the colonial desire to dominate, but with the implacable, inert force of language to signify. Language, rather than serving subversive desire, often dominates it by its signifying structures, even where these run contrary to that desire. Thus, if Césaire's text attempts to cannibalize colonial discourse, it can be cannibalized in turn by linguistic translation.[5]

One technique used by Césaire is particularly informed by the problems of translation: the enunciation of place names and the repetition of the names of local flora and fauna. In the original text, this is already a problem of translation: what names will be rendered, from Creole, for instance, into French versions; what rendered by an equivalent French term; what will remain untranslated?

We know Césaire's familiarity with Martinican place, flora, and fauna. During his early years, he was educated by Eugène Revert, a teacher who "attempted to interest his students in the peculiar geographical characteristics of Martinique at a time when standard examination questions were based on mainland French history and geography" (Eshleman and Smith 1). In his poetry, he uses that knowledge of local place: the dominance of France is contested by insisting on the presence of Martinique as a real, specific location. *Notebook of a Return to the Native Land* is filled with details about Martinique. Early in the poem, for instance, he rotates the local seasons: "After August and mango trees decked out in all their little moons, September begetter of cyclones, October igniter of sugar-cane, November who purrs in the distilleries, there came Christmas" (39). However, while this may be a description of quotidian Martinican ordinariness, it also summons up a landscape straight out of Western travel brochures. Thus, despite Césaire's intent to reclaim this landscape, the question remains whether it is possible to name without first plugging into the codes of domination and exoticism and, second, without evoking the representative power of language to render extraordinary.

According to John Searle, enunciation of ordinariness itself marks out extraordinariness. To say, to name, is also to make deviant, to remove from the "normal":

[T]o remark that [something] is standard is to suggest that its being standard is in some way remarkable, and to imply or suggest that is often, or in general, to imply or suggest that there is some reason for supposing that it might not have been standard or that the audience might need to be reminded that it is standard. . . . The point is not, "no modification without aberration," but "no remark without remarkableness." (37)

In my view, it is not only remarking on ordinariness that has the effect of making language extraordinary. Remark alone, that is, enunciation alone, makes what is enunciated extraordinary in the same way that a frame can turn an ordinary object into a work of art. Césaire's desire to make the Martinican landscape "standard" by naming place, flora, and fauna may result in, contrary to his intention, making them remarkable. To return to Suzanne Césaire and hibiscus, her renunciation of the flowers' names is one way to refuse the exotic. But the enunciation of the same names can reconstruct it. In other words, the problem is not that Suzanne Césaire, having refused hibiscus, frangipani, and bougainvillea, should be faced with their presence. Rather, the problem is that they must be named in order to be present, that is, in order for that tropical landscape to be reappropriated in Césaire's text.

I do not wish to argue the success or failure of Césaire's subversion of the exotic here. Rather, I am concerned with the problem of the translator who wishes to be faithful to Césaire's subversive desire. What license must that translator take with Césaire's text in order to respect it?

Gregory Rabassa, the translator of Gabriel García Márquez and other Latin American writers, discusses "this problem that arises when an environment that is commonplace in one culture becomes exotic in the other" in "If This Be Treason":

I recall that the Peruvian novelist Mario Vargas Llosa was concerned that the English translation of his novel *The Green House,* which I was working on, would give an exotic tone to what in Peru was commonplace. He was worried about the names of flora and fauna that have no translation, since they do not exist in English-speaking countries and no Anglo-Saxon Adam had passed through to give them lexical identity. . . . The Peruvian trees remained with their aboriginal names, for, as I explained to the author, many commonplace aspects of Peru are, per se, exotic to the outsider. If a novel is universal, the universality should not be hindered by the strange. . . . So the transfer of the ordinary from one culture to another is apt to be another impossibility of translation. (24–25)

However, such acceptance of exoticism and the impossibility of transferring the ordinary would be specifically at odds with Césaire's texts. But leaving the Peruvian trees with their "aboriginal names" can have an effect quite other than Rabassa allows. Rather than just stressing Peru's "strangeness" and "exoticism," enough "aboriginal" or at least untranslated names can direct the reader's attention to the translation itself. This can help the translator who wishes to respect Césaire's desire to make the Martinican landscape ordinary and to make it universal.

Traditionally, translation has posited "*accurate rendering* of an original" as its goal (Jackson 82).[6] To be "accurate" in terms of Césaire's texts would mean to de-exoticize the landscape and simultaneously mythologize it. The ideal has been an "invisible" translator and a translation which reads so fluently as to give the impression of having been written originally in the target language. Lawrence Venuti argues against both invisibility and fluency, advocating instead what he calls "resistant" translation, one which makes the reader constantly aware that he or she is reading a translation, a text shaped by the translator's choices. The problem of translating place in Césaire, it seems to me, can be handled by a similar kind of opaque translation, which by refusing fluency can guide the reader to question the easy codes of the exotic.

Since Césaire uses enunciation—the incantatory repetition of naming as a subversive technique—the translator, too, can manipulate enunciation in the text. The translation can refuse to translate, be silent, not enunciate—that is, leave the trees with their aboriginal names. It can also name excessively, provide an excess of translation. Both insufficient and excessive translation, through their very opaqueness, refusing to allow the reader to forget that this is a translation, can effectively foreground the ordinariness and the otherness of place, subvert the colonizing power of language, and accurately render Césaire's movement between de-exoticization and reglamorization.

The operation of insufficient translation, or not-naming, the refusal to translate, may best be demonstrated by a specific instance of enunciation and translative silence. We know that Césaire studied and knew a great deal about the flora and fauna particular to the Caribbean. In fact, the February 1944 edition of *Tropiques* published two articles discussing this subject: E. Nonon's "La faune précolombienne des Antilles françaises" and Henri Stehlé's "Les dénominations génériques des végétaux aux Antilles françaises. Histoires et légendes qui s'y rattachent." Some representative names from these two articles include: *balaous, coulirous, titiris, orphie*. If animals and plants are commonplace to readers of the English translation, then there is no enunciatory problem, but then they are not particular to the Martinican landscape. One possibility for translation is to anglicize names, as in transforming *genipa* into *genipap*. What the act of enunciation does here is to establish *genipa* as remarkable, as exotic, by attempting to standardize it into a more English-sounding form. What is the effect of leaving such words untranslated? While this may at first seem to insert the exotic in very obvious ways into the text, in fact not-naming, silencing translation has a different kind of effect. Nontranslation establishes these names, *balaous, coulirous,* as the original and only names. *Not* remarking on the names through translation means that their ordinariness remains uncontested; silence, nonenunciation, renders them standard, unremarkable. Not-naming, silence in translation, can be powerfully subversive. Consider the effect of the nontranslation in the following poem, "Barbarity":

> This is the word that sustains me
>
> . . . .
>
> Barbarity
> the single article

> barbarity the tapaya
> barbarity the white amphisbaena
> barbarity I the spitting cobra
> awakening from my putrefying flesh
> suddenly a flying gecko
> suddenly a fringed gecko
> and I adhere so well to the very loci of strength
> that to forget me you must
> cast the hairy flesh of your chests to the dogs.
> (Eshleman and Smith 213)[7]

Or this speech by Ariel in *A Tempest*:

Tree! One of those words that exalts me! I've often thought about it: Palm! Like a fuse, rising into a nonchalance where swims the elegance of the octopus! Baobab! The sweetness of the entrails of monsters! Ask the calao bird who cloistered herself there one season. Ceiba! Deployed in the fierce sun! Bird! The talons planted in the quick of the earth! (10–11)[8]

The refusal to translate words like *tapaya*, *calao*, or *ceiba* is particularly powerful in "worlding" the Martinican landscape because that refusal stresses that they are proper names. Derrida makes the point that proper names do not "properly belong to the language" (172). A noun can be translated (*pierre*) but proper names cannot (*Pierre*). The untranslated names of these flora and fauna show their utter linguistic ordinariness: these are the only names; there are no others (translation always implies the idea of the linguistic alias). But at the same time, because the names are unknown, they stress the otherness of the place. That otherness may be taken as potent, powerful mythologizing or as a falling back into exoticism: this is the same risk taken by Césaire's original text.

Silence in translation can also take the form of not-translating words for which equivalents or cognates do exist in English. In *Et les chiens se taisaient* (*And the Dogs Stopped Barking*), the central character is a sacrificial, deified epic hero named only "the Rebel." When his mother faints, he bends over her body and says,

> Woman, your face is more worn than pumice rolled by the river
> much more, much more,
> your fingers are more tired than cane crushed by the mill,
> much more, much more.

The next line offers the translator a choice:

> Oh, your hands are shredded bagasse,
>   much more, much more

or

> Oh, your hands are shredded sugar cane pulp,
>   much more, much more.

(And the Dogs 49)[9]

To translate *bagasse* as "sugar cane pulp" not only disrupts the high poetic timbre of the speech, but also introduces an almost ethnographic note. While it is possible to translate *bagasse*, it is not possible to do so without remark.

What is lost or gained by refusing translation here? Information about the vocabulary of sugar production is suppressed—but this is in any case irrelevant or disruptive. More, it directs attention away from the mother and son relationship and toward the idea of Black women working in sugar cane fields—an image whose power diffuses the emphasis on the Rebel. "Meaning" is also lost; *bagasse* moves from referential signifier to nonreferential sign: it, like pumice rolled by the river, cane crushed by the mill, points to the Rebel's love and pity for his mother and his recognition of the extent of her use and abuse by the world. The loss of information is a gain in faithfulness to the text.

Insufficient translation results in a kind of naturalization of the foreign, if not a pure "transfer of the ordinary," to use Rabassa's phrase. It also causes a kind of reading that is the opposite of "fluent": a slow, almost stumbling reading that pauses, puzzles, and, unsatisfied, must move on—a reading with cognitive holes in it. Excessive translation or overly naming can also be a powerfully subversive technique. If translative silence refuses to allow nonstandard status by not remarking (and so making remarkable), translating the same thing repeatedly suggests not so much irreducible foreignness, otherness—although it does that, too—as it does the inadequacy of translation itself. The name, the place, and so on, are not necessarily "naturalized," standardized; translation, how-ever, *is* marked as an unnatural act; it is revealed as unable to transform one text or word into another smoothly, invisibly, unremarkedly. The self-reflexivity of surplus translation, by remarking upon itself, enunciates itself as remarkable. One example of surplus translation might be a disruption of the text with a catalogue of possible translating options. The word *quinquiliba,* for instance, could be rendered by more than a single equivalent; other possible names for it are: zépiante, herbe puante, café marron, caroubier de l'Inde, capalier, casse puante, pois puant, café nègre, café bâtard. Translated into English, the catalogue nature of such a translation remarks upon the fact of translation.

In addition, glossaries, appendices, endnotes, footnotes, and translator remarks all function as excessive translation. With a writer as erudite and deliberately esoteric as Césaire, such extratextual apparatus seems to be desperately needed. For example, Eshleman and Smith bracket their elegant translation of his collected poetry with an introduction that includes translators' notes before the translated poems and notes after them. They do not disrupt the smooth reading of the poems themselves with any excessive apparatus like footnotes. Rather, discreet asterisks appear beside lines where a word or phrase is more fully explained in the notes. If readers wish to know that fuller explanation immediately, they must turn to the endnotes, surely a more disrupting interpolation than footnotes. If readers choose the "fluent" reading offered by this translation, they can read without knowledge, for the sound or for the contextual sense. Thus, this particular translation offers either the fluent reading or the stumbling one, the reading with cognitive holes.

The Présence Africaine 1970 edition of *La tragédie du Roi Christophe* presents another possibility, one answering to Césaire's cultural translation. Occasional pages contain footnotes explaining creole expressions. Page 24 is the most interesting:

Marchande: Rapadou (1)! Rapadou! Par ici pour tout ce qu'un homme peut désirer. Tafia! Clairin. Tabac en boulons (2)! Tabac en andouilles (3)! Viande en aiguillettes! Tassau (4)! Tassau!
(S'addressant à Hugonin.)
Du rapadou, Papa? ou du tassau?
Hugonin: Dis donc la belle, ce n'est pas du rapadou que je veux, c'est de toi, doudou! Pas de tassau! Te donner l'assaut, ma doudou!
Marchande: Mal élevé! Polisson! Messieurs, par ici pour l'akassan! Akassan! Akassan (5)!
Hugonin: L'agaçant, ce n'est pas ton akassan, c'est autre chose qui me remue le sang.
Marchande: Vaurien! Goujat! Police, police, à moi!

---

(1) Rapadou: sucre de canne grossier.
(2) Boulons: feuilles de tabac tordues.

(3) Andouilles: feuilles de tabac local pressé dans de longues *tâches,* pédoncules désséchées du tronc de palmier.
(4) Tassau: de l'espagnol *tasajo:* viande coupée en aiguillettes.
(5) Akassan: bouillie de maïs.

Here is the translation:

Market Woman: Rapadou!(1) Jaggery! Look here for all a man can desire! Tafia! Light rum! Tobacco twist!(2) Tobacco sausage,(3) meat jerky! Tasso! Tasso!(4)
(addressing Hugonin)
Hey daddy, like brown sugar? Like some jerky?
Hugonin: Listen, sweetie, it's not sugar I want; it's you, honey! Not a piece of jerky! A jerk of your piece, love!
Market Woman: You dirty boy, you! Little rascal! Come, this way, gentlemen, if you want some warm corn mush.
Hugonin: It's not porridge that heats me up; it's something else that's got me cooking.
Market Woman: Scoundrel! Scamp! Help, Police, Police!

---

(1) *Rapadou:* unrefined cane sugar, jaggery.
(2) *Tabac en boulons:* tobacco leaves twisted together.
(3) *Tabac en andouilles:* locally grown tobacco leaves rolled and pressed tightly together, with the appearance of andouilles sausages.
(4) *Tassau:* from the Spanish *tasajo:* meat cut into small pieces.
(5) *Akassan:* corn meal porridge.

The presence of footnotes—and several of them at that—has an interesting effect. Not only do they work against invisibility and fluency, they set up, as Shari Benstock explains, a place to question "authority in fiction" (205) and actively engage the reader in the text. This kind of surplus translation can serve Césaire's subversive purposes by preventing fluency, by not allowing the reader to accept the exotic easily. By setting up alternative ways of speaking, of telling the story on the same page, excessive translation distances the reader from the narrative, focusing instead on the fact of translation. This reminds us that what is extraordinary to us is ordinary to others—this landscape, its plants, products, and people are not different in some absolute sense, only in relation to what we, as foreign readers, don't know.

Of course, opaque translation, either in its insufficient or its excessive forms is not the only way to remain faithful to a subversive text; it is, however, one effective way of maintaining faith by taking license. Both the refusal to translate and the overeagerness to translate are useful in that they faithfully adhere to the subversiveness of Césaire's project. As his texts attempt to resist the domination of the exotic, opaque translation resists the naturalizing impulse of linguistic transformation. The traditionally desired invisible, transparent translation of the original text misreads, replaces, and displaces that text—erases it, in fact. But an opaque translation, drawing attention to its own presence in the text, foregrounds the difference between original and reproduction. This is a self-reflexive translation, a thick translation, drawing attention to its own presence and the ideological nature of translation as a colonizing act. In its opacity, silent and excessive translation can be appropriately resistant for Césaire's narratives of resistance.

Notes

1. Linguistic translation into English also presupposes, for the purposes of this paper, cultural translation for an audience unfamiliar with the Caribbean landscape, fauna, and flora.

2. Some critics would argue that Césaire, far from combating the exotic, reinscribes it. Rather than arguing the effectiveness of Césaire's project, I would rather focus on the ways his texts work with and against exoticism, both wishing to de-exoticize (make ordinary), and to create mythic stature, which may re-exoticize. Of course, the problem of the exotic is only one part of Césaire's project to re-center Martinican subjectivity.

3. In "Le cri du morne," J. Michael Dash convincingly shows the centrality of the Martinican landscape, especially the upthrust mornes and the volcanic Mont Pelée. Clayton Eshleman and Annette Smith, the translators of *Aimé Césaire: The Collected Poetry*, remark on the omnipresence and the thematic importance of Césaire's use of Martinican place names, as well as the names of flora and fauna, in their introduction. They also discuss the difficulty of translating them in their translators' notes:

Let us pass quickly over the large number of rare and technical words (there exist quantitative and qualitative analyses of them), which keep the translator bent over various encyclopedias, dictionaries of several languages (including African and Creole), botanical indexes, atlases, and history texts. If he is fortunate enough to identify the object, then he has to decide to what extent the esoteric tone of the poetry should be respected in the English. Dispatching the reader to the reference shelf at every turn in order for him to find out that the object of his chase is nothing more than a morning glory (convolvulus) or a Paraguayan peccary ("patyura") hardly encourages a sustained reading. Here, again, a delicate balance must be maintained between a rigorously puristic stand and a systematic vulgarization. The case of plant names is especially complex, as one must be wary to betray neither Césaire's use of vegetable forms as a symbol of black culture nor his concrete interest in Caribbean flora demonstrated in *Tropiques*. (26)

4. This can be seen very clearly in his *A Tempest*, which claims to be an "adaptation" of Shakespeare's play for a black theater, but so incorporates what it adapts that it permanently changes the understanding of the original. Césaire's history plays also demonstrate this desire to supplant, rather than supplement. As Shakespeare does for England, Césaire creates the histories chronicling the development of the "Black nation" through its epic heroes, Christophe and Lumumba.

5. That language is a category highly resistant to social change has been much discussed by, among others, the French feminists. Their concern with the recalcitrance of language to change, and the ways it "speaks" in ways contrary to the intentions of the speaker informs much of this discussion. Césaire and other Caribbean and African writers prior to and involved in the negritude movement also wrote about this question of language in many ways. For Césaire, as he has said in interviews and articles published in, for example, *Tropiques*, the French language was the only possible language for literature; he did not consider Creole weighty enough. But he also declared his desire to *marroner* the French language, to escape it, to subvert it, to distort it.

6. See also Bassnett-McGuire, who assumes the ideal of invisible, fluent translation. To achieve this goal, she argues for "equivalence," even where this seriously (in my view) distorts the historical context of both the source language and the target language. In one example, she approvingly cites Tony Harrison's translation of *Phèdre, Phaedra Brittanica* (produced in 1976). Harrison substitutes colonial India for Greece, creating a translation Bassnett-McGuire finds well adapted for production in contemporary theater:

And just as *Phèdre* deals with the coming together of disparate world systems—the passions of a doomed house and a world of order and rationality, in this vision of colonial India two similar worlds come into contact: the world of English order, so helpless in its new context, and the forces of darkness, typified by an alien culture in revolt against the colonizers. (127)

That India may not be "the forces of darkness" simply does not matter here.

In another example, seemingly contradictory to the above, Basnett-McGuire cites Ben Belitt's translation of Pablo Neruda's *Fulgor y muerte de Joaquín Murieta*, which renders speech in very colloquial Americanisms. Bassnett-

McGuire disapproves on the grounds that the "translator has altered the ideological basis of the text through over-emphasis of extralinguistic criteria—in this case, according to Belitt's own preface, the expectations of the American audience" (124). Venuti argues against her position convincingly in "The Translator's Invisibility." Of course, Harrison's use of India as an easily available symbol of the "forces of darkness" also distorts the ideological basis of *Phèdre*. Both Harrison's and Belitt's decisions are influenced by ideology and are attempts to find equivalence relations. Invisibility of translation seems most possible if the ideology of the translator agrees with that of the reader/viewer. The desire for fluency can lead into dangerous ideological waters.

  7. In French:

BARBARE

                 C'est le mot qui me soutient.

                 . . . .

                 Barbare
                 l'article unique
                 barbare le tapaya
                 barbare l'amphisbène blanche
                 barbare moi le serpent cracheur
                 qui de mes putréfiantes chairs me réveille
                 soudain gekko volant
                 soudain gekko frangé
                 et me colle si bien aux lieux même de la force
                 qu'il vous faudra pour m'oublier
                 jeter aux chiens la chair velue de vos poitrines
                                            (Eshleman and Smith 212)

  8. In French:

Arbre, un des mots qui m'exaltent! J'y ai pensé souvent: Palmier! Fusant très haut une nonchalance où nage une élégance de poulpe. Baobab! Douceur d'entrailles des monstres! Demande-le plutôt à l'oiseau calao qui s'y claustre une saison. Ceiba! Éployé au soleil fier! Oiseau! Les serres plantées dans le vif de la terre! (Césaire, *Une Tempête* 23)

  9. The original reads:

                 Femme, ton visage est plus usé que la pierre
                        ponce roulée par la rivière
                 beaucoup, beaucoup,

> tes doigts sont plus fatigués que la canne broyée
>   par le moulin,
> beaucoup, beaucoup,
> Oh, tes mains sont de bagasse fripée, beaucoup,
>   beaucoup.   (*Et les chiens* 72)

The translation by Eshleman and Smith, *And the Dogs Were Silent*, reads:

> Woman, your face is more worn than a pumice stone
>   tumbled along by a river
> utterly, utterly,
> your fingers are more fatigued than cane crushed
>   by the mill,
> utterly, utterly,
> Oh, your hands are crumpled bagasse, utterly,
>   utterly.   (41)

Works Cited

Bassnett-McGuire, Susan. *Translation Studies.* London: Methuen, 1980.

Benstock, Shari. "At the Margins of Discourse: Footnotes in the Fictional Text." *PMLA* 98. 2 (March 1983): 204–25.

Césaire, Aimé. *Aimé Césaire, The Collected Poetry.* Trans. Clayton Eshleman and Annette Smith. Berkeley: U of California P, 1983.

———. *And the Dogs Stopped Barking.* Trans. Indira Karamcheti and Gérard Georges Pigeon. Unpublished ms., 1990.

———. *And the Dogs Were Silent. Lyric and Dramatic Poetry: 1946–82.* Trans. Clayton Eshleman and Annette Smith. Charlottesville: The UP of Virginia, 1990. 1–74.

———. *Et les chiens se taisaient.* Paris: Présence Africaine, 1956.

———. "Notebook of a Return to the Native Land." *Aimé Césaire, The Collected Poetry.* Trans. Clayton Eshleman and Annette Smith. Berkeley and Los Angeles: U of California P, 1983. 35–85.

———. *La tragédie du Roi Christophe.* Paris: Présence Africaine, 1963, reissued 1970.

———. *The Tragedy of King Christophe.* Trans. Indira Karamcheti and Gérard Georges Pigeon. Unpublished ms.

———. *A Tempest.* Trans. Gérard Georges Pigeon and Indira Karamcheti. Unpublished ms., 1990.

———. *Une Tempête.* Paris: Éditions du Seuil, 1969.

——— and René Ménil, eds. *Tropiques: Revue culturelle.* Nos. 1–13/14 (April 1941–Sept. 1945). Rpt. Paris: Jean-Michel Place, 1978.

Césaire, Suzanne. "Une Misère d'une poésie." *Tropiques* 4 (Janvier 1942): 48–50. Rpt. 1978.

Dash, J. Michael. "Le cri du morne: Le poétique du paysage Césairien et la littérature Antillaise." *Soleil éclaté: Mélanges offerts à Aimé Césaire à l'occasion de son soixante-dixième anniversaire par une équipe internationale d'artistes et de chercheurs.* Ed. Jacqueline Leiner. Tubingen: Gunter Narr Verlag, 1984. 101–10.

Derrida, Jacques. "Des tours de Babel." Trans. Joseph F. Graham. *Difference in Translation.* Ed. Joseph F. Graham. Ithaca, N.Y.: Cornell UP, 1985. 165–207.

Eshleman, Clayton and Annette Smith. "Introduction." *Aimé Césaire: The Collected Poetry.* Trans. Clayton Eshleman and Annette Smith. Berkeley: U of California P, 1983. 1–28.

Jackson, Thomas H. "Theorizing Translation." *SubStance* 64 (1991): 80–89.

Klor de Alva, Jorge. "Language, Politics, and Translation." *The Art of Translation.* Ed. Rosanna Warren. Boston: Northeastern UP, 1989. 143–62.

Neruda, Pablo. *Splendor and Death of Joaquín Murieta.* Trans. Ben Belitt. New York: Farrar, Strauss & Giroux, 1972.

Nonon, E. "La faune précolombienne des Antilles françaises." *Tropiques* 10 (Février 1944): 45–52.

Rabassa, Gregory. "If This Be Treason: Translation and Its Possibilities." *Translation: Literary, Linguistic, and Philosophical Perspectives.* Ed. William Frawley. Newark: U of Delaware P, 1984. 21–29.

Said, Edward W. "Yeats and Decolonization." *Nationalism, Colonialism, and Literature.* Minneapolis: U of Minnesota P, 1990. 69–95.

Searle, John. *Speech Acts.* London: Cambridge UP, 1969.

Spivak, Gayatri Chakravorty. "Criticism, Feminism, and the Institution." *The Postcolonial Critic.* Ed. Sara Harasym. New York: Routledge, 1990. 1–16.

Stehlé, Henri. "Les dénominations génériques des végétaux aux Antilles françaises. Histoires et légendes qui s'y rattachent." *Tropiques* 10 (Février 1944): 53–87.

Venuti, Lawrence. "The Translator's Invisibility." *Criticism* 28. 2 (Spring 1986): 179–212.

Translating Space: Russia's Poets in the Wake of Empire

Harsha Ram

How does poetry meet history? If the rhythms of empire and decolonization have provided a scansion for the modern era, how, if at all, might they impinge on the opacities of the poetic craft? I pose these questions, strangely enough, in response to the crisis in what was once the Soviet Union. The recent and spectacular implosion of the Soviet state and the concurrent decolonization of Central Asia, Eastern Europe, and the Baltic states provoked in me the desire to translate. From the coarse-edged grandeur of the eighteenth-century poets Derzhavin and Lomonosov and the alienated lyricism of Lermontov to the modernist densities of Mandel'shtam and Khlebnikov, the poets of Russia have spoken to me for much of my adult life. In search of a language adequate to the events that swept the Soviet Union, I began in 1991 to translate Russian poetry.

The reflections that follow are themselves a translation. They try to reformulate the translator's "gut feelings" as a properly critical response, negotiating between the local triumphs and failures of intuition and a broader attempt to historicize or—as will become clearer—*spatialize* the translator's enterprise. To encounter a poem is always to confront the intimacies of history and literary form; to translate it is to register the subtler dislocations of culture that insinuate themselves into language and its voices. My own struggle in this regard has been at least twofold: to seek out in the poetry of Lomonosov, Pushkin, Lermontov, Khlebnikov, and Aigi precedents that anticipate and articulate Russia's ongoing transformation and to situate this sense of change in the English lan-

199

guage. This translation of cultural moments—English and Russian in a densely global present—is the occasion for what follows.

Trans-latio, we know, is etymologically a *carrying across:* if the term's erosion suggests the banality (if not the ease), today, of cross-cultural encounter, does the act of translating still evince something of this primordial crossing as a space to be explored? And could this complex formal movement in turn evoke something of the wider displacements that have marked our era: the reterritorializing forces of conquest, the peripheralization of vast areas and peoples and the waves of migration following in its wake?

Certainly even the routine difficulties of translation force us to discard the fantasy that language might be transparent to other languages or to the world "at large." Yet *trans-latio* suggests the subtler possibility of intimating historical change in the very movement of language; the task of the translator might then be to elicit and highlight a spatial idiom already intrinsic to poetry and which in turn allows it to bear unique witness to imperial histories.

To translate poetry, I would suggest, is to work out within a privileged register the very historical questions which arise when translation occurs in the wider sense as the interpretive burden of transcultural encounter, but where, muffled by daily interaction and the abstractions of exchange-value, it is seldom posed in the full density and difficulty of language. If imperialism can be taken as a constitutive if not the exclusive condition of cultural crossing, then the problem of translating a foreign lyric mode becomes one of registering a spiral of forces. These forces are the complexities of indirection that allow the lyric to be an oblique yet resonant locus of historical violence, forces that must be located and remobilized within the uncanny doubling that any translation performs. Whereas an original poem all too often repatriates the fact of power—which is equally the power of and over language—for a national literary tradition, a translation relocates political and poetic force as an encounter *between* entities: nations, languages, structures, and their agents.

The disintegration of the Soviet Union and the emergence, in its place, of a cluster of tentative national polities including Russia are events crucial to today's global politics. Despite the poetic precedents of Aimé Césaire or Pablo Neruda as well as the recent theorizations of colonial discourse, the collapse of this the last classically territorial empire appears remote from the dilemma of poetic language. The shock of this juxtaposition, however, is perhaps an effect of our own disciplinary laziness: while imperialism has been thought primarily through the already "classical" examples of France and Britain, Russian literature owes its currency abroad to a different if related pathos, the martyrologies of Russian culture that have pitted Pushkin, Pasternak, or Solzhenitsyn against the Kremlin.

A history of Russia's literatures of empire in the wake of decolonization is still to be written; more immediate is the task of contemplating the collapse of the Soviet Union, in its suddenness and its historical depth, as an event for translation. I began to translate a series of poems from Russian into English under the provisional title "Poems Beyond Russia." The title stuck just as the collection grew; if I have played nurse to its progress the project and its name appear to me less as a personal choice than as the meeting—and translation—of at least three histories:

(1) The history of poetry translation in English as an escalating form of international culture which, through the exemplary figures of Ezra Pound and—more recently if in a different way—Walter Benjamin, has circulated as a paradigmatic case of a global if fragmented modernity,

(2) The history of Russian poetry itself as a tradition with a deep national-linguistic valency as well as a sustained engagement in the fact of power,

(3) The history of the Caucasus and Central Asia (among other regions of the Russian empire) as newly autonomous configurations, in their past as two of Russia's imperial playgrounds and through their canonical assimilations within the body of Russian literature.

Translating Time

The historicity of the English-language translator should not be psychologized too hastily as a personal investment. A translator's personal taste and poetic culture are dwarfed by the wider phenomenon of the internationalization of English. The now global dimension of the English language should always remain a problem of and for translation; yet the loss of a defining center in Anglophone literary culture has, regrettably, often been resolved in the terms we have inherited from Anglo-American and European modernism.

The ascendancy of Ezra Pound in the theory and practice of poetic translation is a case in point. Pound dissolved the false options of parochial modernization and historical fidelity in favor of an absolute but estranging sense of the contemporary: where Pound strove to reshape the original, then, it was not for the sake of increased familiarity. The range of Pound's response was vast: if his renderings of Guido Cavalcanti and the Provençal troubadors are beguilingly meticulous in their attention to rhyme sequences and verbal archaisms, Pound's translations of the Chinese suggest a more radical collapsing of lexical registers and formal markers: here the historical accretions of English are pulverized and reorganized into smaller units, isolated image-phrases devoid of meter and rhyme, much like the prosodic revolution that Pound's own poetry was to achieve. A generic modernism has become, after Pound, the routinized if often highly productive stance of poetry translation in English, even in its furthest cultural reach: we need think only of A. K. Ramanujan's translations from the Tamil and Kannada or Peter Lamborn Wilson's recent renderings of Persian Sufi lyrics.

If the reverberations of Pound's practical legacy are still being felt, the great theoretical models of modernism in translation, such as Ernest Fenollosa's *The Chinese Written Character as a Medium for Poetry* and Benjamin's "The Task of the Translator," read today like brilliantly suggestive anachronisms. These manifestos of modernist sensibility in language succeed in yoking a translator's radical intuition of the foreign to an experience of time that we can no longer call our own. This experience is a lived sense of sheer flux, the acceleration of elapsing time that may or may not shatter into the instants that compose and over-whelm it. Modernist time is this flow in all its permutations: what Fenollosa celebrates Benjamin will reject as a viable temporalizing of language. In both cases the foreignness of interlinguistic crossing is meditated upon as the *temporality* of translation.

What is it about time, modernist time, that once functioned as a measure of cross-cultural encounter? If modernism was coeval with the heyday of European imperialism, how might the time of translation have served to condense the dislocations of imperial history into a hesitation between sheer flux and the messianic hope of a discontinuous moment that is filled, in Benjamin's words, "by the presence of the Now"? These were the options for translation represented, in turn, by Fenollosa and Benjamin.

The Chinese Written Character as a Medium for Poetry stands as a significant monument of modernist orientalism; written by Ernest

Fenollosa, it was edited and published posthumously in his name by Ezra Pound in 1920. Much as historical linguistics and its revelation of the Indo-European family served as the scholarly apparatus for Western romanticism, Fenollosa's observations on Chinese writing, however philologically discredited, buttressed Pound's own poetic program. This episode in modernist poetics interests us for its intersection of concerns: the relevance of Chinese writing, Fenollosa suggests, lies in its "throwing light upon our forgotten mental processes" (21), in its vindication of the temporal basis of language which European culture, through its grammatical formalism and elaborate syntax, has lost. If all poetry is, for Fenollosa, "time-art" (6), the Chinese ideogram returns us to the original temporality of language:

A true noun, an isolated thing, does not exist in nature. Things are only the terminal points, or rather the meeting points, of actions, cross-sections cut through actions, snap-shots. Neither can a pure verb, an abstract motion, be possible in nature. The eye sees noun and verb as one: things in motion, motion in things, and so the Chinese conception tends to represent them. . . . The truth is that acts are successive, even continuous; one causes or passes into another. And though we may string ever so many clauses into a single compound sentence, motion leaks everywhere, like electricity from an exposed wire. (10–11)

Fenollosa's conception of time is, of course, Bergsonian and he rediscovers Bergson's *élan vital* in Chinese syntax. Time is the thrust of active movement, and language finds its authentic voice in reproducing this ineluctable order of sheer succession. An astonishing reversal of Hegel who had dismissed the Chinese ideogram as pure space, Fenollosa's vision of Chinese time finally remains, like Hegel's, compensatory.[1] The vitalism of Chinese poetry is the translator's antidote to the accelerating abstraction of European time: the struggles of organized labor over work-time, the Italian futurist notion of *velocità* and the hypertrophy of memory in high modernism (we need think only of Proust's *Recherche*, Osip Mandel'shtam's *Tristia* or Giuseppe Ungaretti's *Sentimento del tempo*) all share a common apprehension of older rhythms disintegrating into the alienated passage of random moments.

This compensatory link between Chinese and European time is for Fenollosa the temporality of translation itself. Translation occurs, in Fenollosa, as the passage, through syntax, of *force:* "All truth has to be expressed in sentences because all truth is the *transference of power.*" Language is primordially nothing more than the transitive force that passes from subject to object—"farmer pounds rice," "man sees horse"—and which moves just as easily, we are told, from Chinese to English. English, like Chinese, lacks grammatical inflection: this "likeness of form . . . renders translation from one to another exceptionally easy" (Fenollosa's emphasis; 12, 16).

Fenollosa's peculiar accomplishment is to have located in the putative structure of Chinese writing a formal homology for American imperial encroachment; indeed, this contextualization begins the essay as its premise:

Vistas of strange futures unfold for man, of world-embracing cultures half-weaned from Europe, of hitherto undreamed responsibilities for nations and races.

    The Chinese problem is so vast that no nation can afford to ignore it. We in America, especially, must face it across the Pacific, and master it or it will master us. And the only way to master it is to strive with patient sympathy to understand the best, the most hopeful and the most human elements in it. (3–4)

For America, a potentially global force "half-weaned from Europe," translation is necessarily a mode of appropriation. The translator situates him- or herself as a conduit in this desire for mastery, rechanneling the vital forces of Chinese culture into an analogous English form. Hesitating between the humanistic premise of empathy and a more menacing call for imperial mastery, the translator finally discovers the appropriate idiom for transcultural contact in the ascendant discourse of modernist time.

Walter Benjamin's "The Task of the Translator" (1923), written not long after Fenollosa's article, reached the English-speaking world much later—appropriately enough, in a translation the validity of which has, in turn, become a source of controversy. A densely obscure text that questions many of the existing folk-theoretical premises of translation, "The Task of the Translator" owes much of its recent currency to its role as a transitional text. It anticipates, I would suggest, a shift from an older modernist poetics in which an alienated self meets an exoticized and reified other to more recent postmodern debates on translation in which the primacy of language, however understood, has eclipsed the drama of the historical subject, and difference appears ontologically prior to the social world.

To explore the import of this shift as well as the fecund misreadings that have made Benjamin its emblem is beyond the scope of this essay. What interests me in Benjamin is precisely what he reveals of the modernist culture that he still shared, however remotely, with Fenollosa and Pound. "The Task of the Translator" resonates as part of a lifelong search for alternative categories through which to think time: Benjamin's recourse to heterodox Marxism, kabbalistic mysticism, and romantic oriental philology are, if eclectic, consonant with the skepticism he nurtured, and which intensified with the onset of fascism, toward all official forms of historicism. The boldness of his recourse to mystical speculation can be understood as an attempt to work through his despair at the homogenizing chronologies of progress and the crudity of clockwork time.

Translating Baudelaire, one suspects, was for Benjamin yet another form of guerilla warfare against the assumptions of historicist culture. Like Fenollosa's article on Chinese writing, "The Task of the Translator" is an attempt to theorize translation as an alternative temporality of language. At stake is the nature of a translation's relationship to its original: For Benjamin their link is a *temporal* conundrum that he models according to the paradigms of scriptural meaning and messianic history. Benjamin's spirituality is never simply nostalgic (if nostalgia is ever simple); it is deployed, rather, as a considered anachronism that allows him to think outside the range of both natural-organic and cumulative, humanistic time. Translation, for Benjamin, is always belated, a *Fortleben* or life-after-death of the original:

For a translation comes later than the original, and since significant works never find their chosen translators at the time of their origin, their translation signifies the stage of their afterlife. . . . In translation the original rises to a higher and purer linguistic air, as it were . . . in a singularly impressive manner, it at least points the way to this region: the realm, predestined and denied, of the reconciliation and fulfillment of languages. (58, 62)[2]

The temporal tardiness of translation is, however, also a kind of anticipation: the encounter between languages is finally their consummation into the "one, true language." If Benjamin's project can be seen as a kind of linguistic eschatology, then its structure of hope is nonetheless no longer defined by the meaning of the divine. In the Holy Writ, says Benjamin, "meaning (*der Sinn*) has ceased to be the watershed for the flow of language and the flow of revelation"; hence, the preponderance, in successful translations, of syntax over sense. If there is anything resembling a prescriptive rather than a speculative poetics in Benjamin, it stems from this translation of the structure of eschatological time into a kind of pure signifier rather than a signified: the good translator rediscovers this structure not in the *meaning* of the original but through a "literalist approach to syntax" (69, 65 [82, 79]).

Benjamin's poetics of translation shares much with Fenollosa's. To be sure, Benjamin's speculative scaffolding is subtler and far from the vitalist pretensions of Fenellosa's pseudolinguistics. In both, however, a privileging of syntax over meaning coincides with a metaphysics of time, and the resulting paradigm, I would suggest, constitutes the defining limits of high modernist theories of translation.

Are these, today, our limits? For the culture of metropolitan modernism, translation—both narrowly textual and broadly transcultural—provided a kind of alternative and compensatory time irreducible to the simpler chronologies of the clock and calendar. What remained untheorized (if secretly present) in the idiom of modernist time was the intransigence, the refractory nature, of transcultural space. Our distance from European modernism might then be measured in a new imperative for translation: to discover the timeliness of a poem as its space. The act of translating must elicit the situatedness of both languages at play: if the Romantic and modernist moments in Western Europe and Russia evolved their own shifting sense of the foreign, these sensibilities must be rendered within the emergent global spatialization of English. Such a premise is not another call for translator's license; indeed, it suggests a greater vigilance toward the formal markers of space that situated the original poem from within but which the temporalizing rhetoric of the modernist era has obscured.

A highly visible instance, in global English, of this nascent spatial idiom is Salman Rushdie. In one of the Sternian asides that pepper the narrative of *Shame*, Rushdie reflects:

When individuals come unstuck from their native land, they are called migrants. When nations do the same thing the act is called secession . . . we have come unstuck from more than land. *We have floated upwards from history, from memory, from Time.*

I may be such a person. Pakistan may be such a country.

It is well known that the term "Pakistan," an acronym, was originally thought up in England by a group of Muslim intellectuals. . . . *So it was a word born in exile which then went East, was borne-across, trans-lated, and imposed itself upon history; a returning migrant, settling down on partitioned land, forming a palimpsest upon the past.* (91, emphasis added)

After the exilic pathos of decolonization and migration has been lived out, the burgeoning new constituencies of a loosely Anglophone world rediscover linguistic community in the idiom of space. Coming unstuck from the older hypostases of Time and History, the postcolonial translator paradoxically restores the metaphoricity of *trans-latio* by literalizing its etymology. In the silent *e* that alone remains to distinguish *borne* from *born* there is a quickening of space that collapses the gap remaining between the rooted claims of birth and the nostalgia of distance that makes home and nation necessary. Translation as spatialization, in this tension between letter and figure, becomes a mode equal to the spiraling dislocations of imperial history, in which the narratives of nation and selfhood, metropolis and colony are equally, if differently, implicated.

Russia's Poetry of Empire

This premise could remain a new critical piety unless tested within poetic form and outside the territories familiar to Anglophone culture. For the peculiar intensities of its history and in the wake of the Soviet Union's collapse, Russian poetry provides one such site for exploration.

Russia's poetic canon is narrow and still young; after its astonishingly rapid modern birth it has peaked mainly in two epochs, Pushkin's and the modernist era. During this time poetry in Russia has carried a unique social valency: it has been the genre through which linguistic form itself is asserted as an ethical value. Whether literariness has been pursued in the mode of direct civic engagement or as the freedom to disengage, the poetic experience in Russia has ranged from violent repression at the hands of the state to a complex collusion in celebrating the Russian national body.

In the brief but fiercely lived history of Russian poetry the question of empire arises crucially if obscurely. Thematically speaking, it is most easily and frequently read as the "Caucasian question" in Russian literature. Generally cited in this regard are the major literary works which deal, biographically and picturesquely, with Russia's escalating presence in the Caucasus and Central Asia. The southern poems of Pushkin and Lermontov are the most canonical literary expression of this tradition, whose early modern roots can be traced back to the eighteenth-century panegyric ode and which continues to resonate well into the twentieth century in the great utopian-futurist syntheses of Velimir Khlebnikov, in the more muted but difficult modernism of Mandel'shtam and the nervous exuberance of Pasternak. Under the integrationist aegis of the pan-Soviet state, this "southern" tradition outlived the Stalinist terror primarily through the very act of translating from regional languages, which became something of a rite of passage and mode of survival for later poets. More significantly for the future of Russian literature, the postwar period has also seen the emergence of Soviet writers from outside Russia proper adopting the imperial linguistic medium.

This vast genealogy, and the Asiatic regions that gave rise to it, have hardly been neglected by Russian criticism or the culture at large: mostly they have circulated as a biographical motif, a source of inspiration that marks a stage in a given writer's evolution. Among more philologically grounded critics the Caucasus have been seen as Russia's own "southern question," either unrelated to Western orientalism or linked to it in terms of a largely literary genealogy: such an approach has at best gathered a vast array of undifferentiated historical data in which literary sources and the broader modes of imperial information-retrieval coexist in a kind of philological abstraction where causal links and formal homologies are never discerned. Where the rare critic has suggested that the southern or Caucasian problematic in Russian literature is fundamentally implicated in the growth of the Russian empire, their correlation has been thought in terms of a simple conflation of literature and imperialist ideology. The few critics, from Pushkin's contemporary Prince Viazemskii onward, who have frowned on the claims of a literature of empire, have thus read this question as an author's thematic distance from the clichés of imperialist rhetoric. The figuration of the poetic voice becomes the degree of empathy with which it depicts the foreign and its ability to undo stereotypes that mark the limits of one's humanity.

These readings of empire, thematicist or biographical in orientation, appear at a certain remove from what might be called poetry's essential drama: its *space*. What, in the broadest terms, have been the spatial contours of the modern lyric that allow it to contemplate the shifting and imagined realms of nation and empire?

Our critical culture has often viewed literary geography as "imagery," the landscape against which a contrasted self may be foregrounded. However *figuratively* understood, this sense of landscape continues to operate at the level of purely phenomenal or pictorial vision until it is grasped in its essential tension with narrative time. The Russian formalists first theorized the figural power of space as something interruptive: for critics such as Viktor Shklovskii (204) space emerges implicitly as the deformation or complication (*siuzhet*) of sequential time (*fabula*). Space gains a sudden vigor when seen in this negative capacity of resisting the temporalizing mode of narrative. In lyric poetry, which weakens or eliminates the temporal coordinates of plot, this dynamic crucially escalates: the lyric offers the volatility of landscape a privileged locus to fashion itself beyond the familiar dichotomy of time and space that is normally seen as a duration opposed to a structuring stasis.

Any insistence on the productivity of literary and historical space militates against an entire tradition that has privileged time as the current of change. To conceive literature as a spatial history is to investigate a mobile geography as an alternative means of defining, through poetic language, the morphologies of cultural collision and literary-historical transformation. What might have been the concern of cultural anthropology or at least the sociology of literature, however, becomes, for the translator, a formal moment of the text. The translator must grasp poetic history as a series of evolving locative modes: the place names, shifters, and broad lexical registers that situate the poem and the poet.

Within the canonical genres of modern European literature the topoi of nation and empire are perhaps the overarching modes of location. Nationhood has generally been evoked in the evolutionary and particularizing temporal idiom of growth or development. This ascendant sense of national time, however, is seldom quite secure as territory: its boundaries are subject to the thrust and retreat of imperial aggression that superimposes on national time the secondary imperative of space. It is in the overlapping of national time and imperial space that modern poetic language has circulated; what remains for us is to situate Russia and Russian poetry with respect to the blurred and shifting layers of this palimpsest.

Most histories of Russia speak of the crystalization of Russian national consciousness as a legacy of the eighteenth-century post-Petrine state. Russia's sense of nationhood, we are told, evolved according to the urgency of its political and finally cultural competition with the great metropolitan powers of Europe. Russia Asiatic dimensions, by contrast, are archaicized as the ancient and bitter memory of the Tartar yoke. Received opinion has conflated Russia's process of acculturation with a

rivalry that is inter- and intra-European, while reducing the great south-
ward drive which saw Russia's absorption of the Kazakh steppe, the
Caucasus, and Central Asia over two centuries to a case of sheer territorial
expansion. The latter process, even when materially or psychologically
motivated, has been articulated by historians of Russia in a kind of
deculturated idiom.

Denied the power of a properly cultural dialectic, the impact of
Russia's expanding Asiatic peripheries on the national body has been
nonetheless dramatic. This difficult connection, the "inner incom-
patibility" that Benedict Anderson (89) sees linking nation and empire,
was often pondered within Russia as her unique geographical burden. To
be sure, the banishment to the Caucasus of such poets as Pushkin and
Lermontov often allowed Russia's relationship to her peripheries to be
posed in the romantic idiom of literary exile. The conceptual intractability
of Asiatic terrain was thus reduced to a distance from the Russian mother-
land that was only as far as the return journey. It remained only for critics
to reenact the poet's eventual repatriation as the fact of his posthumously
entering the patrimony of national culture.

Yet from Chaadaev to Solov'ëv and Derzhavin to Blok, the
philosophers and poets of post-Petrine Russia evolved a more complex
projection of the nervous intimacy of nation and empire. We find it
crudely but effectively summarized in Dostoevskii's words hailing the
Russian General Skobelev's massacre of the nomadic Turkmen forces at
Goek-Tepe in 1881: "In Europe we were hangers-on and slaves, whereas
to Asia we shall go as masters. In Europe we were Tartars, whereas in
Asia we too are Europeans. Our mission, our civilizing mission in Asia
will bribe our spirit and drive us thither" (513).

Behind Dostoevskii's confident assumption of a civilizing role lies a
more anxious awareness of Russia as a kind of threshold between Europe
and Asia, a liminal zone whose contours and edges are always open to
revision. This dilemma does not belong only or even primarily to physical
geography; its constant shifts of perspective betray what are in effect
discursive adaptations to the modalities of nation and empire as conceptual and political limits. We cannot assume that these limits coincide,
and it is the struggle of Russia's writers to negotiate both modalities that
renders their rhetoric so complex. Dostoevskii first orientalizes Russia as
barbaric, a Tartar despotism, yet calls also for the annexation of the East
(or South) for a Russia that is consequently no longer, or not yet, oriental.
Despotism is what, for Western Europe, renders Russia Asiatic, yet is also

the occasion that permits Russia's subjugation of its own Orient in the name of a European civilizational mission. These are the necessarily blurred contours of a political allegory that will haunt Russian literature, from the eighteenth century through Pushkin and Tolstoi to the Russian avant-garde.

Translating Space

The topos of threshold, then, has dictated Russia's spatial formation, folding East into West as empire into nation. How has Russian poetry responded in turn to the oscillating Eurasian space that was its outcome? In one of the founding texts of modern Russian poetry, the "Ode on the Taking of Khotin in 1739," Mikhail Lomonosov, an essential figure of the Russian eighteenth century, writes:

> Восторг внезапный ум пленил,
> Ведёт на верьх горы высокой,
> Где ветр в лесах шуметь забыл;
> В долине тишина глубокой.
> Внимая нечто, шум молчит,
> Которой завсегда журчит
> И с шумом вниз с холмов стремится.
> Лавровы вьются там венцы,
> Там слух спешит во все концы,
> Далече дым в полях курится.

> A sudden rapture seized the mind,
> And led it high upon a mountain,
> Where forest winds forgot to roar;
> Deep silence stills the valley floor.
> The roar heard something and abating
> It stops its clamor's downward pour
> That ever drowns the hills descending.
> There winding laurels wreathe the air,
> And hearing quickens everywhere;
> Smoke drifts in fields on the horizon.

These sonorous if somewhat stilted lines mark Lomonosov's debut as poet and progenitor of modern Russian verse; they also inaugurate the remarkably consistent rhetorical mode in which the Russian lyric voice has articulated its own sense of location within the interstices of nation and empire. This mode, which we first discern in the odes of Lomonosov and which is revived, almost as an anachronism, at different junctures in Russian poetry, is the sublime.

The roots of the sublime as a rhetorical mode, both in Russia and Western Europe, go back to a tract of late antiquity, Longinus's *On the Sublime,* that was revived through Boileau's French translation of 1674. Longinus explains the sublime as a form of elevation, a loftiness or excellence of diction that forces the reader beyond aesthetic appreciation to a sense of wonderment, an apprehension of grandeur. In Greek the sublime is *hypsos,* height itself, whose proportions can be gauged only in the emotional turbulence it provokes. The sublime, then, is chiefly a cluster of affective reactions through which the subject registers the pathos of transport or uplift, an experience that is both empowering and radically privative: "with its stunning power," the sublime has "a capability and force which, unable to be fought, take[s] a position high over every member of the audience" (Longinus 1.3).

How does this psychology of the sublime evolve as a geography? In tracing, through translation, a spatial genealogy of Russian poetry, my premise has been that Russia's poetic tradition, after its rapid modern genesis, elaborates what I shall call an *imperial sublime.* The topographies of the sublime map out the complex relation of Russia to its Asiatic peripheries through a rhetoric closely linked to what is generally known as eighteenth-century classicism. The thematics of oriental space will become inseparable from a rhetorical mode that is perceived increasingly to be archaic, an anachronism that will become essential precisely for the ways in which it will render the space of imperial Russia itself and the writer's place within it.

How might the emergence, with Lomonosov, of a Russian sublime affect strategies of translation? Traditional poetics have stressed fidelity to the original rhyme and meter. Modernism, by contrast, insisted on a more defamiliarizing sense of rhythm that I have called the modernist temporality of translation. Both of these poetics appear at a certain remove from the peculiar drama of Lomonosov's poem: although formulaically sublime in the tradition of the French precedents Lomonosov knew, the opening lines of the "Ode on the Taking of Khotin" struck a radically new note in Russia. It is this note, the now outdated novelty of

the Lomonosovian sublime *as a nascent sensibility of space,* that is chiefly
at stake in any new rendering of the poem.

Older premises of translation, such as fidelity to rhythm and syntactical literalism, need not be discarded. I have tried to preserve the faintly
clumsy versification of the Russian eighteenth century, lexically dense,
syntactically knotty, yet generally devoid of enjambments. Yet the traditional dilemma of the translator—should I try to write an eighteenth-
century English poem or modernize the original?—must be redefined.
The readability of a translation is located in its space and not in its time.

There is, to be sure, an overriding literary-historical dilemma in
translating this and other poems of the Russian tradition. This is the
temptation of translating the Russian sublime into a readily available and
immensely powerful idiom: the sublime of English romanticism, of
Wordsworth, Coleridge, or Shelley. Yet the Russian sublime, even after
Byron and his Russian equivalents, remains *un*romantic rather than
simply *pre*romantic. Its psychologism is weaker and its lexical choices
more archaic; its apprehensions of the world have less to do with the
mind-nature dialectic we know from the *Prelude* than with an intuition
of peripheral space and the stakes of power.

To translate Lomonosov into Wordsworth or one of his English
predecessors risks a kind of domestication. The struggle not to roman-
ticize the Russian poet is not only lexical or syntactical; it must be gauged
as the translator's ability to render the peculiarities of a poem's developing
topography. The strangeness of the stanza quoted is primarily the absence
of an active human subject. The wind, or rather the noise the wind makes,
is the only agent, registering through its silence a landscape that effectively
shapes its own vista. "The roar heard something," the poem tells us; if
hearing as a quintessentially temporal faculty replaces the spatial quality
of sight, it is rather because hearing is itself here visual. "And hearing
quickens everywhere; / Smoke drifts in fields on the horizon": this
quickening of time into space in the visualization of hearing and its
growing autonomy as a faculty unconnected to any organ is the stanza's
odd triumph and the principal challenge for the translator.

Vertical uplift is the essential axis of the lyric sublime: the mind is
thrust upward by the sudden onset of poetic rapture over which it has
no control. Where the difficulty of height consumes the first seven lines
of Lomonosov's poem, the final period provides a compensatory horizontal axis of extension. The wind's elevation grants it a panoramic view:

potentially infinite, this horizontal space will nonetheless become local-
ized as the historical occasion that is the poem's real object.

Horizontality is the site of conflict; its field of attraction is territorial
aggression, the surge of battle, the line of advance, victory or retreat.
Poetry encounters history at the intersection of two axes, the point at
which the terror of lyric afflatus is resolved in a compensatory and
transformative identification with imperial power. The uplifted poet,
slave to his vision, becomes Russia's heraldic eagle surveying the horizontal spread of the retreating Ottoman forces:

> За холмы, где паляща хлябь
> Дым, пепел, пламень, смерть рыгает,
> За Тигр, Стамбул, своих заграбь,
> Что камни с берегов сдирает;
> Но чтоб орлов сдержать полет,
> Таких препон на свете нет.

> Beyond the hills where raging pools
> Belch death in flame and smoke and ashes
> Beyond the Tigris, Istanbul,
> Retreat your men, that rends its passage;
> To stop the eagle's soaring flight
> There is no hindrance left nor might.

The sublime emerges, in Russian poetry, as an allegory of poetic
possession that invariably anticipates an instance of imperial power. This
power is finally shared, by poet and tsar, in a scenario of territorial
aggression, such as the capture of the Ottoman fortress of Khotin by
Russian troops in 1739. Yet if the imperial eagle is unstoppable, its
progress is secondary, in the poem, to the movement of Asiatic space
itself: in the remarkably tortured syntax of the middle lines, as twisted as
the flow of the Tigris, the zone of conquest emerges as a process of
continuous withdrawal through a shifting and sublime "beyond." This
"beyond" is no more than the endless displacement of its own boundaries,
like the river Tigris that, in the English spatialization, "rends its passage"
(the Russian reads: "that tears the stones from its own banks"), just as it
is itself syntactically cut off from the clause that defines it.

Lomonosov's poetry stands as a dated example of a tradition that
evolves according to the same displacements of force. In the nineteenth
century the Russian sublime deepens beyond a simple celebration of

imperial force. In the great "prophetic" poems of Pushkin and Lermontov, in the metaphysical geographies of Tiutchev, in the cultural nostalgia of Mandel'shtam and the utopian visions of Khlebnikov the drama of imperial space ramifies into a more complex evocation of the liminal. These poems inhabit the edges of culture, the shifting borders that split and transform the bodies, voices, and nations that cross them. Lermontov's poem, "A Dream," is a case in point:

В полдневный жар в долине Дагестана
С свинцом в груди лежал недвижим я;
Глубокая еще дымилась рана,
По капле кровь точилася моя.

Лежал один я на песке долины;
Уступы скал теснилися кругом.
И солнце жгло их желтые вершины
И жгло меня—но спал я мертвым сном.

И снился мне сияющий огнями
Вечерний пир в родимой стороне.
Меж юных жен, увенчанных цветами,
Шел разговор веселый обо мне.

Но в разговор веселый не вступая,
сидела там задумчиво одна,
И в грустный сон душа ее младая
Бог знает чем была погружена;

И снилась ей долина Дагестана;
Знакомый труп лежал в долине той;
В его груди дымясь чернела рана,
И кровь лилась хладеющей струей.

As midday's heat besieged the desert valley,
I lay inert, a bullet in my breast.
My wound was deep, its path still smoking freshly
And bleeding gently on the splattered dust

Of Daghestan's valley where I lay alone,
Surrounded on all sides by clustered rock.

The sunlight baked the clifftop's burnished yellow
And burnt the deathly slumber that I kept.

And in my dream I caught the glow of fires
That light the twilight feasting in my land,
Where talk of me rang out among the women,
Their hair wreathed festively in floral bands.

But of their company one spurned the laughter
And sat apart, in melancholy's throes;
A wistful sleep withdrew her youthful spirit,
What force and whence it came God only knows.

She dreamt of Daghestan's deserted valley;
Upon it lay a corpse she seemed to know;
She caught its breast shine blackly through the bleeding
That hardened as it soaked the valley floor.

The protagonist of "A Dream" is a Russian imperial officer. Lying
mortally wounded in the Caucasian valley of Daghestan, his body offers
what is structurally the most exquisite instance I know in Russian poetry
of the violence of the imperial sublime deflected and internalized as a
kind of melancholy that I name explicitly in the translation. The complex
and obsessive roundness of the poem, which rests on a circuit of intimacy
linking the soldier to his beloved, is achieved through a dream of recipro-
cal mourning. The soldier's body inhabits this oneiric landscape as a
conduit between the lost narrative of nationhood (the "land" native to
both lovers) and the sublime territory of conquest where he now lies
dead. The enjambment that links and divides the first two stanzas ("the
splattered dust / Of Daghestan's valley") is absent in the original, an
interpretive liberty that allows me to convey the sense of spatial crossing,
the transgression and separation, that lie at the heart of the text.

The soldier, we find out at the poem's end, is already dead, a fact
that operates retrospectively to make the flow of time strangely redun-
dant. The intimacy of poet and lover—that is the source and focus of
the poem's spatial dynamic—draws them together into a zone where
premonition and recollection are interchangeable. This crucial distortion
of sequential time prompted my translation's rendering of the somewhat
more disingenuous original "by God only knows what" as "what force
and *whence it came* God only knows." Here the problem of direction
replaces that of recollection: if the voice that speaks in the poem can still

be called a memory, then it recalls as this zero-point in time, which becomes the sheer space of encounter. I tried to make this resonance more explicit through the repetition of knowing (more obscure in the original as *znaet/znakomyi)* that resurfaces in her recognition of a body "she seemed to *know.*" The poem thus embraces the erasure of sequential time, which it survives just as the poet's'body lingers beyond its death in the phantasmatic bond that links the spaces of nation and empire.

The yearning that haunts much of Lermontov's poetry, to repatriate and heal the poet's body and thereby close the gap between nation and empire, is perhaps the principal if frustrated legacy of the nineteenth-century imperial sublime. Velimir Khlebnikov's revolutionary transformation, in the twentieth century, of the question of poetry and empire takes up this very question as the touchstone for a new poetics. In 1922, passing the last months of his life in conditions of extreme privation and illness, Khlebnikov wrote:

Баграми моров буду разбирать старое строение народов,
Чернилами хворей буду исправлять черновик,
                    человеческий листок рукописи,
Крючьями чум после пожара буду выбирать брёвна
                    и сваи народов
Для нового сруба новой избы.
Тонкой пилой чахотки буду вытачивать новое здание,
Выпилю новый народ грубой пилой сыпняка.
Выдерну гвозди из стен, чтоб рассыпалось Я,
                    великое Я,
То надевающее перстнем ваше это солнце,
То смотрящее через стекло слёз собачонки.

With these plague-hooks I'll take on the old house of nations
With the ink of each illness I'll correct its rough draft,
                    humanity's manuscript,
With these hooks of contagion I'll take from the embers
                    beams and stakes of each nation
To build anew the new house.
With the thin saw of consumption I'll put it newly together,
I'll hew the new nation together with typhoid's coarse blade.
I'll pull every nail from the wall to let the I scatter,
                    I, the great I,

That can put a ring round the sun you call yours,
Or look through the glass of a dog's eye weeping.

Khlebnikov's universalism is equally a poetic abandonment of the very metropolis in whose name modernism was proclaimed, a centrifugal impulse that led him to privilege the Asiatic peripheries of Russia over its Europeanized centers. His vision remained unrealized, truncated by the Stalinist terror and its territorial consolidations. Yet his heritage has survived in complex ways, in the voices of other nationalities who have come to inscribe their history and its constitutive alienations into the Russian language.

The case of Gennadii Aigi is an isolated but important one: a native of Turkic Chuvashia, Aigi has been writing poetry in Russian since the Khrushchev era. As a poet Aigi has altered the Russian lyric tradition like almost no other writer before him: moving between the archaic shamanistic culture of his region and the transnational avant-gardes of Europe, Aigi has effectively leapt over the Russian national space, shattering its linguistic conservatism, its civic and moral pieties from without. Aigi is not a "political" poet: he contemplates the phenomenal and metaphysical conditions of sight and space for its alienating and redemptive possibilities:

а в зрении было—словно что-то белое:

без веса—мраморное;

и без вещественности!—

от этого родства оно как будто
открытые провалы чувствовало:

и в мраморе в саду:

и в белизне бумаги—

прокладывались сквозь воздух—как сквозь
                                                    шёлк!

в руке они внезапно раскрывались
пустыми
где-то
гроты оставляя—

и в общей и пустой раскрытости
(так долго небом неким отступающей)
самоисчёрпавшихся роз—

изрезано и ярко плакалось
сырой
воздушной будто известковостью

seeing had in it—something white:

weightless—marble:

even thingless!—

this kinship made it almost feel
the open gaps:

out where the marble was:

or in a page's whiteness—

they paved the air as if—they cut through

$\qquad\qquad\qquad\qquad\qquad\qquad$ silk!—

abruptly unfolding in the hand
empty
leaving
scattered grottos—

and in the wide empty unfoldedness
(receding slowly like a sky)
of roses bloomed to their exhaustion—
the sound of weeping
shredded bright
like the damp
hovering
of lime   ("August: Nietzsche in Turin")

The Task of the Translator

In the wake of empire and with the temporal impulse of modernism
becoming slowly exhausted, the translator must now look to the space

of poetry. In addressing the peculiar horizons, edges, and limits upon which any poetic tradition rests, the translator's task is to expose the gap existing *within the original itself* between language as a national patrimony and the project of empire.

The spatial imperative of translation is not necessarily a new anachronism, for it is retroactive only in being firstly transverse. It reads a spatial anxiety back into modern literary experience by highlighting the abstracted markers of imperial space that modernism itself had blurred. Where modernism sought a defamiliarizing sense of time, the translator now seeks to render the alienation of the original text from its own quest for national space, reviving the canonical poems of a given tradition as powerful allegories of empire. This has been my implicit task in "Poems Beyond Russia."

Translation is always a liminal activity: it operates at the threshold of languages, bodies, and histories. Far from reaffirming the boundaries that separate cultural entities—English and Russian, Russia and Asia—or celebrating a text as a repository of cultural uniqueness, translation asserts the essential discontinuity between language and nationhood which makes its task possible.

Notes

1. Compare Hegel's speculations on Chinese calligraphy in Hegel, §459: "Written language passes into the sphere of immediate spatial intuition where it takes and produces its signs. Better still [*Näher*], it is the *hieroglyphic* [or Chinese] script that signifies its *representations* through spatial figures; *alphabetic writing*, by contrast, signifies *sounds* that are themselves already signs."

2. I translate from the German; compare Zohn's English version in *Illuminations* 71, 75 (henceforth given in square brackets in the text). I have read this article alongside the more temporally oriented later essays "Theses on the Philosophy of History" (312–13), (*Illuminations* 255–66) and the "Theologico-Political Fragment." The most widely circulating postmodern readings of Benjamin's essay are by Carol Jacobs, Paul de Man, and Jacques Derrida. A treatment of modernist time and space that permits an alternative historicization of Benjamin and high modernism can be found in Jameson's *The Political Unconscious*, 260–69, and in his article "Modernism and Imperialism."

Works Cited

Aigi, Gennadii. *Otmechennaia zima: Sobranie sochinenii v dvukh chastiakh.* Paris: Sintaksis, 1982.

Anderson, Benedict. *Imagined Communities: Reflections on the Origin and Spread of Nationalism.* London: Verso, 1983.

Benjamin, Walter. "Die Aufgabe des Übersetzers." *Illuminationen: Ausgewählte Schriften.* Frankfurt: Suhrkamp Verlag, 1961.

———. "The Task of the Translator: An Introduction to the Translation of Baudelaire's *Tableaux Parisiens*" and "Theses on the Philosophy of History." *Illuminations.* Trans. Harry Zohn. New York: Harcourt Brace & World Inc., 1955.

———. "Theologico-Political Fragment." *Reflections: Essays, Aphorisms, Autobiographical Writings.* Trans. Edmund Jephcott. New York: Harcourt Brace Jovanovich, 1978.

Bergson, Henri. *L'Évolution créatrice.* Geneva: Éditions Albert Skira, 1945.

Derrida, Jacques. "Des Tours de Babel." *Difference in Translation.* Ed. Joseph F. Graham. Ithaca: Cornell UP, 1985.

Derzhavin, Gavriil R. *Almazna sypletsia gora.* Moscow: Sovetskaia Rossiia, 1972.

Dostoevskii, F. M. "Goek-Tepe. Chto takoe Aziia dlia nas?" *Polnoe sobranie sochinenii.* St. Petersburg: Samoobrazovanie, 1896. Vol. 21.

Fenollosa, Ernest. *The Chinese Written Character as a Medium for Poetry.* Ed. Ezra Pound. 1936. San Francisco: City Lights Books, 1969.

Grossman, Leonid. "Lermontov i kul'tura vostoka." *Literaturnoe nasledstvo.* Vol. 43–44 (1941): 181–262.

Hegel, Georg Wilhelm Friedrich. *Vorlesungen über die Naturphilosophie als der Encyklopädie der philosophischen Wissenschaften im Grundrisse, Zweiter Teil.* Ed. Carl Ludwig Michelet. Berlin: Verlag von Duncker und Humblot, 1842.

Iusofov, R. *Dagestan v russkoi literature kontsa XVIII i pervoi poloviny XIX v.* Moscow: Nauka, 1964.

Jacobs, Carol. "The Monstrosity of Translation." *Modern Language Notes* 90 (1975): 755–66.

Jameson, Fredric. "Modernism and Imperialism." *Nationalism, Colonialism and Literature.* Minneapolis: U of Minnesota P, 1990.

———. *The Political Unconscious: Narrative as a Socially Symbolic Act.* Ithaca: Cornell UP, 1981.

Khlebnikov, Velimir. *Tvoreniia.* Ed. M. Ia. Poliakov. Moscow: Sovetskii pisatel', 1986.

Lermontov, M. Iu. *Polnoe sobranie stikhotvorenii v 2 tomakh.* Leningrad: Sovetskii pisatel', 1989.

Lomonosov, M. *Polnoe sobranie sochinenii.* Moscow: Akademiia Nauk SSSR, 1950–59.

Longinus. *On the Sublime.* Trans. James A. Arieti and John M. Crossett. New York: The Edwin Mellen Press, 1985.

Lotman, Iu. M. *Aleksandr Sergeevich Pushkin: Biografiia pisatelia.* Leningrad: Prosveshchenie, 1983.

de Man, Paul. "Conclusions: Walter Benjamin's 'The Task of the Translator.'" *The Resistance to Theory.* Minneapolis: U of Minnesota P, 1986. 73–105.

Mazour, Anatole. *Modern Russian Historiography.* Princeton: D. Van Nostrand Co. Inc., 1958.

Miliukov, P. *Glavnye techeniia russkoi istoricheskoi mysli.* 2nd ed. Moscow: Kushnerev and Co., 1898.

Pound, Ezra. *Translations.* 1953. London: Faber & Faber, 1984.

Pushkin, A. S. *Sochineniia v trekh tomakh.* Moscow: Khudozhestvennaia literatura, 1974.

Ramanujan, A. K., trans. *Speaking of Shiva.* London: Penguin, 1973.

Rogger, Hans. *National Consciousness in Eighteenth-Century Russia.* Cambridge: Harvard UP, 1960.

Rushdie, Salman. *Shame.* New York: Vintage International, 1989.

Serman, Il'ia. "Russian National Consciousness and Its Development in the Eighteenth Century." *Russia in the Age of Enlightenment, Essays for Isabel de Madariaga.* London: Macmillan, 1990.

Shklovskii, Viktor. *O teorii prozy.* Moscow: Federatsiia, 1925.

Vel'tman, S. *Vostok v khudozhestvennoi literature.* Moscow: GIZ, 1928.

Wilson, Peter Lamborn, and Nasrollah Pourjavady, trans. *The Drunken Universe: An Anthology of Persian Sufi Poetry.* Grand Rapids: Phanes Press, 1987.

Religious and Cultural Considerations in Translating Shakespeare Into Arabic

Amel Amin-Zaki

Translation from any language into another is difficult enough at the best of times. Translation from one West-European language to another may be problematic, but it is less so than translation from English into Arabic. European languages share common linguistic origins. They are thus more compatible in terms of language than Arabic and English. Complicating factors which arise in translating Shakespeare into Arabic, for instance, include the difficulties of capturing puns, wordplay, and similar linguistic humor of his poetic dramas. Equally important is the shared cultural heritage of European languages. In this respect, translation is further complicated since Shakespeare assumes that his audience is familiar with classical and Renaissance cultures and literatures. Many misinterpretations, for example, reflect the translator's unfamiliarity with the cultural background of the Elizabethan period. Finally, religious considerations are also important. In the Arab world, Islamic culture predominates. While there have always been significant numbers of Christian and Jewish Arabs, Islamic culture—in the use of language, for instance—has exerted a tremendous influence even on non-Muslims in the Arab world. Accordingly, translators usually eschew those references which might give offense to a Muslim audience.

One example of this phenomenon occurs in a passage from *Romeo and Juliet* when the nurse exclaims, "Give me some aqua-vitae" (III.ii.88).[1] Kittredge (989) glosses the expression as "brandy," Harrison (494) as "Spirits," Schmidt (vol. 1, 49) as "Ardent spirits," and Evans

(1078) as "Strong alcoholic spirits." The nurse, then, informing Juliet that Tybalt has been killed by Romeo, calls for a drink. She does so again later in the play (IV.v.16). Despite this unanimity of the commentators that "aqua-vitae" is a reference to alcoholic drink, the term has been translated several times into Arabic as *mā' al-ḥayāt* ("water of life"), an expression which has no connotation of alcoholic beverage to the Arab listener. While it is possible that this translation represents a misunderstanding, this explanation is extremely unlikely. What is far more probable is that the translators all believed that it would seem indecorous to their audience to have someone who drinks alcoholic beverages in charge of a family's only child.

This essay will focus on two areas in which the translator of a Shakespearean play into Arabic must consider whether an audience might be so offended by a character's statements that its appreciation of the larger work might be compromised. The first section will deal with how translators have rendered Shakespeare's various oaths. Many such oaths are blasphemous and would be highly offensive to any audience in the Islamic world. Others have, for one reason or another, little or no meaning when rendered literally into Arabic. These oaths have typically been "Islamized" by the translators; that is, they have been rendered into Arabic in such a way as to make their usage and occurrence consistent with Islamic beliefs and the habits of an Arabic speaker. I will show that the predilection of translators to do this is consistent from the earliest trans-lations of Shakespeare until the present. The second section of this essay concerns bawdiness in Shakespeare and the ways in which the translators have dealt with this ribaldry in the face of an audience unaccustomed to having bawdy or ribald material dealt with in public. In this context, there are far fewer certainties in predicting how translators deal with bawdy expressions, as the translation of these expressions depends instead primarily on individual choices.

There were several translators of Shakespeare's works into Arabic in the late nineteenth and early twentieth centuries. Their efforts, however, were by and large quite inferior and have had neither wide scholarly nor lasting popular acceptance. These early translators frequently ignored Shakespeare's plots to such an extent that their efforts sometimes had only a passing resemblance to Shakespeare's works. In addition, these "translations" were characterized by an unaesthetic use of Arabic, a lan-guage whose highly developed poetic traditions date to pre-Islamic times. Among the first serious translators of Shakespeare's plays into Arabic were

Muḥammad al-Sibāʿī, Muḥammad ʿIffat al-Qāḍī, ʿAlī Imām ʿAṭiyah, Khalīl Muṭrān, and Sāmī al-Juraydīnī.[2] Of these five, Muṭrān's translations cannot be said to be authoritative from a scholarly point of view; however, they have gained wide acceptance by the broad popular audience, so I have included a discussion of his *Hamlet* and *Romeo and Juliet* in this essay. The works of these earlier translators were chosen with a view toward being able to compare and contrast the earlier translations with more recent examples from the same plays.

Of the contemporary translators it must be stated at once that Jabrā Ibrāhīm Jabrā, ʿAbd al-Qādir al-Qiṭṭ, and ʿAbd al-Wāḥid Luʾluʾah represent a new and unprecedented development in the hitherto not-too-promising field of Shakespearean translation into Arabic.[3] These three men are well acquainted with the multifarious aspects of their self-appointed task; they seem to be deeply aware of Elizabethan culture and have a sound grasp of Shakespearean language. Despite minor flaws, they have succeeded in producing the best translations of Shakespeare in Arabic; their work is characterized by accomplished scholarship, accuracy of rendition, and an elegant style.

Other translators considered in this essay include ʿAlī Aḥmad Bākathīr, Muʾnis Ṭāhā Ḥusayn, ʿAwaḍ Muḥammad, and Muḥammad Muḥammad ʿAnānī.[4] While these translators achieved varying degrees of popularity, they failed, by and large, to produce good translations. Their prime drawback was their failure to render accurately many phrases and expressions from the original into Arabic, apparently because they did not seem to comprehend (or did not wish to convey) the implications of many of them. Their translations also fall short because these translators apparently lacked good knowledge of Elizabethan, Renaissance, and Greco-Roman literature, lore, and culture. I discuss these translators, however, because, as stated, some of them achieved some level of popularity, and because they, particularly Bākathīr, sometimes put forward interesting solutions to problems.

The Islamization of Shakespeare's Oaths

Both Christians and Muslims are enjoined by their respective scriptures from oath-taking and swearing. The Old Testament injunction against taking God's name "in vain" (Exod. 20:7) is amplified by Christ in the Sermon on the Mount. There, Christ instructs his followers "not to swear at all" (Matt. 5:34), for oath-taking "comes from the devil" (Matt. 5:37). Similarly, the Qur'ān teaches its adherents to eschew those who too easily invoke God in their speech: "Heed not the type of despicable man, ready with oaths"[5] (al-Qalam, lxviii:10). The Qur'ān further instructs that one should "make not God, by your oaths, a hindrance to your being righteous" (Pickthall, al-Baqarah, ii:224).

Despite a common belief by both Christians and Muslims that excessive oath-taking and swearing are blasphemous, such oaths are common in both European and Arabic literature. As Walter Raleigh Coppedge demonstrates, Shakespeare's work is no exception. His characters, whether from the nobility or common people, men or women, all use the name of God. Sometimes they swear by Him, sometimes they appeal to Him, and sometimes they put their trust in Him. The names of well-known saints are sometimes used for such purposes too. Often, the names of the pagan Greek and Roman gods are invoked instead of Christ, the Virgin, and the saints.

Since there are differences in belief between Islam and Christianity, some of the oaths that are used by the Shakespearean characters might sound particularly blasphemous to a Muslim audience. Some of these oaths, moreover, are likely to lose their meaning in translation even if rendered literally, since their usage is intricately tied to Christian beliefs. Still others might be completely lost on a broad Arabic-speaking audience since many oaths in Shakespeare refer to classical Greek or Roman characters, with whom the audience would likely be unfamiliar. The translators in most cases, when faced with such problems, change the oath to make it suit Islamic beliefs or omit it entirely, presumably to avoid embarrassment. But surprisingly, on occasion, the translators themselves—most especially Bākathīr—provide an oath when none exists in the original text because they apparently feel that an Arabic speaker might use one in that particular context. In addition to concentrating on these issues, this section of the essay will also discuss in passing the treatment of so-called mild oaths by Arabic translators and will conclude with a brief consideration of instances where the oaths spoken by Shakespeare's characters have different apparent and actual meanings, thus confusing the translator. This situation underscores the need for careful attention to accepted commentaries when translation is attempted.

Caius Marcius in his conversation with Menenius uses the oath "'Sdeath" (*Coriolanus* I.i.203), which means, according to G. B. Harrison, "by God's death" (1272*n*221). Of course, the expression refers to the Christian belief that Christ, the second person of the Trinity, died on the cross to atone for humanity's sins. This oath is anathema to a Muslim audience because God, for a Muslim, is everlasting and eternal. The Qur'ān states that "All that is on earth will perish: but will abide (forever) the face of thy Lord—full of Majesty, Bounty and Honour" (al-Rahmān iv:27). Furthermore, Islam rejects the divinity of Christ (al-Mā'idah v:19, 75) as well as his death on the cross (al-Nisā' iv:157). A translator, therefore, cannot render the oath as Caius Marcius utters it, for it would be considered blasphemous by his audience. In addition, such an oath, which has a visceral meaning to Shakespeare Christian audience, striking at the very heart of Christian understanding of salvation, would have no meaning to a Muslim audience. The power of the oath would be utterly lost, and the Muslim audience would regard "God's death" as merely an absurd utterance. Accordingly, this oath has either to be changed drastically or omitted.

Al-Sibā'ī's solution is to change the oath to one which any Muslim might utter: "Uqsimu bi al-mawt al-zu'ām" ("I swear by sudden death") (14.14). 'Atiyah, whose translation follows in al-Sibā'ī's footsteps, renders it as "qasaman bi al-mawt" ("I swear by death") (16.10). Jabrā gives it a completely different, though no less Islamic, interpretation: "ya lalla'nah" ("O, damnation") (51.3).

The identical considerations discussed above obtain regarding the expression "zounds," which appears twice in Mercutio's lines, "Zounds, consort" (*Romeo and Juliet* III.i.46) and "Zounds, a dog, a rat, a mouse, a cat, to scratch a man to death" (III.i.96). The word, according to all the standard commentators, is an oath which means "by God's wounds" (Kittredge 987*n46;* Harrison 492*n52;* Schmidt 1410; Onions 256; Evans 1075*n49),* a reference to the wounds which Christians believe were suffered by Christ before and during his crucifixion. Although he believes in Jesus Christ as a prophet and as the Messiah, as discussed above, a Muslim rejects the divinity of Christ. Thus to translate the expression literally would again confound the sensibilities of a Muslim audience just as "God's death" would. It would also be nonsensical to a Muslim audience, since God, in the absence of a belief in Christ's dual nature, is incapable of being wounded.

On both occasions, Husayn omits the words. 'Anānī also omits the expression entirely, as, indeed, do most translators. Interestingly, Bākathīr renders the expression as "*yā jurūh al-Masīh*" ("O Christ's wounds" [76.4]). Although this oath is not used in Arabic, and is purely Bākathīr's invention, it is an ingenious adaptation on several levels. First, the oath is not as offensive as a verbatim translation of the original would be. Although Islam rejects explicitly the crucifixion of Christ, the Qur'ān is silent on the question of whether Christ might have been tormented prior to his Ascension. Second, a Muslim audience is likely to be aware of the Christian doctrine of Christ's suffering, so that the power of the oath is conveyed by Bākathīr's rendition of the literal meaning of the utterance. Third, Muslims often invoke the Prophet Muḥammad in oath-taking. Indeed, Bākathīr's oath is quite similar in form to common Arabic oaths such as *wa ḥayāt al-nabī* ("by the Prophet's life") or *wa ra's al-nabī* ("by the Prophet's head"). The invocation of Christ in an oath would, therefore, not strike a Muslim audience as so unusual, even if it might find the exact wording of the oath somewhat distasteful.

Hamlet's contemplation on the skulls tossed up by the clown as he digs Ophelia's grave causes a similar problem for Arab translators. Hamlet states, "This might be the pate of a politician, which this ass now o'erreaches; one that would circumvent God, might it not?" (V.i.73–75). On the face of it, the phrase "would circumvent God" might seem blasphemous to an Arab-Muslim audience, touching on the very core of Islamic beliefs. Perhaps the most succinct statement in the Qur'ān of the core beliefs of Islam occurs in the so-called Verse of the Throne:

God! There is no god save Him, the Alive, the Eternal. Neither slumber nor sleep overtaketh Him. Unto Him belongeth whatsoever is in the heavens and whatsoever is in the earth. Who is he that intercedeth with Him save by His leave? He knoweth that which is in front of them and that which is behind them, while they encompass nothing of His knowledge save what He will. His Throne includeth the heavens and the earth, and He is never weary of preserving them. He is the Sublime, the Tremendous. (Pickthall, al-Baqarah ii:255)

Thus, God's absolute sovereignty over the created order is central to Islamic belief. It is inconceivable to posit to an Islamic audience that any created being can oppose, much less circumvent, the Divine Will.[6] A Muslim audience would likely be far too shocked by the suggestion to understand the irony of Hamlet's question.

Mutrān's solution to this problem is to rewrite the lines completely: "amā yuḥtamal anna ṣāḥib hādhihi al-jumjumah kāna siyāsiyyan aẓīman? Aw kāna rabb ṣawlah wa dawlah, wa ʿalayhi lamḥah min ʿizzat rabb al-ʿālamīn?" ("Would it not be possible that the owner of this skull was a great politician? Or a master of despotic position and power, on whose visage appears some of the glory belonging to the Lord of the Universe?" [118.9–12]). Clearly, Muṭrān's interpretation has little to do with the original, implying not that the politician might have circumvented God, but, quite the opposite, that God's favor was upon him. Al-Qiṭṭ, in his version, also evades the embarrassing expression, rendering it as "*siyāsī yaghlib dahā'uh al-ālihah*" ("a politician whose subtlety subdues the gods" [240.15]). Thus, al-Qiṭṭ keeps the spirit of the original, but makes the phrase more palatable by removing reference to the Almighty and substituting a pagan allusion. Jabrā's version manages to remain close to the original and yet contains no offense: "*aḥad al-sāsah al-ladhīna yuḥāwilūn al-kayd ḥattā li rabb al-'ibād!*" ("one of the politicians who try to outwit even the Lord of Mankind!" [143.15–16]). The joke has been rendered at the expense of the politician without damaging the original.

In *Twelfth Night*, Antonio uses the oath "'Slight" in his conversation with Fabian (III.ii.10). Kittredge reads the exclamation as "by God's light" (415*n10*). This oath does not violate any religious conviction of the translators' audience. There is no obvious reference to specific Christian beliefs which are rejected by Islam, as was the case with "'Sdeath" and "zounds." The problem with this oath is that it is simply not used in Arabic. If the translators were to translate the expression literally, the audience would, no doubt, understand the meaning; however, it would recognize the expression as being obviously a foreign one. Accordingly, Ibrāhīm translates the oath as "*bi ḥaqq al-samā' wa nūrihā*" ("by heaven and its light" [96.10]); Jabrā's rendition is "*billāh 'alayk*" ("for God's sake" [175.11]). Both translators give the sense of the oath, but, although Ibrāhīm comes closer to conjuring the same image as the original, Jabrā uses a more common Arabic oath.

Shakespeare's frequent references to classical Greek and Roman figures, particularly the pagan gods, present a distinct problem for the Arabic translator. Here the fear is not so much that an audience might be offended by the allusions, but that such allusions would be lost upon an Arab audience which has no cultural affinity to these characters and may be wholly unfamiliar with them.

Al-Sibā'ī faced this dilemma in translating Marcius's curse, "Pluto and hell" (*Coriolanus* I.iv.36). Marcius utters this curse against the Roman soldiers who had retreated before the enemy. For al-Sibā'ī to have transliterated the name of Pluto into Arabic would have meant that the overwhelming majority of his audience would not have understood the allusion. Thus, he coins an expression which sounds as if it were uttered by a Muslim amidst a Muslim group: *"ayna anta yā Mālik wa ayna jahannam fatabtaliʿuhum?"* ("Where are you, O Mālik, and where is Hell to gulp them down?" [30.15]). So, Pluto, the god of the infernal regions, is replaced by Mālik who, in the Qurʾān (al-Zukhruf xliii:77), is said to be the angel in charge of hell. The substitution of an Islamic figure, Mālik, for the Roman god Pluto works extremely well in this context. The audience would immediately recognize the role of Mālik as guardian of hell, and the line as rendered, though not translated literally, conveys the precise meaning of the original.

Other references to such classical figures were not always so easily dealt with by al-Sibāʿī's contemporaries. An example is Hamlet's lines, "So excellent a king, that was to this / Hyperion to a satyr" (I.ii.140). There is no easy counterpart in Arab-Islamic culture for Hyperion or satyrs, as was the case for Pluto. Accordingly, both al-Juraydīnī and Muṭrān completely ignore these two lines. As contemporaries of al-Sibāʿī (though he did not translate *Hamlet*), these two early translators were writing for the same audience. They were aware that the majority of their audience would be unfamiliar with Greco-Roman mythology, nor would the audience be acquainted with the symbolic value for which these figures stood.

More recent translators, however, have treated these lines much differently. Jabrā, Muḥammad, and al-Qiṭṭ each translated *Hamlet* into Arabic within fifteen years of one another, and did so some fifty to sixty years after al-Sibāʿī's contemporaries. By the time these three translators were doing their work, the names of the major classical gods and, in a general sense, Greek and Roman mythology, were far more familiar to the educated classes in the Arab world. Thus, Jabrā transliterated the names of the classical figures into Arabic, but used footnotes to explain their significance. Muḥammad did the same thing, except that he gave *satyr* the designation *"tays"* ("billy goat" [44.1]). Al-Qiṭṭ, as if in an effort to spare the reader the toil of wondering what those names were and of having to read multiple footnotes, Arabicized the Greek names. He rendered "Hyperion" as *"ilāh al-shams"* ("the sun god" [65.1]), and "satyr" as *"rabb al-shahawāt"* ("god of lechery" [65.2]).

This generational difference in treating classical figures for whom there are no Arab-Islamic counterparts is consistent. Muṭrān and al-Juraydīnī, for instance, both delete any reference to Niobe from Hamlet's lines: "A little month, or ere those shoes were old / With which she followed my poor father's body / Like Niobe, all tears" (I.ii.147–49). The later translators, Jabrā, Muḥammad, and al-Qiṭṭ, all render Niobe's name into Arabic, explaining her significance in a footnote.

Rather an unusual situation occurs, however, with the use of the name *Jove* in Shakespearean texts (e.g., *Twelfth Night* III.i.42, III.iv.69; *Timon of Athens* IV.iii.107). The letter *v* does not exist in Arabic, and when foreign words which contain this letter are rendered in Arabic, the translator uses the next closest letter, *f*. Thus, *Jove* would be transliterated as *jawf*. A difficulty arises because the word *jawf* in Arabic means interior, hollow, or cave. To avoid any confusion, both Jabrā, in his translation of *Twelfth Night*, and Lu'Lu'ah, in his translation of *Timon*, render "Jove" as "Jupiter." This substitution operates to eliminate any ambiguity for the audience while not imposing any meaningful alteration on the original meaning.

Up to this point, I have focused on instances where translators have had to omit or change Shakespeare's oaths for a variety of reasons; however, there are instances in which translators supply an oath where none exists in the original. Bākathīr is the premier example of this phenomenon. The oath most frequently added by him is "*ī wa rabbī*" ("ay, by my Lord"). An example of this usage occurs when Benvolio asks Montague if he knows why Romeo keeps to himself and avoids other people. Montague replies that he has asked him, as have many other friends. His line, containing no oath in the original, is, "Both by myself and many other friends" (I.i.140). He is made by Bākathīr to say: "ī wa rabbī, kam tawakhkhayt bi nafsī wa kathīr min siḥābī dhāk" ("ay, by my Lord many a time I tried that myself and so did a good number of my friends" [15.4–5]). Bākathīr adds this oath because a modern Arabic speaker would likely utter this or a similar oath in expressing his exasperation as Montague does. Thus, the addition serves to Arabicize the line while not doing violence to the original text.

Another occasion where Bākathīr inserts his favorite oath occurs later in the same scene. Benvolio, discussing Rosaline with Romeo, asks, "Then she hath sworn that she will still live chaste?" Romeo answers, "She hath" (I.i.211–212). Rather than merely responding affirmatively, Bākathīr's Romeo says instead "ī wa rabbī" ("ay, by my Lord" [18.11]). In this context, where the chastity of a lady is in question, an Arab audience would expect the proponent of the lady's chastity to take an oath affirming it. His failure to do so would be noticeable and might even be understood as equivocation on his part; hence, Bākathīr's added oath.

Bākathīr's Capulet also utters an oath where none exists in the
original. Capulet is arguing with Tybalt that it would not befit his dignity
to mistreat Romeo while the latter is under his roof: "I would not for
the wealth of all this town / Here in my house do him disparagement"
(I.v.67–68). In his Arabic version, Bākathīr adds the following line just
before the above-quoted line 67: "*wa alladhī nafsī fī qabḍatih law
qaddamū lī*" ("by him, in whose grip is my soul, if I were offered" [38.1]).
This is a paraphrase of an oath attributed to the Prophet Muḥammad
and would be recognized as such by any educated Muslim audience. It
is an extremely uncommon oath, hardly ever uttered in spoken language.
The Prophet is quoted as saying, "By Him, in Whose hands is my soul,"
or, "By Him, in Whose hand is Muḥammad's soul." Muslims regard
Muḥammad as God's quintessential prophet. Thus the power of the
image of the Prophet taking an oath imperiling his own soul cannot be
overstated. In the context of the play an Arab audience would understand
Capulet's horror at the suggestion that he would harm Romeo in his own
house. Treating those in one's house not only with civility but with
hospitality is considered by Arab and Islamic culture to be inextricably
linked with one's honor (just as Capulet himself understood it to be).
Indeed, this duty rises to the level of a religious obligation. Thus,
Bākathīr's invocation of this powerful image in expressing Capulet's
horror at Tybalt's suggestion is one that his audience would well have
understood—and one which it would have shared.

In contrast to Bākathīr's insertion of a powerful oath where none
exists in the original, he does precisely the opposite a few lines after the
ones discussed above. While remonstrating with Tybalt, Capulet utters
the oath, "God shall mend my soul" (*Romeo and Juliet* I.v.77). According
to Onions, this oath is supposed to be used in "asseverations" (139).
Bākathīr, who is fond of serious oaths, renders this one quite mildly as
"*waḥayātī*") ("by my life or by my soul" [38.16]), which is a very gentle
form of swearing in Arabic. No readily apparent reason comes to mind
to explain why Bākathīr chose to express this oath in so understated a
fashion. Perhaps he felt that, having used a most potent oath only a few
lines earlier it would be surplusage to use a stronger oath here. In this
one instance, however, Bākathīr does a disservice to his audience by
downplaying the vexation Capulet feels in having to restrain Tybalt from
acting against Romeo at that moment. By contrast, both Ḥusayn and
'Anānī render the line correctly, giving it its full weight and meaning.
Ḥusayn renders it as "*Allāhumma rahmatak*" ("O God [bestow upon me]

Your mercy" [90.89]), while 'Anānī translates it as "*raḥmatak yā rabb*" (["bestow upon me] your mercy, O Lord" [88.36]). Both of these expressions are familiar to modern Arabic speakers, but they are understood as being far weightier oaths than Bākathīr's.

There are times, of course, where the Shakespearean character utters a mild oath because a stronger oath would be out of place. In those situations, the translators can generally find a suitable Arabic oath which conveys the meaning of the original without overstating it. For instance, the first line in *Romeo and Juliet* starts with a mild oath by one of the servants of the Capulet house: "Gregory, on my word, we'll not carry coals" (I.i.1). Bākathīr renders the oath as "*qasaman*" ("I swear" [1.1]), while 'Anānī gives the variant "*uqsim*" ("I swear" [80.1]). These two renderings are virtually literal translations of the original. Ḥusayn's version reads "*lal amrī*" ("upon my life" [17.1]). This rendering may appear to the English speaker as a more serious oath than the original intends; however, this oath is extremely common in Arabic speech, so that it expresses more or less the same meaning as the original.

One notable exception to the generality stated above is with respect to the oath "marry," an oath frequently used by Shakespeare. In *Romeo and Juliet*, it first occurs shortly after the lines quoted above, in the conversation between the servants (I.i.34). According to Marian Edwardes, *marry* "is an exclamation derived from the Virgin's name" (154). An oath derived from or alluding to the name of the Virgin Mary is unknown in Arabic, although the Virgin is revered as Christ's mother since the virgin birth of Jesus is accepted in Islam. Thus no literal or approximate rendition is available. Accordingly, all three translators ignore the line completely. In any case, very little meaning of the original is lost by the omission, since the oath appears to have no more function than to provide slight emphasis.

It is quite interesting to notice that sometimes when Shakespeare uses an oath which has a seemingly equivalent Arabic oath, some of the translators tend to be baffled. They try to be so literal in their translation that they make the oath sound quite different. This mistake usually occurs when the oath as written in the original appears to have a verbatim analogue in Arabic, when in fact the meaning or severity of the original is much different from its apparent Arabic equivalent (rather like a false cognate).

An example of this situation occurs in the oath used by Horatio after witnessing the appearance of the ghost: "Before my God, I might not

this believe / Without the sensible and true avouch / Of mine own eyes"
(*Hamlet* I.i.56–58). Muṭrān translates the oath as: "*aʿtarif bayn yaday rabbī*" ("I confess in the presence of the Lord" [13.6]). Muḥammad's rendition is: "*uqsim amām Allāh*" ("I swear before God" [31.19]). Al-Qiṭṭ's translation reads: "*ushhid Allāh*" ("God is my witness" [51.7]). These translators, particularly Muḥammad, give the oath what appears to be the literal translation. In fact, they miss the nuance of the simplicity and spontaneity of Horatio's exclamation by supplying cumbersome renditions which provide for their Arab audience a much harsher and powerful oath than Shakespeare intends. An Arab-Muslim speaker would take an oath invoking the presence of God only in extremis. In contrast, Schmidt glosses Horatio's oath as "by God" (vol. 1, 95), which has a simple translation in Arabic: *wallāhi*. It is not hyperbole to state that this oath is the most commonly used oath in the Arabic language for Jewish, Christian, and Muslim Arabs. The seemingly literal, but actually excessive oaths used by Muṭrān, Muḥammad, and al-Qiṭṭ, are inferior to the simple rendition of both al-Juraydīnī and Jabrā, *wallāhi*, which is truer to the meaning of the original. This example illustrates that it is imperative that translators study the standard commentaries to ensure that Elizabethan usages are correctly understood.

    Among the most successful examples of a translator not being confused by the apparent and finding the actual meaning of Shakespeare's oaths occurs in al-Sibāʿī's *Coriolanus*. In the same speech in which he invokes Pluto, Marcius again swears while threatening the soldiers: "By the fires of heaven, I'll leave the foe / And make my wars on you" (I.iv.39–40). The "fires of heaven," according to both Kittredge (1383*n*39) and Harrison (1276*n*39), are the stars. Al-Sibāʿī understands this meaning and quotes an oath directly from the Qurʾan itself (al-Ṭāriq lxxxvi:1–4), rendering the expression as "*Wa al-samāʾ wa al-ṭāriq*" ("By heaven and the piercing bright star" [31.2]). Although it sounds rather elaborate in English, al-Sibāʿī's version actually gives the correct gist of the line. It has the virtue not only of rendering the line accurately but of doing so within the cultural/religious ethos of al-Sibāʿī's audience.

Bawdiness in Shakespeare

The Shakespearean text is full of sexual innuendos and obscene hints and remarks. Most of them depend on witticisms, wordplay, and puns. They are part and parcel of the text and have to be taken seriously in translation. In the Arab world, however, the question of obscenity is still quite sensitive. In mixed society, unsavory expressions are avoided. Hence, this question poses a problem when a play is supposed to be presented on the stage for the general public. I will look at the way in which the translators deal with this rather sensitive issue by showing that, where a line has only one meaning—that is, a ribald one—the translators frequently deal with it by deleting it altogether, just as in the case of certain oaths discussed above. On the other hand, where the ribald expression takes the form of a pun or double entendre, the translators are likely to ignore the sense which involves the indecent hint, translating only the superficial, innocent sense.

It should be stated at the outset that, unlike the translators' treatment of Shakespeare's oaths, there are very few generalities which can be stated with respect to their treatment or ribaldry. There is little unanimity among the translators as to how much their respective audiences will tolerate. This situation is one to be expected, however. Unlike the oaths, which touched upon fundamental religious beliefs, there are no established, universally accepted guideposts when it comes to treating ribaldry and bawdiness. Of necessity, this issue must be tied more closely to the translator's own personal preferences and tastes, as well as his assessment of how far his audience will allow him to go.

It would be tempting to posit a general rule that the earlier translators were less likely to render obscene meanings than their more modern counterparts. This temptation must be resisted, however. It is true that earlier translators, such as al-Qāḍī, Muṭrān, al-Juraydīnī, Amīn, and Ibrāhīm tend to be quite cautious in their translations, generally preferring to delete or soften ribald allusions. As to the later translators, no general statement encompassing all of them can be made. Muḥammad, al-Qiṭṭ, and most particularly Bākathīr are usually quite conservative in their renditions. Ḥusayn and, to a lesser extent, 'Anānī, usually omit or rewrite ribald expressions, although they sometimes include them. On the other hand, Jabrā seems to be the least inhibited of the translators, as he is not at all shy about rendering as accurately as possible Shakespeare's ribald expressions.

In the conversation between Hamlet and the clown, the latter tells Hamlet that "Water is a sore decayer of your whoreson dead body" (V.i.158–59). Muṭrān ignores the line completely, while al-Juraydīnī drops the obscene word and translates the line as: "*laysa ka al-mā' mufsid lil juthath"* ("there is nothing like water in decomposing corpses" [112.19]). Muḥammad and al-Qiṭṭ also delete the obscene reference, interpreting the line respectively as: *"al-mā' aqwā 'anāṣir al-fasād fī al-jasad"*("water is the strongest element in decomposing bodies" [187.8–9]) and *"Al-mā' 'āmil muhim fī taḥallul al-jasad al-mayyit"* ("water is an important factor in decaying a dead body" [246–47.14–15]). Jabrā is the only translator who renders the line correctly (if somewhat awkwardly when retranslated into English): *"Al-mā' mufsid la'in lil jasad al-mayyit ibn al-zāniyah"* ("water is a detested decomposer of the son-of-a-strumpet dead body" [146.2–3]).

In *The Tempest*, during the storm in the first scene, Gonzalo, referring to the boatswain, says, "I'll warrant him for drowning, though the ship were no stronger than a nutshell and as leaky as an unstanched wench" (I.i.42–44). Among the earlier translators, 'Umar 'Abd al-'Azīz Amīn and Ibrāhīm delete these lines completely. Al-Qāḍī changes their meaning entirely: "innī kāfil lahu bi'an lā yamūt gharaqan walaw 'ann al-safīnah laysat bi 'akbar wālā amtan min qishrat al-jawzah wa annahā akthar tahayyu' li qubūl al-miyāh min al-arḍ al-mujdibah" ("I warrant that he will not die by drowning though the ship were no larger and no sturdier than the shell of a walnut and it were more susceptible to accepting water than arid ground" [3.14–16]). The later translator, Jabrā, on the other hand, maintains the precise meaning of the original, representing the ribald expression as *"mūmis nāzifah"* ("a discharging harlot" [79.48]).

Although the above examples fit the hypothesis stated at the beginning of this section, I should caution against a false sense that there is a hard and fast rule about which translators do or do not retain these ribald remarks. A few lines after the ones quoted above, the clown happens upon another skull. He says, "A whoreson mad fellow's it was. Whose do you think it was?" (V.i.163–64). Hamlet, of course, responds that he does not know. The clown curses the owner of the skull, recalls some trivial indignity once offered by him, and identifies it as having belonged to Yorick. Of course, Hamlet recounts with great feeling the love shared between him and Yorick, whom Hamlet recalls "hath borne me on his back a thousand times" (V.i.173). The juxtaposition of the clown's callousness and Hamlet's love of Yorick is jarring. Hamlet's dear childhood companion is nothing to the clown but another whore's son. Though all but one translator of the identical word are unwilling to translate it correctly a few lines earlier, all the translators, except one, render "whoreson" correctly and accurately in Arabic for this line. They appear to understand that without the use of this word, it is impossible to convey to the audience the profundity of this scene. Where it is indispensible to the integrity of the scene to translate this bawdy expression correctly, these translators do not hesitate to do so. Only al-Qiṭṭ refuses to translate the line correctly, using an inferior word, *mājin* ("jester," although it could also mean "profligate" [247.6]), thus damaging the image Shakespeare creates.

In other instances, where the bawdy implication is of no comparative importance to the scene, the translators respond by deleting the implication altogether. The following example illustrates a line where a simple, innocent meaning is correctly translated into Arabic, but the sexual innuendo is utterly omitted. The nurse in *Romeo and Juliet* recalls that Juliet, when she was a child, had fallen on her face, prompting the nurse's husband to comment, "'Yea,' quoth he, 'dost thou fall upon thy face? / Thou wilt fall backward when thou hast more wit'" (I.iii.41–42). Ḥusayn's version is: "ahākadhā taṣquṭin 'alā wajhik? Sataṣquṭin 'alā ẓahrik ḥīna yakūn lakī min al-'aql akthar mimmā laki" ("do you fall like this on your face? You will fall on your back when you have more sense than this" [43.39–40]). 'Anānī renders the lines as "Hal waqa'ti 'alā wajhik? Sawfa taqa'īn 'alā ẓahrik ḥinamā yakbar 'aqluk" ("did you fall on your face? You will fall on your back when your mind matures" [85.43–44]). These lines do not contain the innuendo in Arabic that they do in English, and the translators do not explain the double entendre in a footnote. Apparently unwilling to allow even any hint of impropriety, Bākathir deletes the line entirely.

Although the contrast between where a ribald expression is or is not important to a scene may be used as a guidepost in whether the translators will render the expression correctly, it is by no means a litmus test. There are instances where even an unimportant line containing a sexual innuendo is translated accurately in Arabic, where the line is not likely to be overly offensive. A few lines after the ones quoted above, the nurse, still referring to Juliet's fall when she was a toddler, describes the lump which the child had on her forehead as "A lump as big as a young cock'rel stone" (I.iii.53). Naturally, in Bākathir's version this line goes with the rest of the lines which he deletes. But Ḥusayn renders it as: "*waram ka khiṣyat al-dīk al-saghīr*" ("A swelling [as big] as a young rooster's testicle" [43.52]). 'Anānī uses another word, "*baydah*," which is more or less like the nurse's "stone" and which sounds somewhat milder in Arabic, although it implies the same meaning. Here, the two translators do not hesitate to translate the ribald expression, in all probability because the reference is not to a human being. Thus the line is comparatively inoffensive to the audience, but its humor remains.

Later in the play, when the nurse approaches Mercutio, he, without provocation and seemingly only for comic effect, exclaims, "A bawd, a bawd, a bawd! So ho!" (II.iv.116). Obviously, this line can be deleted without materially affecting the play. It goes without saying that Bākathīr does precisely that. Surprisingly, however, both Husayn and 'Anānī render "bawd" exactly as "*qawwādah*" ("pandress"). No definitive explanation for this inclusion can be put forward. It is, however, true that use of this word in Arabic is quite common in its masculine form (*qawwād*), although not in polite society. The translators, then, may feel that the audience would not take extreme offense, particularly in light of the comedic quality of the scene.

There are occasions when even Jabrā does not translate a ribald expression. This occurs when a pun is simply incapable of being rendered into Arabic. A typical instance of this situation is in the first scene of *King Lear*. Gloucester attempts to tell Kent, using veiled words, that Gloucester's son, Edmund, is illegitimate. Kent does not understand and states, "I cannot conceive you." Gloucester responds, "Sir, this young fellow's mother could; whereupon the mother grew round-womb'd, and had indeed, sir, a son for her cradle ere she had a husband for her bed" (I.i.11–14). This play on the double meaning of the word *conceive* would be completely lost in Arabic. Jabrā translates Kent's comment as "*lam 'afhamka*" ("I do not understand you"), to which Gloucester responds, "*'umm hādhā al-fatā fahamatnī*" ("This young man's mother did understand me" [15.9–10]). Jabrā explains the pun in the original in a footnote. He translates the remainder of Gloucester's response accurately.

Conclusion

The question of oaths and religious beliefs has never been a basic question as far as the Shakespearean text is concerned (Nādir 166). Shakespeare, after all, did not intend to use his plays for religious advocacy. Yet, in translation into Arabic, this point as it relates to the audience's religious sensitivities has to be taken into consideration when oaths are dealt with. Some of the most successful translators have recognized that it may be more important to choose an image which conveys to the Muslim audience the meaning of Shakespeare's original, rather than rendering literally Shakespeare's imagery—a practice Kamāl Nādir also recommends (145–59). The translators seem consistently to assume that to render these blasphemous oaths literally would so offend their audiences as to drive them away.

In the examples provided respecting Shakespeare's use of bawdy language and innuendo, the translators seem to be guided by what they understand of their own culture and times and how far they believe their audiences will allow them to go. The success of Jabrā's translations is an indication that audiences have become more sophisticated with time, and that they may be far more willing to tolerate ribaldry than one might have supposed. It is an intriguing question—perhaps only to be answered by future translators—whether the wider Arab/Islamic audience might be equally willing to tolerate irreligious and blasphemous utterances in literature. Future translators must consider whether they might be cheating their audiences by censoring Shakespeare.

At the same time, however, translators must also maintain balance in their understanding of the two cultures they represent. Some scholars and translators are becoming better versed in Western traditions than their predecessors, but they are losing touch with their own cultural roots. For instance, Nādir, in his doctoral thesis, comments on Iago's line, "She that, so young, could give out such seeming / To seel her father's eyes up close as oak" (*Othello* III.iii.209–10). Nādir states that he had to change the metaphors because they are "incomprehensible to our audience who are familiar neither with falconry nor with oak" (265–66n212). This statement is not true. Falconry originated in the Middle East circa 2000 B.C., and has been continuously enjoyed there up to the present.[7]

A different aspect of this problem is demonstrated by Muṭrān's translation of a farewell in *Hamlet*. M. B. Twaij translates Muṭrān's phrase, "*alā al-ṭā'ir al-maymūn* ("good luck or Godspeed"), as "on the blessed bird," a literal rendition of the Arabic expression, but one which utterly fails to grasp the meaning of the original phrase. Twaij comments: "Strangely enough, this is an Arabic farewell used mostly for people who travel in aeroplanes, but Shakespeare did not live to Muṭrān's age to see such means of transportation" (105). Actually, this farewell existed in Arabic even before Islamic times and has nothing to do with airplanes, but was related to the ancient Arabs' belief in omens. The practice was this: A person, when he set out on a journey, or when he had a serious decision to make, used to let a bird fly. It was considered a good omen if the bird flew to the right. If it flew toward the left, however, whatever one had in mind had to be canceled.

To be sure, successful translation of Shakespeare's works into Arabic can only be accomplished as the translators become more and more familiar with Shakespeare's culture; however, if future scholars succeed in that endeavor only at the expense of understanding their own Arab/Islamic heritage, they shall have accomplished very little, indeed. The point of successful translation is to bridge the two cultures; it is not to eviscerate the translators' own culture.

Notes

1. All lines citations to Shakespeare's works are from the edition of Ribner and Kittredge.

2. Muḥammad al-Sibāʿī, who died in 1931, is one of the most famous Egyptian translators according to Muḥammad Yūsuf Najm, who highly praises him for being accurate and specific in handling the different foreign literary materials. He had to his credit several Shakespearean translations, such as *Coriolanus, Henry V, Julius Caesar,* and *Romeo and Juliet.* He also translated Byron's *Childe Harold's Pilgrimage,* Fitzgerald's *Rubāʿiyāt al-Khayyām,* and Carlyle's *On Heroes and Hero-worship,* in addition to numerous other titles and articles (Najm 249).

Muḥammad ʿIffat al-Qāḍī stated, in the introduction to his 1909 translation of *The Tempest,* that he translated the play from the original with the help of the French version. A judge in the Egyptian courts at the time he was translating the plays, he also translated *Macbeth* in 1911 into Arabic monorhyming verse. He had other translations from French into Arabic, including Voltaire's *Mérope* in 1889 (Najm 230–32).

Khalīl Muṭrān (1871–1949) is considered to be an important poet who strove and succeeded in revitalizing the tradition of Arabic poetry. His diction in Arabic was superb, but his translations of Shakespeare were neither faithful to the original nor accurate. Some critics think that Muṭrān may have relied rather heavily on the French translation, although he appeared to have frequently consulted the original text. M. M. Badawī, however, states that Muṭrān "did not translate directly from the English text, but from the French text of Georges Duval" (181–96). This fact may account for the many inaccuracies which appear in Muṭrān's text. Nevertheless, Muṭrān's translations, despite their glaring faults, were still popular up to the late seventies and were reprinted almost every year.

Muṭrān's translations include *Othello, Hamlet, Macbeth, The Merchant of Venice,* and *Julius Caesar.*

Sāmī al-Juraydīnī, in addition to *Hamlet,* translated *Henry V, Julius Caesar,* and *King Lear.* He also translated several other novels and essays from English into Arabic. Al-Juraydīnī's translations shared some of Muṭrān's defects in that they contained many errors and inaccuracies. He was neither a Shakespearean scholar nor an expert on Elizabethan literature. He oftentimes omitted what he did not understand and did not hesitate to summarize whole passages when he felt they were not important. Najm makes the point that al-Juraydīnī failed to be a more accomplished translator because his knowledge of English was deficient (Najm 22–25, 254). It must be pointed out that al-Juraydīnī translated directly from the English text while Muṭrān had been completely dependant on a French translation.

3. Jabrā Ibrāhīm Jabrā received his undergraduate and master's degrees from Cambridge University, and did postgraduate work at Harvard. He is an accomplished novelist, short story writer, poet (Arabic and English), painter, and literary and art critic. His translations include *Hamlet, Macbeth, King Lear, Othello, Twelfth Night, Coriolanus,* and the sonnets.

'Abd al-Wāḥid Lu'lu'ah received his M.A. and Ph.D from Harvard University. He is a noted literary critic in the Arab world. In addition to his translation of Shakespeare's *Timon of Athens* and *Pericles,* he translated T. S. Eliot's *The Wasteland* and some fourteen volumes of the *Encyclopaedia of Critical Idioms.*

4. 'Alī Aḥmad Bākathīr (1910–69), was a poet, a playwright, and an author who had more than thirty published works. He was influenced by the poetic plays written by Aḥmad Shawqī, the Arab poet laureate, while still studying at the university, hence his poetical monorhyme translation of *Twelfth Night* (Bākathīr), *Fann al-Masraḥiyah,* pp. 6–9.

5. All citations to the Qur'ān are from Abdullah Yusuf Ali's translation unless otherwise noted.

6. The Qur'ān, therefore, makes no mention of Jacob striving with God "and prevail[ing]" (Gen. 32:28). On the authority of the Verse of the Throne (and other qur'ānic verses), such a proposition is untennable. Similarly, the Qur'ān rejects any notion of God being involved in aquatic battles, such as are found in Psalm 74 or Isaiah 51:9–11.

7. For details on the falconry metaphor, see Kittredge, *Othello* III.iii.210; and Harrison, *Othello* I.iii.270, III.iii.210. On falconry, see Adham ibn Muḥriz al-Bāhilī. The original text of this work was written by al-Bāhilī during the reign of the Caliph Hārūn al-Rashīd, who reigned in Baghdad from 786 to 809 A.D. Also see Mark Allen, Zakī Muḥammad Ḥassan, and "Bayzara" in the *Encyclopedia of Islam.*

Works Cited

Ali, Abdullah Yusuf, trans. *The Holy Qur'ān*. Washington: American Interna-
    tional Printing Co., 1948.
Allen, Mark. *Falconry in Arabia*. London: Orbis Publishing, 1979.
Amīn, 'Umar 'Abd al-'Azīz. *Al-'Āṣifah*. Cairo: al-Maktabah al-Mulūkiyah,
    1930.2
'Anānī, Muḥammad Muḥammad. *Al-Masraḥ: Romeo wa Juliet*. Cairo: April,
    1965.
'Aṭiyah, 'Alī Imām. *Coriolanus*. Cairo: Al-Maktabah al-Mulūkiya, 1911.
Badawī, Muḥammad Muṣṭafa. "Shakespeare and the Arabs." Cairo Studies in
    English. Cairo: The Anglo-Egyptian Bookstore, 1963–1966. 181–96.
Al-Bāhilī, Adham ibn Muḥriz. *Manāfiʿ al-Ṭayr wa ʿIlājat Dāʾihi*. Ed. Saʿīd
    Salmān Abu 'Ādhirah. Abu Dhabi: Markaz al-Wathaʾiq wa al-
    Dirāsāt, 1983.
Bākathīr, 'Alī Aḥmad. *Fann al-Masraḥiyah min Khilāl Tajāribī al-Shakhṣiyah*.
    Cairo: Maʿhad al-Dirāsāt al-'Arabiyah al-'Āliyah, 1964.
———. *Romeo wa Juliet*. Cairo: Maktabat Miṣr, 1946.
Coppedge, Walter Raleigh. "Shakespeare's Oaths and Imprecations." Diss. U
    of Indiana, 1967.
Edwardes, Marian. *A Pocket Lexicon and Concordance to the Temple
    Shakespeare*. London: J. M. Dant, 1974.
The Encyclopedia of Islam. Leiden: E. J. Brill, 1927.
Evans, G. B., ed. The Riverside Shakespeare. Boston: Houghton Mifflin, 1974.
Harrison, G. B., ed. Shakespeare: The Complete Works. New York: Harcourt,
    Brace and World, Inc., 1952.
Ḥassan, Zakī Muḥammad. *Hunting as Practiced in the Arab Countries*. Cairo:
    n.p., 1937.
Ḥusayn, Mu'nis Ṭāhā. *Romeo wa Juliet*. Cairo: Dār al-Ma'ārif, 1968.
Ibrāhīm, Muḥammad 'Awaḍ. *Al-Laylah al-Thāniyatah 'Asharatah*. Cairo: Dar
    al-Ma'ārif, n.d.
———. *Al-'Āṣifah*. Cairo: Dār al-Ma'ārif, 1958.
Jabrā, Jabrā Ibrāhīm. *Al-'Āṣifah*. Baghdad: Dār al-Ma'mūn lil Tarjamah wa al-
    Nashr, 1986.
———. *Coriolanus*. Kuwait: Wazārat al-'I'lam, 1974.
———. *Hamlet*. Cairo: Dār al-Hilāl, 1960.
———. *Al-Laylah al-Thāniyatah 'Asharatah*. Baghdad: Dār al-Ma'mūn lil
    Tarjamah wa al-Nashr, 1989.
———. *Al-Malik Līr*. Cairo: Dā al-Hilāl, 1971.
al-Juraydīnī, Sāmī. *Hamlet*. Cairo: al-Maṭba'ah al-Raḥmāniya, 1912.
Lu'lu'ah, 'Abd al-Wāḥid. *Taymūn al-Athīnī*. 2nd ed. Beirut: al-Mu'assassah al-
    'Arabiyah li al-Dirāsāt wa al-Nashr, 1984.

Muḥammad, M. 'Awaḍ. *Hamlet.* Cairo: Dār al-Maʿārif, 1972.

Muṭrān, Khalīl. *Hamlet.* 1918(?). Cairo: Dār al-Maʿārif, 1971.

Nādir, Kamāl. "Shakespeare and the Arabic Speaking Audience." Diss. Birmingham U, 1958.

Najm, Muḥammad Yūsuf. *Al-Masraḥ fī al-Adab al-'Arabī al-Ḥadīth 1847– 1914.* Beirut: Dār al-Thaqāfah, 1967.

Onions, C. T. *A Shakespeare Glossary.* Oxford: The Clarendon Press, 1946.

Pickthall, M. M., trans. *The Meaning of the Glorious Koran.* New York: New American Library, n.d.

al-Qāḍī, Muḥammad 'Iffat. *Al-'Āṣifah.* Cairo: n.p., 1909.

al-Qiṭṭ, 'Abd al-Qādir. *Hamlet.* Kuwait: Wazārat al-'I'lām, 1971.

Ribner, Irving and Kittredge, George Lymon, eds. *The Complete Works of Shakespeare.* Waltham, Mass.: Ginn, 1971.

Schmidt, Alexander. *Shakespeare Lexicon.* 2 vols. New York: Benjamin Blour, Inc., 1968.

al-Sibāʿī, Muḥammad. *Coriolanus.* Cairo: Maktabat al-Taʾlīf, 1911.

Twaij, M. B. "Shakespeare in the Arabic World." Diss. Northwestern U, 1973.

A Gift of Tamil:
On Compiling an Anthology of
Translations from Tamil Literature

Paula Richman and Norman Cutler

Late in 1990 we learned that Professor K. Paramasivam was dying of cancer. K. P., as we all knew him, had been our teacher during the early years of our study of Tamil, a language spoken by more than fifty million people, primarily in South India. Over the years, K. P. had been a tremendous source of advice and knowledge about Tamil literature. We and his many other former students and colleagues realized the enormous impact he had had upon two generations of American scholars of Tamil. We decided that, in his honor, we would compile and present to him an anthology of translations from Tamil literature into English.[1] In the course of compiling the volume, we encountered a number of seemingly intractable problems. Although some of these problems were technical in nature, it became apparent over time that many of them were political in origin, insofar as they involved delicate negotiations between and across cultures, negotiations concerning definitions of bodies of knowledge, and the appropriateness of various modes of translation. The process of creating this book involved "cultural commuting" of several different kinds.

Whenever one compiles an anthology of translations, difficult decisions must be made. In retrospect, we see that our decisions involved three kinds of negotiations. First, because the project originated in response to a specific situation in the life of K. P., the selection of our contributors and our timetable for the project were shaped by contingent factors.[2] We were determined that K. P. receive this volume before he left us; the contributors were all students or colleagues of K. P. Second, we were maneuvering within a complex literary tradition that had been self-critical about its own verbal art for hundreds of years. Tamil is a language with a continuous literary tradition from ancient times (circa first century B.C.E.) to the present. One of the oldest regional literatures from the Indian subcontinent, Tamil literature is known for the beauty of its classical love poetry and heroic poetry, the variety of its religious texts, and the existence of a sophisticated and self-critical commentarial tradition. Certain decisions regarding selection and categorization of translations involved negotiations between competing notions of what comprises "Tamil literature." In addition, in conformity with Tamil literary tradition, we needed to pay attention to Tamil notions of how a book should be formally "released" before being made available to a general audience. Third, certain decisions involved the particular and dual-faceted nature of our intended readership. We were compiling an anthology of literature from the "Third World" for readers located *both* in India and in the United States. On the one hand, we compiled the book for a reader at ease with both the Tamil and English languages, who is at once familiar with Tamil linguistic and cultural conventions and attracted to the idea of reading Tamil poetry in a fresh way through the lens of English translation. On the other hand, we hoped to reach a reader who was unfamiliar with the Tamil language and its literature by making this literature accessible through careful selection, translation, and annotation.

As we engaged in the process of compiling the anthology we found ourselves confronted by issues regarding ways of honoring a teacher, perceptions of what constitutes "Tamil literature," strategies for representing Tamil words and Tamil literary categories in English, ways in which literary works are transformed by inclusion in an anthology such as ours, and culturally determined notions of the social life of a book. This essay analyzes these issues, highlights certain problems that arose, and explains what was at stake when we grappled with and attempted to solve these problems. Our conclusions concerning our negotiations of those problems may be helpful to others compiling anthologies under similar circumstances.

Conceptualizing a Mode of Honor

The conception for the volume emerged in response to two different cultural models for honoring a teacher or scholar. Initially we sought to create a volume in the form of a European-style festschrift, a compilation of scholarly essays by contributors who have all studied with a particular teacher. We also considered another model, the Indian felicitation volume presented to celebrate the sixtieth birthday of a prominent professor by students and admirers. Yet neither model was entirely satisfactory. The festschrift tends to be heterogeneous in content, and consequently few are motivated to read it from beginning to end, let alone purchase it. As editors, we wanted to create something more coherent than a festschrift. Since K. P. was a couple of years short of his sixtieth birthday and would not live to see it, the felicitation volume proved inappropriate. Rejecting each of these alternatives, we began considering other options. The idea of creating an anthology of translations from Tamil literature into English occurred to us. It struck us as an appropriate way to honor K. Paramasivam because it would create a volume symbolic of his extensive involvement with projects of translation.

Much of K. P.'s life involved moving across and between the assumptions of Indian academic culture and American academic culture. After teaching Tamil literature for many years at a college in Madurai (a medium-sized city in South India), he came to the University of Chicago in midlife to earn his doctorate in linguistics while teaching courses in the Tamil language to graduate students. He then returned to teach in Madurai where he continued to serve as a mentor for Western students and scholars who came there to pursue doctoral research in Tamil studies. Later he served as head of the Tamil language program run by the American Institute of Indian Studies, which provides language instruction for advanced students enrolled in American universities.

For over twenty years, in various capacities, K. P. designed pedagogical materials for nonnative students of Tamil. Such efforts bore fruit in a three-volume introductory textbook for Tamil language studies, which he co-authored with a colleague (Paramasivam and Lindholm). He also co-translated into English a commentary on a work of Tamil love poetry with a former student (Buck and Paramasivam). Furthermore, over the years he had been the consultant for many American translators who encountered problematic, obscure, or enigmatic passages in the Tamil texts that they were translating as part of their research. Clearly, translation was at the center of his scholarly interests.

K. P. was also a translator of English literary works into Tamil. In his early years he had translated into Tamil, in abridged form, over twenty

Western "classics," including novels by authors such as Jane Austen, Emily Brontë, Charles Dickens, and Sir Walter Scott. These translation projects gained part of their impetus from a tendency of the postindependence government of India to privilege English literature in public and private schools, following the earlier model of the British colonial government of India. At the same time, such a translation agenda grew out of a new form of cultural nationalism that asserted that the Tamil language is equipped to serve as an expressive medium for all the written texts that other languages had to offer. K. P. translated English novels for the South Indian Saiva Siddhanta Publishing Works Society, which pioneered such English-Tamil translations as part of its explicit program of promoting and glorifying the Tamil language. Later he wrote, in Tamil, an introduction to modern linguistics in which he presented to Tamil readers an overview of Western schools of modern linguistic analysis as it is practiced in Western universities (Paramasivam).

We felt that an anthology of translations would be an appropriate way to honor K. P. not only because of his personal connections with translation, but also because the concept of the literary anthology is well established in Tamil literary tradition. The tradition of compiling anthologies of poetry was central to the earliest corpus of Tamil texts, which bears the name "sangam" poetry, poetry composed by an "assembly" or "group."[3] Legend tells us that the authors of these poems were members of a literary academy patronized by one of the royal houses of the ancient Tamil land. Even if formal academies did not actually exist, the poems were perceived as a unified corpus, and the eight extant anthologies of sangam poems were compiled within a few centuries of the composition of the poems themselves. Most of the sangam poems were probably composed between the first century B.C.E. and the third century C.E., though some of the poems are later. The sangam anthologies constitute a highly unified literary corpus, defined not only by its chronological placement in Tamil literary history, but also by a shared repertoire of situations, settings, characters, and poetic figures. But there are also precedents in Tamil literary tradition for anthologies of selected verses from a range of texts representing a wide variety of genres and periods.[4] Thus, although our endeavor would be different in scope and focus from previous Tamil anthologies, in a sense it could be seen as the continuation of a long tradition in Tamil.

On a more practical note, such an anthology would have a cross-cultural audience, and hence, market. As editors, we were faced with the task of convincing a publisher that the book would appeal to a reasonably large group of readers. Recently a number of educational institutions in America have developed courses on world literature in translation. Yet no recent anthologies of Tamil literature in English translation spanning the full range of Tamil literary history existed, despite the fact that some superb English translations of particular Tamil texts, or texts belonging to a specific genre, have been published in the last two and a half decades (Ramanujan, Cutler, Hart and Heifetz, Peterson, Shulman). Thus, this volume seemed to fill a "market niche" for readers outside of India. Within India as well, English readers who could not read Tamil in the original could get a taste of one of India's most significant regional literatures through these translations.

Even in the course of conceptualizing the volume, the three spheres of negotiations identified at the beginning of this essay came into play. As for the specific context, we chose this kind of volume partially because translations would be symbolic of K. P.'s numerous achievements as a translator and because an anthology allowed us to include the work of many people who had studied Tamil with him. Second, Tamil literary tradition itself values anthologies, and thus the form is one well suited to garner the respect that we sought to express for K. P. Finally, because there was a market in the United States for translations of world literature, we could argue that this book was worthy of publication. Nonetheless, by deliberately aiming at two audiences—one composed of those with almost no knowledge about the tradition and one composed of those who hold a number of assumptions about the nature of Tamil literature—we encountered a series of problems.

Categorization and Representation: Defining the Scope of the Anthology

When we undertook this project we had, of course, a certain sense of what we meant by "Tamil literature," and thus of the range and kinds of texts we considered to be appropriate for inclusion in our anthology of translations. But at the same time the scope of the anthology was limited by our pool of potential contributors—the American students of Tamil literature and culture who had studied or worked with K. P. over the years. Thus the structure of the anthology was shaped by a combination of contingent as well as theoretical considerations. Though we knew that it would be impossible to produce a comprehensive anthology of translations from Tamil literature given the limited size of our pool of contributors, the choices we made in arranging and categorizing the contributions we received were informed by a model of the field of Tamil literature which includes certain kinds of texts and not others.

The anthology includes translations of twenty-one texts or selected portions of texts including some that, prior to their appearance in translation in our volume, had never before appeared in written form. The selections are grouped in six sections: classical poetry, wisdom literature, long narrative poems, devotional poetry, folk literature, and modern literature. Like certain other aspects of this project, these categories are as much intuitive as they are systematic. Some of these categories correspond closely to traditionally acknowledged corpora, while others reflect a perspective that would have been unknown to the Tamil literary academy until relatively recently. Retrospectively reflecting on the volume we had created, we were led to consider our implicit assumptions concerning the field of Tamil literature and the categories that articulate the internal structure of this field.

One question we were forced to confront was whether the very notion of "literature" as it is commonly understood by English speakers is a foreign importation in the context of textual production in Tamil. Today, the word *ilakkiyam* is commonly used as a signifier for the wide variety of texts that fall within the purview of the English word *literature,* but this is a relatively recent development.[5] Traditionally, *ilakkiyam* denoted a far more restricted corpus of texts, namely, the sangam poems and their direct descendants that exemplify the rules of grammar and poetics found in formal treatises on these subjects. In Tamil these rules are known as *ilakkaṇam.* At least in theory, the poems included in *ilakkiyam* texts embody the principles of poetic composition presented in normative terms in *ilakkaṇam* texts. Among the selections included in our anthology, only the poems included in the first section, classical poetry, qualify as *ilakkiyam* in the most restricted and formally correct sense of this term.

Besides *ilakkiyam,* the lexicon of Tamil offers several other terms that overlap in part but do not coincide precisely with our working model of the field of Tamil literature. Among these is *pāṭal* or its variant *pāṭṭu,* both derived from the verb *pāṭu* ("sing"). As one might expect, *pāṭal* or *pāṭṭu* may denote any text that is intended to be sung. Thus the defining criterion of a text that may described as *pāṭal* or *pāṭṭu* is not its content or poetic structure, but what Northrop Frye called its "radical of presentation."[6] Several of the texts included in the devotional poetry section are traditionally sung and thus could be and often are associated with the word *pāṭal*. But the majority of the texts included in the anthology are not traditionally found in musical settings, and thus *pāṭal*, though a term that may be applied to a wide variety of texts, excludes many that are included in our anthology.

Two other terms that come to mind are *ceyyuḷ* and *nūl*. *Ceyyuḷ*, derived from the verb *cey* ("do," "make"), denotes an autonomous verse or a stanza of a multistanzaic text that is composed in accord with formal rules of prosodic structure—a *ceyyuḷ* is a particular kind of linguistic "fashioning." The semantic field of *ceyyuḷ* in some ways exceeds and in some ways falls short of our working model. On the one hand, verses from texts that we would not consider to be candidates for inclusion in our anthology, such as the verses that compose grammatical texts, may be described as *ceyyuḷ*. On the other hand, the texts included in our folk literature and modern literature sections fall outside the purview of *ceyyuḷ* because they are not composed in formal stanzas. Like *ceyyuḷ*, the semantic field of *nūl* both exceeds our model in some ways and falls short in others. There are many texts which could be designated *nūl* that we would not have considered including in our anthology, such as technical treatises on rhetoric. But on the other hand, a text designated as *nūl* is necessarily a written text. It is therefore not an appropriate designation for the oral tales included in our section devoted to folk literature.[7]

Rather than as a domain of texts delimited by a single defining criterion, another way to think of the field of Tamil literature is as the sum total of a number of definable literary types. This approach is implicit in many of the Tamil literary histories produced during the past several decades in which the chapters are usually organized according to a combination of chronological and genre-based criteria (Purnalingam Pillai, Jesudasan and Jesudasan, Meenakshisundaram, Zvelebil). From this perspective the relevant question becomes, to what extent do the categories we relied upon to organize our anthology correspond to literary types or corpora that are recognized in Tamil literary tradition? The answer varies, depending upon the category.

Although the title of the first section of the anthology, "Classical Poetry," is not a translation of a Tamil term, it does indicate a specific body of literature; it is commonly understood among English-speaking scholars of Tamil language and literature as a designation for approximately 2,380 poems of varying length. This corpus is often referred to as "sangam poetry" because according to legend, as mentioned above, they were composed by members of a literary academy. Understood in these terms, Tamil classical poetry is a finite corpus of poems defined not only by their chronological placement in Tamil literary history, but also by a repertoire of situations, settings, characters, and poetic figures. These are, in fact, the poems that constitute *ilakkiyam*, "literature," in the most restricted sense of this word.

We titled the second section of the anthology "Wisdom Literature," a phrase which is a very free translation of the Tamil term *nitinūl*, more literally, "ethical text." This term in and of itself does not designate a finite corpus of texts, but many of the texts that would be described by traditional Tamil scholars as *nitinūl* do belong to such a corpus, the "eighteen shorter texts." (Eleven of these eighteen texts are so classified.) The translated verses included in this section of our anthology are from a text called *Tirukkuṟal*, by far the best known and most influential of Tamil *nitinūl* texts, which was probably composed during the fourth or fifth century C.E. *Tirukkuṟal* contains 1,330 couplets on a wide range of topics pertaining to family life and life in society, asceticism, kingship, and the protocol of love. The text is seen as a repository of wisdom about how to live one's life and, hence, our choice of the title.

The third section contains translated passages from two long narrative poems. In Tamil the genre to which these poems belong is called *kāppiyam*. One group of scholars of Tamil argues that the term *kāppiyam* is a Tamil transliteration of the Sanskrit *kāvya*, a genre of ornate literary creations, although the semantic range of the term has clearly shifted in Tamil. Another interpretation of the term is put forth by scholars from a different school of Tamil scholarship, who reject what they perceive to be the cultural imperialism of Sanskritic tradition. Representatives of this movement, who are devoted to the cause of "Pure Tamil," challenge claims for the supposed Sanskritic etymological origin of *kāppiyam*, arguing that the term is derived from the Tamil root "to contain" and owes nothing to North Indian linguistic sources.[8] If we were to translate the term *kāppiyam* into English, we would be forced to take a stand on this political issue, which has not been definitively resolved and is highly inflammatory. More crucial than this charged etymological controversy is the question of whether or not the poems designated *kāppiyam* in Tamil really constitute a definable literary genre. Not infrequently these poems are referred to as "epics" in English; but the Tamil poems categorized as *kāppiyam* do not exhibit many of the features commonly associated with the term *epic*. We wanted to avoid the misleading connotations of *epic*, but we also wished to avoid terminology that would be unfamiliar and perhaps alienating to a nonspecialist audience. We settled on the relatively neutral section title "Long Narrative Poems," which at least is an accurate, if not particularly specific, description of the two works represented in this section.

The fourth section, "Devotional Poetry," closely corresponds to a category which, though it may be found in histories of Tamil literature written in this century, does not have deep roots, as a category in Tamil poetic tradition. Five texts are represented in this section, and to varying degrees all express attitudes characteristic of *bhakti*, the devotional strand within Hinduism in which a devotee expresses personal love for a deity. Modern-day scholars employ recently devised Tamil terms such as *pakti ilakkiyam*, "devotional literature," or *pakti pātalkaḷ*, "devotional songs," to encompass the full range of texts that express a sensibility commensurate with personal love for a deity.[9] But prior to the nineteenth century such a categorization probably would have been puzzling if not incomprehensible. What is most untraditional about the modern category of "devotional literature" is that it does not acknowledge the distinction between the two major Hindu sectarian traditions—the Vaishnava (in which the god Vishnu is regarded as supreme) and the Saiva (in which the god Siva is regarded as supreme). Based on their formal and thematic similarities, we have included poems found in both the Vaishnava and Saiva canons of devotional poetry in this section of the anthology.

The last two sections of our anthology, devoted to folk literature and modern literature, are the most far removed from any traditional Tamil textual categories. In recent years the academic establishment has undertaken the task of collecting oral songs and tales in circulation among Tamil speakers. These songs and tales have no clearly attributable author, and prior to the act of recording by folklorists they did not appear in the form of fixed texts. There are no traditional textual categories to account for such "texts" other than simply "story" (*katai*) or "song" (*pāṭṭu*). But in the modern academic environment, folklore has acquired the status of a category of Tamil literature, and Tamil terms coined as equivalents for English "folktale," "folksong," and "folk literature" have entered the vocabulary.[10]

The last section of our volume is devoted to a few examples of modern literature. There are many variables that individually or in various combinations identify a text as "modern" besides the date of its composition.

These may include elements of textual form and content as well as extratextual variables such as circumstances of authorship, publication, and dissemination. Undeniably, India's contact with the West has had an enormous impact on the kinds of writing in Tamil that have arisen since the mid-nineteenth century. To take one example, traditionally, except for commentaries on texts composed in verse, there were virtually no prose texts in Tamil. Nowadays, however, there is an enormous output of short stories and novels in Tamil, and the most widely disseminated verse form is the "cinema song." The section "Modern Literature" is represented in our anthology by two original short stories, a prose poem, and a modern writer's retelling of a folktale.[11]

In our efforts to categorize and represent Tamil literature, we found ourselves carrying out a number of laboriously negotiated decisions. Our anthology needed to take into account traditional commentarial categories of literary texts, the political agendas of various schools of scholarship within Tamil studies, the distinctiveness of texts claimed by sectarian religious traditions, the influence of the academic study of folklore, and the impact of modern literary sensibilities. The negotiations within Tamil tradition, in combination with the needs of two very different audiences, led us to create an anthology that reflected a number of compromises.

Representing Tamil Titles and Tamil Terms

As editors we were faced with decisions concerning whether to use Tamil or English when naming the categories that organize the anthology, whether or not to translate the titles of texts, and how to represent Tamil words where they appear in the translations themselves and in the editorial apparatus. From the foregoing discussion it is apparent that we decided to rely upon English in naming our categories, even though some of these categories correspond to traditionally recognized genres of Tamil literature and could be more precisely identified by Tamil terms. We felt that our goal of ensuring that the anthology be maximally accessible to our intended audience of nonspecialists dictated that we use English to identify the sections of the anthology.

However, at the risk of appearing to be inconsistent, we concluded that the titles of some of the texts represented in the anthology should appear in the original Tamil and others should be translated. In the case of the traditional texts, it seemed appropriate to retain the Tamil titles, given the nature of one of our intended audiences. These works are widely known by their Tamil titles, and readers unfamiliar with Tamil literature can easily find short critical introductions to these texts, identified by their Tamil titles, in a number of surveys of Tamil literature written in English. Further, aside from the fact that the titles of some of these works are virtually untranslatable, to translate the titles of these works into English runs the risk of alienating our readers who are familiar with Tamil literature.

In contrast, we felt we needed to provide English titles for the folk narratives and selections from modern literature. The titles of the folk narratives were in most cases provided by the translators. In addition, there is no secondary literary history that gives a critical introduction to the folk narratives, since they were first recorded and translated by our contributors. In the case of the modern literary pieces, the Tamil titles of the selections do not have the recognition value of the titles of the traditional literary works. Some of the selections are fine pieces of writing, but relatively unknown to the Tamil public because they were published in serials or collections that are considered avant garde and are not widely disseminated among the Tamil reading public. Further, no standard histories of Tamil literature include all our translated modern selections, so the nonspecialist reader cannot easily consult other sources for background about these texts. Thus we decided that the needs of our diverse audiences would be better served by using English titles for these selections.

The texts that appear in the anthology with Tamil titles, as well as untranslated Tamil words that appear in some of the selections, forced us to confront the issue of how to represent the Tamil language. Tamil has its own script, but it is common in English writing dealing with Tamil subject matter to represent Tamil words in roman transliteration. The question was, what system of transliteration should we employ? We had the choice of using either the transliteration system most commonly employed by scholars in their academic publications or more informal Anglicized spellings.

The advantage of the standard academic system of transliteration is its precision. In this system each Tamil letter is discretely represented by a roman letter, sometimes with an accompanying diacritical mark. This transliteration system adapts the roman alphabet to phonemic distinctions in Tamil which it is not otherwise well equipped to represent. If one knows the transliteration system, one can easily and quickly reconstruct the original Tamil spelling by consulting the transliteration. And yet, for a reader who is not familiar with the system's conventions, a transliterated word may appear quite strange and provide little guidance to correct pronunciation. For example, as noted above, the name of the classical period in Tamil literature is commonly spelled "sangam" when native Tamil speakers represent the word in roman script. The term "sangam" is as well-known there as the word "medieval" is in the West. Yet, if we spell this term according to the scholarly system of transliteration, it becomes *caṅkam*. Those unfamiliar with the system invariably try to pronounce it as they see it spelled, something like "kankam" or "chunkam," neither of which replicates the Tamil pronunciation accurately. We did not want to produce a volume which employed spellings that alienated the nonscholarly segment of our audience; on the other hand, we wanted to ensure that we provided the most accurate transliterations possible.

Although standard editorial policy for scholarly consistency called for the same usage throughout the volume, in materials drawn from the modern period special problems arose. For example, some selections, especially in the folk literature section, mention characters whose caste is identified; often caste identity was crucial to the outcome of the story. The names of a number of castes have acquired familiar Anglicized spellings as a result of several projects undertaken by India's colonial rulers, such as compendia of caste communities (for example, Thurston) and the census, and also in the context of the policy of India's postindependence government to impose caste quotas on admission of candidates to educational institutions and in hiring of candidates for government jobs. These spellings are recognizable to almost everyone who reads English in the state of Tamilnadu. For instance, according to the standard scholarly system, *dhobi*, a term commonly used to denote the washerman caste, should be written *tōpi*, but this spelling would tend to alienate and confuse our Tamil readers unfamiliar with the scholarly transliteration system and more accustomed to the Anglicized spelling widely in use.[12] The alternative was to use more informal Anglicized spellings that, for the nonspecialist, may provide a more accessible guide to pronunciation.

Eventually our wish to create a volume accessible to both of our intended audiences led us to adopt a hybrid transliteration plan. Generally, we used the scholarly system with the premodern texts and omitted

or minimized formal transliteration in the sections devoted to folk literature and modern literature, though some words appear in familiar, informal Anglicized spellings throughout the volume. We felt that this was
an appropriate compromise because this dual system acknowledged that
the British colonial presence had shaped the way Tamil phonology was
represented in roman script by Indians during the colonial and postindependence periods.

The Anthologizer as Translator

Our volume "translates" not only because it contains English versions of
texts originally composed in Tamil, but also because the activity of
compiling an anthology involves other kinds of translating. Traditionally,
the texts represented in our volume are or were composed, deployed, and
consumed in a number of markedly different environments. The two
canonical poems included in the section on devotional poetry, for instance, have traditionally been employed as liturgy and as a basis for
theological discourse. From the perspective of traditional devotees, the
authors of these poems are saints and the poems represent a spontaneous
expression of their authors' devotion rather than the product of their
authors' schooling in techniques of literary composition. This model of
the creative process stands in direct contrast to the model implicit in
legends concerning the composition of the sangam poems by poets who
belonged to a literary academy patronized by the kings of an early South
Indian dynasty. Also implicit in this legend is the implication that the
classical poems were intended for consumption by the literary connois-
seur, not, like the devotional poems, as verbal acts of worship.

Audience and medium of consumption are major variables that
distinguish the texts from one another. The classical poems, while they
are not exclusive to members of any particular religious group, are
composed in a very erudite and now archaic form of the Tamil language,
and even in their own day their audience would have been restricted to
the educated few. The saints' poems, in contrast, while more exclusive
in the sense that they traditionally "belong" to particular religious
communities, are much more accessible than the classical poems in
linguistic and stylistic terms. A revealing contrast can also be made
between the oral tales included in the folk literature section that, in
their original form, circulate primarily among a rural audience whose

members are not necessarily literate, and the selections included in the modern literature section which are intended for a largely urban, literate audience and are consumed through the medium of print.

Another factor that distinguishes these texts and the implicit models of "literature" they embody in their original contexts is the intended ends they address: The *telos* of some of these texts is their aesthetic effect; for others, it is to express or stimulate a religious experience. Others may be valued primarily as entertainment, as social commentary, or as moral instruction. Or a single text may combine several of these ends. Brought together in our anthology, in many instances these ends are muted, if not effaced altogether. What then is the *telos* of these texts after they have undergone transformation by being brought together in our anthology? If there is a single teleological and selective principle operative in our anthology, it is perhaps that we have valued the works we have included first and foremost as creative acts of the imagination.

When the contents of our anthology are considered in these terms it becomes apparent that the anthology represents a "translation" of far-reaching proportions, whereby the differences in the literary models and literary pragmatics that distinguish these texts from one another are leveled and subordinated to a model that assumes an audience that will read them in a foreign language and, except for the selections in the modern literature section, in an alien medium.[13]

Releasing the Book

In light of this transformative process our anthology can be described as an innovation; however, the book was received in a very traditional fashion—on the occasion of a book-releasing ceremony. Initially, we assumed that our goal of honoring K. P. would be met when we completed the volume. But our conversations with Tamil friends and colleagues indicated that, according to the norms of traditional Tamil "book" culture, the volume, once complete, should be "released" in an appropriately coded ritual.[14] Although we both had editorial experience which assisted us in compiling the anthology of translations, neither of us had the specialized knowledge needed to plan this particular event. In attempting to construct the symbolism and structure of the book-releasing ceremony, we once again found ourselves trying to bridge two cultural worlds while trying to be sensitive to the constraints of each.

Essentially, the book-releasing ceremony is one among a series of celebratory events, often referred to as "functions" in contemporary South Asian culture. There are marriage functions, betrothal functions, first haircut functions, sacred thread investiture functions, retirement functions, opening of a new concert hall functions, first classical dance recital functions. The list is long. A function generally includes a core of fairly standard key ceremonies that can be condensed or elongated, ceremonies geared to the symbolic significance of the event.[15]

In a book-releasing function, a prominent person presents the first copy of the book to another prominent person while an audience of well-wishers observes. Although our project did not exactly fit into the pattern of a function for a teacher's sixtieth birthday (as mentioned earlier), some nuances of that kind of function seemed to color the celebration as well. In addition, there was an award for distinguished service presented by a representative of the International Studies Office at the University of Wisconsin-Madison. Such an addition also gave the ceremony something of the tenor of an American academic honors or award assembly. Because the final ceremony contained elements of all three kinds of events, it possessed a hybrid cultural content and tone.

Initially we envisioned a simple ceremony for a few people held in the building where K. P. taught Tamil, followed by some tea and snacks, but Tamil friends insisted that proper procedure called for a far more elaborate and formal event than we had planned. The ceremony that finally occurred was structured according to elaborate social and ritual practices. The event took place in a high status hotel, multicolored invitations were sent, more than one hundred and thirty guests attended, and a company that specializes in weddings videotaped the entire affair. A cake in the shape of a book, with the Tamil word *vāḻttukkaḷ* ("felicitations" or "best wishes") written on it, was the centerpiece of the post-ceremony reception. During the ceremony there were many testimonials, much praise, numerous garlands, several gifts, and many awards. References to K. P.'s good character and excellent teaching, to the auspiciousness of the city of Madurai, and to the greatness of Tamil abounded.

We had assumed that the ceremony would focus upon honoring a single individual, but it ended up celebrating the achievements of K. P.'s employer as well as his place of residence, Madurai. The costs of the ceremony, as well as a grant to help defray costs, were paid by the American Institute of Indian Studies (AIIS), the academic institution that employed K. P. as a Tamil teacher for the last fourteen years of his life.

The AIIS is a consortium of American educational institutions that awards research grants to students and faculty at American universities and colleges to study in India, conducts advanced South Asian language training programs in India, and develops various kinds of research resources. All the top officers of the institution in India and two from the United States were present at the ceremony and were honored at the function. The occasion also celebrated Madurai, with many references to it as a place which respects Tamil and is connected with the ancient Tamil academies of legend. True to the Tamil social context, at the book-releasing ceremony honor was widely distributed.

Just as the ceremony was less exclusively oriented to K. P. than we had expected, it was also more hierarchical. The determination of who received honor focused to a large extent on the group of people permitted to sit on the dais, a raised platform at the front of the hall. Those qualified to sit on the dais were restricted to the presider, the book releaser, the chief guest who receives the first copy (the president of AIIS), the master of ceremonies, K. P., his wife, and the editors of the book. Other people—a colleague from the college where K. P. had taught who gave a speech about K. P. as a teacher, the student who presented a velvet purse of money, and the person who proposed a vote of thanks—all sat in the audience and mounted the dais when it was time to perform their prescribed role. The people on the dais received brightly colored garlands made of high-quality silk and a greater share of the honor than those who merely sat in the audience.

The core of the event was two ritual sequences. First the book needed to be officially "released," that is, unwrapped and presented to the chief guest. At first this ritual seemed puzzling to us because it directed attention away from K. P., for whom the ceremony was being held, and toward the book-releaser and chief guest. Eventually it became clear that the prominence of each of these two people was critical: the status of the person to be honored was enhanced by the status of the chief guest and book-releaser. Second came the felicitation. K. P., his wife, the presider, and the editors each received a shawl, a gift traditionally given to indicate respect for the wearer and to bestow prestige upon him or her. The culminating vote of thanks expressed gratitude toward everyone who had anything to do with the project, including the proofreader, the person who typed the manuscript, the publisher, the manager of the hotel, and all the guests who attended. Clearly a link between the book and this wider community had been established by the ceremony.

The videotape of the book-releasing ceremony reached us two months later, and we needed to have it transferred from the Indian video format to the American one, yet another instance of the cultural translations needed to bring this project to a close. We had noticed certain similarities between the book-releasing ceremony and an elaborate Tamil wedding at the time of the event. The videotape brought these similarities to the fore. The genre of matrimonial videos has been influenced both by the Indian film industry and the recent introduction of computer graphics. The video of the book-releasing ceremony began with an extremely long sequence, set to upbeat music, in which the information on the invitation to the book-releasing ceremony was reproduced using computer graphics in sequences with temple chariots and other auspicious symbols interspersed.

In comparison to the book-releasing ceremony in Madurai, the introduction of the book to the U.S. market was rather dull. It appeared first at a book exhibit at the Association of Asian Studies meeting in Washington, D.C., three months after its appearance in India, having survived the long trip by sea mail. But there it was just one among a number of books on Indian literature, politics, religion, art, economics, and other topics, laying on a table while convention-goers perused the books in the booths.

During the several months when we were busy with the time-consuming arrangements for the book-releasing ceremony, we viewed the ceremony at times as a weighty and burdensome addition to the task of completing the anthology of translations, an addition loaded with excessive ceremony and sentimentality. To our surprise, however, we found the event to be a deeply moving tribute to a Tamil scholar about whom all involved cared a great deal, as well as a meaningful way to send the anthology of translations out into the world. The ceremony showered K. P. with honor, and when, a few days later, he was released from this world and his physical pain, he died an appreciated man. In the end the final product, the anthology compiled in his honor, seemed to justify the delicate and complex cultural negotiations involved.

Conclusions

As we learned during a year's time, the process of compiling an anthology of translations from Tamil into English entailed a number of problems.

We did not fully understand that behind the debates about book section titles, the morass of transliteration issues, and extensive discussions about who should be permitted to sit on the dais, there were unacknowledged cultural assumptions which were structuring conflicting alternatives. The opportunity to write this essay has enabled us to analyze our experience in light of the issues raised in this volume. We have come to see that the assembly and presentation of an anthology of translations from Tamil literature by two American scholars has certain implications that bear careful examination. All three categories of decisions we made—in relation to the specific and contingent circumstances of the project, the self-perceptions within Tamil literary tradition, and the dual audience for which the book was intended—shaped the final product in ways significant enough for us to conclude that these categories of decisions may be operative in significant ways for other such enterprises involving compilation of anthologies.[16]

Anthologies do not simply come into being. There has to be the impulse, motivation, or necessity to create them. This anthology of translations came about because of a specific historical circumstance, our desire to honor a Tamil scholar at a particular point in his life. The identity of the contributors to the volume and the manner in which the man honored was involved in its release shaped the production and dissemination of the volume. It is likely that many anthologies of translations are at least partially the result of similarly contingent factors—in the lives of the translators, the compilers, the publishers, or some combination of the three.

As for the second category, negotiations within Tamil literary culture, surely the act of translating from one language to the other will, at some level and at some point in time, affect the way the members within a literary tradition view their own tradition—whether they reject the outsider's representation, embrace it, defy it, or transform it. The use of indigenous categories to classify texts can give an anthology a certain kind of faithfulness. Yet totally faithful adherence to traditional literary categories propagated by a literary elite with certain vested interests may obscure other kinds of literature that exist within the culture. Thus, the process of classification entails certain kinds of assumptions that should be scrutinized.

Finally, by compiling this anthology we hoped to create a bridge between Tamil literature and readers of diverse cultural backgrounds. We found that because we tried to address the needs and expectations of two very different audiences, we could not avoid making certain compromises and that our book must in certain ways remain a hybrid of competing strategies for representing Tamil literature in translation. We hope that this analysis of the problems inherent in compiling an anthology of literature from the "Third World" for consumption by both "Third World" and "First World" audiences will suggest to others who undertake similar projects the range of issues involved in this delicate and problematic enterprise.

Notes

We are grateful to Anuradha Dingwaney, Carol Maier, Sandra Zagarell, and Abbie Ziffren for helpful comments on an earlier version of this essay.

1. This was the beginning of the project that eventually culminated in Norman Cutler and Paula Richman, eds., *A Gift of Tamil: Translations from Tamil Literature* (New Delhi: Manohar and American Institute of Indian Studies, 1992).

2. Although this essay focuses primarily upon the "political"—in the broad sense defined above—aspects of the compiling of the anthology and our sadness at K. P.'s illness and suffering gave the task a personal urgency that is largely outside the bounds of this academic essay, except insofar as the knowledge that he had only about a year to live did affect the timetable for our project: It was crucial to us that K. P. be alive to enjoy the honor the volume would bring to him.

3. For an illuminating discussion of sangam poetry, as well as some widely acclaimed translations of selected sangam poems, see Ramanujan.

4. Among the most noteworthy of such anthologies is a text called *Puṛattiraṭṭu*. (*Tiraṭṭu* is one of several words in Tamil that may be translated "anthology.") This text, which was probably compiled in the fifteenth century, contains 1,570 verses selected from thirty texts spanning approximately one thousand years of Tamil literary history and which represent a number of genres. Beginning in the mid-nineteenth century, many anthologies of Tamil poetry have been compiled. Such projects have sometimes been undertaken in the interest of preserving literary works that might otherwise be lost and also to provide sources of quotations for orators and essayists.

5. The word *ilakkiyam* and other italicized Tamil words appearing in this essay are transliterated according to the *Tamil Lexicon* system, the transliteration system most widely used in the scholarly community. In the Madras University *Tamil Lexicon,* the most complete and authoritative Tamil-English dictionary,

ilakkiyam is defined as follows: "(1) The thing defined (2) Example from classical writings to illustrate a rule of grammar, or the different meanings of a word or an expression, or to justify the use of a word or expression (3) Classical writings which form the basis for inductively framing the rules of grammar, literary works (4) mark, butt."

6. "The basis of generic distinctions in literature appears to be the radical of presentation. Words may be acted in front of a spectator; they may be spoken in front of a listener; they may be sung or chanted; or they may be written for a reader." (Frye 246–47).

7. The word *nūl* is used in a number of contexts, both literary and non-literary. In the latter it means "string" or "thread," and this may be related to its common use in a sense similar to English "text," because traditionally South Indian texts were inscribed on palm leaves which were perforated and tied together to form a "book" (*nūl*). One of the meanings for *nūl* found in the *Tamil Lexicon*, "systematic treatise, science," suggests the kinds of texts denoted by this word which fall outside the purview of our anthology.

8. The Sanskrit etymology is found, for example, in the *Tamil Lexicon*. The opposite view is found, for example, in Balusamy (163).

9. *Bhakti* is a Sanskrit word. Adapted to Tamil phonology, it is transliterated as *pakti*.

10. In modern Tamil discourse on folklore one encounters terms such as *nātōti katai* ("folktale"), *nāṭṭuppurappāṭal* ("folksong"), and *nāṭṭuppura ilakkiyam* ("folk literature"). All these terms include forms of the word *nāṭu,* which may be loosely translated as "country."

11. A number of terms have been introduced into Tamil to denote modern literary forms. For "short story," the loan translation *ciṟu katai* is commonly used. Similarly, *vacana kavitai* is the term used to denote "prose poem." English "novel" (spelled *nāval* in Tamil) has been borrowed as a signifier for this very popular modern genre.

12. In fact, the term *dhobi* is a word of North Indian origin, and the Anglicized spelling in common use is actually more faithful to the phonology of this word as it would be written in North Indian scripts than is the Tamilized spelling *tōpi.*

13. However, nowadays many of the older texts have been absorbed into the modern culture of print, for instance, as components of high school, college, and university literature curricula.

14. "Book" here is in quotes because even in the days when poets wrote on palm leaves, an elaborate ritual initiated the dissemination of the text.

15. The term *function* has been borrowed from English and taken on its own particular semantic range in several South Asian languages. The term is used somewhat loosely to indicate a big event. Compare the Marathi term *tamasha.*

16. For an article about the politics of editing anthologies of Latin American literature, see Myriam Díaz-Diocaretz, "Framing Contests."

Works Cited

Balusamy, N. *Studies in Maṇimēkalai.* Madurai: Athirai Pathippakam, 1965.

Buck, David, and K. Paramasivam, trans. "A Translation of Nakkīraṉār's Commentary on Iraiyaṉār's Study of Stolen Love." Forthcoming.

Cutler, Norman. *Songs of Experience: The Poetics of Tamil Devotion.* Bloomington: Indiana UP, 1987.

Cutler, Norman, and Paula Richman, eds. *A Gift of Tamil: Translations from Tamil Literature.* New Delhi: Manohar and American Institute of Indian Studies, 1992.

Díaz-Diocaretz, Myriam. "Framing Contexts, Gendered Evaluations, and the Anthological Subject." *The Politics of Editing.* Ed. Nicholas Spadaccini and Jenaro Talens. Minneapolis: U of Minnesota P, 1992. 139–55.

Frye, Northrop. *Anatomy of Criticism: Four Essays.* Princeton: Princeton UP, 1957.

Hart, George L., III, trans. *Poets of the Tamil Anthologies.* Berkeley: U of California P, 1979.

Hart, George L., and Hank Heifetz, trans. *The Forest Book of the Rāmāyaṇa of Kampaṉ.* Berkeley: U of California P, 1988.

Jesudasan, C., and Hephzibah Jesudasan. *A History of Tamil Literature.* Calcutta: YMCA Publishing House, 1961.

Meenakshisundaram, T. P. *A History of Tamil Literature.* Annamalainagar: Annamalai U, 1965.

Paramasivam, K. *Ikkāla Moḻiyiyal Aṟimukam.* Madras: South India Saiva Siddhanta Works Publishing Society, 1984.

Paramasivam, K., and James Lindholm. *A Basic Tamil Reader and Grammar.* 3 vols. Evanston, IL: Tamil Language Study Association, 1980.

Peterson, Indira Viswanathan, trans. *Poems to Śiva: The Hymns of the Tamil Saints.* Princeton: Princeton UP, 1989.

Purnalingam Pillai, M. S. *Tamil Literature.* 1929. Thanjavur: The Tamil U, 1985.

Ramanujan, A. K., trans. *Poems of Love and War from the Eight Anthologies and the Ten Long Poems of Classical Tamil.* New York: Columbia UP, 1985.

Shulman, David Dean. *Songs of the Harsh Devotee: The Tēvāram of Cuntaramurttināyaṉār.* Philadelphia: U of Pennsylvania Department of South Asia Regional Studies, 1990.

Tamil Lexicon. 6 vols. 1924–36. Madras: University of Madras, 1982.

Thurston, Edgar, assisted by K. Rangachari. *Castes and Tribes of Southern India.* 7 vols. 1909. Delhi: Cosmo Publications, 1975.

Zvelebil, Kamil Veith. *Tamil Literature.* Wiesbaden: Otto Harrassowitz, 1974.

Translation, Cultural Transgression and Tribute, and Leaden Feet

Mary N. Layoun

At every moment, the foreign language, whose power is limitless, can draw back into itself, beyond any translation. He told himself, I am a middle ground between two languages: the closer I get to the middle, the further I am from it. . . . Teach me to speak in your languages.

—Abdelkebir Khatibi, *Amour bilingue*

It has become clear that translational thinking is fundamental to all acts of human communication and that indeed all acts of communication are acts of translation. . . . [are] an integrating force in a fragmentary and discontinuous world.

—R. Schulte & J. Biguenet, *Theories of Translation*

Translation is a funny thing—something you often find yourself doing even when you think you are not. Disciplined in comparative literature, I would resolutely insist that I didn't "do" translations; I worked "in the original." Translation was a literary/scholarly task for which I had neither training nor desire. Then, in a large midwestern university, at the front of a lecture hall teaching one of the masters' great pieces (Homer's *Odyssey*, I think), I fell into translation. Not from classical Greek into modern English. I could have, but someone had already done that and bound it between two suitably dark and ancient-looking covers. I was, in any event, less interested in that aspect of translation and more interested in a translation of what most students were trained to think of (almost idly) as *their* cultural tradition into something *not* so assuredly theirs. Something obviously distanced by time and space and language, but also by multiple and complex acts of appropriation or interpretation—or translation. Something that had been claimed in their name and, in the claiming, "carried over" into a "western tradition" as an originary moment in a master narrative of "western civilization"—as exemplary oral

267

epic, as the emergence of the individual and reason, as the story of a peripatetic and cleverly scheming storyteller, as a "cradle" for European culture. In that context, then, the more appropriate translation of Homer's masterpiece seemed an insistence on distance and unfamiliarity. This notion of translation is not a violation of "the task of the translator." For the grittiness of a cultural text made strange rather than neatly "ours" is also translation's "bearing across." Rather than translation as the rendition of the "foreign" into the "familiar," it is translation as a multivalent configuration of the attempt to make familiar, of the strange and silent, of the inapprehensible, and of the drawn-near. And such a configuration—the task of the translator, her translation, and the audience(s) for it—is virtually unintelligible without a consideration of the context of and reasons for, the frame narrative of, the act and product of translation.

To begin with this notion of translation as the attempt to make unfamiliar is not, however, to postulate some untransgressed purity of the original and selfsame text, language, or culture—regardless of what the *Odyssey* is in the (familiar) original and might be in multiple (foreign) translations. Nor, obviously, is this making unfamiliar and distant the only direction of translation as practice or idea.[1] But I begin with this notion in the attempt to underscore the situatedness of the production and the consumption of translation—of both its practice and idea. Even as translators are "between language and cultures," they are also very much of, in, and subject to specific languages and cultures at a given moment. The audiences who eagerly consume translations—savoring, in the process, the pleasures of "global connection"?—are as situated, remaining most often (quasi-safely) in their language(s), their space(s), their time(s). For translation can titillate with the distant and strange while simultaneously reinforcing the solidity and familiarity of the implacably here and now. And yet that here and now is itself almost invariably already a translation; it is already a heterogeneous complex translated as and into order and coherence. In the context of this problematic movement-between—a movement without ethereal wings or high-tech transporters (indeed, with often "leaden feet") and most often on unequal terms—I would like to consider translation as both transgression and tribute. And that transgression and tribute is of and to cultures *and* of and to their boundaries. Of course those boundaries have been and continue to be crossed variously. But their crossing so as to bring back or over the challenge of the "foreign" is the notion of translation that I would like to foreground for the moment.

This direction—translation as bearing-across-challenge—might appear to run counter to Talal Asad's charge that "a good translation should always precede a critique" (Asad 156). But Asad's astute discussion of (a once and perhaps still imperial) British social anthropology and its cultural translations, and his critical reading in that context of Gellner's essay, "Concepts and Society," tracks the practice and idea of a particular translation with a distinct subtext. What is finally at issue in that context might not be translation as necessarily separate from and precedent to critique. For if translation is always an intervention (and I would argue that it is) and always an interpretation (as many accounts and theories of translation insist), then to postulate the separation of translation from critique or interpretation or "transcending stories" (Crapanzano 76) is to postulate an impossibility. What might be far more possible, efficacious, and to the point is to foreground—and contest—the frame story (or stories) in which both translation and critique are situated, the story (or stories) of which they are a part. The intracultural or intercommunal translation in which I am interested here is, on the one hand, distinct from the translation/critique between British social anthropology and the cultures which are objects of its discipline. But these different translations are scarcely unrelated or without implication for one another. The focus of what follows is the ways in which acts of (a perhaps more metaphorical) translation in fiction can simultaneously be critical acts of contestation, both within the same culture and society *and* between different ones.

To engage in the vexed process of translation, then, is not only to translate a book, an oral story, a film script, a cultural practice—the literary and cultural works of which translation is a relatively more familiar process. Translation is, but not only, this putative transfer from one language and culture to another. It is, but not only, the making strange of the apparently familiar. It is, but not only, the interpretive re-presentation of the strange and foreign as, if not familiar, at least plottable and arguably comprehensible in more or less familiar terms. It can be and often has been—as Asad and others so astutely point out—the imperial rendering and domination of another culture.

But translation can also be moving—often violently—between genders, between nationalities, between dominant and counterdominant communities, between histories. Translation can also be the attempt to bear across sometimes fierce divides stories of difference and the foreign that are not necessarily thereby to be eliminated or subsumed. Translation can also be to carry across the challenge or charge of the different, a charge to reconsider our cultural mappings of a putative sameness and difference *and* our practices (as those Asad contests in Gellner) based on those maps. It can be to respond to stories of injustice or ignorance or displacement by "bearing across" those stories to and for others and ourselves. It is this sense of translation that underlies what follows as, I would suggest, it informs the notions of translation in *Sitt Marie Rose* by Etel Adnan and *Al-jabal al-saghīr / The Little Mountain* by Elias Khoury. These novels trace the sometimes frantic movement in between and across, bearing stories of the foreign and different from which the same is always-already differentiated. And the foreign there is a direct challenge to business-as-usual of the same.[2]

A more leisurely (and privileged) tempo of that movement "in between" and "across" has recently acquired a particular and even fervent resonance in the citation of the post-, the trans-, and the multi- as appropriate spatial and temporal markers of translation. But, in this citation, there is a tendency to ignore or collapse the time- and space-*between,* the interstices of, languages and cultures. In the idea and practice of carrying across or translating something—a text, a cultural artifact, a historical incident—the both temporal and spatial between or across is often elided as beside the point. The point is to get there, to reach the destination. The in-between is a space or time to be transversed as quickly as possible on the way from the "source" tongue or culture or discourse to the "target" tongue or culture or discourse. Here, that space-between is obviously metaphorical (though it need not necessarily be so). Yet for all of that, the space-between is crucial to translation. It is decisive to the end "product" of translation and to the consumption of that product. For who can make it between and across? And bearing what? From whom (and not just from where) do they come? To whom do they arrive? And what happens in that space-between, however metaphorical, not only to the translation, but to the translator, and, most especially to the audiences from and for whom the translation is born across?

And if the between is diminished, its tenancy is more difficult as well, as the demands of the space proper sound more insistently and, at the same time, its demarcations become ever more problematic.[3] For multiple mappings—of languages, of cultures, of social organization—clearly underlie the acts of producing and consuming translation. Yet translation is, at least initially, a confrontation of sorts with cartographic aporia. That is the collision of a (variously generated) desire to map and know with apparently unmappable or only partially knowable contradiction, multiplicity, and difference. To address (if not answer) such an aporia, pristine refusal—a chaste abstinence from mapping—is scarcely adequate. It is, in any event, inconsequential. Mapping occurs nonetheless, even in the face of selective abstinence. And the maps drawn include (and plot) the abstainer as well. The older imperial plottings are (and were) unable to accommodate the spaces or times of either imperial centers or of their objects of territorial desire. And so translation and the between on which it plays—between nations, states, languages, cultures—are increasingly caught by and in an economic trans-, post-, multi- that simultaneously vacates and depends on operative notions of nation, state, language, and culture.[4] In this scheme of things, if arguably for cultural and intellectual purposes than rather more clearly for economic and political ones, the space-between is scarcely exempt from discipline, exploitation, or mapping. On the contrary, the space-between is equally administered with the aid of a plethora of hyphens and prefixes.

But, again, it is not mapping itself that is the issue. Nor translation. It is how, by whom, and for whom those maps or translations are drawn and maintained. Translation, too, depends on maps of the knowable and the plottable. If those maps of bearing across and moving between were compelled by the manifest power of (an older imperial) cartography (of locations, identities, boundaries), contemporary border crossings, remappings of terrain, reconfigurations of locations—and "translations"—are not utterly fated to reduplicate those earlier ways of plotting space or time. Translations and border crossings may well still be implicated in imperial maps. But they might sometimes also suggest other ways of knowing and mapping.

If translation is implicated in mapping and mapping in domination, to refrain from translation/mapping is not thereby a protection of the original. Silence or an insistence on the incommunicable "original" language/text/culture does not necessarily ensure its sanctuary. Even if such privileging of an "original" were possible, its object—the "original"—is already permeated with the "foreign" and the non-"original" tongue, text, culture. Not only the space-between but the space-proper is contested, rife with multiple struggles. This is not, by extension, to postulate that there is only always more of the same. However, that "difference" between cultures, literatures, societies, languages is not necessarily discernible, comprehensible, or sustainable as we choose. Nor are the authorial intentions of the translator the final determinant of meaning or practice. The familiar terms—the apparently incontrovertible compass points, the orderly plotting of time, the sometimes almost formulaic invocation of other than the same—may well be inadequate. Translation as carrying "across" and "between" the different brings with it obligation—not least of all to what might be the distant, the unplottable, the incomprehensible. And it bears with it a charge, not only for translators and those from whom they come but also for those *to* whom they come. Translation, then, is always an interpretation and an intervention, even in the most "literary" of instances.[5]

What might seem obtuse insistence here will be perhaps less so in the context of a novel of "translation" itself—Etel Adnan's *Sitt Marie Rose*. Originally written in French, the novel is also available in translation. It is, then, a translation in the most literal and conventional sense of the term. But, more to the point, *Sitt Marie Rose* is a novel that both performs and tells the story of "translation" and its attendant obligations. In that context, Adnan's novel is, first of all, a fictional translation of a historical incident. Marie Rose Boulos—a Christian Lebanese woman from Beirut and the historical basis for the character Sitt Marie Rose of the eponymous novel—was in fact kidnapped by the Phalange in the first year of the Lebanese civil war and killed. Both in terms of the novel's content—the stories of Marie Rose, of her deaf-mute students, and of her captors and murderers—and of its structural organization, a historical incident is "brought over" / translated into fictional narrative.[6]

That translation of historical incident to fiction is accomplished most especially through the deft ordering of the narrative. The novel is divided into two asymmetrical parts: "Time I: A Million Birds" and "Time II: Sitt Marie Rose." "Time II" is, obviously, framed by and a drawing out of the implications of "Time I." So too, "Sitt Marie Rose" is, metaphorically and literally, one of the "million birds" that are the prey in "Time I." In the latter time and space, the unnamed but clearly female narrator retraces the spatial and temporal map of the wealthy, Maronite Christian Lebanese and of the assigned place for women on that map. This is (one of) the mother tongue(s) from which Marie Rose, too, translates/sets out. In *Sitt Marie Rose*, it is a map/mother tongue organized under a violent series of images, metaphors, and analogic parallels. In "one of [east] Beirut's most beautiful houses," a small group of Lebanese men and women watch a film of the men's hunting trip in Syria. The narrator observes that as the men kill the birds that are their prey, "their faces glow. . . . None of them has ever found in a woman the same sensation of power he gets from cars. An auto rally is more important than a conjugal night and the hunt is better still than the rally. There is a hierarchy even in the world of sport" (8–9).

When Mounir, whose house is the setting for this gathering, comments that women would never be able to experience firsthand the pleasure of the men, the narrator concurs:

It's true. "We women" were happy with the lesser power from this little bit of colored and imperfect film which, for twenty minutes, gave a kind of additional prestige to these men whom we see every day. In this ultra-circumscribed circle [*un cercle ultra-restreint*] the magic which these men exert is once again reinforced. The whole world plays quite well at this game. (10)[7]

Perhaps, though, contrary to what the narrator asserts here, everyone does not play at "this game" in quite the same way. Nor does everyone stay within that charmed circle. But the stakes for moving between and across are high. If Marie Rose is a translator, attempting to bodily and metaphorically articulate a translation from Lebanese Christian east Beirut to (a Palestinian area of) Muslim west Beirut (and back again), her translation proves to be fatal.[8] In that move back and forth between east and west Beirut, Marie Rose is *both* translator and translation. As a divorced woman with three children living with a Palestinian doctor in west Beirut while teaching in and directing a resident school for deaf-mute children in east Beirut, Marie Rose translates across multiple boundaries. But Marie Rose is not only a translator; she is also translated by the Christian Lebanese of her ethno-religious and class community into a symbol of violated (and violating) womanhood, a symbol of the Lebanese nation putatively "taken" by Palestinians. In her move across the lines between east and west Beirut, Marie Rose translates multiply. Her translations—or violations, according to her captors—are of her class, ethnic, and religious place; her familial place; her place as a woman and lover. In that translation/violation, she carries across maternal love to her biological and nonbiological children; sexuality and love to a man who is a stranger to her confessional, national, and class communities and to the religious and legal boundaries of marriage; and political alliance with and commitment to the Palestinian refugees in Lebanon. But the "charge" of translation to those for and to whom Marie Rose translates is only partially recognized in the novel.

And so, in "Time II," translating, crossing over from that "ultra-circumscribed circle" on the basis of a different map, results literally in Marie Rose's "dismemberment." The narration of the single claustrophobic narrator in "Time I" gives way in "Time II" to a carefully plotted series of seven narrators, each speaking in turn three times.[9] "Time I" and its narration are that of the restrictive and circumscribed— the time and space of the "normal" and "everyday" which allows a kind of "deadly survival" as long as everyone follows the same map in the same way. "Time II" and its plural narration are those of the abnormal and extraordinary, terms that recur often in this part of the novel. Yet the narration(s) of the abnormal in "Time II"—execution and death, violence, and extraordinary love—is systematically organized in careful sequence. There is, then, a grim structural order to the abnormal.

Linked to the textual translation of the "historical" into the "fictional," of the unspeakable and nonspeakers into that which can be narrated by those who cannot speak, and to the multiple translations in which the fictional character Marie Rose and her interlocutors engage, is another sense of translation in Adnan's novel—the translation of everyday "normality" (and violence) into the "abnormality" and violence of civil war. The "translation" of "Time I" into "Time II" consists precisely of this latter translation. So the four men of the "charmed circle" in "Time I"—the men of "magic" and "prestige"—are, in "Time II," torturers and murderers.

Yet, though the violence of these four men dominates "Time II," they are introduced as narrators only *after* the deaf-mute children and Marie Rose herself. There is a careful "hierarchy" here too, not of sport, but of a symbolic order—a mapping of narrative priority, a translation of the unspeakable. The narrative privilege of first place in "Time II" is given not even to Marie Rose, but to "US, the deaf-mutes." The children introduce themselves as collective narrator and as themselves translators in their own right:

We are all here, enrolled to learn special languages that will help us communicate with the others. We read words on lips whose sounds never reach us. We utter sounds that seem to make others shudder. We don't understand or hear them. We use our fingers to make an alphabet. But, above all else, we dance. Our hands, pressed against the radio, recognize the music; we dance like charmed snakes, the vibrations guiding us. (37)

For the deaf-mute children, as for Marie Rose, the "normal"—the "original text" of translation—is only tenuously so in the first place. The problematic demarcation of "the space proper"—its insistent demands and its blatant contradictions—render the space-between and the consequent translation no more "abnormal" than the "original" in the final analysis. For the children and for Marie Rose, the process of translation is a back-and-forth movement. It travels equally, if not with the same effects, in more than one direction—from "original" to "translation" and back again. The children, for example, translate others' inaudible words into their own (equally inaudible) sounds. And their sounds are translated back to them as the shudders of their audience. Or inaudible music is read as vibration and translated into dance as a kind of body language.

This image of translation and dancing-as-response is darkly reiterated in the concluding lines of the novel as Pierre narrates the aftermath of Marie Rose's murder. The deaf-mute children (and Pierre) watch the four men (Mounir, Tony, Fuad, and Bouna Lias) standing over Marie Rose's body on the desk at the front of the classroom:

An execution is always a celebration, whether you like it or not. It is a dance of Signs and their stabilization in Death; it is the swift ascent of silence without pardon; it is the explosion of absolute darkness among us. What can one do at this counter-festival if not dance? The deaf-mutes rise and, moved by the rhythm their bodies pick up from the bombs once again battering the earth, they begin to dance. (115)

The death and dismemberment of Marie Rose, the grim and violent (mis)translations of the civil war, and the bombs falling on Beirut are here translated into a celebratory dance on the part of the deaf-mute children. Bizarre as this closing image might seem, it is—with Pierre's metamorphosis from Marie Rose's captor and prosecutor to her analogic counterpart—a final textual indication of the power (and necessary intervention) of translation.

Marie Rose is at once translator (now dead) and "original text" (neither pristine nor unproblematic). And finally, in conclusion, she and her death become the object of yet another series of translations. For her captors and murderers, it is a brutally literal translation as "transgression" in "tribute" to a paranoid, chauvinist, exclusivist image of the same—the Lebanese Maronite community. For the deaf-mute children and for Pierre, translation is "tribute" to and love for Marie Rose but it is, also, "transgression." The children are as fascinated by the interaction between Marie Rose and her captors as they are horrified. They reiterate and reciprocate her love for them at the same time as they are compellingly transfixed by the brutal power of the four men. Their final translation of this "text" is in and as their dance to the "music" of civil war, murder, and bombs falling. And Pierre-as-translator was initially one of Marie Rose's abductors, though, like Marie Rose, his occupation of "the space proper"—as a Christian (and Phalangist) Lebanese—was not unproblematic. Nonetheless, he too engages in a violently transgressive "translation" of Marie Rose, at least initially. In spite of his increasingly critical assessment of the events in the deaf-mute children's schoolroom, he is unwilling or unable to prevent the culmination-in-murder of the other four men's "translation" of Marie Rose. Still, he occupies an ambiguous place in the normality of "Time I" and his position in "Time II" shifts substantially, though not altogether conspicuously. It is, at first, only apparent from the carefully repetitive structural organization of "Time II" that Pierre is in fact the increasingly sympathetic, perceptive, and critical narrator of these sections. And, even then, the movement from Marie Rose's captor to (potentially) her differently sexed analogue is elusive and implicit. A critical distance in Pierre's narration of the events in the classroom gradually becomes apparent; the narrative sections attributed to him in "Time II" increasingly move beyond the lethally neat circles of "order" which the other four men occupy and police. The ways in which the "ultra-circumscribed" circles of "Time I" figure even more ominously in "Time II" as "circles of oppression" and "of betrayal" (114), and finally "of repression" (115) grow increasingly explicit to Pierre. The circle, as exclusionary and restrictive, is to be broken, crossed over, translated into another language of nonexclusionary and nonrestrictive relationship:

One remembers again, from time to time, the famous image of concentric circles drawn by Gamal Abdel Nasser: Egypt in the middle, and then the Arab world, the Islamic Third World, the rest of the Third World. . . . But this hero of Arab History should, instead, have denounced the concentric circles of oppression and taken on the task of breaking them.

In the center is the individual surrounded by the circle of the family. Then there is the circle of the State, then that of the "countries of Arab brothers," that of the Enemy, of the superpowers, and so on. . . . The circles of oppression are, inevitably, circles of betrayal. In their interior spaces, all lively forces are crushed, annihilated in a sorrow always reinvented, and an apparent confusion is maintained through a mortal order. (114)

This concluding section of *Sitt Marie Rose*, in which Pierre is narrator and mourner of Marie Rose's death, is in stark contrast to the narrative and narrator of the opening sequence(s). The closed circle of a "whole world which plays quite well at this game" is at least implicitly challenged by Pierre—who not only stops playing that game but haltingly attempts to indicate a different way of crossing over the circumscription of the circle. His effort is a distinctly limited one, though. For within the text we are told of no shift in Pierre's relations with the living; Marie Rose is, after all, dead as he laments the practice and idea which makes her murder possible. If Pierre is an analogue of sorts to Marie Rose, her differently sexed counterpart, it is primarily in his understanding of (and/or persuasive story about) her motivations and fears. His is an understanding that implicitly enfolds *and* indicts his own narrative position. In the penultimate paragraph of the novel, followed by his closing account of the deaf-mute children's dance to the rhythm of the civil war, Pierre maintains "the true Christ doesn't exist except when someone stands up and defends the stranger against their own brothers. [Then] Christ is the manifestation of innocence" (115).

The referent here is clearly, if not explicitly, Marie Rose, who confronted her "brothers" in defense of multiple strangers—the Palestinians in Lebanon, the Muslims among the Christians, the deaf-mute children in a society that would rather ignore them. And, if Pierre enacts his idea, if he practices that which he has apparently recognized in his narration of Marie Rose's life and death, he too must necessarily defend the stranger against his own brothers. His narration, in its gentle and astute account of Marie Rose—and of her murderers—is itself perhaps an *implicit* defense of Marie Rose as stranger to his brothers. But the darkly lyrical world of Pierre's perception is still *not* the world of active endeavor. Nor is it one of "innocence." Marie Rose is dismembered on the classroom desk in front of Pierre and the deaf-mute students in a macabre school lesson; Pierre does not confront his "own [Phalangist] brothers" in defense of the stranger there. He is unable or unwilling to alter their deadly fraternity. Instead, in the forcefully noncircular construction of the novel itself, a defense of the stranger is launched against an audience—an implied reader—who might be tempted to condemn the apparent "naivete" of Marie Rose, the apparent "absurdity" of the deaf-mute children, the apparent "intrusion" of the Palestinian refugees in Lebanon. Still, if no such confrontation of "one's own brothers" is possible for Pierre within the story of *Sitt Marie Rose* itself, in the textually structural imperative that opens already shifting circles, the implied reader is a kind of *propre frère* ("one's own brother") against whom "the stranger"—Marie

Rose, the deaf-mute children, the Palestinians in Lebanon, even Pierre as (a former?) Phalangist—is defended.[10]

If the circles which mark the contours of this map of translation/civil war fatally enclose Marie Rose, they are, metaphorically at least, forced open with Pierre's narration and with the children's dance in celebration of Marie Rose's death. To refuse the circle is to accept the presence of the stranger, the bearer-across/mover-between different stories. But the circles are rigidly reinforced with the refusal of "one's own brothers" to accept the stranger, with an insistence on brutally excising the stranger from the circle.

In Adnan's *Sitt Marie Rose*, as in Elias Khoury's *Al-jabal al-saghīr*, the topography of the city of Beirut is explicitly foregrounded as map. It is narrated as circular, as enclosure, as—in Mounir's strategic military mapping, "a city without exit. On one side there's the sea, and we [the Phalange] control the east. We'll advance westward with a vast circular movement. We'll clear out the pockets of resistance, one after the other. Next, we'll bomb the airport south of the city. And the circle will be closed" (41).[11] Mounir's lethally conservative vision of Beirut as a circle expunged of the foreigners (Palestinians), the unbelievers (Muslims and heretical Christians), and the unclean (in this instance, women like Marie Rose), is predicated on (a perversely familiar) notion of defensive sameness and purity (of which women are cast as markers). But Mounir's plan for a "definitive and clean" takeover of the city is told differently by the first person narrator(s) of *Al-jabal al-saghīr*. It is *against* such an expurgative plan that the stories of Khoury's novel—like the narrative frame of *Sitt Marie Rose*, if not each of the stories within it—are narrated. It is *against* circular communities that resolutely refuse translation or bearing-across as they attempt to resolutely foreclose on the space-between. For Khoury's novel too, translation is intervention *and* contestation. The act of translation between and across different ethno-religious communities and their languages and cultures is also an act in coalition with others—a coalition that structurally contests exclusionary circles. Even as the apparent defeat of those translations and coalitions across boundaries is told, *The Little Mountain* testifies to the power (destructive and alternatively productive) of coalitions and of the translations in which they necessarily engage.

The narrative organization of *Al-jabal al-saghīr* and its stories of the Lebanese civil war, not unlike *Sitt Marie Rose*, suggest a map of concentric circles—if one under erasure. This configuration is implied in the succession of the novel's five chapters where, if the circles are of shifting circumference, the landmarks remain minimally recognizable or are explained as such.[12] The first chapter of Khoury's novel—"The Little Mountain"—traces the (already breached "interior") circle of the family; the second—"The Church"—that of religion and the church (not insignificantly for a society organized on confessional lines); the third—"The Last Option"—that of the aesthetic and of love and the erotic; the fourth—"The Stairs"—in a recasting of the third, that of state bureaucracy (an institutionalized version of artistic or aesthetic labor) and of marriage (an institutionalized version of love and sexuality); the fifth— "The King's Square"—that of "civilization"—here that of the foreign and formerly colonial metropole of Paris.

But, from the opening lines of the novel, the boundaries of the family or the church or erotic love or even the formerly colonial metropole are not available—or narratable—in stark and fixed outline. This non-availability/narratability of secure boundaries and what they contain and exclude is a source of no little narrative unease—not least of all to the narrator of *Al-jabal al-saghir.* "It isn't possible for us to go through life like this, without a stable point of reference" (143), he protests to Mariam, the young woman who is the object of his desire.[13] But here, on the terrain of Khoury's novel, circle and circumference are unstable and at least potentially mutable—sometimes shifting (or exploding) in response to love, to violence, to the child's relationship to his father and mother, to memory, to desire.

And then, too, Mariam herself is unstable as the narrator's object of desire, shifting even within a single sentence. She is a young, brown-skinned woman with short, curly hair; she is "a slender young African boy"; "she becomes a circle" (61). Like the dislocated little-mountain-that-is-not-a-little-mountain, the landscape-marker-that-is-not-one, so Mariam is alternately a gendered character "marker" that is not one in the narrative—disembodied, dislocated as a fixed point of reference or narratorial desire.

And "the little mountain" itself—like the floating narrator of the novel and Mariam as the object of his desire—is dislocated/disembodied, a detached and abstracted geometric shape, a floating triangle. What might, in the opening chapters of the novel, seem a fanciful metaphoric tenacity about the little mountain as (non)marker is, in the final chapter, made explicit:

Everything seems to be like that, ambiguous and inexplicable. But in the end it comes together and is incorporated into triangles. It isn't possible for you to discover something utterly exposed [naked] like that. All of it fits into triangles and a triangle is a beginning or something resembling it [a beginning]. And a triangle fits into a circle. Every triangle, regardless of its shape or the size of its angles, fits into a circle. And the circle inevitably ruptures. (144)

The operative narrative principle of *Al-jabal al-saghīr*, then, is not the strictly demarcated ordering of narrative voice, the translation of violent content as orderly narrative structure. Rather, it is permeability—as violent destruction *and* alternative community. That "permeability" is mapped or articulated here in the iteration and reiteration of detached triangles that, encircled or encircling themselves, break open. It is articulated in the floating first-person narrator, himself permeated by other stories, other potential (and perhaps actual) narrators.

Retrospectively for the narrator of Khoury's novel, the circle of the (nuclear) family—of the (memory of) relationships between (the triangle of) father, mother, and child—is already permeated with and by others; it is a circle already broken open. The eponymous first chapter of *Al-jabal al-saghīr* opens with the repetitive recitation of the ("false" but conventional) name for a major marker on the terrain of childhood/familial memory:

They call it the little mountain and we call it the little mountain. . . . They call it the little mountain; we know that it isn't a mountain; and we call it the little mountain too.
    A single hill or a group of hills. I don't remember any more; no one remembers any more. A hill on the eastern edge of Beirut which we called a mountain, because the mountains were far away. We sat on its slopes and stole the sea.
    The little mountain. . . . The little mountain is [only] an exposed [rock] crest that we encroach on in amazement and pride.
    They call it the little mountain . . .
    We fear for the mountain . . .
    They call in the little mountain. And we know it isn't a mountain; but we call it the little mountain. (9–10)[14]

The almost consistent present tense of the narration in the first section of chapter 1 suggests an overflow of the past into the present—an overflow that runs through the remainder of the novel as well.[15] The narrator is clearly recalling his childhood—thus, obviously, a time and story past—from the different time of the narrative present. But his memory of the (story) past is carried over into the (narrative) present as still present. Even though, in the past *and* in the present, "we know" that the little mountain is not one, we (continue to) participate in its (mis)naming—"we call it." Yet, that participation is equally one of the past; "we called [it] a mountain" when "we sat" on the hillside and "stole" the sea. For the narrative moment at least, the remembered past of childhood is not so clearly disassociable from the present.

This ubiquitous past that pervades the present, though, takes a different turn in the next section of chapter 1.[16] There the past asserts itself unequivocally, at least in the opening sentence: "Five men arrived, jumping from what looked like a military jeep" (10). We are in a narrative present distinctly set off from the story past of completed action: the men "arrived." But as soon as they arrive the narration shifts back into a (continuous) present tense of memory: "They carry automatic rifles in their hands and surround the house." This account of five armed men searching the narrator's house is reiterated twice again in the first chapter. The breaking into and searching of the narrator's family home, the confrontation of the paramilitary with his mother, erupt continuously into the narrative present, even retrospectively into the narrator's memory of his childhood past. This is linguistically apparent in the alternation of verb tenses; it is evident as well in the structural sequence of narrative content. The memory of invasion and violation continually disrupts the narrative present and its recollection of childhood:

They search the house for me. I'm not there. They rifle through books and papers. I'm not there. They discovered a book with a photo of Abdel Nasser on the back cover. I'm not there. They scattered the papers and overturned the furniture. They cursed the Palestinians. They ripped apart my bed and searched it. They cursed my mother and [my] corrupt generation. I'm not there.

I'm not there. My mother was there, trembling with grief and resentment, pacing the house nervously. . . . She sat on a chair in the entranceway, guarding her house, while inside they searched for Palestinians and Abdel Nasser and international communism. She sat on a chair in the entranceway, guarding her house, while inside they tore papers and memories to shreds. (11)

The narrator's mother "guards" her home not unlike her son "guards" his memories of the past—and in a similar context: home and memory are already assaulted (and reassaulted). There is no such "guarding" possible. Neither childhood nor home are inviolable spheres; quite the contrary.

The conclusion to the first chapter is the final reiteration of this memory of violation and of the narrator's absence from the scene. "I was," he concludes, "east of the city, searching with short, barefoot young men, wearing rubber shoes on their feet that didn't keep out the cold. I was east of the city looking for the little mountain" (24–25). The relentlessly linear and ordered narrative direction of *Sitt Marie Rose* that leads to Marie Rose's death (and Pierre's "birth") invokes as metaphor (the necessary challenging of) concentric circles. *Al-jabal al-saghīr* in its narration and its floating first-person narrator traces otherwise rather similar circles.

In each chapter then—arguably another circle—the spatial and temporal narrative markers are already in disarray; the circles, the chapters, the narrative thread, are already disrupted and broken open. And the "translation" between those circles is only scarcely more possible than the safeguarding of home/memory/childhood in the first chapter. So it is not surprising that in the second chapter, the church as signpost of refuge and faith is, like the "little mountain" as signpost on the terrain of memory and childhood, beyond recognition—not the spatial marker convention supposes it to be:

I see the church and I don't see it. . . . Butros wanders around looking for the church.
   "We're *in* the church Butros."
   "But I don't see anything. . . . What's this? This isn't a church."
   Christ is on the ground. The statue of Christ is twisted, his right cheek on the ground and his left hand stretched out open toward the sky, searching for his shattered right hand. (29–31)

The attempt of the young men to right the statue fails; the church, with its symbols and spiritual markers, has slipped from its conventional place. The retranslation of the church and its symbols across the temporal divide of the past is divided into five "acts" ("*al-mashhad*"). "The church" as chapter and narrative site is also a confrontation between the anticircular coalition of young fighters occupying and seeking refuge in the church and the faded circle of two old priests who also, if differently, occupy and seek "refuge" in the church. The old priests, most explicitly Father Marcel, seek refuge from the civil war and its defenses of and challenges to the present order of things in memories of a very different (and colonial) past from that of the narrator in the first chapter. This confessional drama-in-five-acts is a tragedy of grim errors and mistranslations. Reiterating or resituating things the way they used to be is "impossible because the base [of Christ's statue] is broken." But, at least within the two covers of *Al-jabal al-saghir*, it is grimly unclear if the new translations will stand any better or longer than the broken religious statue.

The past(s) of childhood, of confessional boundaries, of desire and art/marriage and bureaucratic paper pushing, or of the postcolonial European metropole escape the first-person narrator(s) of Khoury's novel. They are not retrievable or narratable in a steady fashion. They are urgently in need of alternative translation, of another crossing of the space-between. The narrator of *The Little Mountain* struggles anxiously in the face of such urgency to begin that retranslation—to make a different sense of things. And he insists to Mariam on his singular ability to do so: "I am the last option, I told her and we walked along the long seashore" (59). But the narrator is not quite able to maintain this narrative bravado in the face of so mutable a map. It seems fitting that he should deliver this ultimatum of sorts at the water's edge—trying to fix a definitive boundary in sight of the sea, his feet "rooted" in the sand. Mariam (and perhaps the sea as well) laughs at his desperate boldness and calls him "a romantic." But at the end of "The King's Square," the final chapter, our narrator is no longer so confident. He returns once again to geometry:

The triangle fits into the circle. But we didn't realize that the war had begun. We believed that the point would remain one of questioning the premises of the triangle and realigning its terms. But when the triangle ruptured, the bloodshed was boundless. It flowed on until the circle collapsed completely. Every circle is doomed to collapse. That is the rule. And when it does, it fractures the sides of the triangle. And we sit in the rain looking for new triangles. (148)

The solid geometry of circles and triangles and squares is overrun (here, at least in one sense, with blood) and yet the narrative desire for that solidity-which-is-not-solid remains. In fact, the narrator's (and the novel's) concluding line is another "return"—not to geometry but to desire (and arguably to the beginning of another familial triangle). The (violated) circle that holds the familial "triangle" of the opening chapter is reconfigured here in the geometry of the metropolitan "square." For the narrator, "all squares look alike," but they are "reassuringly" not

triangles or circles. Yet the four orderly sides of the square in the center
of the "solid and stable" city of Paris form a thick and impassable wall;
the "continuity of civilization" (a linear continuum intersecting the
square) of which Mariam sings becomes an ominous heap of "civilization"
on top of "civilization"; the squares themselves gray prisons or white
hospitals or—even when they are green—the site for a hanging.

The convention of geometry as the reassuring calculation of distinct
lines, angles, surfaces, and solids is desperately evoked and exploded
throughout *Al-jabal al-saghīr*. Such corporeal or material calculation is
an impossibility in Khoury's novel; the tangible line, surface, or angle
that would lend itself to precise measurement or calculation has "collapsed." Or, perhaps more properly, what has collapsed is the notion
that the world is so assuredly assessable and organizable on geometric
terms. At least here, geometry is itself a translation—of the world
("*geo*"/the little mountain/belief/love/work/Mariam) into the schematic
and of the schematic into numbers, measurements, and formulae. From
the opening lines of *Al-jabal al-saghīr*, the apparently tangible and
concrete—as in the little mountain itself—is problematic. Even before
(mis)measurement, naming is ("mis")translation. But perhaps—in spite
of the narrator's insistent repetition of the *mis*naming of the little
mountain, in spite of his *mis*apprehension of Mariam, and the *dis*location
of his narration on the embattled terrain of civil war—the point is *not*
simply the reconstruction and reinforcement of geometric boundaries.
Nor is it exactly insistence on "correct" or "accurate" naming and
measuring; the ominous implications of a naming and measuring made
and maintained in the name of "correctness" and "accuracy" is precisely
the pretext for civil war. Neither is the point just the "realignment" of
existing configurations. Those existing configurations with their
"geometric" boundaries have not held in any case. Even the "tangible"
boundaries of the individual fictional character and his or her narration
have not held. Not for Mariam as narrated by the narrator nor for the
narrator himself: "I am the last option," he claims to Mariam. And she
laughs. An apt response to an arrogantly foolish assertion. He tries one
last time to master the object of his desire, his language, and geometry:
"I grabbed and threw her into the water. But she wasn't a fish, she
was a woman. So she began to sink. The water flowed across her face
and between her breasts. But she wasn't a fish. I grabbed her and
scaled/scalded her to the end but the end was impossible. That is the
point" (144).

And so, like the deaf-mute schoolchildren and Pierre in *Sitt Marie Rose*, the narrator struggles to learn another more "appropriate" language in the face of horrific violence and of "inappropriate" desire. For both Khoury's and Adnan's novels, violence is on the one hand and first of all the grim and bloody Lebanese civil war. But their narratives of civil war, of the simultaneous and ferocious policing and explosion of circle(s), are equally an indictment of the (narratives of the) "normal" as well: "normal" languages and their translations, "normal" geographies (and geometries) and their maps, "normal" relations between various communities and the laws they engender. It is these "normal" narratives, too, of which *Al-jabal al-saghir* and *Sitt Marie Rose* are translations, of which the stories and characters in Khoury's and Adnan's narratives speak.

If the "last option," then, is not the narrator/"me" of Khoury's novel is it perhaps the deaf-mute/"us" of Adnan's? "Us" as deaf-mutes—witnesses to and participants in violence that can neither be forgotten nor ignored; reading words on lips whose sounds are inaudible; trying to communicate—to talk back—in the face of disdain, embarrassment, repugnance, or bemused benevolence at best? Yet for all of that, in an almost macabre translation of their own, the deaf-mutes dance—to vibrations from bombs, to music. Their bodily translation of their love for Marie Rose and of the violence that saturates all of their lives is paralleled by the symbolic translations of Pierre—finally, as a potential Marie Rose.

The narrator of *Al-jabal al-saghir* is equally witness to and participant in "abnormal" violence, the civil war of course, but also his attempt to conquer and contain Mariam and his memories, to learn another language (and geometry?) that will allow him to translate, to bear across, a different story. Standing in the center of Paris in "the square of the king," the narrator finally addresses the king himself: "What's the true/real ("*al-qissa al-haqiqiya*") story, your Majesty?" (154) Not surprisingly, there is no answer from the "king" or anyone else. Nor has there been an answer for him from Mariam to a similar question. But it is to her that the narrator races at the end of the novel, hoping that she will still be waiting where he left her.

If translation is always an intervention of one sort or another and if translation is not finally disassociable from interpretation and critique, then the stories that we tell with our translation (and critiques), the narratives in which our languages situate those translations, are scarcely unimportant. For it is precisely there—in those narratives, with those stories—that not only the *text* and *translator* are foregrounded (historically, these two seem to be habitually situated front and center). It is there that the audiences from whom the texts-for-translators are carried across are implied. And there that audiences *for whom* the translations are produced are implied as well. If in traditional literary translation, the emphasis is on the production of translation, on the producer (the translator) and the product itself (the translation, its faithfulness to the original, and so on), perhaps we can tell a story or two about the audiences for and of translation too. Perhaps we can translate in yet other languages. Not "true" or "correct" or "pure" languages, for Khoury's and Adnan's novels make brutally clear the costs to all concerned of making *that* argument about language and translation. But both novels suggest, however tentatively, something else about translation in yet other languages. Both *Sitt Marie Rose* and *Al-jabal al-saghīr*, in the multiple translations in which their narratives and stories engage, suggest other ideas and practices of translation or bringing across. They suggest other notions of language. We are in urgent need of such other ways. The ways with which we are most familiar too often conclude—as they do for the character Marie Rose in Adnan's novel or most of the characters in Khoury's novel—in death, dismemberment, or dismissal. The "failed" but exuberant proposition held out in the conclusion of Abdelkebir Khatibi's *Amour bilingue* is an equally fitting and impossible invocation here: "teach me to speak in your languages."

Notes

1. Vincent Crapanzano, in his "Hermes Dilemma" aptly locates a central predicament of the translator/ethnographer: "He has to make sense of the foreign. . . . He aims at a solution to the problem of foreignness . . . he must also communicate the very foreignness that his interpretations (the translator's translations) deny . . . he must render the foreign familiar and preserve its foreignness at one and the same time" (52). Crapanzano's insistence throughout, however, that translation/ethnography dispense with "transcendent stories" and be "convincing" (without specifying for and to whom) is a puzzling elision of his essay's most powerful implications.

2. Both *Sitt Marie Rose* and *Al-jabal al-saghīr* are novels of the Lebanese civil war. But if national crises (and civil wars) are not simply disruptions of or deviations from the "normal" but a more radical and explicit rendering of that "normal," then these two novels are most exemplary novels of translation.

3. For, like "the original," the "space proper" is scarcely some seamlessly unproblematic and coherent category either—a phenomenon to which both Adnan's and Khoury's novels testify.

4. The extent to which late eighteenth- and nineteenth- century discussions of translation were also and simultaneously discussions of the national is striking. See Wilhelm Von Humboldt's introduction to his translation of Aeschylus's *Agamemnon* or Nietzsche's "On The Problem of Translation" (Schulte and Biguenet 55–60, 68–71), for example. More recent theories of translation struggle with maps still—even if it is with attempts to locate alternatives to the national.

5. Gayatri Spivak's translator's foreword to and translation of Mahasweta Devi's short story, "Draupadi," and the story itself, are a keen commentary on "knowing" and "translating" (Spivak 179–96). In a different but not unrelated context, the narration of the deaf-mute children in Etel Adnan *Sitt Marie Rose* also comments suggestively on the notion of "silence"—and that from physically silent children as collective narrator.

The managers of the multi-, trans-, and inter-national can project that flattened image of omnipresent sameness quite well on their own; though the extent to which they depend in that effort on assistance from peripatetic "translators" (area experts, language and literature specialists, popular culture analysts, etc.) is an interesting question.

See also Asad's observation about the authority of the ethnographer or translator: "In the longer run, therefore, it is not the personal authority of the ethnographer, but the social authority of his ethnography that matters" (163).

6. The front cover of the novel's French edition suggests translation both linguistic and historical in its image of a page from an Arabic language newspaper splattered with blood. Though I have consulted the (excellent) translations of both Adnan's and Khoury's novels with interest, the translations here are my own. The "sitt" affixed to Marie Rose's name in the title of Adnan's novel is a respectful term of address toward women who are married or older or toward one's biological grandmother—as in, *sitti*, "my grandmother." Its use is suggestive in the context of Adnan's novel for it alludes, of course, to respect for Marie Rose. But it also suggests a loosely familial relationship with her—on the part of the implied audience? *Sitti* could also be used in addressing a woman older than the speaker who is not a biological grandmother but to whom one is close—"related"—nonetheless.

Phalange, or, in Arabic, the *Kataeb* (originally, the *Phalanges Libanaises*) is a right-wing party and militia of Maronite Christians. For an astute account of the 1975–76 Lebanese civil war and its (continuing) aftermath, see Tabitha Petran, *The Struggle over Lebanon*.

7. Mounir specifies that the women's inability to understand or share this pleasure is because they are incapable of using compass and map to find their

way across already charted terrain—implicitly at least, an ominous comment on Marie Rose's attempt to map and move across the terrain differently.

8   On the back cover of the novel's French edition, in a statement "signed" by the author is the blunt declaration: "Marie Rose pays with her life for a situation in which weapons replace dialogue.

9. There are, then, twenty-one narrative segments in "Time II," divided into three sections, each section narrated by seven different narrators in consistent sequence. That sequence is (1) the deaf-mute children, (2) Marie Rose, (3) Mounir, (4) Tony, (5) Fuad, (6) Bouna Lias (a Maronite priest), and (7) Pierre.

10. Although here too, as there is no pristine and "natural" original text, there is no such translator—not in Marie Rose, not in Pierre's narration, and not in the structural organization of the novel itself.

11. The military map that Mounir traces is reiterated in his linguistic map as well—in his short, simple, blunt statements. The contrast between the tone, style, and grammatical construction of his narration or that of Fuad or Tony or even the priest, on the one hand, and that of Pierre or Marie Rose or the deaf-mute children on the other is appropriately distinct.

12. The Arabic text offers an occasional footnote or intratextual explanation of local terms for various locations; the translation provides maps and footnotes for those who are strangers to Beirut.

13. The point is made even more explicitly in the original Arabic text; what I have translated here as "stable point of reference" is, more literally, "a fixed star [or constellation to navigate by]."

14. "The little mountain is a popular name for the Ashrafiyya district of Beirut" (footnote in the original).

15. Examples of overflows of the past into the present: *yasmūnaha* ("they call it"); *nasmīha* ("we call it"); *na'arafa* ("we know"); but later, *jalasnā* ("we sat") (on the hillside) and *saraqnā* ("we stole").

16. The five chapters are each composed of a number of relatively distinct segments, designated by extra spacing or by a small square or, as in chapter 2, "The Church," with subtitles: Act One, Act Two, etc. Often the narrative focus and story time—and arguably the narrator—shift with these markers.

Works Cited

Adnan, Etel. *Sitt Marie Rose*. Paris: Des femmes, 1977. Trans. Georgina
        Kleege. Sausalito, CA: The Post-Apollo Press, 1982.
Asad, Talal. "The Concept of Cultural Translation in British Social
        Anthropology." Clifford and Marcus 141–64.
Clifford, James, and George Marcus. *Writing Culture: The Poetics and Politics
        of Ethnography*. Berkeley: U of California P, 1986.

Crapanzano, Vincent. "Hermes Dilemma: The Masking of Subversion in Ethnographic Description." Clifford and Marcus 51–76.

Gellner, Ernest. "Concepts and Society." *Rationality*. Ed. B. R. Wilson, 18–49. Oxford: Basil Blackwell, 1970.

Khatibi, Abdelkebir. *Amour bilingue*. Paris: Fata Morgana, 1983. *Love in Two Languages*. Trans. Richard Howard. Minneapolis: U of Minnesota P, 1990.

Khoury, Elias. *Al-jabal al-saghīr*. Beirut: Mu'assasa al-abhāth al-arabīya, 1977. *The Little Mountain*. Trans. Maia Tabit. Minneapolis: U of Minnesota P, 1989.

Petran, Tabitha. *The Struggle Over Lebanon*. New York: Monthly Review Press, 1987.

Schulte, Rainer, and John Biguenet. "Introduction." *Theories of Translation*. U of Chicago P, 1992. 1–10.

Spivak, Gayatri. *In Other Worlds: Essays in Cultural Politics*. New York: Methuen, 1987.

IV.

Translation, Pedagogy, and Cross-Cultural Texts

"Translation, Pedagogy and Cross-Cultural Texts" returns to the pedagogical imperative which this collection was undertaken in response to. bell hook's "'this is the oppressor's language, / yet I need it to talk to you': Language, a place of struggle" asks us to look at two interrelated dimensions of this imperative: First, the need to re-make and re-invent the oppressor's language, as, for example, black vernacular does, to make it "speak beyond the boundaries of conquest and domination," to make it function as a counter-language that maps the space for "alternative cultural production and alternative epistemologies"; second, the need on our part as readers (and listeners) of these "rupture[s] of standard English" to attend to those "moments of not-understanding [the black vernacular] as a space to learn," for in those moments rests the "opportunity to listen without 'mastery,' without owning or possessing."

Anuradha Dingwaney and Carol Maier's "Translation as a Method for Cross-Cultural Teaching" is concerned, practically and concretely, with "the need for a pedagogy [that] will guide the teaching of cross-cultural texts," and with their own work as mediators—in classroom situations and in critical commentaries. They analyze *I . . . Rigoberta Menchú* to disclose various mediations—Elisabeth Burgos-Debray's, Ann Wright's, and, not the least, their own. At the same time as they make visible the theoretical and critical baggage and disciplinary training that informs their interpretation, they fix attention on Menchú's "active agency in crafting her narrative" through which she seeks to achieve what

293

is for her an urgent political task. Their analysis of *I . . . Rigoberta Menchú* provides them with the occasion to reflect more generally on a pedagogy for teaching cross-cultural texts—a pedagogy in which the theory and practice that inform the activities and processes leading to translation provide an enabling means.

"this is the oppressor's language / yet I need it to talk to you": Language, a place of struggle

bell hooks

Language like desire disrupts—refuses to be contained within boundaries. It speaks itself against our will, in words and thoughts, that intrude, violate even, the innermost private spaces of mind and body. I was in my first year of college when I read Adrienne Rich's poem "The Burning of Paper Instead of Children" published in the collection *The Will to Change*. That poem, speaking against domination, against racism and class oppression, attempts to graphically illustrate that stopping the political persecution and torture of living beings is a more vital issue than censorship, than burning books. This poem contained a line that moved and disturbed something within me. So much so, that in the years of my life since first reading this poem, I have not forgotten it. And perhaps could not have forgotten it had I tried to erase it from memory. This illustrates what I mean to suggest in the opening lines of this essay—that words impose themselves, take root in our memory against our will as the words of this poem begat a life in my memory that I could not abort or change.

Now, when I find myself thinking about language, these lines are there, as if they were always waiting to challenge and assist me. I find myself silently speaking them over and over again in my head, with such intensity they seem like a chant. These words that say: "this is the oppressor's language / yet I need it to talk to you." Startling me, shaking me into an awareness of the link between language and domination, I initially resist the idea of the oppressor's language, certain that this construct has the potential to disempower those of us who are just learning to speak, who are just learning to claim language as a place where we make ourselves subject. "This is the oppressor's language / yet I need it to talk to you." Adrienne Rich's words. Then, when I first read these words, and now, they make me think of standard English, of learning to speak against black vernacular, against the ruptured and broken speech of a dispossessed and displaced people. Standard English is not the speech of exile. It is the language of conquest and domination. In the United States it is the mask which hides the loss of so many tongues, all those sounds of diverse native communities we will never hear, the speech of the Gullah, Yiddish, and so many other unremembered tongues.

Reflecting on Adrienne Rich's words: "this is the oppressor's language / yet I need it to talk to you," I know that it is not the English language that hurts me, but what the oppressors do with it, how they shape it to become a territory that limits and defines, how they make it a weapon that can shame, humiliate, colonize. Gloria Anzaldúa reminds us of this pain in *Borderlands/La Frontera* when she asserts: "So, if you want to really hurt me, talk badly about my language." We have so little knowledge of how displaced, enslaved, or free Africans who came or were brought against their will to the United States felt about the loss of language, about learning English. Only as a woman did I begin to think about these black people in relation to language, to think about their trauma, as they were compelled to witness their language rendered meaningless within a colonizing European culture where voices deemed foreign could not be spoken, were outlawed tongues, renegade speech. When I realize how long it has taken for white Americans to acknowledge diverse languages of native Americans, to accept that the speech their ancestral colonizers declared were merely grunts or gibberish was indeed *language*, it is difficult not to hear in standard English always the sound of slaughter and conquest. I think now of the grief of displaced "homeless" Africans forced to inhabit a world where they saw folks like themselves, inhabiting the same skin, the same condition, but who had no shared language to talk with one another, who needed "the oppressor's language." "This is the oppressor's language / yet I need it to talk to you." When I imagine the terror of Africans on board, slave ships, on auction blocks, inhabiting the unfamiliar architecture of plantations, I consider that this terror extended beyond fear of punishment, that it resided also in the anguish of hearing a language they could not comprehend. The very sound of English had to terrify. I think of black people meeting one another in a space away from the diverse cultures and languages that distinguished them from one another, compelled by circumstance to find ways to speak with one another in a "new world" where blackness, the darkness of one's skin, and not language, would become the space of bonding. How to remember, to reinvoke this terror? How to describe what it must have been like for Africans whose deepest bonds historically forged in the place of shared speech to be abruptly transported to a world where the very sound of one's mother tongues had no meaning?

I imagine them hearing in spoken English "the oppressor's language," yet I imagine them also realizing that this language would need to be possessed, taken, claimed as a space of resistance. I imagine that the moment they realized "the oppressor's language" seized and spoken by the tongues of the colonized could be a space of bonding was joyous. For in that recognition was the understanding that intimacy could be restored, that a culture of resistance could be formed, that would make recovery from the trauma of enslavement possible. I imagine then Africans first hearing English as "the oppressor's language" and then rehearing it as a potential site of resistance. Learning English, learning to speak the alien tongue was one way enslaved Africans began to reclaim their personal power within a context of domination. Possessing a shared language black folks could find again a way to make community, and a means to create the political solidarity necessary to resist.

Needing the oppressor's language to speak with one another they nevertheless also reinvented, remade that language so that it would speak beyond the boundaries of conquest and domination. In the mouths of black Africans in the so-called "new world," English was altered, transformed, and became a different speech. Enslaved black people took broken bits of English, fragments, and made of them a counterlanguage. They put together their words in such a way that the colonizer had to rethink the meaning of English language. Though it has become common in contemporary culture to talk about the messages of resistance that emerged in the music created by slaves, particularly spirituals, less is said about the grammatical construction of sentences in these songs. Often, the English used in the song reflected the broken, ruptured world of the slave. When the slaves sang "nobody knows de trouble I see," their use of the word "nobody" adds a richer meaning than if they had used "no one" for it was the slave's body that was the concrete site of suffering. And even as emancipated black people sang spirituals, they did not change the language, the sentence structure, of our ancestors. For in the incorrect usage of words, in the incorrect placement of words, was a spirit of rebellion that claimed language as a site of resistance. Using English in a way that ruptured standard language usage and meaning so that often white folks could not understand black speech made English more than the oppressor's language.

An unbroken connection exists between the broken English of the displaced, enslaved African and the diverse black vernacular speech black folks use today. In both cases the rupture of standard English enabled and enables rebellion and resistance. By transforming the oppressor's language, making a culture of resistance, black people created an intimate speech that could say far more than was permissible within the boundaries of standard English. The power of this speech is not simply that it enables resistance to white supremacy but that it also forges a space for alternative cultural production and alternative epistemologies—different ways of thinking and knowing that were crucial to creating a counterhegemonic world view. It is absolutely essential that the revolutionary power of black vernacular speech not be lost in contemporary culture. That power resides in the capacity of black vernacular to intervene on the boundaries and limitations of standard English.

In contemporary black popular culture, rap music has become one of the spaces where black vernacular speech is used in a manner that invites dominant mainstream culture to listen—to hear—and to some extent be transformed. However, one of the risks of this attempt at cultural translation is that it will trivialize black vernacular speech. When young white kids imitate this speech in ways that suggest it is the speech of those who are dumb, stupid, or only interested in entertaining or being funny, then the subversive power of this speech is undermined. In academic circles, both in the sphere of teaching and writing, there has been little effort made to utilize black vernacular or, for that matter, any languages other than standard English. When I asked an ethnically diverse group of students in a course I was teaching on black women writers why we only ever heard standard English spoken in the classroom they were momentarily rendered speechless. Though many of them were individuals for whom standard English was a second or third language, it had simply never occurred to them that it was possible to say something in another language, in another way. No wonder then that we continue to think: "this is the oppressor's language / yet I need it to talk to you."

Realizing that I was in danger of losing my relationship to black vernacular speech because I too rarely use it in the predominately white settings that I am most often in both professionally and socially, I have begun to work at integrating the particular southern black vernacular speech I grew up hearing and speaking in a variety of settings. It has been hardest to integrate black vernacular in writing, particularly for academic journals. When I first began to incorporate black vernacular in critical essays, editors would send the work back to me in standard English. Using the vernacular means that translation into standard English may be needed if one wishes a more inclusive audience to understand the meaning of what is said. In the classroom setting, I encourage students to use a first language and translate it so that they do not need to feel that seeking higher education will necessarily estrange them from that language and culture they know most intimately. Not surprising when students in the black women writers class began to speak using diverse language and speech, white students often complained. This seemed to be particularly the case with black vernacular. It was particularly disturbing to them because they could understand the language but not comprehend its meaning. Pedagogically, I encouraged them to think of the moment of not understanding what someone says as a space to learn. Such a space provides not only the opportunity to listen without "mastery," without owning or possessing speech through interpretation, but also the experience of hearing non-English words. These lessons seem particularly crucial in a multicultural society that remains white supremacist, that uses standard English as a weapon to silence and censor. June Jordan reminds us of this in *On Call* when she declares:

I am talking about majority problems of language in a democratic state, problems of a currency that someone has stolen and hidden away and then homogenized into an official "English" language that can only express non-events involving nobody responsible, or lies. If we lived in a democratic state our language would have to hurtle, fly, curse, and sing, in all the common American names, all the undeniable and representative participating voices of everybody here. We would not tolerate the language of the powerful and, thereby, lose all respect for words, per se. We would make our language conform to the truth of our many selves and we would make our language lead us into the equality of power that a democratic state must represent. . . . This is not a democratic state. And we put up with that.

That students in the course on black women writers were repressing all longing to speak in tongues other than standard English without seeing this repression as political was an indication of the way we act in complicity with a culture of domination without conscious awareness.

Recent discussions of diversity and multiculturalism tend to downplay or ignore the question of language. Critical feminist writing focusing on issues of difference and voice have made important theoretical interventions that call for recognition of the primacy of voices that are often silenced, censored, or marginalized. This call for the acknowledgment and/or celebration of diverse voices and consequently diverse languages and speech necessarily disrupts the primacy of standard English. When advocates of feminism first spoke about the desire for diverse participation in the women's movement, there was no discussion of language. It was simply assumed that standard English would remain the primary vehicle for the transmission of feminist thought. Now that the audience for feminist writing and speaking has become more diverse, it is evident that we must change conventional ways of thinking about language, creating spaces where diverse voices can speak in words other than English or in broken/vernacular speech. This means that at a lecture or even in a written work there will be fragments of speech that may or may not be accessible to every individual. Shifting how we think about language and how we use it necessarily alters how we know what we know. Now at a lecture where I might use southern black vernacular, the particular patois of my region, or where I might use very abstract thought in conjunction with plain speech, responding to a diverse audience, I suggest that we do not necessarily need to hear and know what is stated in its entirety, that we do not need to "master" or conquer the narrative as a whole, that we may know in fragments. That we may learn from spaces of silence as well as spaces of speech. That in the act of being patient as we hear another tongue we may subvert that culture of capitalist frenzy and consumption that suggests all desire must be satisfied immediately or disrupt that cultural imperialism that suggests one is worthy of being heard only if one speaks in standard English.

Adrienne Rich concludes her poem with this statement:

I am composing on the typewriter late at night, thinking of today. How well we all spoke. A language is a map of our failures. Frederick Douglass wrote an English purer than Milton's. People suffer highly in poverty. There are methods but we do not use them. Joan, who could not read, spoke some peasant form of French. Some of the sufferings are: it is hard to tell the truth; this is America; I cannot touch you now. In America we have only the present tense. I am in danger. You are in danger. The burning of a book arouses no sensation in me. I know it hurts to burn. There are flames of napalm in Cantonsville, Maryland. I know it hurts to burn. The typewriter is overheated, my mouth is burning, I cannot touch you and this is the oppressor's language.

To recognize that we touch one another in language seems particularly difficult in a society that would have us believe that there is not dignity in the experience of passion, that to feel deeply is to be inferior, for within Western metaphysical dualistic thought, ideas are always more important than language. To heal the splitting of mind and body, marginalized and oppressed people attempt to recover ourselves and our experiences in language. We seek to make a place for intimacy. Unable to find such a place in standard English, we create the ruptured, broken, unruly speech of the vernacular. When I need to say words that do more than simply mirror and/or address the dominant reality, I speak black vernacular. There, in that location, we make English do what we want it to do. We take the oppressor's language and turn it against itself. We make our words a counterhegemonic speech, liberating ourselves in language.

Translation as a Method for Cross-Cultural Teaching

Anuradha Dingwaney and Carol Maier

"Third World" cultures, peoples, texts are "in"; they have been, to adapt Guillermo Gómez-Peña's remarks about the sudden attention being showered on "Latinos," declared "fashionable and grantable" by major cultural institutions (24). This includes academic institutions, where more and more courses about "Third World" cultures are being tacked on to already existing curricula. Although we both welcome this challenge to the canon, our experiences in teaching such courses have often proved disconcerting. In particular, the repeated appropriation of these cultures under the categories of the familiar (same) or of the unfamiliar (different)—which inevitably characterizes student/reader responses—has made us aware of the need for a pedagogy that would guide the teaching of cross-cultural texts and has led us to question our own work as mediators.

The possibility that translation itself might offer a method for making students aware of the organizing principles at work in their readings of "Third World" texts, thereby enabling them to read the "other," resulted unexpectedly from a short story in English translation. After a presentation about Rosario Ferré's "Pico Rico Mandorico" that Carol Maier made to one of Anuradha Dingwaney's classes, a student asked if a basket of Puerto Rican fruit would really contain cherries. In fact, in her translation, Diana Vélez had replaced several tropical fruits, whose names would most likely be unfamiliar to north American readers, with cherries, bananas, and passion fruit (68). The student's question led to a discussion about

303

the difficulties of translating culture-bound terms. It also led to the first of many conversations between the two of us about the possibility of merging Carol's theory and practice in translation with Anuradha's work on postcolonial theory and "Third World" writers. What gradually evolved was a conceptualization of translation as a cross-cultural activity in which the goal of immediacy or readability is tempered by a simultaneous willingness—even determination—to work in difference. Practicing within this definition, a translator does not strive to make possible a rush of identification with an "other" unencumbered by foreignness. Rather, the goal is a more complex verbal "transculturation" in which two languages are held within a single expression.[1]

Translation has long been considered a rather questionable tool for language acquisition. When one grants to the practice of translation, however, the broader task of mediation discussed by contemporary theorists, translation involves far more than looking for the closest lexical equivalent.[2] Rather, it involves the creation of a complex tension.[3] That is, translation, ideally, makes familiar, and thereby accessible, what is confronted as alien, maintaining the familiar in the face of otherness without either sacrificing or appropriating difference. This means that the translator must have a foot in each of two worlds and be able to mediate self-consciously between them. It is our belief that cross-cultural reading based on this model of translation can give rise to a potentially disquieting but highly interactive situation by ensuring that the mediations in cross-cultural literary texts, including the mediation of reading itself, will be recognized and scrutinized.

In order to illustrate our model and its development, we have chosen *I . . . Rigoberta Menchú: An Indian Woman in Guatemala* as our primary text. This is an exemplary text for two principle reasons: (1) it is multiply mediated; (2) it is rapidly acquiring canonical status among scholars and students of minority experience, who do not necessarily attend to these multiple mediations. In the account that follows, we describe the process we underwent as we read and reread *Rigoberta Menchú*, critically examining our initial assumptions and expectations to expose their fault lines. In class, we try to provoke our students to undertake a similar (if not identical) process.

When we decided to write about *Rigoberta Menchú*, our discussions revolved around the many textual layers of discourse that distance Menchú's testimony from her readers. We were, after all, reading Ann Wright's English translation of *Me llamo Rigoberta Menchú: Y así me*

nació la concienca based on Elisabeth Burgos-Debray's transcription and
reworking of Menchú's testimony. The testimony had been spoken in a
Spanish only recently acquired, and tape-recorded in a metropolitan
setting, Paris, where Burgos-Debray lives. There were other mediations
as well. Our own, for instance, informed by years of interpreting literary
texts—in Carol's case, by acts of interpretation she brings to bear on her
translations—and by our more recent reading of critical commentaries
on transcription and reworking of life histories by ethnographers who
seek to understand and render the experiences of non-Western cultures
and peoples. Contemporary critical analyses of life histories insist that
these histories are not transparencies through which we glimpse the
"reality" of the cultures being described; nor do these histories simply
speak for themselves. Rather, "oral history depends for its existence on
the intervention of an ethnographer who collects and presents a version
of the stories gathered" (Patai 1–2). The ethnographer's acknowledged
and unacknowledged assumptions—social, cultural, political—about the
speaker and her culture are implicated in the rendering of the life history.
Mediations, therefore, are very much at issue, in that readers, with their
expectations and assumptions, interpret a life history, which is an
ethnographer's interpretation of a speaker's oral testimony. And the
speaker's testimony is an account constructed by an individual who has
her own agendas and motives for telling the story and therefore has a
stake in what gets represented and how.[4]

As we focused on the role of the ethnographer, Burgos-Debray, shut-
tling back and forth between her introduction and her textual rendition
of Menchú's oral testimony, we were struck both by what Burgos-Debray
says and by what she either leaves unsaid or actively suppresses. In her
introduction, she explains how she became involved in the project, explicitly identifying her potential handicaps as an ethnographer. Because
she had never studied Maya-Quiché culture and never done field work
in Guatemala (xix), she was worried at first about the quality of her
relationship with Menchú—the anxieties and stresses that her lack of
background might generate (xiv). As soon as they met, however, Burgos-
Debray says, she "knew that [they] were going to get along together" (xiv).
We felt, however, that Burgos-Debray glossed over her handicaps, not
overcoming them so much as displacing them by appropriating Menchú's
identity, her world, her cause, even her voice itself—an impression con-
firmed by the Spanish version where Burgos-Debray is named as the
author of *Me llamo Rigoberta Menchú*. Furthermore, a quick, not-fully-

monitored reading of *Rigoberta Menchú* allows the "I" of the introduction
to slide seamlessly into the "I" of Menchú's testimony, conflating, indeed
conjoining Burgos-Debray's identity with Menchú's. Here we might also
recall Burgos-Debray's problematic assertion that "for the whole of that
week, I lived in Rigoberta's world" (xv), when, in fact, it is Menchú who
lives for a week in Burgos-Debray' home in Paris. Who inhabits whose
world, then, becomes an appropriate question to ask.

Our discomfort with Burgos-Debray's claims about her complete
identification with Menchú ("I lived in Rigoberta's world"; "I became
her instrument, her double" [xv, xx]) undoubtedly arose from our experiences teaching and analyzing literary texts from the "Third World,"
or non-Western cultures, in universities in the United States, which is
viewed as part of the "First World." The sheer inequities in the material
and discursive power the "First World" wields over the "Third" necessarily affects "First World" readings of such texts. For this reason, it is
important to disclose and scrutinize the prior understandings and
ideological stances vis-à-vis the "Third World" that U.S. readers bring to
bear upon their reading. Such disclosure and scrutiny will, of course, not
guarantee an informed understanding, but they could clear the ground
for it. More importantly, a revelation of the interpreter's ideological
investments, her "location"—political, intellectual, and so on—will make
those investments explicit to other (subsequent) readers. We should add
that contemporary criticism on life histories emphasizes that self-
reflexivity is required of an ethnographer who edits and interprets life
histories from (an)other culture. In such instances, as in teaching and
writing about "Third World" texts, a great deal is at stake in terms of
representations and evaluations about (an)other culture.

Burgos-Debray, as John Beverley notes, is a "Venezuelan social scien-
tist, [who was] living in Paris at the time she met Menchú, with all that
[that] implies about contradictions between metropolis [read "First
World"] and periphery [read "Third World"], dominant and emergent
social formations, dominant and subaltern languages" (19–20). She actively fosters the impression of a single first person, however, by erasing
all marks of her "intrusions" in and her "refashioning" of Menchú's story:
"I soon reached the decision to give the manuscript the form of a mono-
logue: that was how it came back to me as I reread it. I therefore decided
to delete all my questions" (xx). Although Burgos-Debray explains the
erasure of her "intrusions" as a gesture that allowed her to become
Menchú's "instrument"—her "double"—we questioned whether, in fact,

anyone (Burgos-Debray included) can simply abandon her identity and take on that of another. Or, less charitably, we questioned whether this gesture did not violate Menchú's identity: in the chapter headings, for example, Menchú is referred to in the third person, and the epigraphs are attributed to her, as if she herself were not already speaking.

None of these contradictions is given "voice" in Burgos-Debray's introduction or in the "refashioned" testimony that follows. The reader's awareness of them is nevertheless crucial to an understanding of Burgos-Debray's project. As readers, teachers, and "translators," we felt it incumbent upon us to attend to Burgos-Debray's suppressions and evasions and to reconstitute the text according to its silences and invisibilities.

Ironically, at first, our attempt to reconstitute Menchú's text by looking insistently for signs of mediation Burgos-Debray might have suppressed had the peculiar (and undesired) effect of displacing Menchú's testimony: Burgos-Debray increasingly came to occupy the foreground of our interpretive concerns, while Menchú's story receded into the background. At the same time, however, this realization directed us toward the following question: What if Burgos-Debray had deliberately erased most signs of her mediation to let Menchú's testimony speak to its readers in all its immediacy and urgency? Menchú's testimony, as we began to recognize, is, after all, the testimony of a political activist; indeed, that testimony is a form of activism ("a manifesto on behalf of an ethnic group" is how Burgos-Debray characterizes it [xiii]) insofar as it seeks to engage the reader's sense of morality, justice, and compassion through its graphic account of the atrocities and dehumanization the Maya-Quiché suffer at the hands of a minority *ladino* population. "Words are her only weapons" (Burgos-Debray xi) in making a distant, alien culture and a community's struggle for survival *real* to an audience that has not, in all likelihood, ever experienced the kind of repressions Menchú describes. Words matter. To call their referentiality into question, as our emphasis on Burgos-Debray's mediating presence tended to do, defuses their intense political charge and could even be considered the "irresponsible luxury" (Sommer 120) we should have been trying to avoid.[5]

This discomfiture with our initial interpretive move and its displacement of Menchú's testimony also provoked a complementary question: what if Menchú had collaborated with Burgos-Debray in producing this textual simulation of an unmediated narrative?[6] By concentrating on Burgos-Debray's (lack of) mediation, our initial discussion had evaded, perhaps ignored, Menchú's active agency in crafting her own narrative.

Such a view failed to account for "the authority and creativity of the speaker weaving her own text" (Patai 8). Our assumption that Menchú had no agency also risked reproducing the classic colonizing gesture, identified by Edward W. Said, whereby representatives of a hegemonic (colonizing) culture invest themselves with *the* authority to speak about, describe, represent the colonized/subaltern subject (*Orientalism:* "In the Shadow of the West").

How, we asked ourselves, do we go about accounting for Menchú's active role in the construction of her story? Where to begin? As an activist for her community and as a representative of the Guatemalan activist group 31 January Popular Front in Europe and the United States, it was only reasonable to suppose that Menchú had—and continues to have—a stake in telling her story. For example, *Report on Guatemala* notes Menchú's appearance at a conference where "she requested solidarity from North American friends in supporting the demands of popular organizations and of Guatemala's indigenous majority" (Gorin 14). Telling her story was, and is, for her, a political task. To influence a diverse, international audience, that story had to be readily accessible, which meant that Menchú may well have had a far more active role in the construction of her story than Burgos-Debray's retelling of it first suggests.

Once we had granted Menchú this accessibility as a strategy, the extended descriptions of her culture—its presiding deities, its rituals, family, and community life—could be read as marks of a deliberate effort to render an unfamiliar culture less alien to her readers in the West to enlist their support. Certainly a great deal of her extended descriptions about her culture are a part of her political program: "I'm an Indianist, not just an Indian," Menchú declares, "I defend everything to do with my ancestors." But this is not her sole motivation. As Burgos-Debray notes, "she talked to me not only because she wanted to tell us about her sufferings but also—or perhaps mainly—because she wanted us to hear about a culture of which she is extremely proud and which she wants to have recognized" (166, xx). Nevertheless, some of these descriptions also seem designed to accommodate Western notions about "primitive" peoples.

This self-consciousness about her political task and about the self-representations Menchú mobilizes are signaled at various moments in her testimony. We will mention only two examples. First, she reflects on her community's subversive uses of the Bible to underscore her peoples' more "moral" grasp of its precepts and teachings:

We began studying [the Bible] more deeply and, well, we came to a conclusion. That being a Christian means thinking of our brothers around us, that everyone of our Indian race has the right to eat. . . .

For us the Bible is our main weapon. It has shown us the way. Perhaps those who call themselves Christians but who are really only Christians in theory, won't understand why we give the Bible the meaning we do. But that's because they haven't lived as we have. And also perhaps because they can't analyze it. (132, 134)

Second, Menchú accounts for her transgressive move to learn Spanish, despite her father forbidding it because he feels it will take her away from the community, by spelling out its political implications: "They've always said, poor Indians, they can't speak, so many speak for them. That's why I decided to learn Spanish" (156).

Those instances of reflection and the explicit use of language as a political strategy made clear to us the fundamental paradox that Menchú's testimony turns on, and of which she was certainly "conscious." On the one hand, to affect its readers with its full and urgent political force, the testimony must be, or seem to be, unmediated—a transparency that makes *visible* the brutalities and repressions it witnesses. On the other hand, such *immediacy* can so overwhelm readers that they identify with—indeed, feel they become—Menchú. This "identification," of course, is problematic at best, dishonest at worst. Menchú's reader is not Menchú. Protected and distanced from Menchú's "battlefield"—her severe material conditions and struggle for survival—the "First World" reader can only masquerade as a "Third World" oppressed, subaltern subject.[7] As Menchú insists, "It's not so much that the hungrier you've been, the purer your ideas must be, but you can only have a real consciousness if you've really lived this life" (223). Her challenge, then, is to enable a reader to *identify* with her cause, her political agenda, without assuming her identity, even though to identify with her cause may entail imagining oneself in her place.

Menchú's testimony ensures this im-mediated response by deploying another paradox. Her testimony is replete with details about her culture, community, family, even the events that lead to her politicization and development into a leader for her people. At the same time, however, she insists that there are secrets she will not disclose, and she concludes her testimony by reminding us: "Nevertheless, I'm still keeping my Indian identity a secret. I'm still keeping secret what I think no-one should know. Not even anthropologists or intellectuals, no matter how many books

they have, can find out all our secrets" (247). This maneuver compels
readers to inhabit that space of uncertainty where they know that they
do not know everything. Moreover, it compels readers to respect the
"prior" text—Menchú's testimony—knowing all the time that, from
their first encounter with it, the text has been interpreted (and transformed) in their consciousness—an act for which they bear responsibility.[8]

When we thought of Ann Wright's mediation in *Rigoberta Menchú*,
our initial response was quite negative, much as it had been with Burgos-
Debray. Wright had done a creditable job of rendering Menchú's Spanish
into English, but she had just as clearly taken pains to repeat some of the
gestures in the Spanish edition that we felt might lead to a reader's
unexamined compassion. Like Burgos-Debray, Wright wants her own
words to be as much like Menchú's as possible. As she explains in her
translator's note, she hopes that her own presence as mediator will go
virtually unnoticed, and this goal of transparency has determined her
practice (viii–ix). She has followed Menchú's "spontaneous narrative"
and "original phrasing," even at times when Menchú's expression might
seem awkward, and she has transcribed rather than translated many words
in Quiché. Indeed, in large part her translator's note reads like a translation of the Spanish *introducción* that it replaces. In that *introducción*
(7), which is omitted in the English (where the introduction is in fact a
translation of Burgos-Debray's *prológo*), Burgos-Debray reiterates her
determination not to "betray" Menchú by altering the content of her
narrative.

What is more, as if to follow Burgos-Debray's example and insert
herself unobtrusively into the same space Burgos-Debray occupies vis-à-
vis Menchú—and therefore insure for her reader "the impact" Menchú's
words had on her—Wright draws no attention to specific strategies she
might have used to prepare the English version. Nor does she speculate
about the changes in Menchú's narrative Burgos-Debray may have made
when she translated Menchú's spoken words to written prose. This allows
her to state, for example (and without qualification), that "I have tried,
as far as possible, to stay with Rigoberta's original phrasing" (viii).[9] In
addition, ironically, not only is Wright absent from the photograph of
Menchú and Burgos-Debray, on the back cover of the English edition
of the book, she is not even mentioned. A translator, of course, can hardly
be blamed for a publisher's failure to acknowledge her and her work.
Wright's apparent determination to make herself as invisible as possible,

however, in effect contributes to a second layer of mediation or, to use Richard Seiburth's term (239), "covering" of Menchú's text which, with respect to the reader in English, acts as a second distancing or even a second erasure.

What is curious about this second erasure, however, as we discovered as we began to study Wright's version with a view to Burgos-Debray's Spanish, is that Wright does, in fact, give evidence that she translates not only Burgos-Debray's invisibility but also Burgos-Debray's editing of Menchú's tapes. This is to say that, contrary to what her translator's note might lead a reader to believe, Wright has apparently been guided as much by Burgos-Debray's mediating principle as by a "fidelity" to the words in her text. "I only hope that I have been able to do justice to the power of their message . . . and convey the impact they had on me when I first read [Menchú's words]" (ix). As we studied her own English words we found in them definite indications of will or agency.

The substitution of Burgos-Debray's *introducción,* for instance, is just one of several alterations that suggest Wright believed she could do more "justice" to the "power" of Menchú's testimony by making it accessible to the English-language reader. Other alterations include the "I" at the beginning of the English title, the absence of *conciencia,* and the use throughout of word "Indian" rather than "Quiché." What's more, Wright has not reprinted either Burgos-Debray's acknowledgments or her dedication to Alaide Foppa. She has changed the epigraphs of several chapters, shortened many chapter titles, and omitted an appendix of documents about the Comité de Unidad Campesina (CUC). Finally, her use of ellipsis is not consistent with the Spanish, and on several occasions she has Menchú speak to a second person, something that does not occur in the Spanish. These last two alterations are especially important because they lead one to speculate about whether Wright believed her changes could restore some of the orality sacrificed in Burgos-Debray's initial transcription: "Something I want to tell you" (165), Menchú says in Wright's English, or "It's not so much the hungrier you've been" (233), or "I'd need a lot of time to tell you all about my people" (247). (The changes involved in the transcription of oral narratives are discussed in Patai, Tedlock, and Watson and Watson-Franke.)

As our discussion of *Rigoberta Menchú* demonstrates, our grasp of the "demands" Menchú's testimony makes on its readers was achieved through a circuitous route. We constantly interrogated our premises—repeatedly doubling back on our initial assumptions and expectations—at the same time that we tried to be alert to the various positions (Menchú's, Burgos-Debray's, Wright's) implicated in the crafting of Menchú's testimony. In this way our work revolved around diverse mediations, including those involved in erasing the marks of mediation itself, the readings and retellings that intervene between the reader and the "realities" Menchú describes.

Our assessment that the simulation of an unmediated narrative in order to engage Menchú's reader is almost as important as insisting on the very fact of mediation can be extended, we believe, so as to formulate a theory of reading other cross-cultural "Third World" texts as well. In these texts, as we have come to understand them, the sense of unmediatedness or immediacy is the means by which some form of identification is produced. Simultaneously, however, mediation assumes distance (and difference) between readers and the subjects/objects of their reading. Reading, then, can be based on a similar subtly dialectical interplay of identity (identification) and difference. The dangers of mobilizing solely one or the other category are many. An uncritical assumption of identity is, as we have shown through *Rigoberta Menchú,* a mode of appropriation. Similarly, identification is a function of recuperating the unfamiliar "other" in terms of the familiar; reading this way relies on the stereotypes one culture utilizes to understand, and domesticate, (an)other. An uncritical assumption of difference, which presumes that (an)other is never accessible, allows readers to abandon, indeed exonerates them from, the task of ever reading cross-cultural texts. Deployed solely, each category produces an impasse.[10]

Invoking the idea and activity of translation and attending to the specific strategies translators employ offers one way out of this impasse. As an activity, translation starts from the assumption that something of one language *can be* "borne across" or recovered in another. Although translation is often construed as an activity that simply "copies" or "repeats" a "prior" text, it is also, and more importantly, construed as one that interprets (and transforms) a "prior" text. It is, after all, an activity that presumes a translator, a subject who intervenes, mediates, between one language and another. Thus, recent theorists emphasize not the "accuracy," or even the product of translation, but rather the appropriateness of a translator's choices, the strategies used to render one language in terms of another, the inclusions and exclusions.

When a cross-cultural work is seen as an author's translation of a culture, it becomes possible to read that text itself as a reading—a construction of social, political, cultural "realities"—by an individual who inserts herself and her work (and is embedded) in that culture in particular ways, for particular purposes. Such a view warns against easy judgments about how an individual or a work represents (or is representative of) a culture.[11] When readers see their reading as an activity involving translation, it becomes possible for them to scrutinize their own "locations"—the interpretive choices and strategies—which are implicated in their readings. At the same time, however, this emphasis on individual and individualized interpretation involved in translation should not lead to a domain of pure relativity, where every reader can only read in terms of personal experience. The text being translated resists and constrains the reader from this absolute appropriation. While translation requires, according to James Boyd White, "an act of creation, a making of something new . . . the original text cannot be forgotten, for fidelity is always due to it. Indeed, it is upon the prior text that our right to speak at all depends. One has no authority to disregard it and substitute for it texts of one's own composition" (246).

In light of what we have said above, a desirable goal in teaching (and reading) cross-cultural texts as an exercise involving translation is to nudge students (readers) to occupy that space or tension where they are "faithful" to the text at the same time as they acknowledge that their "fidelity" is itself refracted through their ideological formations as "subjects" in the "First World." As Catherine Belsey notes in a different context, "it is here that we see the full force of Althusser's use of the term 'subject,' originally borrowed, as he says, from law. The subject is not only a grammatical subject, 'a center of initiatives, author of and responsible for its actions,' but also a *subjected* being who submits to the authority of the social formation represented in ideology as the Absolute Subject (God, the king, the boss, Man, conscience)" (49). Being "faithful," then, entails constructing, in as informed a way as possible, the author's "purposes"—examining, that is, "the process of production—not the private experience of the individual author, but the mode of production, the materials and their arrangement in the work" (Belsey 54).

How might this function in class? More specifically, to return to our first thoughts about using informed translation as an antidote to translation practiced unawares, how might it function with respect to *Rigoberta Menchú?*

Even students who have no knowledge of Spanish might be asked to look carefully at the book's front cover and consider it with respect to the statements in Menchú's opening paragraph. They could be asked about the "I" at the beginning of the title, in the context of Menchú's assertion that "it's not only *my* life, it's also the testimony of my people" (1); about the use of the word *Indian* or the advertisement of a film "featuring" Menchú. They could be asked to find information about the publisher, about Burgos-Debray, or about similar testimonials in English and to discuss what they find in light of Menchú's narrative. The changes Wright made when she translated the title could be pointed out and discussed as well, and the difficulties of translating the work could be explained.

For students whose Spanish allows them to work in both languages, a discussion of the cover and title could be followed by an examination of terms in passages that presented particular challenges to the translator. Depending on the extent of their language skills, they could be asked to discuss, for example, the role of *conciencia* in the Spanish and its appearances in English as "consciousness" or "awareness." This type of exercise would no doubt be richer for students who had some familiarity with Spanish (and should in fact suggest many similar activities). But even students unable to work in Spanish could be asked to examine the English text for examples of the experience Menchú points to as the one that guides her as she talks to Burgos-Debray. *Conciencia* implies awareness—"waking up" in the sense of seeing clearly—an "illumination" that, when its development is traced through passages selected in Spanish, leads from the raising of a young woman's consciousness to a complex strategy for bringing to light certain secrets in order to protect their integrity.[12] Regardless of the language in which students carried out this exercise, they would confront not only the difficulties implied in rendering Menchú's story in English, they would also need to consider the issue of translation with respect to this central experience. What is more, once *conciencia* is placed in the context of Menchú's very deliberate and conscious decision to risk betraying her people in order to make outsiders aware of their suffering, students should recognize that their own role within the narrative is one of potential intruder, one for whom Menchú is constantly mediating or translating from Quiché to Spanish (to English), not only words but also the very incidents of the story.

Although we did not think of Menchú's narrative in this way until we had discussed it several times, the more times we read her reminder that "I'm still keeping my Indian identity secret" (247), the more we considered her a translator in the widest possible sense of the word. This means that we have come to view the marketing of her story, whether in Burgos-Debray's Paris apartment or on the English-language cover, as absolutely consistent with her decision to learn Spanish and leave her village. "My name is Rigoberta Menchú, and here's how I woke up," Menchú might say in the English title that could be proposed to students as they were encouraged to think of how she might sound if she were able to cast her story in their idiom. What might she want from you, they could be asked, how would she expect you to insert yourselves in her story? How do you think she might have envisioned you as she gave permission to Wright to make an English-language translation of her book? How well do you think Wright has made way for a realization of the "you" Menchú envisioned?

And how do you think *Wright* envisioned you as she prepared that translation? Students could be queried as the discussion was returned, inevitably, to the English-language version. Why do you think she placed a first person pronoun in the title, or made her other adaptations? Why, for example, is the second person addressed in Wright's version? Who is that "you" in Wright's text?

None of those questions would be answered easily, and some might not be possible to answer at all. By considering them, however, students would be enabled to see Wright, and Burgos-Debray, and Menchú, and themselves engaged in a collaboration that results not from passivity and transparency on the part of the "translators," but from assertiveness and interchange. They should also realize that to make Wright or Burgos-Debray or Menchú visible is not to "criticize," but to acknowledge them. In the same way it should be evident that a translator's visibility does not lessen the impact or immediacy of a story for its readers but actually intensifies that immediacy by compounding an awareness of translation and bringing the act of mediation to light. "Im-mediation" results from the simultaneous distancing and participation that characterizes translation directed by *conciencia* as both self-consciousness and conscience as ethical responsibility.

Notes

1. We use "transculturation" thinking of Pérez Firmat's discussion of it with respect to "the Cuban condition": "the word properly designates the

fermentation and turmoil that *precedes* synthesis." It is thus "a coinage that denotes transition, passage, process" (23).

2. See, for example, the work by Lefevere, Venuti, and White, and the articles in Warren.

3. See Warren's "celebration of otherness" (5), or White's description of the translator's identity "split irremediably in two" (231), or Maier's "compact" (628).

4. Among the essays and books we looked at, the following were especially useful: Crapanzano, Watson and Watson-Franke, Frank, Geiger, Patai, and Tedlock. We use the terms *life history* and *testimony* interchangably because Menchú employs both "genres" when she "turn[s] her life story" (Burgos-Debray xiv) into a *testimonio* that bears witness to the "problem of repression, poverty, subalternity, imprisonment, struggle for survival"—all experiences that characterize the *testimonio*, according to Beverley (14). See, however, Beverley's discussion of the distinctions between *testimonios* and oral histories (13–14).

5. A danger comparable to displacement haunts the work of interpreters who wish to signal their self-reflexivity clearly with regard to their acts of interpretation; one of the effects of extensive self-reflection on one's "location" is that it can displace the "real" subject of their interpretation. In extreme cases, such self-reflexivity becomes a mode of self-aggrandizement whereby the interpreter mobilizes a host of personal details to keep herself at the "center" of an interpretive "performance." In some instances, self-reflexiveness can be (and is) deployed not as a way of accounting for one's position, but as a way of explaining it away, a way of exempting oneself.

6. This question and the discussion that follows arose simultaneously with the question that frames our discussion of Burgos-Debray's suppression of her presence in Menchú's testimony. We saw them as complementary questions. For purposes of clarity, however, we present them in a linear narrative. But, in a classroom situation, we would encourage both questions to be asked, and discussion around them to proceed simultaneously in order to minimize the risk of one subjectivity being subsumed under the other.

7. "We live down the street from what I consider to be the prettiest park," one of Carol's former students from a class on Central American politics and poetics wrote to her recently from a university town in the Pacific Northwest, evoking her reading of *Rigoberta Menchú:* "It includes a big rose garden with 300 different types of roses. There is a community garden where neighbors plant corn or beans or whatever side by side. Almost like Rigoberta Menchú's community."

8. White uses respect to refer to "a set of practices by which we learn to live with difference" (257).

9. It is odd that Wright should refer to Menchú's "original," since there is

no evidence that she had access to the tapes of Menchú's voice from which Burgos-Debray worked.

10. Trinh T. Minh-ha analyzes a somewhat different move where "difference" is invoked to disempower some and empower others: "Let difference replace conflict. Difference as understood in many feminist and non-western contexts, difference as foreground in my filmwork is not opposed to sameness, nor synonymous with separateness. Difference, in other words, does not necessarily give rise to separatism. . . . Many of us hold on to the concept of difference not as a tool of creativity to question multiple forms of repression and dominance, but as a tool of segregation, to exert power on the basis of racial and sexual essences. The apartheid type of difference" (74).

11. Consider the reception of Salman Rushdie and his two works about India and Pakistan, *Midnight's Children* and *Shame*, in the West, where they have been read as representative of the "realities" of the subcontinent. Clarke Blaise, for example, describes *Midnight's Children* as "a continent finding its voice" (see Dingwaney). The same could be said of *Rigoberta Menchú:* the blurb on the back cover packages the book as "one of the few complete expressions of Indian self-knowledge since the Spanish conquest."

12. In Spanish, where *conciencia* is "born," and birth is commonly expressed as a "giving of light" ("*dar a luz*"), this strategy is formulated in the language itself as well as conceptually.

Works Cited

Belsey, Catherine. "Constructing the Subject: Deconstructing the Text." *Feminist Criticism and Social Change.* Ed. Judith Newton and Deborah Rosenfelt. New York: Methuen, 1985. 45–64.

Beverley, John. "The Margin at the Center: On *Testimonio* (Testimonial Narrative)." *Modern Fiction Studies* 35 (Spring 1989): 11–28.

Burgos-Debray, Elisabeth. *Me llamo Rigoberta Menchú: Y así me nació la conciencia.* Barcelona: Argos Vegara, 1983.

Crapanzano, Vincent. "Life Histories: A Review Essay." *American Anthropologist* 86 (December 1984): 953–60.

Dingwaney, Anuradha. "Author(iz)ing *Midnight's Children* and *Shame:* Salman Rushdie's Construction of Authority." *Reworlding: The Literature of the Indian Diaspora.* Ed. Emmanuel Nelson. Westport, CT: Greenwood Press, 1992. 157–68.

Ferré, Rosario. "Pico Rico, Mandorico." *Reclaiming Medusa: Short Stories by Contemporary Puerto Rican Women.* Ed. and trans. Diana Vélez. 64–72.

Frank, Gelya. "Finding the Common Denominator: A Phenomenological
    Critique of the Life History Method." *Ethos* 7 (Spring 1979): 68–94.
Geiger, Susan N. J. "Women's Life Histories: Method and Content." *Signs*
    11 (Winter 1986): 334–51.
Gómez-Peña, Guillermo. "The Multicultural Paradigm: An Open Letter to the
    National Arts Community." *High Performance* (Fall 1989): 18–27.
Gorin, Joe. "National Conference." *Report on Guatemala* 11.3 (1990): 14.
Lefevere, André. "Translations and Other Ways in which One Literature
    Refracts Another." *Symposium* 38 (Summer 1984): 127–42.
Maier, Carol. "Notes After Words: Looking Forward Retrospectively at
    Translation and (Hispanic and Luso-Brazilian) Feminist Criticism."
    *Cultural and Historical Grounding for Hispanic and Luso-Brazilian
    Feminist Criticism.* Ed. Hernán Vidal. Minneapolis, MN: Institute
    for the Study of Ideologies and Literature, 1989. 625–53.
Menchú, Rigoberta. *I . . . Rigoberta Menchú: An Indian Woman in
    Guatemala.* Ed. Elisabeth Burgos-Debray. Trans. Ann Wright. Lon-
    don: New Left-Verso, 1984.
Minh-ha, Trinh T. "Not You/Like You: Post-colonial Women and the Inter-
    locking Questions of Identity and Difference." *Inscriptions* 3–4
    (1988): 71–77.
Patai, Daphne. *Brazilian Women Speak: Contemporary Life Stories.* New
    Brunswick, NJ: Rutgers UP, 1988.
Pérez Firmat, Gustavo. *The Cuban Condition: Translation and Identity in
    Modern Cuban Literature.* Cambridge: Cambridge UP, 1989.
Said, Edward W. *Orientalism.* New York: Vintage Books, 1979.
————. "In the Shadow of the West." *Wedge: The Imperialism of Repre-
    sentation, the Representation of Imperialism* 7–8 (Winter–Spring
    1985): 4–12.
Seiburth, Richard. "The Guest: Second Thoughts on Translating Hölderlin."
    Warren 237–43.
Sommer, Doris. "'Not Just a Personal Story': Women's *Testimonios* and the
    Plural Self." *Life/Lines: Theorizing Women Autobiography.* Ed. Bella
    Brodzki and Celeste Schenck. Ithaca, NY: Cornell UP, 1988.
    107–30.
Tedlock, Dennis. *The Spoken Word and the Work of Interpretation.* Philadel-
    phia: U of Pennsylvania P, 1983.
Vélez, Diana, ed. and trans. *Reclaiming Medusa: Short Stories by Contemporary
    Puerto Rican Women.* San Francisco: Spinsters/Aunt Lute, 1988.
Venuti, Lawrence. "The Translator's Invisibility." *Criticism* 28 (Spring 1986):
    179–212.
Warren, Rosanna, ed. *The Art of Translation: Voices from the Field.* Boston:
    Northeastern UP, 1989.

Watson, Lawrence, and Maria-Barbara Watson-Franke. *Interpreting Life Histories: An Anthropological Inquiry.* New Brunswick, NJ: Rutgers UP, 1985.

White, James Boyd. *Justice as Translation: An Essay in Cultural and Legal Criticism.* Chicago: Chicago UP, 1990.

V. Responses

A Comment on Translation, Critique, and Subversion

Talal Asad

There are a number of fascinating themes in this rich collection on translating literature. I have learned something of value from each of the essays, but I am not competent to deal with all the topics they address. So instead I shall discuss briefly—and inadequately—a question that surfaces in several of the contributions: translation as an act of fidelity and/or subversion.

Translation, in the most common contemporary sense, is used to denote the process by which meanings are conveyed from one language to another. In ecclesiastical usage, however, the removal of a saint's remains, or his relics, from an original site to another is also known as translation. (So, too, the transfer of a cleric from one office to another, or of a feast from one date in the calendar to another.) In medieval Christendom the narratives relating such events were called *translationes.* As a subgenre of hagiography, translations displayed a typical structure: first, there was the search for the saintly relic, then the miracles marking its discovery, the initial failure in moving it followed by prayer and invocation and eventual success, and finally its joyful and reverent reception and placement in the new shrine. Relics were sometimes stolen, and the translations would proudly say so (see Geary). Translation is thus (like history) at once a sequence of human acts and a narrative recounting it, both being and representation.

The transfer of relics involved the retention of something essential despite the change of location. What was transferred was not merely a relic but the power inherent in it (such as curing sickness or ensuring success in some enterprise). Disturbing a relic—sometimes in secrecy— was a critical and dangerous thing to do. It involved a deliberate act of transgression. Hence translation required a faithful—even reverential— relocation of the relic.

The *translationes* make it clear that the relics gave the new site its significance, and the inscription was undertaken to articulate this significance. A *translatio* was therefore never a neutral representation; it was situated in a particular way of life and a particular set of practices. For apart from authorizing the relic's new context, the *translatio* was a text to be recited in the liturgy celebrating the anniversary of the translation.

Translation, of whatever kind, is never a neutral process, but it does not follow that it must therefore be an act of moral criticism or political subversion. The process of translating always involves discrimination, interpretation, appraisal, and selection. It calls for a constant awareness of the limits and possibilities of translating adequately from one language to another. And, of course, one translates texts for a variety of purposes, some benign and some hostile to the producers of the original texts. But none of this implies that the *practice* of translation can't be distinguished from the practice of critique.

Translation is one of the things that ethnographers undertake (together with analysis and description) in order to give readers an understanding of the beliefs and practices of unfamiliar peoples. Such an understanding is likely to be impaired if the task of translation preempts that of moral and political critique.

I have written about a mode of public argument in contemporary Saudi Arabia that is based on theological premises and directed at the Saudi ruling establishment (see my *Genealogies* ch. 6). In the course of doing so, I summarized and translated several audiocassettes of sermons by a number of young preachers who have emerged as critics of the regime. The cassettes can be purchased at bookshops in Saudi Arabic selling religious literature. They are also widely copied and distributed in private circles within the country as well as abroad. I secured several of these, including one that expounded in detail the practical principles of theologically based public criticism. At every step in my account I was, of course, obliged to select, interpret, and make decisions. From the *recorded voice* of a publicly delivered lecture where information about gesture, stance, facial expressions, and so on, was missing, to a *transcription* where references to such things as intonation, stress, repetition had to be virtually eliminated, through to *translations* of selected passages that I thought were in one way or another significant, my major concern in translating was to bring out as clearly as possible the preacher's style of reasoning, based as it was on religious commitments and limits. I tried, through my translations, to make the speaker's point of view (presented in Arabic to a Muslim audience in a Muslim country) understandable to an English-speaking, non-Muslim readership. That task did not require a critique—let alone a subversion—of that point of view. Nor, for that matter, did it call for a justification or defence.

This doesn't mean that in that essay I offer a view-from-nowhere about these preachers and the kinds of public criticism they have mounted. I was interested in developing and presenting a more complex understanding of the Islamic movements and traditions that are called "fundamentalist" by Western writers. I was opposed to the political tendency implicit in the homogenizing use of this term, and at the same time I wished to question some of the background assumptions about rationality, political tolerance, and religious authority that the social sciences in the modern Western university have inherited from the Enlightenment. In brief, although the Saudi sermons are acts of criticism, my translation of them is not.[1]

For readers unfamiliar with the Arabic language and Islamic tradition, access to these sermons and the movement to which they belong can only be through translations. Yet insofar as discourse is enmeshed in particular ways of life, its translation from one language to another is never completely successful. The habitual practices, assumptions, and feelings of readers in the target language limit the possibilities open to a translator and confront him or her with various kinds of resistance. Conversely, resistance is a sign of untranslatability—and therefore of incommensurability. Critiques that draw on translations only will be affected accordingly.

But critique is not necessarily dependent on translations. Strictly speaking, critiques do not presuppose translations but familiarity with the tradition to which the discourse to be criticized belongs and the ability to conduct an argument in terms of that tradition. A crucial component of what the discourse means derives from the vocabularies, debates, and preoccupations of a tradition. That is why I hold that, for moral criticism to be responsible, it must be addressed to an audience belonging to the tradition criticized who can respond to it (see my "Concept" 156). One might object here that this rules out the possibility of criticizing one's

ancestors who, being dead, cannot respond. That objection could only
be made by readers who haven't understood what is involved in belonging
to a living tradition. Criticisms of the past are morally relevant only when
that past still informs the present—when contemporaries invoke the
authority of founding ancestors against each other. In criticizing the dead,
one is therefore questioning what they have authorized in the living. (To
reject everything that preceding generations have authorized is, of course,
to abandon the tradition as a whole, to call for a severance of all links
between the living and the dead.) If one can criticize the living from
within their tradition, one does not depend on translation. One learns
to speak their language and to understand their life in its own terms.
That is why I maintain not only that critique is an activity different from
translation, but that translation as such is not essential to morally responsible critique.

Too often we use the terms *critique* and *subversion* as though they
were interchangeable. It is useful to distinguish them. True, both carry
an agonistic sense, yet it is only the former that refers to the process of
rational appraisal and judgment. Subversion, on the other hand, is a
matter of overturning, undermining, and destroying. Whereas critique
has pretensions to shared standards of reasoning and justice, subversion
assumes a state of war and a determination to eliminate the enemy—or
at least his power. For purposes of subversion, anything goes. The instruments available to criticism are more narrowly defined.

In my view, translation can play an important part in subverting
values, practices, and modes of life quite independent of critique. In order
to appreciate this fact we need to shift our focus from literary works of
imagination to texts of a more mundane sort. Let me explain by reference
to a recent text on the politics of translation.

In an interesting essay on the translation of French literature into
Arabic, Richard Jacquemond writes about "the Thousand Books project
. . . [which was] launched in 1955 with the explicit purpose of allowing
the Egyptian audience to read the most essential books of modern world
culture in cheap, subsidized paperback editions" (144), books that included a large number of translations from contemporary French
philosophy, novels, and drama. Twenty-five years later, notes Jacquemond, the picture was very different: "More than half of the translations
from the French published in the 1980s concern Egyptology, Orientalism, or Arab, Islamic, and Third World affairs. In this case, translations
can no longer be seen as springing from the urge to have access to Western

intellectual production, but rather as a way for the national culture to examine and reassure itself in the other's mirror" (146).

This change is surely significant. Jacquemond does not tell us the proportions falling into the categories "Egyptology, Orientalism, or Arab, Islamic, and Third World affairs," nor how these categories were constructed. But I find more problematic the assumption that the unconditional reception (through translation) of French philosophy and imaginative literature constitutes an entry into "modern world culture," and that the distanced utilization of other translations from the French constitutes something much less edifying: a form of cultural narcissism. Thus "modern world culture" is equated with "Western intellectual production" and presented as the proper historical destiny of countries that are not yet fully part of it.

I find this familiar view striking for two main reasons: First, "modern world culture" is represented as a state of consciousness (a beatitude) that precludes narcissism. (Respect for modern world culture, so one is given to understand, is reverence for a transcendent power, not for oneself.) The second, connected, reason is that the relationship between translated literature and its consumption is represented entirely in nonpractical terms. "Culture" in this context is a cognitive category; it relates to what people think, not to what they do.

Yet it is precisely what people do, and what they are able to do, that has received inadequate attention from those who are interested in translation theory. I would suggest that we need a more systematic consideration of the social preconditions and consequences of translating Western discourses on a range of social practices: law, banking, public administration, education, health, accounting, insurance, policing, war, mass communication, natural sciences, and so on. The translation into Arabic of Western manuals and reports on the techniques used in these domains has had momentous consequences for Egyptian culture. It has subverted old practices, knowledges, and powers and has helped to create new ones. And even if this process hasn't always reproduced Western models, the newer arrangements could not have come about without the (generally forcible) translation of Western discourses to Egypt. These changes were rarely the outcome of persuasive critique. But more relevant for translation theory is the thought that Western discourses thus helped to create "Egyptian society" analogous to other "societies," each with its national culture, all represented by modernizers as moving painfully into the modern world.

In this consideration of translation, what is called modern world culture turns out to be rooted not in images (perceptions of "self" and "other") but in social practices of power. Access to "modern world culture" by "local audiences" becomes a matter of translating from "stronger" languages to "weaker" ones, a change from "worse" ways of living to those that are "better." The subversion of dominated ways of life by transcendent powers becomes the order of the day. In this process, translation generates not only ambiguity in the reading of translated texts, but ambivalence in cultural relations between colonizer and colonized. The former invites the colonized into "modern world culture" but insists, as its authentic originater, on being the judge of successful enculturation. The latter often accuses the colonizer of injustice in the name of "modern world culture" precisely because he concedes that he is not yet accorded full membership.

Accessibility in a major European language is a precondition of entry into modern world culture. "Why are they not translating my work?" says the colonized writer: "Am I not inventive in the way modernity values inventiveness? Do I not demonstrate the sensibilities that modern culture requires? Can I not criticize everything even as moderns do?" (The non-colonized writer asks no such questions.) Literary subversion cannot constitute an adequate response to the colonized writer's (or critic's) discontent because its effectiveness is a matter of canonical judgment, and he or she has no authority to make that judgment. The structures of power the colonized writer confronts are institutional, not textual.

From the colonizer's standpoint the issue is not whether the colonized writer is "modern," but whether he or she is "good enough" to be accorded serious critical attention as part of what is called modern world culture. Rightly or wrongly, it is the colonizer who has the power to make this judgment. When someone pleads with the colonizer to make a judgment in a particular writer's favor, to have him or her translated and read "seriously," what is sought is the modern world culture's transcendent power to redefine that writer's value as "universal." (The plea, let it be noted, is always for translating the writer into English, or into French, but never into Chinese or Hindi—although there are nearly as many Chinese speakers as there are English, and more Hindi speakers than French.) And even if a novel, such as Tahar Ben Jalloun's *La nuit sacrée*, is properly described as "the model of the francophone North African text that is both resister and liberator" (Mehrez 127), it is the Prix Goncourt that locates it unequivocally within "modern world culture."

Contrary to what some critics argue, its bilingual resonances do not make it oppositional to that culture. (Let us recall that from Ezra Pound and T. S. Eliot to the Surrealists, European writers and artists have employed devices of intertextual quotation from several languages and of startling iconic juxtaposition in their effort to question or undermine bourgeois values. The result, notoriously, was an enrichment of modernism, a cultural movement patronized by the European bourgeoisie and endlessly glossed by Western university professors.) Modern world culture has no difficulty in accommodating unstable signs and domesticated exotica, so long as neither conflicts radically with systems of profit.

Perhaps this state of affairs is historically inescapable. But should one not, in that case, be skeptical of the liberating claims of postcolonial literary subversion?

In their exemplary essay on the translation of Rigoberta Menchú's autobiography, Dingwaney and Maier warn that the current "emphasis on individual and individualized interpretation involved in translation should not lead to a domain of pure relativity, where every reader can only read in terms of personal experience." I couldn't agree more with this statement. What it implies is that the original text constrains in a way that a translation of it does not; that while one argues *about* the original one cannot, as a translator, argue *with* it. The latter activity can be properly carried on only in relation to the translation. Like the medieval *translationes,* all translations must seek to articulate the power of the relic in its new habitat, and remain faithful to that power.

Note

1. So, too, an imaginative work of art—like Salman Rushdie's *The Satanic Verses*—may aim to subvert religious beliefs and attack political practices, but a successful translation of it from the English is not itself a critique.

Works Cited

Asad, Talal. "The Concept of Cultural Translation in British Social
        Anthropology." *Writing Culture.* Ed. J. Clifford and G. Marcus.
        Berkeley: U California P, 1986. 140–64.

————. *Genealogies of Religion.* Baltimore: Johns Hopkins UP, 1993.

Geary, P. J. *Furta Sacra.* Princeton: Princeton UP, 1978.

Jacquemond, Richard. "Translation and Cultural Hegemony: The Case of French-Arabic Translation." *Rethinking Translation: Discourse, Subjectivity, Ideology.* Ed. Lawrence Venuti. New York: Routledge, 1992. 139–58.

Mehrez, Samia. "Translation and the Postcolonial Experience: The Francophone North African Text." *Rethinking Translation: Discourse, Subjectivity, Ideology.* Ed. Lawrence Venuti. New York: Routledge, 1992. 120–38.

On the Virtues of Not Understanding

James Boyd White

Because every attempt distorts the original, perfect translation is impossible. Is it the task of the translator to make this impossibility seem to disappear, to produce a text that flows effortlessly in the new language, presenting no problems of understanding, or should the translator somehow find a way to bring the reader to share a sense of the foreignness of what he is reading, and hence this much of the reality of the unknown text, its language, and its world? Several of the authors in this volume raise this issue one way or another, especially Indira Karamcheti, who argues for the virtues of "opaque translation," a translation with "cognitive holes." And I myself have made a similar argument:

To translate at all requires that one learn the language of another, recognize the inadequacy of one's own language to that reality, yet make a text, nonetheless, in response to it. Should it accordingly be a constant and central aim of the translator to bring his own reader to a new consciousness of the limits of his language in relation to another? Not by changing English, say, into some foreign thing, but far more subtly, by reminding the reader that one is always at the edge of what can be done; that beyond it is something unknown and if only for that reason wonderful; that, like a grammar, a translation can be only a partial substitute for an education (White 252–53).

To do otherwise, to create a seemingly effortless text, would be to erase the reality of the other language—the possibilities for life and feeling it offers, the experiences of those who live on its terms—which would be an ethical as well as an aesthetic wrong, a violation of the translator's duty of fidelity to the original. This is especially so where speakers of the

333

other language are politically subordinate to those to whom the translation is addressed. (There may be a greater obligation to recognize the reality and validity of "Third World" languages in an English translation than to recognize the value of English when one is translating the other way.) The issue can be seen in even more general terms, as another instance in which it is valuable to be conscious of one's language and its limits.

But there is something to be said on the other side too. I think of John Gardner's claim that the heart of fiction writing (and he could have included writing of other kinds as well) is the creation of a "vivid and continuous dream" in the reader's mind: "One of the chief mistakes a writer makes is to allow or force the reader's mind to be distracted, even momentarily, from the fictional dream" (Gardner 31–32). If the text we are translating has this quality, as of course many great ones do—think of the *Odyssey*, for example—are we not unfaithful to it in an important, indeed essential, way if our translation lacks it? If the text does anything it creates a world in which one can for the moment believe, and should the translator not aim at that too? Fidelity to the original requires no less.

It is the tension between these views that I wish to address here, with the idea not so much of resolving it as complicating it, by suggesting a way to think about it somewhat more fully.

My first point is that this is an issue not only in translating between languages, but in translating from one dialect or discourse within a language into another, indeed in every act of reading or listening. To take an especially clear example, think of translation in the law: the story of the client is translated into the discourse of the law, the authoritative texts of the law are translated into the new context that is provided by the client's story, and both processes are full of imperfection. This becomes especially clear in a lawsuit, for both processes are explicitly contested. The lawyers for the two parties argue for different versions of the key events in legal discourse and for different versions of that discourse itself. How far should the speakers acknowledge the fact that the law results in the choice of one story, in one language, over another, which is erased? One function of the judicial dissent, so important in the rhetoric of appellate decisions, is to make just this acknowledgment; but should something like this happen elsewhere in the process? When and how should legal speakers recognize the limits of their own discourse? This question, which is obviously political and ethical, is also a question about the virtues of opacity or transparency in translation.[1]

But it is not only in such interdialectical translations but in the rest of life, in the reading of virtually every human utterance, that the texts we make about other texts represent them imperfectly. Everything we read has opacities as well as transparencies, as do all of our own expressions. Dealing with this fact is a part of ordinary human competence. Think of the way a child learns the language in which she is raised, for example, by repeating sounds and gestures. She may be confident of her capacity to do this without understanding very much of what the words "mean" to the grown-up she is imitating or responding to. But that is all right, for her capacity is usually sufficient to her needs, and she can be confident in the rightness of her own gestures in the context in which she makes them. But sometimes the degree of not understanding, or of not being able to speak confidently, becomes overwhelming, and this creates a painful lacuna she must try hard to fill.

With this imagined experience of a child, compare your own reading of Chaucer or Shakespeare: you read right along, wholly engaged, even though if someone asked you to do it, you would be hard pressed to explain this particular word or that phrase; but somehow you get enough sense of its function and its flavor to enable you to go on. If the text is important to you, you may go back, focusing on the moments of not understanding, and then you are likely to realize that there is more to understand about the meaning of the words and phrases than you could ever master. We can never understand completely; what is more, our sense of incompleteness is itself a spur to investigation, learning, invention. I am here reminded of the remark of bell hooks in her essay for this volume, that she tries to get her students to see "not understanding as a space for learning."

Let me give one more example, a sentence I am sure every one of us in some sense will understand just fine: "I'll bet you never went there." But that is a sentence abstracted from any real context, and what we "understand" is also rather abstract. Imagine, for example, reading it with the emphasis on the "I": what social circumstances would produce that intonation? (Answering this question, for example: "Will nobody bet that I never went there?") Go through the whole sentence, emphasizing each word in turn, and see how the sentence changes meaning as it is variously pronounced to suggest a range of contexts in which it works as a gesture. Or imagine it spoken by different voices: by a grandchild to a grandfather, or a grandmother; a taxi-driver (male or female) to a passenger (male or female); a soldier to a civilian, or vice versa; one ten-year-old boy to another, and so on. The sentence shifts tone and emphasis with each imagining, yet these are all still incomplete: exactly what grandchild to what grandfather? My colleague the linguist A. L. Becker has often made this assignment to students: go out into the world and listen until you overhear a sentence that strikes you; write it down; now observe or recall as much of the context as you can, in as great detail as possible, and record that too; finally explain how this specification of context gives meaning to the sentence you have written.

While in one sense we all "understand" the sentence, "I'll bet you never went there," in another sense we do not. Our understanding—unknown to ourselves—is full of empty spaces or "cognitive holes" and "ignorance."[2] It is part of Becker's achievement to suggest a way in which these aspects of not understanding can be made visible to us and hence the occasion for learning. More generally, one of the great virtues of asking students to translate in the classroom, or to read translations with an eye to the original, is that the opacities are more easily seen, the need for learning more obvious. And what needs to be learned is not a set of politically proper pieties, about diversity or difference, but the actual language of another person.

As a contrast with these opacities, think of what you would regard as the most nonproblematic speech of all, the most completely understood: what would it be? A set of stereotyped cliches, a ritual of verbal gestures? (see Coles 134). At the end of the spectrum that approximates complete transparency, I think one finds no life at all, but a kind of death of mind and self.

This is the way of saying that there are opacities in all our speech, all our reading, and that part of one's competence at life includes managing this fact. Translation, then, is not a unique practice, but one case of a more general phenomenon, and one we already know something about, whether we are aware of that knowledge or not.

One can learn to see "not understanding" as a "space for learning," I think, in part because some of the texts we read and hear invite us to do just that, and in ways that prove valuable. Or, to put it slightly differently, one way to evaluate texts is by asking how productive their opacities and uncertainties are. Here, for example, is the opening sentence of Jane Austen's *Mansfield Park:* "About thirty years ago, Miss Maria

Ward of Huntingdon, with only seven thousand pounds, had the good luck to captivate Sir Thomas Bertram, of Mansfield Park, in the county of Northampton, and to be thereby raised to the rank of a baronet's lady, with all the comforts and consequences of a handsome house and a large income."

In one sense this is perfectly accessible, though on reflection one will realize that one may not exactly know what a "baronet" is, or how much "seven thousand pounds" should be thought to be, or what the "comforts and consequences" of the position are, or with what deprivations they are to be compared. The novel will indeed give meaning to each of these terms. But this is not the major opacity of the sentence: the real question is how we are to regard this voice, so officious and mercenary, which can speak so coldly of "good luck" and "captivating." This will in fact be a major problem of the novel, for its heroine, Fanny, grows up in a world in which almost everybody speaks in one or another version of this voice, against which she must find her own way of talking; this defines a problem for the reader too, who must struggle in his own way with these various speakers, starting with this one. In this way, the difficulty of the opening sentence is made productive of thought and life by the rest of the novel of which it is a part. But that is by no means necessary: one could imagine a novel continuing in the same voice without a break, or one in which it was made the object of crude or heavy-handed irony.

One way to think of reading a book like this is that one learns its language: the ways in which one gesture plays off against another, perhaps freshly defining both; the ways in which its central terms are given meaning by particular uses in particular contexts; the ways in which its central tensions are accordingly defined and perhaps resolved. Think of the way Emily Dickinson gives meaning to central terms like *noon* and *circumference,* for example, across the range of her poems. Reading as learning a language, then, just what the translator must do as the first stage of her work.

What all this means about translation is that it cannot be wholly transparent—the idea of a continuous dream is itself a dream—and that it cannot be wholly opaque, if the translation makes any effort to speak the language of its audience at all. It is important to ask not where it lies on this spectrum, as if that were a test of value, but rather what it does with its opacities and clarities, that is, whether it makes them productive or not. The translator can focus mainly on what is problematic in the original work—for example, the manliness of Odysseus, implied in the very first work of the *Odyssey* (*andra*) as a term of praise; yet this hero ends up dependent upon a boy, a swineherd, and a woman for his success—or mainly on what is problematic in the interaction between the two languages, in the act of translation itself. She cannot do one to the exclusion of the other: the continuous dream is impossible, and at the other extreme there is only a language lesson. Instead, she must find her own mix of emphasis, the one she thinks right for this text or genre, in the situation in which she is working. She may try for consistency in this respect, or may choose to alternate between moments of transparency and moments of opacity. The range of her possibilities cannot be defined ahead of time, for she is engaged in creative art; but the performance can be judged afterwards, by asking how well it invites its reader to make its moments of "not understanding," of both kinds, into "spaces for learning."

Notes

1. What of the fact that translations in the law are mandatory, exercises of official power, in this sense acts of domination? Since they are contested, they also are to some degree open to dispute; and in many cases the act of translation gives power to those who should have it. The furniture store cheats you; the law provides a place to tell that story, and a language in which to do so, that may give you the power to get your money back. The fact that the law naturally reflects power distributions in our world, and in ways that make it in some respects systematically unfair, should not obscure two other things: that many of those who have unfair power through the law would have much, much more without it; and that our law itself is meant to be fair, including, and sometimes especially, to the powerless. It is neither to be rejected as polluted, nor revered as flawless, but subjected to intelligent scrutiny, judgment, and change.

2. Our false sense that we do "understand" such a sentence, abstracted from any context, is itself the product, I think, of a false image of language, one that reduces meaning to structural relations among semantic units.

Works Cited

Coles, William E., Jr. "Freshman Composition: Circle of Unbelief." *College English* 31 (1969): 134–40.

Gardner, John. *The Art of Fiction*. New York: Knopf, 1984.
White, James Boyd. *Justice as Translation: An Essay in Cultural and Legal Criticism*. Chicago: U of Chicago P, 1990.

Untitled Structures

Fred Maier

Photography by Albin Dearing

The two untitled structures in the photographs that introduce each section of *Between Languages and Cultures* belong to an ongoing series in which I explore an intersection of sculpture and architecture. Some of those structures are paired, as in this presentation; others are grouped, and still others stand alone. They are constructed of common building materials: wood, drywall, metal, alone or in combination. The photographs of them here are presented at random.

The structures are roughly of human scale. Placed together they remain isolated. Each proposes and simultaneously denies entrance. While they permit limited viewer participation, they offer no response. The pair photographed appears to be consociate. Other structures in the series are physically linked but are held apart by the inflexibility of their connection. Despite the apparent potential, these associations deliver nothing of relevance to either structure. This is a circumstance that may prompt collaboration.

Notes on Contributors

Agha Shahid Ali, a poet from Kashmir, is on the poetry faculty of the MFA program at the University of Massachusetts, Amherst. He has published several volumes of poetry, including *Half-Inch Himalayas* (Wesleyan University Press), *A Nostalgist's Map of America* (Norton), *Belovèd Witness* (Viking Penguin). He has also translated the poetry of Faiz Ahmad Faiz, *The Rebel's Silhouette* (Peregrine Smith), and is the author of *T. S. Eliot as Editor* (UMI).

Amel Amin-Zaki has been professor of Shakespearean drama at the Baghdad University and the University of the United Arab Emirates, where she chaired the Department of Foreign Languages. Amin-Zaki has also taught courses on the history of English literature and modern English and American drama. Her writings, both in English and Arabic, have focused primarily on Shakespeare and on the problems associated with translating Shakespeare into Arabic. She has also published works on Dickens, modern Arabic literature, and other aspects of comparative literature.

Talal Asad, a member of the graduate faculty at New School for Social

Research, teaches contemporary anthropological theory. Author most recently of *Genealogies of Religion* (Johns Hopkins University Press), and editor of a collection of essays entitled *Anthropology and the Colonial Encounter*, his research extends to questions of religion and power in the Middle East and European Christianity. He has also published essays on issues of cultural translation.

Sharon Masingale Bell teaches at Kent State University and is also affiliated with the Institute for Applied Linguistics. Her translation of Jacques-Stéphen Alexis's *Romancéro aux étoiles* won the American Literary Translators Association's Gregory Rabassa prize for 1989. Her recent translations of two abolitionist pieces by Germaine de Staël appear in *Translating Gender and Race: Women Writers in France, 1783–1823*, ed. Doris Kadish and Françoise Massardier-Kenney. Kent, Oh.: Kent State UP (1994).

Tim Brennan teaches English, comparative literature, and cultural studies at the State University of New York at Stony Brook. Author of *Salman Rushdie and the Third World* (St. Martins Press), he is currently at work on a book-length study of cosmopolitanism. He edited a special issue of *Modern Fiction Studies* on *Narrative and Colonial Resistance* (1989) and has published widely in such journals as *Transition, Cultural Critique, American Literary History, Race and Class*, and *Social Text*.

Norman Cutler, who teaches Tamil in the Department of South Asian Languages and Civilizations at the University of Chicago, has explored the relationship between Tamil literature, Tamil poetics, and literary criticism. His publications include *Songs and Experience: The Poetics of Tamil Devotion* (1987) and "Interpreting *Tirukkural:* The Role of Commentary in the Creation of a Text," *Journal of the American Oriental Society* (forthcoming). With Joanne Punzo Waghorne he edited *Gods of Flesh/Gods of Stone: The Embodiment of Divinity in India* (1985) and with Paula Richman, *A Gift of Tamil* (1992).

Anuradha Dingwaney teaches Anglophone literature of the "Third" World at Oberlin College. She has published essays on the British Romantic writers Wordsworth and De Quincey, Salman Rushdie, Chinua Achebe, on feminist pedagogy, and on pedagogical issues relating to cross-cultural "Third" World texts. Her current research initiatives include a book-length study of discursive resistance in the work of writers from the African and Indian diaspora, for which she was awarded an NEH Fellowship for 1992–93.

Rosario Ferré is a Puerto-Rican–born writer who lives and works in San Juan. Her work in fiction includes *Papeles de Pandora* (1976), a collection of short stories that was published in English as *The Youngest Doll* (1991), mainly in her own translations. She has also translated her novel *Maldito amor*, which was published as *Sweet Diamond Dust* (1988). In addition she has written poetry—*Fábulas de la garza desangrada* (1982)—and essays—*Sitio a Eros* (1980) and *El coloquio de las perras* (1990). Her most recent book is *Las dos Venecias* (1992), a collection of poetry and autobiographical prose.

Jacinto R. Fombona I. teaches Spanish at Tulane University. His teaching and research interests include travel literature as a turn-of-the century cultural practice in Spanish America, Spanish-American essay, and the history of ideas, writing "class" and "gender" in Spanish America, poet-modernity and the cultural market in Latin America, and Spanish reading and theory of translation. He has lectured and published on Enrique Gómez Carrillo, José Donoso, and Severo Sarduy.

bell hooks has written extensively on issues of gender, race, and sexuality. The author of several books and essays, her most recent publications include *Sisters of the Yam, Black Looks: Race and Representation, Breaking Bread: Insurgent Black Intellectual Life* (with Cornel West), and *Yearning: Race, Gender, and Cultural Politics*—all from South End Press.

Indira Karamcheti teaches postcolonial literature and theory in the English Department at Wesleyan University in Connecticut. With a colleague, she has translated the complete plays of Aimé Césaire. She has written on authors such as Salman Rushdie, Rita Dove, V. S. Naipaul, Anita Desai, and Simone Schwarz-Bart, as well as on the Indian diaspora, the question of the native anthropologist, and interpretative strategies for reading postcolonial literature. She is working on a book, *Postcolonial Theory*, which examines the formation of postcolonial studies as a discipline within U.S. academia.

Mary N. Layoun teaches in the Department of Comparative Literature at the University of Wisconsin at Madison. She is the author of *Travels of a Genre: Ideology and the Modern Novel* (1990) and the editor of *Modernism in Greece?: Critical Texts on the Margins of a Movement* (1990). She teaches and writes about colonial and "post-colonial" literatures and cultures, nationalism and gender, political culture, fascism, disciplinary histories, and institutional politics. Her current project is a book-length manuscript on cultural responses to nationalism-in-crisis, provisionally titled "Boundary Fixation?"

Carol Maier teaches Spanish at Kent State University, where she is also affiliated with the Institute for Applied Linguistics. Her translations include Severo Sarduy's *Written on a Body* (1989), Octavio Armand's *Refractions* (1994), and Rosa Chacel's *Memoirs of Leticia Valle* (1994). She has edited, with Noël Valis, *In the Feminine Mode: Essays on Hispanic Women Writers* (1990) and, with Roberta L. Salper, *Ramón María del Valle-Inclán: Essays on Gender* (1994). Current projects include translations of work by Valle-Inclán and María Zambrano.

Fred Maier did social and community work, woodworking, and construction prior to his formal training in sculpture. He recognizes—and pursues—the potential of collaborative art projects as a socially constructive mechanism.

Lawrence Needham has written essays on the rhetoric(s) of Romanticism and is coediting a collection of essays with Don H. Bialotosky on that subject. He has also published on the impact of expansionism/colonialism in Romantic literature. A research associate at Oberlin College, he is currently working on Indian poets who write in English, for which he has been awarded an American Institute of Indian Studies fellowship for travel and work in India.

Harsha Ram was born in India and educated in Australia. He currently teaches in the Department of Slavic Languages and Literature at the University of California at Berkeley and has recently completed a dissertation on orientalism in Russian and French lyric poetry from the eighteenth century to the modernist avant-garde. He has recently begun to translate poetry and literary criticism.

Paula Richman teaches South Asian Religions at Oberlin College and has focused on Tamil religious texts from the perspective of the history of religions. She is author of *Women, Branch Stories, and Religious Rhetoric in a Tamil Buddhist Text* (1988), editor of *Many Rāmāyanas: The Diversity of a Narrative Tradition in South Asia* (1991), and coeditor, with Caroline Bynum and Stevan Harrell, of *Gender and Religion: On the Complexity of Symbols* (1986). Currently she is writing a monograph on the political uses of the *Rāmāyana* in Madras from 1873–1962.

Edward W. Said is University Professor of English and Comparative Literature at Columbia University and is the author of numerous works, including *Beginnings: Intentions and Method; Orientalism; The Question of Palestine; The World, the Text, and the Critic; Musical Elaborations; Culture and Imperialism* (1993).

Mahasweta Sengupta teaches at Visva Bharati University, Santiniketan. She has also taught in the Department of Comparative Literature at the University of Massachusetts, Amherst. Her essay about "Translation, Colonialism, and Poetics: Rabindranath Tagore in Two Worlds," appeared in Susan Bassnett and André Lefevere's *Translation, History and Culture*. The essay in *Between Languages and Cultures* is part of a larger study on cultural perceptions and the way they work through translation.

James Boyd White is the Hart Wright Professor of Law, professor of English, and adjunct professor of classical studies at the University of Michigan. His books include *The Legal Imagination* (1973), *When Words Lose Their Meaning* (1984), *Heracles' Bow* (1985), and *Justice as Translation: An Essay in Cultural and Legal Criticism* (1990).

Index